COMMUNITIES OF
# FRANK
# LLOYD
# WRIGHT

# COMMUNITIES OF
# FRANK
# LLOYD
# WRIGHT

## TALIESIN AND BEYOND

MYRON A. MARTY

*To Don Chamberlain*

*Best wishes,*

*Myron A. Marty*

*Oct. 2, 2009*

NORTHERN
ILLINOIS
UNIVERSITY
PRESS

© 2009 by Northern Illinois University Press

Published by the Northern Illinois University Press, DeKalb, Illinois   60115

Manufactured in the United States using postconsumer-recycled, acid-free paper.

Design by Julia Fauci


Library of Congress Cataloging-in-Publication Data

Marty, Myron A.

Communities of Frank Lloyd Wright : Taliesin and beyond / Myron A. Marty.

     p.   cm.

Includes bibliographical references and index.

ISBN 978-0-87580-396-8 (clothbound : alk. paper) 1. Wright, Frank Lloyd,
1867–1959—Friends and associates. 2. Taliesin Fellowship. 3. Architectural studios—
United States. 4. Architecture—Study and teaching—United States—History—20th
century.  I. Title.

NA2127.S66M38 2009

720.92—dc22

2008054054

Frontispiece—Taliesin Studio in 1925. Courtesy of the Frank Lloyd Wright Foundation

TO SHIRLEY

# CONTENTS

# PREFACE

The response to *Frank Lloyd Wright's Taliesin Fellowship*, coauthored with Shirley Marty and published a decade ago, persuaded me that a larger study of the Fellowship was needed. Former apprentices, many belonging to the alumni organization known as Taliesin Fellows, insisted that while they appreciated what the members of the Fellowship who remained in it through the years had done to maintain it as a "learning-by-doing" community and to preserve the buildings at Taliesin and Taliesin West, their perspectives, too, deserved to be recorded.

The next step, therefore, required visiting and corresponding with former apprentices, doing research in the Frank Lloyd Wright Archives at Taliesin West in Scottsdale, Arizona, and occasionally offering seminars for the apprentices there and at Taliesin in Wisconsin. I also engaged in research in other archives and various libraries, principally Cowles Library at Drake University, and the libraries at the University of Illinois at Champaign-Urbana.

This volume treats some of the same subjects as the earlier one, but many of the principals' perspectives are different, just as every apprentice's experiences were different. "Not just different," as one former apprentice told me, "but very different." Naturally, then, perspectives represented here vary widely, but they all contribute to a comprehensive portrait of the Fellowship and, in a limited way, of Wright's earlier communities.

The narrative does not follow the plot I had in mind when I began my research and writing. I anticipated telling a story based almost entirely on recollections of men and women who had belonged to the Fellowship for varying lengths of time between 1932 and the early years of the twenty-first century. As my research progressed, however, I found it necessary to explore the Fellowship's roots, going back to Frank Lloyd Wright's arrival in Chicago in 1886 or 1887 and tracing his experiences with assistants, apprentices, and other architects in the forty-five years before he and his wife Olgivanna welcomed the first apprentices to the organization they founded in 1932. I also concluded that although Mrs. Wright had kept the Fellowship going for twenty-six years after her husband's death, her demise in 1985 brought the Fellowship into a phase covered well in our earlier book. The epilogue in this book summarizes the senior fellows' role in leading the Fellowship, the Frank Lloyd Wright Foundation, the School of Architecture, the Frank Lloyd Wright Archives, and Taliesin Architects into a new era, extending the work done by its irreplaceable leaders. It also presents reflections on Fellowship experiences by former apprentices, known as Taliesin Fellows, as they seek to preserve a record of their Fellowship years and support the School of Architecture.

Given the abundance of resources at my disposal—the voluminous writings by Frank Lloyd Wright; responses to a survey of former apprentices; hundreds of interview transcripts archived at Taliesin West; many articles and reviews dealing with Wright and the Fellowship; the complete sets of the *Journal of the Taliesin Fellows,* the *Newsletter of the Taliesin Fellows,* and the *Frank Lloyd Wright Quarterly;* first-hand accounts of Fellowship experiences by former apprentices found in books and articles; and many other books—it is essential for readers to understand that I have used a strategy of sampling in the manner that pollsters sample opinions from small groups to draw broad conclusions. No one knows better than I that countless good stories had to be omitted, that significant events invite greater elaboration than can be offered here, that many other events are bypassed, that names that might have been included receive no mention, and that the emphases and interpretations are different from what another writer's might have been. With apologies to persons who provided me with good recollections that I cannot draw upon directly or completely, I must acknowledge that much good material remains, so to speak, on the cutting room floor. But it will not be swept away or shredded, for almost all of my sources, if they are not already there, will be deposited in the Frank Lloyd Wright Archives and made available to other Wright scholars.

Readers should also be aware that following a strict chronological framework in telling the Fellowship story is impossible, as episodes in it overlap. Consequently, to ensure clarity in identifying individuals and events in separate episodes, occasional redundancies are unavoidable.

In her *Bird by Bird: Some Instructions on Writing and Life,* Anne Lamott cites a remark by E. L. Doctorow: writing a book, he said, "is like driving a car at night. You can see only as far as your headlights, but you can make the whole trip that way." In other words, Lamott continues, "You don't have to see where you're going, you don't have to see your destination. You just have to see two or three feet ahead of you." Very few writers, she adds, "really know what they are doing until they've done it" (18, 22).

That is what I discovered. I hope you profit from your journey with me.

# COMMUNITIES OF
# FRANK LLOYD WRIGHT

# INTRODUCTION

When my wife, Shirley, and I arrived for a month-long sojourn at Taliesin West in November 1994, senior members in the Taliesin Fellowship greeted us warmly. "We knew you would return," they said, citing Frank Lloyd Wright's remark that visitors and departing apprentices would leave Taliesin with rubber bands attached to snap them back. No matter how far away people went or how long they stayed away, the rubber band would remain in place and do its job. During earlier visits, in 1992, at both Taliesin West and Taliesin, we had not yet heard about the rubber bands, but we, too, knew that returning was a certainty.[1]

We have been snapped back many times, on some occasions to lead seminars in the Frank Lloyd Wright School of Architecture and on others to conduct research in the Frank Lloyd Wright Archives. Frequently we also were at one site or the other for weekend meetings of the board of the Frank Lloyd Wright Foundation or simply to visit friends. Through the Wright-designed buildings, as well as through the senior fellows who have lived at the two Taliesins for decades and the young apprentices who come and go, we have always felt Wright's presence.

To visit Frank Lloyd Wright's Taliesin and Taliesin West is to discover experiences found nowhere else. Both are popular tourists sites, but our visits during the past sixteen years were more than tourists' adventures. At Taliesin West we participated in accreditation visits, led seminars in the School, observed "box-project presentations" in which apprentices demonstrated progress in their work, engaged in archival research, recorded interviews with senior fellows, assisted in the Archives and the Library, attended meetings of the Frank Lloyd Wright Foundation's Board of Trustees, enjoyed the dinners and entertainment offered in Taliesin's formal evenings, and gained insights into communal living.

Given the warmth and openness of the senior fellows, it was easy to make ourselves at home. We set tables in the dining room, dined with the community, washed dishes, and engaged in conversations with apprentices, sometimes at the daily teatime. Shirley edited early drafts of Cornelia Brierly's *Tales of Taliesin,* assisted several of the women in dealing with other transitions in their lives, and took part in an Indian sweat-lodge ritual. Both of us enjoyed the incomparable experiences of life in the Fellowship.

Living in quarters designed by Wright has been a recurring privilege. At Taliesin West we have been lodged in the Sun Cottage, the most recent incarnation of Mr. and Mrs. Wright's first enclosed living quarters (see Chapter 16). We stayed also in the Cottage's additions, one a guest apartment, the other known as Eve's apartment, built for their granddaughter, Iovanna Wright's daughter. Several times we found ourselves in a desert cottage, constructed in its first phase by Jack and Lu Howe and expanded and modernized by Kenn and Susan Lockhart (see Chapter 18). For four weeks we lived in an apartment in the Crescent, designed and built by Taliesin apprentices.

At Taliesin in Wisconsin our first abode was the Rose Room in the lower level of Taliesin; Cornelia Brierly had lived there in the mid-1930s, with only a fireplace providing heat in Wisconsin winters. Later we stayed in other rooms on that level and, upstairs, in the guest apartment, where Mr. and Mrs. Wright lived before their bedrooms were built. Because the apartment is on the house tour, we, like other guests, placed our belongings in the closet during the day. We stayed also in rooms known as Wes's apartment—long the Wisconsin home of Wes Peters. One cannot live in these places without hearing voices from the past and imagining what life there was like in earlier times.

Attending reunions of the Taliesin Fellowship in 1997, 2002, and 2007 gave us opportunities to reflect on Taliesin life with returning apprentices from as far back as the 1930s and '40s and to observe what working with Mr. and Mrs. Wright had meant to these men and women. In one particularly poignant experience, I joined in a ritual led by Eric Lloyd Wright, Frank Lloyd Wright's grandson, and his wife, Mary. As we gathered on the serene hillside behind the Midway Farm buildings, Mary waved a cluster of glowing sage branches over us, in the manner of an Indian purification ritual. Eric invited us to form a circle and, one by one, to recall Taliesin experiences that had continued to influence our lives.

As the only one in the circle who had never been an apprentice, what I heard and observed allowed me to grasp and appreciate what living and working with Eric's grandfather had meant to those who had done so. Although I can recall no specific recollections offered by those present, the profundity of the occasion touched me deeply, and memories of its mystical nature linger.

The men and women in the Taliesin Fellowship whom we came to know understand very well why, fifty years after his death, Frank Lloyd Wright remains America's best-known architect. They share the judgment of many that he was the greatest and, as architectural historian Henry-Russell Hitchcock asserted in 1948, that Wright was "obviously the Michelangelo of the twentieth century. . . ." Hitchcock said this in the presence of architects Marcel Breuer, Walter Gropius, Philip Johnson, and Eero Saarinen, as well as architectural historians Vincent Scully and Edgar Kaufmann Jr.[2]

Even so, Wright's image in American minds is incomplete and often blurred or skewed. Although he is widely regarded as a creative genius, he is often seen as an eccentric and remote figure. For that he bears responsibility, for throughout his life he set himself apart from and above others. In 1930, for example, he said: "I warn Henry-Russell Hitchcock right here and now that, having a good start, not only do I fully intend to be the greatest architect who has yet lived, but the greatest who will ever live. Yes, I intend to be the greatest architect of all time. And I do hereunto affix 'the red square' to this warning."[3]

By then, as historian Thomas S. Hines, tells it, his "unique creative nature demanded and conceived for himself a *persona,* a mythic personality surrounded by a partially mythic world." Two years later Wright's autobiography presented this mythic persona to a wide readership. He was free to do this, Hines said, because "he had no conception of 'truth' as most people define it."[4]

Illustrated studies of Wright's work provide valuable insights into his architecture, and biographers have sought with some success to distinguish the authentic Wright from the mythical persona he created.[5] But there was another Wright—authentic but not found in biographies. This Wright was known to those who worked with him daily in his studios and in the buildings and surroundings he created with their assistance. Meeting this Frank Lloyd Wright by being snapped back to his Taliesin communities again and again has allowed us to understand him as the non-mythical, fully human Frank Lloyd Wright. Further, experiences at Taliesin and Taliesin West helped us to begin to grasp the nature of his genius and to appreciate more fully his remarkable productivity.

My purpose in this book is to tell a fresh story about Frank Lloyd Wright by focusing on his intentions in creating communities of apprentices and coworkers—most notably the Taliesin Fellowship, but also those that preceded it—and revealing how his intentions were realized, or in some instances, not realized.

Early in his career, Wright served apprenticeships in several communities of architects, and in 1893 he began to establish a community of his own in a studio in downtown Chicago. Five years later he took a step toward giving that nascent community stability, maybe even permanence, by moving his studio to a structure appended to his home in Oak Park. He continued there until 1909. Subsequently, until 1932, he presided over a series of small, incidental communities that were shaped by chance and circumstance rather than intention and design.

The Taliesin Fellowship, founded in 1932, was an "intentional community." Under Wright's inspirational leadership, and that of Olgivanna Lloyd Wright, the woman he married in 1926, men and women worked together in common causes, with shared ideals and commitments and a spirit of camaraderie. Attracted by the charisma of Mr. and Mrs. Wright—as they were unfailingly called—as well as the Wrights' pragmatic intentions, the apprentices responded to communal life and the absolute control of the Wrights in various ways: Some cultivated devotion to their leaders and expressed it freely. Some maintained a distance from the community life and devoted themselves to the work at hand. By resisting Mrs. Wright's dictates they risked being sent away. Some *were* sent away. Some left on their own volition, either because they had accomplished their purposes in the Fellowship and were ready to move on, or because life in communal circumstances had lost its appeal.

Following Mr. Wright's death in 1959, Mrs. Wright became the Taliesin Fellowship's sole leader. After she died in 1985 the Fellowship continued on its own into the twenty-first century. Its inspiration lay in ideals and commitments shaped during the fifty-three years of leadership by the Wrights.

This book demonstrates that Frank Lloyd Wright's communities, particularly the Taliesin Fellowship, had profound effects on his life and work: They made possible his extraordinary productivity, helped to sustain his genius, provided him with crucial social outlets, and made it possible for him to remain a creative force outside the mainstream of American architecture.

# 1 FRANK LLOYD WRIGHT, ARCHITECT

BEAUTIFUL BUILDINGS ARE MORE
THAN SCIENTIFIC. THEY ARE
TRUE ORGANISMS, SPIRITUALLY
CONCEIVED; WORKS OF ART,
USING THE BEST TECHNOLOGY BY
INSPIRATION RATHER THAN THE
IDIOSYNCRASIES OF MERE TASTE
OR ANY AVERAGING BY
THE COMMITTEE MIND.[1]

**—FRANK LLOYD WRIGHT**

When Frank Lloyd Wright and his wife Olgivanna established the Taliesin Fellowship in 1932, he at age sixty-five and she thirty-four, their intentions were clear and specific: under their direction, young men and women seeking to become architects would observe the Wrights in their life and work, and serve them as well. The community would be self-sustaining. The daily routines of its members would include farming, cooking, and other chores. Some of them, at least, would engage in designing and constructing the community's buildings and tending its landscapes. In a rural Wisconsin setting, free of the curricular and geographical constraints of colleges and universities, they would learn by doing. For the privilege of community membership they would pay an annual fee of $650, if they could afford to do so. Some could not, but if they contributed to the community in other ways, they were permitted to stay.

## ORGANIC ARCHITECTURE

Mr. Wright—as members of the Fellowship always addressed him, and as past and present members unfailingly do yet today—called his architecture "organic." Although his voluminous writings include few precise definitions of this term, he left little doubt as to its meaning.[2] His apprentices have generally followed his lead, persuaded that there can be no consistently applicable definition, but that the concept, philosophy, and applications of organic architecture are evident in the buildings their master designed, as well as in their own work. Moreover, as they interacted with him they absorbed the meaning of organic architecture through processes of discovery, as Wright explained in one of his lectures to the Royal Institute of British Architects in 1939:

Working with apprentices as I do, I have observed that when this idea of architecture as organic begins to work in the young mind something happens: something definite happens to life. Something larger happens to one's outlook upon life. One becomes impatient of these unfounded restraints, these empirical impositions, these insignificant gestures as in grand opera, these posturings which all the buildings of the pseudo-classic and pseudo-renaissance assume to be art and architecture. One begins to want something a little nearer to the ground, more *of* life not so much *on* it. We begin to want to live like spirited human beings. . . . Always in human scale in all proportions.[3]

Bruce Brooks Pfeiffer, one of the apprentices who worked closely with Wright in the last decade of his life, has provided helpful definitions of the term *organic architecture*. In one instance he writes that organic architecture is "architecture that is appropriate to time, appropriate to place, and appropriate to man." By being appropriate to the era of its creation, he continues, a building satisfies the first criterion. It is appropriate to place if it is "in harmony with its natural environment, with the landscape, wherever possible taking best advantage of natural features." It is appropriate to man if its "first mission is to serve people."[4]

## AN ORGANIC COMMUNITY

By this definition, and as demonstrated by its evolution through the years, the Taliesin Fellowship is an organic community. At its founding in 1932, the Fellowship was appropriate to the times. In the preceding five years, only three of Wright's designs had been built. The nation was in the depth of the Great Depression, and that, combined with the damage done to his reputation by well-publicized scandals in his personal life, made the prospects of architectural commissions bleak. Young men and women wondered whether their generation would be denied a promising future. Along with the Wrights, they found hope in the opportunities promised by the Taliesin Fellowship.

The Fellowship's organic character was apparent in its capacity to change with the times. As part of the Frank Lloyd Wright Foundation and through the operation of the Frank Lloyd Wright School of Architecture, its practices evolved further in the twenty-six years that Mrs. Wright was in charge after her husband's death. The evolution continued after she died in 1985.

The Taliesin Fellowship was also appropriate to its place. In the beginning its place was in the beautiful Wisconsin River Valley, forty-five miles west of Madison. The nearest village, Spring Green, had a population of around a thousand. In this rural Midwestern setting the apprentices would blend the experiences and inspiration of the daily routines into their lives of learning. The Fellowship, in Wright's words, would be "a kind of daily work-life." Its work "in its manifold branches," Wright wrote, would come "directly under the influence of an organic philosophy: organic architecture for organic life."[5]

Frank Lloyd Wright had been an architect for forty-five years when he cofounded the Fellowship. He had designed houses and other buildings for clients in eighteen states, as well as in Canada and Japan. Along the way he had been a member of a number of communities consisting of architects, clients, draftsmen, craftsmen, artists, apprentices, assistants, and secretaries. In his most immediate community—his family—two sons were architects. He had published a handsomely illustrated retrospective on his work to 1910, sixteen articles in the *Architectural Record,* and about that many articles in other journals. His *An Autobiography* appeared months before the first apprentices arrived.[6] What he learned on the long route to the Fellowship, with its twists and turns, triumphs and trials, unquestionably shaped his purposes and designs for the community he would lead for the final twenty-seven years of his life.

## FRANK LLOYD WRIGHT'S EARLY YEARS

That long route began in Richland Center, Wisconsin, the town he claimed as his birthplace. Residents there consider him the town's native son, but without supporting evidence.[7] Family records describe the family's migratory existence during his early childhood, but their accuracy is only partially verifiable.

Moreover, Wright's own accounts of his early years are marked by inventions and discrepancies. His name was Frank Lincoln Wright until he replaced "Lincoln" with "Lloyd," his mother's family's name. Although he was born on June 8, 1867, in the mid-1920s he began to call 1869 his birth year, even though he had a sister born that year. Biographer Meryle Secrest speculates that perhaps the impending birth of his daughter Iovanna prompted him to shave a couple of years from his age. Others surmise that he wanted to honor the memory of Mamah Borthwick, his true love (see Chapter 3), but at least six years passed after her death before he claimed 1869 as his birth year.[8] But like so much else in Frank Lloyd Wright's life, the specific reasons for this discrepancy are unknown.

## AN AUTOBIOGRAPHY

Wright's autobiographical recollections of his years at the University of Wisconsin present more factual discrepancies. Writing of his frustrations and disappointments as a student, he said, "So the university training of one Frank Lloyd Wright, Freshman, Sophomore, Junior, and part-time Senior was lost like some race run under a severe handicap, a race which you know in your heart you are foredoomed to lose: a kind of competition in which you can see nobody winning anywhere."[9] In fact, Wright was enrolled at the University of Wisconsin for only two terms, both in 1886, the year he turned nineteen. He was a special student under the tutelage of Professor Allan D. Conover, the dean of the civil engineering department, in whose office he worked part-time as a draftsman.[10]

As we draw on *An Autobiography* in tracing Wright's career, it is important to understand the nature and purpose of this work, as Curtis Besinger, an apprentice at Taliesin from 1939 to 1955, explains. In a letter to the editor of the *Journal of the Society of Architectural Historians* he said that he found debates over Wright's birthdate to be amusing, as they dealt with an issue of little importance.[11] Six months later in the same journal, Besinger suggested that historians who decried the factual inaccuracies and mythmaking in *An Autobiography* should not compound them by reading into the book what is not there. One does not need to have read very far into *An Autobiography,* he asserted, "to become aware that Mr. Wright was not writing a factual, carefully researched, chronological account. Being a self-confessed romantic, he wrote a poetic account of a 'life of imagination.'. . . As an account of his life as he experienced it, it is a true account. It is true, however, as poetry is true."[12]

Thomas Hines has hypothesized that the discrepancies between the records of Wright's past and his recollections in recounting it resulted from his personal needs as they evolved through the years. Perhaps, he wrote, the discrepancies "suggest in part an explanation of his entire life: that slowly over the years, Wright's unique creative nature demanded and conceived for himself a *persona*, a mythic personality surrounded by a partially mythic world." It is possible that he had "no conception of objective 'truth' as most people define it, but that he determined the truth of all things by the degree to which such things supported or contradicted the 'truths' of his own world."[13]

*An Autobiography* becomes somewhat easier to use when we reach Book Two, for there he begins to write of himself in the first person. But there, too, the autobiographical recollections are occasionally mythical and sometimes misleading or elusive. As we draw further on Wright's writings in recounting his career, we must test them against other sources if factual accuracy is at issue.

## BEGINNING A CAREER IN CHICAGO

When the twenty-year-old Frank Lloyd Wright arrived in Chicago in 1886 or 1887 from Madison, Wisconsin, he had neither a high school diploma nor a college degree. There was little money in his pockets, and his knowledge of the workings of the big city was scant. Chicago struck him as a dreary, dim, smoky, and noisy place. In his autobiography he portrays himself as a poor, wayfaring stranger, probably because he wished to be seen as an independent young man, facing challenges entirely on his own. But he was in Chicago by choice, and now it was time for him to find sustenance through employment and acquaintances, to become part of a community of some sort, or to create one.[14]

The young man's prospects were not as uncertain as he depicted them, however, for he was equipped with several years of experience in drafting with Professor Allan Conover at the University of Wisconsin, and his family connections would serve him well. Those connections no doubt prompted him to stop at the office of Joseph Lyman Silsbee, the architect engaged by his uncle, Jenkin Lloyd Jones, to design All Souls Church in Chicago. Silsbee had also designed the Unity Chapel for the Lloyd Joneses near Spring Green, Wisconsin, and Wright is credited with having done perspective drawings for it. He most likely designed the building's interior, at least the ceiling, and helped with its construction in the summer of 1886.[15]

Silsbee hired him, but at the disappointingly low wage of eight dollars per week. Offsetting that disappointment was the happy formation of a friendship with Cecil Corwin, another draftsman, with whom he went to concerts and the theater. The work at Silsbee's he found to be easy, and he soon made himself useful. After three months his wages were raised to twelve dollars weekly, but when another draftsman with more experience was hired for eighteen dollars a week, he asked for another raise. When Silsbee turned him down he quit. Shortly he found a job at another firm for eighteen dollars a week, but there he was charged with tasks he judged to be beyond his capabilities: he was designing when he should have been learning to design. So he quit that job and went back to Silsbee, where he was reunited with Corwin and given weekly wages of eighteen dollars.[16]

Frank Lloyd Wright in 1887, a newcomer to Chicago. Courtesy of the Frank Lloyd Wright Foundation

Wright learned much from Silsbee, first in observing his sketches, and then in seeing Silsbee's flawed manner, described by Corwin: "He doesn't seem to take any of it or take himself half seriously. The picture interests him. The rest bores him. You'll see. He's an architectural genius spoiled by way of the aristocrat." Wright acknowledged that Silsbee was only making pictures, and the pictures were not very close to what was real in the building. But, he said, he adored Silsbee just the same: "He had style. His work had it too, in spite of slipshod methods. . . . I learned a good deal about a house from Silsbee by way of Cecil."[17] Affiliation with other associates in Silsbee's office, including George Maher and George Elmslie, continued later in Wright's career.

Life was not all work. Wright spent most Sunday mornings at his Uncle Jenkin's All Souls Church. In the church's library he found two books that inspired him to want to learn more about architecture.[18] One of these books, *The Grammar of Ornament,* by Owen Jones, noted that universally approved styles of ornament were always in accordance with laws of nature and set forth thirty-seven general design propositions. Wright's designs strongly suggest that he retained important ideas found in this work, including "1. The Decorative Arts arise from, and should be properly attendant upon, Architecture. 2. Architecture is the material expression of the wants, the faculties, and the sentiments of the age in which it is created. Style in Architecture is the peculiar form that expression takes under the influence of climate and materials at command. 3. As Architecture, so all works of Decorative Arts, should possess fitness, proportion, harmony, the result of all which is repose."[19]

The other book, *The Habitations of Man in All Ages* (1875), was by the French architect Eugene Emmanuel Viollet-le-Duc. According to Frank Lloyd Wright's second son, John, Viollet-le-Duc was a teacher of organic architecture as early as 1860. His profound influence on the elder Wright prompted him to give John a copy of Viollet-le-Duc's *Discourses on Architecture.* So thoroughly did the author cover the subject of architecture, John wrote, "that there were few words Dad could add." His father told him, "In these volumes you will find all the architectural schooling you will ever need." Because the volumes were out of print when John Lloyd Wright published his book about his father in 1946, and because of their basic place in Frank Lloyd Wright's philosophy of life and work, the younger Wright included ten pages of excerpts from Viollet-le-Duc's writings.[20]

According to Wright scholar Donald Hoffmann, historians call attention to "the chasm between Viollet-le-Duc's forceful theory and his lacklustre—not to say awkward—designing," but his theory and rigorous logic were evident in the work of Frank Lloyd Wright. Indeed, Hoffmann contends that a description of a building in Viollet-le-Duc's *The Habitations of Man in All Ages* could well be applied also to Wright's Larkin building (1903) in Buffalo, New York.[21]

With his skill as a draftsman increasing and his knowledge and understanding of architecture growing, Wright grew restless in Silsbee's office, even though Silsbee allowed him to accept a commission of his own in 1887, for the first Hillside Home School, near Spring Green, Wisconsin, for his aunts.[22] Prompted by Wilcox (identified only as "preacher's son number four") and Cecil Corwin, he went to see Louis Sullivan about a position with the firm of Adler and Sullivan.

## WORKING WITH LOUIS SULLIVAN

As Wright recounts it in his autobiography, his interview with Sullivan went well. The man who became his "Lieber Meister" was impressed with the portfolio Wright showed him and offered him a position. When he informed Silsbee of his decision to leave, Silsbee faulted him for his manner of departure. Although Wright regretted his failure to consult with Silsbee before deciding to move on, the opportunity to work with Sullivan was ideal for him at this moment in his life.[23]

Wright began in his new position at the Adler and Sullivan office on the top floor of the Borden Block building (since demolished) the Monday morning following his interview. There he met Paul Mueller, Sullivan's office foreman who was a German immigrant trained as an engineer. Mueller's construction company would later execute a number of Wright's major projects.

After beginning work at his drafting board, Wright looked around to see who was there with him in this, his first community of associates in architecture. In his autobiography he recalled his impressions:

Wright designed Hillside Home School near Spring Green, Wisconsin, for his aunts in 1887. Courtesy of the Frank Lloyd Wright Foundation

Got their names afterwards. Next table to mine Jean Agnas, a clean-faced Norseman. To the right Eisendrath—apparently stupid. Jewish. Turned around to survey the group. Isbell, Jew? Gaylord, no—not. Weydert, Jew undoubtedly. Directly behind Weatherwax. Couldn't make him out. In the corner Andresen—Swedish. Several more Jewish faces. Of course—I thought, because Mr. Adler himself must be a Jew. I had not seen him yet. I marked time, feeling alone in all that strange crowd, drawing on the margin of my "stretch." Had a notion to call up Cecil to say hello and hear his voice.[24]

Soon Sullivan walked in and made clear, Wright recalled, why he wanted him there: he was needed to execute drawings. After an unpleasant confrontation with Weatherwax, Sullivan left and Adler entered. Wright had a pleasant conversation with him. Thus began, Wright wrote, an association lasting nearly seven years. This was 1888, and Sullivan dismissed Wright in the spring of 1893, so once again we see imprecise arithmetic in Wright's writing.[25]

In Wright's recollection, he was clearly Sullivan's favorite, to the point that he was able to bring George Elmslie over from Silsbee's office to help, making the place less lonely for him. But, as he recalled in his autobiography, he paid a price for Sullivan's favoritism. The others in the office conspired to "get" him. Anticipating problems, he went to a boxing academy for lessons. As the nagging at the office persisted, he continued training. The first culmination of the antagonism played itself out two weeks later in the boxing ring at the academy, with Wright prevailing, of course. "By getting angry and sailing into them," Wright recalled, "I made enemies of them all."

So, he says, he made up his mind to stay at Adler and Sullivan's office until he could fire every one of the gang. The next day came another confrontation, this one with a man named Ottenheimer who exhibited his "refined cruelty" with "open taunts and skilled innuendoes." Wright then describes in graphic detail his fight with the "heavy-bodied, short-legged, pompadoured, conceited, red-faced Jew, wearing gold glasses," his face now "red as a turkey-cock's waddles." Wright's fists connected with Ottenheimer's face and his foe retaliated by slashing Wright's back and neck. Stools tumbled and tables were overturned. With Ottenheimer coming at him, Wright grabbed a long, broad-bladed T-square and swung it with all his might, "catching Ottie with the edge of the blade beside his neck just about the collar. . . . The knife dropped from his hand as he wavered a moment. Then he wilted, slowly, into a senseless heap on the floor like a sail coming down."

Ottenheimer lay there, unconscious. Revived by water splashed in his face, "He got up by degrees. Stood white and shaking. 'I'll pay you for this, Wright,' he choked. You'll get yours for this. You'll see.'" He went back to his desk and gathered his instruments as Wright sat smiling, happy to see that he could move, "for I thought I had killed him in that wild moment." He left, and Wright never saw him again. His disappearance, Wright noted, "broke the persecution for a time." Neither Mueller nor Sullivan heard about the feud until Wright had "finally cleaned up the Adler and Sullivan gang" several years later. This altercation occurred in 1888. Wright wrote proudly of it forty-four years later and allowed the story to be included in the 1943 edition of his autobiography. Even during World War II he remained unapologetic for the apparent anti-Semitism in his words and actions.[26] Later, though, he welcomed Jewish apprentices into the Fellowship and had good relations with Jewish clients.[27]

Peter Blake, an architect and architecture critic, tells a story about an experience he had resulting from his reaction to this segment of Wright's autobiography. Blake was new on the editorial staff of the *Architectural Forum* when the 1943 edition of *An Autobiography* was published. The *Forum* editor, George Nelson, assigned him responsibility for reviewing it. "To read, in 1943, Mr. Wright's obscene account of a fight he had with someone in the office of Dankmar Adler and Louis Sullivan," Blake wrote, "was more than startling." After quoting the section abstracted above, he continues, "This was the kind of prose that made *Der Stürmer* a favorite journal among Nazi sadomasochists. . . . Had I known then how badly Mr. Wright needed to assert his manhood . . . I might have laughed this off as an unintentionally revealing self-portrait of the artist as an ambulant inferiority complex; but as it was, I wasn't terrifically amused." That Blake had been born to Jewish parents twenty-three years earlier in Germany (as Peter Jost Blach) no doubt heightened his concern over Wright's tale and moved him to think ill of Wright and the book.[28]

In an earlier work Blake also recounted this episode and excused Wright's conduct, asserting that he was writing as "a rather primitive country-man by instinct," with the "usual run-of-the-mill prejudices." To a Wisconsin farm boy, "Jews were 'Big City' crooks and had to be handled accordingly." In later years, he says, Wright demonstrated again and again his "utter lack of prejudice in the conventional areas of race, color, or creed." To Blake it seemed that Wright included "these faintly nauseating paragraphs in his *Autobiography* as an act of penance," as he continued to demonstrate that "he had no hatred for anything in life except cruelty and sham."[29]

In any event, Blake recalls that he wrote a review that would, he thought, "put this little bigot in his place." He laid the draft of his review on editor George Nelson's desk and went to lunch. While he and Nelson were out, Wright came into the office and riffled through papers on the editor's desk. Finding Blake's draft, he scrawled across it with a red crayon: "George—I always thought you were a son of a bitch, but now I know. FLLW." Fortunately for all concerned, writes Blake, "skillful diplomacy and other written and spoken apologies to the Great Man saved the day; and it seems that he did not demand the scalp of the villain as part of his price."[30]

What he got was a laudatory review by George Nelson, with this conclusion: "*An Autobiography,* like everything Wright has done is on a big scale. In it both faults and virtues are magnified many times. If it shifts, often for no apparent reason, from heights of wisdom and understanding to almost childish petulance and fits of boasting, it is no criticism of the book. Both extremes are human, and this book is one of the most thoroughly human documents of our time. . . ."[31]

As a draftsman at Adler and Sullivan, Wright says he was "a good pencil in the Master's hand." So confident in his relationship with his master had he become that he asked Sullivan to lend him money enough "to build a little house," to be paid back "so much each month." Sullivan agreed,

approved the lot, and lent Wright $5,000 to purchase it. He had money from the $5,000 loan left over for building his small house, but as usual, and as ever after, his tastes were grander than his bank account.[32]

By this time Adler and Sullivan had moved to the top floor of the tower in the Auditorium building, landmark structure of their design on Michigan Avenue. There, Wright said, "I had a small room next to [Sullivan], and a squad of thirty draughtsmen or more to supervise in the planning and detailing that was now my share. Mueller had the engineers and superintendents reporting to him, at the opposite end of the long room." Although Sullivan's attitude and ego separated him from most employees, Wright saw a different side of him, and therein his education as an architect continued.

He loved to talk to me and I would often stay listening, after dark in the offices in the upper stories of the great tower of the Auditorium building looking out over Lake Michigan, or over the lighted city. Sometimes he would keep on talking seeming to have forgotten me—keep on talking until late at night. Probably liking the exercise. And I would catch the last suburban car for Oak Park and go to bed without supper.[33]

The thirty draftsmen might not have formed a community with Wright, or he with them, but there was at least a satisfying relationship with Sullivan. As a "worshipful and sympathetic though critical listener," Wright was soon able to understand Sullivan and to see who his partner in this firm was. "Like all geniuses," Wright generalized, Sullivan was "an absorbed egocentric—exaggerated sensibility, vitality boundless." This egotism, though, he saw as "more armor than character, more shell than substance. . . . the

Louis Sullivan, Wright's employer and mentor. Courtesy of the Frank Lloyd Wright Foundation

usual defense of exaggerated sensibility—a defense become a habit. And with all his synthesis and logical inclination, his uncompromising search for principle, he was an incorrigible romanticist." These characteristics were not inconsistent, Wright concluded, "except as the romanticist degenerates to the sentimentalist."[34] In recalling these qualities in Sullivan, Wright may also have been looking in a mirror, beholding the same qualities in himself.

During Wright's tenure with Adler and Sullivan, he says, his employers resisted requests to build residences. Sometimes the requests came with social obligations that the principals could not avoid. That meant work for Wright, to be done during out-of-office hours. In 1890 he designed six houses for Adler and Sullivan and in 1891 another one. By 1892, with debts closing in on him, he accepted several houses on his own account. When Sullivan became aware of them, he was offended, charged Wright with breaking his contract by doing outside work, and refused to give Wright the deed to the Oak Park house even though the house was paid for. Granting that Wright's work at the office had not suffered, he nonetheless insisted that his sole interest must be at the firm as long as his five-year contract remained in effect. "I won't tolerate division," he said, "under any circumstances."[35]

When Adler's intercession on Wright's behalf not only failed to produce the hoped-for results, but instead offended Sullivan more deeply, Wright threw down his pencil and walked out of the Adler and Sullivan office, never to return. Eventually he received the deed to the home from Adler.

## ON HIS OWN

On his own now, Wright opened an office in the Schiller Building, designed by Adler and Sullivan, in downtown Chicago. On the plate-glass door to room 1501 he and his good friend with whom he shared the office, though not in a partnership, placed these small gold-leaf letters:

FRANK LLOYD WRIGHT, ARCHITECT

CECIL CORWIN, ARCHITECT

To this office came W. H. Winslow of the Winslow Ornamental Iron Works, who wanted him to design a home in River Forest. By seniority Winslow should have been Corwin's client, but Corwin would not have it so.[36]

## A TEMPTING OFFER

At this point in *An Autobiography* Wright interrupts the narrative to describe a purported offer from the renowned Chicago architect Daniel Burnham to send him to Paris for four years of study at the École des Beaux-Arts, then for two more years in Rome. All his expenses would be paid and a job would be waiting for him when he returned. A spirited conversation with Burnham ensued. Burnham's fame had grown as a result of his role in designing and building the 1892 Columbian Exposition in Chicago, and resisting his offer seemed, to Wright's friend and soon-to-be client Edward C. Waller, who was present, to be obstinacy, if not stupidity. "Frank," he said, "don't you realize what this offer means to you? As you choose now, remember, so you will go on all the rest of your life." Wright claimed to have been tempted: "I saw myself influential, prosperous, safe; saw myself a competent leader of the majority rule. . . . It was all so definitely set, too easy and unexciting as I saw it. And it was all untrue. At the very best a makeshift."

Wright could not accept the offer, if in fact it was made, for he could not run away from what he saw as his. Or rather what was his opportunity and others' in America (or Usonia, as he began to call the United States of America). He would go on with what he had started. He was spoiled, he said, first by birth, then by training. Now he had discovered, under the pressure of the need to make a decision, that he must base that decision on his own convictions.[37]

So he continued to live in Oak Park and work there evenings while conducting his business at the Schiller Building downtown. There he had a sad parting with Corwin, who had concluded, according to Wright, that he found no joy in architecture except as he saw Wright do it. He didn't want to continue watching Wright do what he himself could not do. Wright's offers and pleadings were

Dankmar Adler, Sullivan's partner and also Wright's mentor. Courtesy of the Frank Lloyd Wright Foundation

Frank Lloyd Wright and Cecil Corwin, with whom he shared an office and personal interests. Courtesy of the Frank Lloyd Wright Foundation

to no avail. Corwin was going east. There was no bitterness in his departure, Wright said. Rather, it seemed that a load had slipped off Corwin's mind. While he looked happy, Wright was miserable. He never saw Corwin again.[38]

## STEINWAY HALL

Without Corwin, Wright had no desire to stay in the Schiller Building, so in 1897 he moved to the new Steinway Hall, an eleven-story office and theater building designed by Dwight Perkins. A young man himself—he and Wright were both born in 1867—Perkins offered to share space with other architects in the building's loft and on the eleventh floor. Later Wright wrote fondly and appreciatively of his years in Steinway Hall and the community spirit that existed there: "I well remember how the 'message' burned within me, how I longed for comradeship until I began to know the younger men and how welcome was Robert [Bob] Spencer, then Myron Hunt, and Dwight Perkins, Arthur Heun, George Dean, and Hugh Garden. Inspiring days they were, I'm sure, for us all."[39] These young men, he said in his autobiography, "newcomers in architectural practice like myself, were my first associates in the so-called profession of architecture."[40]

According to architectural historian H. Allen Brooks, "Steinway Hall soon became a rallying point and symbol of the *avant-garde* and a variety of occupants were attracted to the eleventh floor." Webster Tomlinson, who was briefly a partner of Wright, mainly for business management purposes, Irving Pond, and Allen Pond were among them. Later came Adamo Boari, Walter Burley Griffin, and Birch Long. This group formed the nucleus of the group of architects whom Wright decades later called "the Eighteen."[41]

Wright also referred to the group as "a little luncheon club" and "the little luncheon round-table." It served as an informal community for exploring ideas in architecture. Writing about it in *A Testament*—sixty years later and thirty-five years after his first recounting in *An Autobiography*—Wright traced its origins to the fact, in his mind at least, that among young architects he was seen as Louis Sullivan's "alter ego." They were "the first converts to the new architecture." Spencer's "classic" comrades in the firm where he was employed saw him as an apostate, and when he and Wright were seen together walking arm in arm down the street, Chicago conformists working in other offices, according to Wright, would say in derision, "There goes God-almighty with his Jesus Christ." "Bob didn't mind," wrote Wright. "He stuck."

## THE EIGHTEEN

"The Eighteen" often wanted to know, Wright recalled—or reconstructed in his memory—"how I convinced my clients that the new architecture was the right thing. 'Do you hypnotize them?' was a common question. The idea of an American architecture fascinated them to a certain degree according to their understanding. Almost all admired what I was doing though they were not yet willing to say it was the right thing." Several never left traditional architectural styles, he noted, "But most of the others fell in with the idea of some sort of modern architecture. I became original advisory exemplar to the group."[42]

Although Wright had written about this group in 1908 and 1932 (repeated in 1943), not until 1957 did he call himself its leader. Brooks regarded this as a mingling of fact and fiction with equal freedom, and he asserted that "Wright's crusade to discredit his contemporaries seemed almost complete. Wright's retrospective attitude is to be regretted," he continued, "especially since he, perhaps more than any other, benefited from this environment." Then he offered this important insight:

Probably it is no coincidence that [Wright's] two most brilliant and productive periods followed closely his intimate involvement with a group of young architects, the first commencing in the late eighteen-nineties at Steinway Hall and continuing in the Studio, and the second beginning after the Taliesin Fellowship was formed in 1932. The Fellowship, in effect, re-created the group milieu that existed about 1900—except that it was an autocracy. And it is precisely this autocratic system that Wright, late in life, wished to think had existed at Steinway Hall.[43]

The common bond of the Eighteen, according to Brooks, was their admiration for Louis Sullivan. Their goal was to do for architecture in general and residential architecture in particular what Sullivan had done for commercial architecture. Drawing upon the strength derived from unity, they played a dominant role in the Chicago Architectural Club, provided leadership in the founding of the Architectural League of America, publicized each other's work, and participated in the Arts and Crafts movement. The Club's major function was to sponsor an exhibition each spring for several weeks, accompanied by a catalogue. By including or excluding work of members and nonmembers and by choosing what would appear in the catalog, the Steinway Hall group exerted considerable influence in the Chicago architectural scene.[44]

### GAINING RENOWN

Brooks notes that Frank Lloyd Wright, consistent with his lifelong anti-joining practice, never belonged to the Chicago Architectural Club, but he derived more direct benefits from it than anyone else. His work was selected for exhibition in 1894, 1895, 1898, 1899, 1900, 1901, and 1902—seven times in nine years. His essay, "The Art and Craft of the Machine," presented earlier that year at a meeting of the Arts and Crafts Society at Jane Addams's Hull House, was published in the 1901 catalogue for the exhibition. The reason all this could happen is that members of the Steinway Hall group dominated the selection juries and publication committees.

That dominance ended in 1902, as the Club's membership apparently rebelled. A room in that year's exhibition devoted to a display of Wright's work prompted a negative review in *American Architect and Building News*. The critic questioned the professional ethics of giving "such a pronounced personal exhibit" a place in a general architectural show and why "Mr. Wright's tables and chairs, and his teazles and milkweeds and pine-branches" covered so much space. By then, though, Wright and his compatriots no longer needed the promotion their dominance of the Club had given them, and they could give fuller attention to their architectural practices.[45]

The second organization that afforded Wright opportunities to learn from others and advance his ideas was the Architectural League of America, founded upon the initiative of the Chicago Architectural Club. Wright's lack of membership in the Chicago Architectural Club did not prevent him from serving as one of its delegates to the organizational meeting in Cleveland in 1899.

At the meeting in Chicago the next year, June 7–9, the Chicago delegation was by far the largest, with more than one hundred listed as being present. Louis Sullivan was greeted enthusiastically and invited to address the convention extemporaneously at the opening session. Sullivan's banquet address, "The Young Man in Architecture," was published in the *Inland Architect and News Record;* the entire issue was devoted to coverage of the convention.[46]

Wright's contribution to the meeting, except as a listener and presenter of one paper, was apparently minimal. The report in the *Inland Architect and News Record* stated simply: "Frank Lloyd Wright read a paper on "The Architect." He prefaced his paper by the remark that 'after listening to the master (Sullivan) it hardly seemed proper to listen to a disciple,' Mr. Wright having been under Mr. Sullivan's special direction for many years before commencing practice."[47] Less kind was the *American Architect and Building News,* which reported that Wright "belabored every existing condition and every ordinary practitioner, right and left, up and down, back and front, without an exception either as to practice or design."[48] Reading his rather poetic paper today, one might conclude that Wright would have been justified in asking for a second opinion.

The Arts and Crafts Society, another organization that attracted Wright's attention, gave him a chance to present his paper at Hull House, but he never joined it. Perhaps he saw it as dominated by persons who did not share his views. Indeed, reflecting autobiographically on his presentation, "The Art and Craft of the Machine"—in comments that Brooks characterizes as bitter, particularly when compared with what he said about his architectural comrades in 1908—Wright expressed regret that his novel thesis, stressing the capabilities and potential of the machine in the hands of artists, did not receive a cordial response from architects and professors who were present. But then his criticism became harsher:

> Never having known Sullivan much themselves, at this time these young architects were all getting the gospel modified through me. And I should have liked to be allowed to work out the thing I felt in me as architecture with no reflections or refractions from them or libelous compliments until I had it all where I felt it really ought to be. But that was not possible. I was out in the open to stay. Premature though it might be.[49]

And out in the open he continued to do what he had been doing, that is, working out principles of design and construction in houses and other buildings for his steady stream of clients. Between 1893 and 1898 he designed about twenty residences, of which some fifteen were built; and six apartment buildings, five of which were built. In addition, he designed several boathouses and stables, a library, a number of commercial structures, and other nonresidential structures; some of these were also built. In 1895 he added a large playroom to his home in Oak Park and three years later the large studio.[50]

## DESIGNS FOR HIS AUNTS

Wright did not forget about Wisconsin or his kinfolk there, even as he embedded himself more deeply in the action of the Chicago area: His aunts, Nell and Jane, decided in 1896 that a "pretty windmill tower," in keeping with the architecture of the Wright-designed Hillside Home School, should be built. Nephew Frank, they said, should design it. His skeptical uncles, who had urged their sisters to have a steel-framed tower built, wondered what "the boy will do."

According to Wright, he sent the aunts a perspective sketch of the tower in the trees, along with the structural details. "The sisters liked it and thought it becoming to the dignity of the beloved school. To the Uncles it looked expensive and foolish." They took the plans to Cramer, the local builder, and came back with this report: "Cramer says wasting time and money to build that tower. Blow down as sure as Death and Taxes." The thing looked crazy to him, Cramer claimed, insisting it should not be built.

So Aunt Nell telegraphed Wright: "CRAMER SAYS WINDMILL TOWER SURE TO FALL. ARE YOU SURE IT WILL STAND?" Wright's answer: "BUILD IT." And that is what the sisters decided to do. Wright called it "Romeo and Juliet," and he found great delight, forty-four years later, in telling the story of its design and construction, and particularly that it had outlasted the skeptics who predicted its early demise. Cramer's reaction, too, continued to amuse him: "'It beats heck,' said he, 'the way those two old maids dance around after that boy. He comes up here with his swell duds on, runs around the hills with the school girls and goes home. You wouldn't think he had a care in the world nor anything but something to laugh at.'"[51]

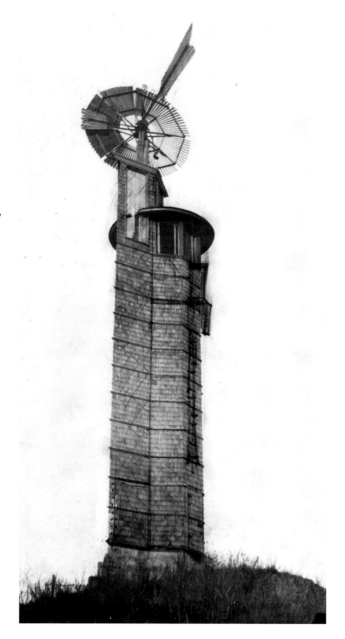

Romeo and Juliet, the windmill at Hillside Wright designed for his aunts in 1896. After several renovations, most recently in 1992, it remains a Taliesin landmark. Courtesy of the Frank Lloyd Wright Foundation

# 2 THE OAK PARK STUDIO YEARS

THE FEW DRAUGHTSMEN SO
FAR ASSOCIATED WITH THIS
WORK HAVE BEEN TAKEN INTO
THE DRAUGHTING ROOM, IN
EVERY CASE ALMOST WHOLLY
UNFORMED, MANY OF THEM
WITH NO PARTICULAR PREVIOUS
TRAINING, AND PATIENTLY
NURSED FOR YEARS IN THE
ATMOSPHERE OF THE WORK
ITSELF, UNTIL, SATURATED BY
INTIMATE ASSOCIATION, AT AN
IMPRESSIONABLE AGE, WITH ITS
MOTIFS AND PHASES, THEY HAVE
BECOME HELPFUL. TO DEVELOP THE
SYMPATHETIC GRASP OF DETAIL
THAT IS NECESSARY BEFORE THIS
POINT IS REACHED HAS PROVED
USUALLY A MATTER OF YEARS,
WITH LITTLE ADVANTAGE ON THE
SIDE OF THE COLLEGE-TRAINED
UNDERSTUDY.[1]
— FRANK LLOYD WRIGHT

Frank Lloyd Wright had reached a point in 1898 when creating an architectural community in a place of its own seemed possible. That place was the studio he had built as an appendage to his Oak Park home. He and his staff began that year to do most of their architectural work in this imaginatively designed and appointed building. His coworkers included well-trained architects, draftsmen, assistants, and a secretary. As Wright's needs and their personal desires changed, members of the community arrived and departed. Some among them were there for only a year or two, some longer. Artists, contractors, and clients also came and went. Wright's growing family lived there too, until he left them and his entire staff in 1909. The office he maintained in downtown Chicago was used primarily for business purposes.[2]

Some of the most renowned Wright designs flowed from the Oak Park studio in these productive years. Between 1901 and 1908 he designed houses for Ward W. Willits, Francis W. Little, Susan Lawrence Dana, Arthur and Grace Heurtley, Burton Westcott, George Barton, Darwin D. Martin, Edwin Cheney, Avery Coonley, Frederick C. Robie, Meyer May, and more than three dozen other houses and cottages. There were also larger projects, including the Unity Temple in Oak Park and the Larkin Building in Buffalo, New York. On a more personal side, Wright built the second Hillside Home School for his aunts near Spring Green, Wisconsin, in 1902; thirty years later this building evolved into the center of activities for the Taliesin Fellowship.[3]

## THE STUDIO COMMUNITY

The concern here is not with these structures, however, but with the nature of the community in which they were designed and Wright's relationships with his coworkers who helped him bring them to reality. At first glance, it might appear that the Oak Park studio served as a prototype for the Taliesin Fellowship he and his third wife founded three decades later. It did not, but experiences in Oak Park no doubt planted seeds in Wright's mind for germination in another time and place.

Wright's autobiographical references to interactions with Louis Sullivan and Cecil Corbin, the Steinway Hall group, and other colleagues in Chicago's

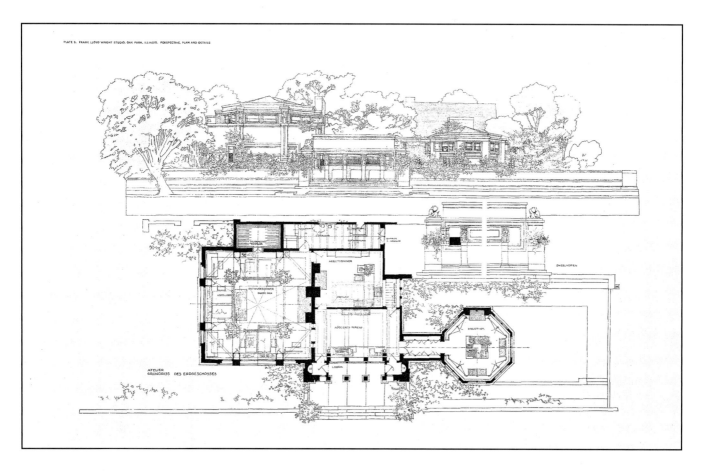

Frank Lloyd Wright's Oak Park Home and Studio. Copyright © 2009 the Frank Lloyd Wright Foundation, Taliesin West, Scottsdale, AZ

architectural enclaves reveal that, his commitment to individualism notwithstanding, he valued comradeship, and he no doubt wanted it in his studio. The fluid nature of his studio staff between 1898 and 1909, however, complicates attempts to speak precisely about the possibility of such comradeship.[4] Nor is it possible to determine the kind of spirit that prevailed there. In general terms, as W. R. Hasbrouck has written, the Oak Park studio "might be considered the first, and for a time the most influential, atelier . . . where a small but intensely loyal and dedicated group of young men, and a few women, worked with Sullivan's acknowledged disciple to invent what amounted to an entirely new architecture."[5] Whether comradeship accompanied the loyalty and dedication is difficult to say, and to what extent Sullivan's disciple interacted purposefully with his own disciples is open to question.

Moreover, as Paul Kruty has shown, the nature of Wright's early practice in the Oak Park Studio years differed in both fact and theory from what it was later. Until around 1906 his assistants were "experienced professionals, most of them with architectural and/or engineering training at universities and several with architectural licenses." He had sought them out and valued their assistance. By 1908, when he wrote the article from which the lead paragraph in this chapter is excerpted, "he saw the unschooled novice as the solution to the problems he had encountered with several studio employees, including Walter Burley Griffin."[6]

Two circumstances kept the studio community fluid: First, Wright employed only as many assistants as the work at hand required; as his commissions increased or diminished, so did the size and composition of his staff. Second, as his assistants responded to his encouragement to have projects of their own, from time to time those projects pulled them away from Wright's studio. For example, in 1903, Walter Burley Griffin designed a residence for William Emery, his neighbor in Elmhurst.[7]

## EXPERIENCING FRANK LLOYD WRIGHT

To discover the characteristics of the studio community, we turn first to Frank Lloyd Wright himself. The March 1908 issue of *Architectural Record* featured eighty-seven photographs of Wright's executed buildings and drawings for other projects. The essay accompanying the illustrations, "In the Cause of Architecture," was Wright's first fully developed statement about the convictions that drove his life and to which he would devote his career. He was forty-one years old and seemingly in his prime, but he apparently sensed a turning point coming. So in addition to addressing the cause of architecture, he also looked back, recalling ten men and two women who worked, or had worked, with him. "These young people," he wrote, "have found their way to me through natural sympathy with the work, and have become loyal assistants."

The members, so far, all told here and elsewhere, of our little university of fourteen years' standing are: Marion Mahony, a capable assistant for eleven years; William Drummond, for seven years; Francis Byrne, five years; Isabel Roberts, five years; George Willis, four years; Walter Griffin, four years; Andrew Willatzen, three years; Harry Robinson, two years; Charles E. White, Jr., one year; Erwin Barglebaugh and Robert Hardin, each one year; and Albert McArthur, entering.

Others, he said, were attracted by the apparent novelty of the work but stayed only "long enough to acquire a smattering of form, then departing to sell a superficial proficiency elsewhere." Still others discovered quickly that "it is all as they would have done it anyway" and set out "to blaze a trail for themselves without further loss of time." They "urge against the more loyal that they are sacrificing their individuality to that which has dominated this work." But Wright did not wish to fault a single understudy on this basis, he said, for what they learned would stay with them as they developed their individualities in their independent work. However, he had noticed "that those who have made the most fuss about their 'individuality' in early stages, those who took themselves most seriously in that regard, were inevitably those who had least."[8]

As might be expected, Wright's list of assistants not only includes a factual error—none of them had joined him twelve years earlier—but it also reflects his romantic capacity for remembering what he wanted to remember and his inclination to mislead when it suited his purposes. Specifically, the only notable person listed who came to him primarily because of his "natural sympathy" for his work was Francis Barry Byrne, and he is the only one who can be aptly described as "wholly unformed" when he arrived. Two of his key assistants, Marion Mahony and Walter Burley Griffin, held degrees in architecture from the Massachusetts Institute of Technology and the University of Illinois, respectively, and had been employed by other architects in Wright's acquaintance. Both were licensed architects and both had left his studio by 1908. They were soon out of his favor and he of theirs. William Drummond had some college-level studies in architecture and was also licensed; he had left Wright and returned. Wright does not say whether the persons he listed were architectural apprentices, architects, or draftsmen or in some other role in the operation of the studio.

Wright's autobiographical reflections on the operation of his "workshop at Oak Park" are similarly misleading. There he recalled that he had "worked away with various boys and girls as helpers and apprentices, to get the houses built that now stand across the prairie." Mahony was only four years younger than he, and Griffin and Drummond were nine years younger.

With this as background, it is useful to consider the assistants' perspectives on the studio's operations. Cheryl Robertson, author of a book on the collaboration between Wright and George Niedeken, an interior designer and curator of an exhibition that displayed their work, drew upon the studies of Wright scholars to maintain that the studio showed signs of being an effective working community. Wright had final control over the designs, but cooperation was the goal. It was "pursued through profit sharing, mutual criticism of drawings, and a fraternal nurturing among the members of the 'rounded individualities' and capacities for contributing 'forms of their own designing to the new [Prairie] school.'"[9]

In some respects the community functioned as family. With the studio's proximity to his living quarters, Wright could work late, he said, tumble into bed, get up again if an idea kept him awake, and go back to the studio. At times his children "were all running around with thumbtacks in the soles of their shoes." One of his assistants, Barry Byrne, recalled that the studio had "an easygoing atmosphere. They had five children who raced through the studio back and forth. The father would pursue them and threaten them with dire happenings. One day someone said, 'What would you do if you caught one of them?' 'Well,' he said, 'I really don't know. I'm very careful not to.' Perhaps it was this feeling of—of improvisation that evoked a sense of delight."[10] And perhaps witnessing this gave Wright's coworkers a sense of being in on something larger than an architectural practice.

The financial rewards of working with Wright were negligible. He paid his assistants enough, he claimed, to meet their needs for board and lodging, and most of them gave him a good return on his investment. "With the exception of six or seven," he recalled, "I have never had reason to complain of their enthusiasm for their work nor their loyalty to me. But, of their loyalty to the cause—yes. And after all, were they not taken in, on that cause?"[11] He readily acknowledged that there was nothing systematic about his way of working:

The system, or lack of it—I have never had an "office" in the conventional manner— has become fixed habit and works well enough—but only because I stay directly with it in every detail, myself. When I go away there is usually trouble and sometimes unpremeditated treachery. No. There was never organization in the sense that the usual architect's office knows organization. Nor any great need of it so long as I stood actually at the center of the effort. Where I am, there my office is. My office is me. And therein is one great difference between my own and current practice.[12]

Wright typically hired assistants referred to him by other architects. The most notable exception was Francis Barry Byrne. Standing at his door one Sunday morning, Wright recalled, was "a small boy, face covered with adolescent pimples, blushing furiously. Wanted to be an architect—liked my buildings, believed he would like to build that kind." What could he do? He could be an office boy, but Wright already had "several boys" doing that. Still, Wright found something touching in the young Byrne, something in his straightforward attempt to fulfill his ambition. Even though he didn't need him, he invited him in. Byrne stayed four years and "turned out better than many who had many years the start of him in every way."

Those who became assistants like Barry Byrne, as he came to be known, or who joined the staff in some other manner, learned that they were not to imagine they were coming to school. Rather they were expected to be as useful to Wright as they could be, to see work going on, and to be taken into the work as far as they could go. They would gain from their experiences in the studio according to their individual abilities and efforts.[13]

## THE NATURE OF THE COMMUNITY

In the absence of systematically maintained records of the Oak Park studio years, other sources must be used to discover who was employed there and to understand the way the community worked. Among these sources are the recollections of the men and women who worked in the studio, chiefly those of Barry Byrne, Charles E. White, Jr., Harry Robinson, and in a different way, Marion Mahony.[14] From them and others we gain insights into their own experiences with Wright, as well as into Wright's ways of dealing with others in the studio and with clients. They help us locate to the fullest extent possible when Wright's assistants—sometimes called students, pupils, or apprentices—came to the studio, what they did while there, when and why they went their own ways, and where their careers took them in later years. This is not the first attempt, of course, to comprehend the goings-on in the studio, so we will also draw upon the research findings of scholars who have studied Wright's Oak Park years or made the experiences of one or another of Wright's associates the focus of their work.[15]

But first we should gain a sense of Wright's attitudes toward those who worked with him. For one thing, he knew that his temperament, standards, and style, his ways of handling financial obligations, and his commitment to individualism rather than collaboration in architectural work would make partnerships impossible, no matter his need for assistance. Seemingly prospective partners among Wright's assistants knew that they could not consider anything but a temporary working relationship with him. Salaries were frequently overdue and sometimes not paid at all. Beyond this, the attitude he expressed toward them in this 1914 statement would also make them wary of assuming an ongoing relationship with him:

I am no teacher; I am a worker—but I gave to all, impartially, the freedom of my work room, my work, and myself, to imbue them with the spirit of the performances for their own sake; and with the letter for my sake, so that they might become useful to me; because the nature of my endeavor was such that I had to train my own help and pay current wages while I trained them.[16]

This statement again ignores or discounts the fact that three of Wright's most relied-upon assistants were trained in architecture schools and had been employed by other architects before coming to him.

Despite his insistence that he was not a teacher, and given his attitudes toward his assistants, his essay published in 1908 shows his commitment to teaching:

This year I assign to each a project that has been carefully conceived in my own mind, which he accepts as a specific work. He follows its subsequent development through all its phases in drawing room and field, meeting with the client himself on occasion, gaining an all-around development impossible otherwise, and insuring an enthusiasm and a grasp of detail decidedly to the best interest of the client. These privileges in the hands of selfishly ambitious or over-confident assistants would soon wreck such a system; but I can say that among my own boys it has already proved a moderate success, with every prospect of being continued as a settled policy in the future.[17]

When Barry Byrne joined Wright's studio staff in the late spring of 1902, Wright advised him to expect little attention. That did not disturb Byrne, he explained in a journal article published sixty-one years later, for he knew, as others in the studio might have told him, that his advancement would depend on his own efforts. Byrne's expression of indebtedness for the counsel and assistance given him by two trained architects, William Drummond and Walter Burley Griffin, provides insights into the studio's operations. To Wright, Byrne was an undemanding "small boy," a perception, he said, that persisted for years. Nonetheless, to Byrne "life at the studio savored, not of dream but rather of the realization of a higher order of things." The studio was a happy place, a rare thing in his life. As for teaching, there was none, at least in Byrne's view. Rather, "It was a true atelier where one learned, if one had the capacity, by working on the buildings that Mr. Wright designed." Byrne continued:

Endowed as he was with an unerring sense of the third dimension, Mr. Wright . . . always arrived at his designs in plan and elevation, the last usually determining one upon which perspectives were based. In the later years of my tutelage, and when projects were turned over to me to develop into working drawings, the original Wright-made studies would come into my hands with the plan established and the main theme of the exterior design clearly defined in elevation. The development of all implied but not delineated portions of the project then became the problem of the student draftsman, subject to the master's approval and often to his correction.

Later in this article Byrne mentions a letter written in 1962 by Walter Gropius, in which Gropius remarked that he had observed Wright's apprentices at work at Taliesin and had seen them doing no more than producing designs in Wright's personal style. That prompted Byrne to wonder whether any architectural school betters that condition. Having judged a number of architectural competitions, he concluded that "what is produced in most schools is of such an indifferent quality that I can only expect the Taliesin product to be better."[18]

After leaving Wright's studio in 1908, Byrne worked briefly for Walter Burley Griffin and Andrew Willatzen, also Wright's alumni, as were two architects with whom he worked in California: Lloyd Wright and John Lloyd Wright, sons of Frank Lloyd Wright. When Griffin moved to Australia in April 1914, he asked Byrne to take over his practice. Before accepting, Byrne consulted with Wright, who counseled him vehemently against such a move, contending it would destroy his chances for a successful career. Perhaps Wright's counsel reflected resentment toward the Griffins for their work in a development in Mason City, Iowa, known as Rock Crest/Rock Glen. He apparently believed that this work should have been his, for he had already designed the City National Bank building, the Park Inn hotel, and the G. C. Stockman residence in that city. In a letter to Mark Peisch, Byrne wrote, "If [Wright] had not gone abroad for a year at that time, we may assume he would have carried out the work at Rock Glen. He certainly thought so, and in those days was bitter in his remarks about Walter and Marion doing the work."[19]

Byrne responded to Wright that he would simply be completing Griffin's buildings and that his career would move forward. Given complete autonomy as a condition of his acceptance, he changed building and landscape designs Griffin had left for him and, to Griffin's dismay, substituted his own in some instances. That is not at all what Griffin had in mind. Paul Kruty, who has called Byrne's management of Griffin's projects a debacle, adds that, in fairness to Byrne, "it appears that more than anything he was overwhelmed with the magnitude of the job and, in addition, lacked Griffin's ability to get along with clients."[20]

Byrne continued on his own when his agreement with Griffin ended. Much of his work thereafter lay in designing Catholic churches and schools, a natural career development for him, for he was a Catholic himself. Howard Dearstyne, paying tribute to Byrne after he was killed when a car struck him in 1967, called him "far and away the most distinguished student of Frank Lloyd Wright."[21] Whether that is so depends on who is counted as a Wright student.

## ONE ASSISTANT'S PERCEPTIONS OF WRIGHT AND HIS STUDIO

Charles E. White, Jr., a young architect from Burlington, Vermont, worked in Wright's Oak Park studio from 1903 to 1906. He described his experiences there in a series of letters to W. R. B. Willcox, an architect practicing in his hometown. The letters ambled impressionistically over six topics: His discoveries in Wright's architecture, which he illustrated with sketches; the work being done in the studio; his own architectural work; personal matters between him and Willcox; the character of the studio's operations; and the contributions of the men and women who worked there. The last two of these topics is of the greatest interest here, but the others invite passing mention for what they reveal about one man's experiences with Wright and in his studio.

Concerning Wright's architecture, White noted that, having come out of Sullivan's office, Wright naturally applied Louis Sullivan's methods. Soon, though, he was simplifying his ornamental designs. His greatest innovation, White believed, was his unit system of design: "All his plans are composed of units grouped in a symmetrical and systematic way." Unlike other architects, he "developes [sic] his unit first, then fits his design to the requirement as much as possible, or rather, fits the requirements to the design."

White considered Wright a "most impractical man." He could be way behind in his work and calmly lay it aside to alter his office. "It makes me nervous," White wrote, "to think of the way he treats his clients, and yet he seems to get the work all the same." The studio, he said, was torn up again, as it was twice a year when Wright rearranged and changed the different rooms. "He says he has gotten more education on his own premises," according to White, "than in any other way."

One of the works in progress at the time was the Unity Temple. The leaders of the Unity congregation, of which Wright was a member, had accepted sketches for it "after endless fighting." Wright's people had all pleaded and argued with the committee until they were "well nigh worn out." It was his personal feeling, White said, that they had a beautiful and consistent design for a liberal church. Because the Unitarian idea calls for an institution rather than a church, Wright was free to follow his natural inclinations. He would be a failure as a designer of an orthodox church, White thought, but for the Unitarians he had produced a building with "the chaste beauty of a Greek temple, and much of the sublimity of . . . the Taj Mahal."

White described for Willcox his own architectural work, as, with Wright's encouragement, he began to establish a practice of his own. Wright told him that he should practice wherever the work came to him and that he would always stand ready to help in any way. Having worked in Wright's studio, White was entitled to use anything he had obtained from him. Against Wright's counsel, White decided to build his own studio in Oak Park. In fact, White told his friend, Wright thought he was a fool for trying to make that village rather than Chicago his home base. But he thought he could be most successful by "butting in" from Oak Park.

In Illinois, White said, dogs and architects had to be licensed (a Frank Lloyd Wright remark), so he was preparing to take the next examination. That required him to use his spare time studying architectural engineering, mechanics, sanitary engineering, plumbing, and related matters, particularly "brushing up on theory." But he also spent a lot of time constructing his own studio, a building he described in detail. And not surprisingly, he fussed about the difficulty of agreeing upon fees with his clients. One wonders whether he had time to follow the advice he passed along to Willcox in the first letter, November 18, 1903: Wright told him to stop reading books for a while, and do nothing but study nature and sketch. He should "continually and eternally sketch the forms of trees," for "a man who can sketch from memory the different trees, with their characteristics faithfully portrayed, will be a good architect."

White wondered whether there was perhaps a place for Willcox in Wright's studio. That might be something to consider, he said, since work was not piling

up for him in Burlington. "You would make an ideal man for Frank Wright," White observed, "but I wouldn't let you go in with him for the world. It would be the worst possible policy for any man who has a family to support, to have his business interests tied up with Wright. If he offered me half interest I wouldn't take it, if there was any possible way to earn a living elsewhere, and yet I owe him more than money can pay—almost an architectural education."

One reason for saying that a place in Wright's studio would not be good for Willcox is that no one could count on being paid, and when pay came it did not amount to much. But beyond that, the setting would not be right for him. For one thing, Wright had not paid attention to taking vacations, and that caused him "to become sort of petered out this last year. For the past three months it had been almost impossible to get him to give any attention to us. As he expressed it, he 'has no appetite for work.'"

In a letter dated May 13, 1904, White noted that everyone in the studio was busy: Isabel Roberts, nominally a bookkeeper and factotum, was working on ornamental glass, and Marion Mahony was preparing a model, sketched by Richard Bock, for a fountain for the Dana House in Springfield. Walter Burley Griffin, White reported, was the "general practical man, writer of specifications and the like." The remaining three, William Drummond, Barry Byrne, and he himself were "draughtsmen in general." He was working almost entirely on the houses for Buffalo, New York.

"The Moon Children," a sculptured panel and fountain in the living room of the Dana House, Springfield, Illinois, designed by Richard Bock and executed by Bock and Marion Mahony. Courtesy of Doug Carr

Andrew Willatzen, who, according to White had been with Wright for three years, had gone to Rockford to work for a friend and earn more than Wright could pay him. Later he reported that Willatzen had gone to work for Robert Spencer, a friend and admirer of Wright. White commented briefly on other colleagues in the studio: Griffin had resigned and was going into practice in Chicago. Wright had told him he was going to let Drummond out when he could. Drummond, according to White, had "some very nasty streaks in his makeup. He is deceitful, among other things," but "very clever." Marion Mahony's great work was evident in her perspectives for the Unity Temple; "she is one of the finest in the country at this class of rendering."

But White had no close friends, not in the studio, none whatsoever in the area, which explained why he was so dependent on his correspondence with Willcox. "There is no one at the Studio who appeals to me in the least," he wrote, "with the exception of young Byrne, and he is only a child [at twenty-one, Byrne was seven years younger than White]. The rest of the bunch are interested strictly in their own affairs. The one thing they need above all else there is the French 'esprit de corps,' instead of each one pulling in an opposite direction. Of course they are all exceedingly friendly, but you feel it comes from the lips instead of from the heart."[22]

**MOVING ON**

Many of Wright's assistants found reasons and ways to move on. After leaving the Oak Park studio in 1905, White continued practicing architecture in the Chicago area until his death in 1936. On several occasions his designs appeared in catalogues of the Chicago Architectural Club. Following Wright's example as a writer, he published articles in *House Beautiful,* the *Ladies Home Journal,* and *Country Life.*[23]

William Drummond came to the Oak Park studio in 1899 and apparently stayed until 1901. After working for other architects, he returned in 1903 as the chief of the drafting room. According to Mark Peisch, he is the one who saw the drawings through the office from start to finish. Grant Carpenter Manson wrote that on the day of Wright's flight from the studio in 1909, the normal volume of work was in progress. Drummond and John van Bergen completed it, overcoming numerous obstacles. When the jobs were finished, wrote Manson, "Drummond and van Bergen closed and locked the Studio door, thereby ending an era in the chronicles of America's greatest architect."[24]

H. Allen Brooks reported the closing differently. In a letter to him, van Bergen wrote that when Wright left, "I was the only one on the payroll. I doubt if I ever received my last few weeks' pay (quite the custom with FLW). I completed the work then in the office, with much help from Miss Roberts. There were many problems to be settled with various contractors (and) as a youngster I had my troubles." One of those troubles was that he and Roberts had to complete work on projects for which Wright had already collected the final fees. Van Bergen also wrote that Drummond left Wright with harsh words as he tried to collect the salary Wright owed him. He continued to practice architecture in the Chicago area. Based on the design of his own home in River Forest and of the First Congregational Church in Austin, both undertaken while he was still employed by Wright,

Brooks concluded that Drummond had the capacity to devise fresh concepts from Wright-inspired ideas. Houses completed in subsequent years confirm this judgment. He partnered with Louis Guenzel from 1912 to 1915 and completed several notable projects. After World War I, however, he found it necessary to compromise with clients who wanted more traditional homes, and he moved away from Prairie-style designs. Brooks says that the depression ruined him and that whatever he did after that was in other offices.[25]

Marion Mahony, the only assistant whose gifts Wright acknowledged in the 1908 article "In the Cause of Architecture," presents a more complicated case study. She was born in Chicago in 1871, and after the Great Fire destroyed large parts of the city that year, moved with her family to Hubbard Woods, a suburb north of Chicago. In 1894 she graduated with a degree in architecture from the Massachusetts Institute of Technology, the second woman to earn a degree there. After about six months of internship with her cousin, Dwight Perkins, the architect for Steinway Hall and one of the Eighteen with whom Wright was associated, she was unemployed briefly before coming to work in 1895 for Frank Lloyd Wright. Her pay was low, and she may have assumed that her title, "superintendent of the office force," was intended to console her.[26] In 1898 she became the first woman ever to be licensed in the practice of architecture.[27] She stayed with Wright, not continuously but as needed, until 1905, when she began an independent practice. However, she also worked with Wright occasionally during the next five years.

Marion Mahony Griffin, an assistant to Wright in his Oak Park office who later criticized him sharply. Courtesy of the Art Institute of Chicago & the New-York Historical Society (Magic of America, IV, 12, 273).

Mahony's studio associate, Barry Byrne, in a 1965 conversation recorded by H. Allen Brooks, referred to her as "a good actress, talkative, and when around Wright there was a real sparkle." Brooks also cites a paper Byrne delivered at a meeting of the Illinois Society of Architects in 1939, in which Byrne said, "Her mordant humor always attracted me as a fellow Celt, and I can well remember welcoming her advent (she came irregularly) because it promised an amusing day. Her dialogues with Frank Lloyd Wright, who, as we all know, is no indifferent opponent in repartee, made such days particularly notable."[28]

Mahony's contributions to the work of the studio were more than conversational. Janice Pregliasco credits her with producing the glass designs for more than a few of Wright's projects, based on his decorative motifs. This enabled Wright to gain recognition for melding art and architecture in art glass and using the designs in such places as the Dana, Robie, Martin, Bradley, Coonley, and Heath homes, as well as Unity Church. Mahony drew freehand, while Wright used rulers and triangles. Several of her fellow assistants considered her to be Wright's superior as a draftsman. Barry Byrne noted that Wright took another draftsman's statement of her superiority "equably."[29]

When Wright left for Europe in 1909, rather suddenly but with considerable premeditation, he asked Mahony to take over his practice. She declined, but she agreed to complete some of his projects, working with Herman von Holst, whom Wright had persuaded to fill in for him. Von Holst had had no previous working relationship with Wright, and the architectural styles of the two men were strikingly dissimilar. That von Holst would accede to Mahony's demand for control of the designing is therefore understandable. "That suited him," Mahony wrote, and "when the absent architect didn't bother to answer anything that was sent over to him the relations were broken and I entered into a partnership with von Holst and Fyfe. For that period I had great fun designing."[30]

When Mahony collaborated with von Holst she moved back to Steinway Hall and was reunited with former colleagues, including Walter Burley Griffin. The work she completed after Wright's departure included the E.P. Irving residence on Millikin Place in Decatur, Illinois, for which she designed the furniture. She also designed the Robert Mueller residence, adjacent to the east, and, two doors to the west, the Adolph Mueller residence. Griffin assisted her on the last of these and landscaped the entire site. Her most notable design was the David Amberg house in Grand Rapids, Michigan. A photograph of this house in the October 1913 issue of the *Western Architect* drew much favorable attention and both von Holst and Wright later claimed it as theirs.[31]

Mahony's professional relationship with Griffin soon took on a personal element. In her memoir, *Magic of America,* Mahony wrote that she was swept off her feet with delight in Griffin's achievements in her profession, "then through a common bond of interests and intellectual pursuits, and then with the man himself. It was by no means love at first sight, but it was madness when it struck."[32] In 1911 she became Marion Mahony Griffin.

It was natural for Walter Burley Griffin, who had grown up in the Chicago area, to return there in quest of employment when he graduated from the University of Illinois in 1899 with a degree in architecture. He found it at Steinway Hall with Dwight Perkins. Among his new acquaintances were Myron Hunt and Robert Spencer, who were members, along with Perkins, of the group Wright many years later labeled "the Eighteen." Although Wright had left Steinway Hall by then, his professional ties with architects based there continued.

Soon after Griffin qualified for his licensure in architecture by the State of Illinois in 1901 he began to work in Wright's Oak Park office. According to Paul Kruty, Griffin quickly became a great asset in the Oak Park studio by lending stability to the "boiling energy" there and by writing specifications, making regular checks on the progress of projects under construction, and attempting to mollify clients and contractors who had been slighted in some way or another by Mr. Wright. His increasingly important role and his growing stature as an architect, however, failed to persuade Wright to acknowledge his capabilities and accomplishments. Even so, Griffin apparently anticipated the possibility of moving into a partnership. Wright had designated him as manager for such large projects as the Hillside Home School for Wright's aunts in Wisconsin and the Larkin Building in Buffalo, New York, and made him the landscape architect for a number of other projects, making such anticipation plausible.

There was another dimension to the Griffin-Wright association: In 1905, when Wright traveled to Japan with his wife and Mr. and Mrs. Ward Willits, his clients, he asked Griffin to manage his office. Griffin apparently managed it well, although he seems to have taken liberties with designs that Wright did not approve. In any case, relations between the two men grew tense. Differences over repayment of a loan Griffin had made to Wright to finance the travel abroad contributed to the tension. When Wright returned, he paid Griffin with Japanese prints rather than cash. Griffin was not pleased. Some years later Wright heard a rumor about Griffin's displeasure over the failure to be paid properly. This prompted him to draft an intemperate letter, suggesting that Griffin was responsible for "petty attacks of inuendo" [sic] and "cowardly blows beneath the belt." Insisting that Griffin was duty-bound to return the prints, Wright said he would then give him the money he wanted, with interest at 6 percent in addition to 20 percent of the profit on his investment. The prints, he said, were worth much more than this, but he wanted to close the unfortunate "episode" or do what he could to "correct an unfair insinuation which I confess touches me to the quick." He did not mail the letter; rather, it apparently remained in the file of Taylor Woolley, his assistant at the time.[33]

In their assessments of the working relationships of Griffin with Wright, scholars note that Griffin always credited Louis Sullivan, rather than Wright, as the inspiration for his architectural ideas. He referred frequently to the address Louis Sullivan gave at the 1900 meeting of the Architectural League of America, "The Young Man in Architecture,"[34] but he rarely spoke about Wright. That Griffin influenced Wright, scholars assert, is evident in Wright's incorporation of "Griffinesque features" in his designs. Marion Mahony, in addition to providing renderings for Wright's designs, also made original contributions to them.[35]

As for Wright, he could not bring himself to acknowledge any of Griffin's accomplishments. In the transcript of an interview for the broadcast on PBS of "Walter Burley Griffin in His Own Right," historian Mark Peisch quotes Wright as saying that "he would not really give Walter any characterization except that he was a very helpful person but one who followed orders, not

Walter Burley Griffin, an assistant in Wright's office who later won the commission to design Canberra, the new capital of Australia. Courtesy of the Art Institute of Chicago & the New-York Historical Society (Magic of America. Negative no. 59228).

one who created." The same was true for Mahony Griffin. His part in their lives, as he saw it, had been to give them the training they needed.[36]

The collaborating Griffins enjoyed successful, interwoven, mutually dependent careers, first in the United States, mainly as designers of homes and in landscape and decorative architecture. In 1912, however, Walter Burley Griffin won the competition to design the new Australian capital in Canberra, an achievement Wright ignored. Griffin benefited immeasurably in the competition from his wife's beautiful renderings of his designs. The couple's success continued in Australia, although frustrations in dealing with bureaucratic wrangling played a part in Walter's decision to move to India in 1935 to supervise the construction of a library he had designed for the University of Lucknow. Marion moved to India in 1936. When her husband died there in 1937, she saw to the completion of some of his projects and returned to the United States, where she wrote her memoir, *The Magic of America*.

In this work she made it clear that Walter Burley Griffin's cause was hers, that his adventure was her story. When she suggested to him "that he might find me a useful person in his office in the matter of the presentation of his work," she became "deeply centered in the task of lending a hand in all the various emergencies that arose. Truly I lost myself in him and found it completely satisfying."[37]

Marion Mahony Griffin had evidently enjoyed a cordial relationship with Frank Lloyd Wright during the years she worked for him, and also with Mrs. [Catherine] Wright; she on occasion spoke favorably of Wright's work. In later years she could not resist denigrating what he had done, although she avoided using his name when allusions identify him sufficiently. Referring to him in her memoir as a "so-called architect," she asserted that his "vanity and malice killed the so-called Chicago movement in architecture," in which he had been a "cancer sore." The delay in the development of creative design was largely due, she charged, to his "malicious vanity," and his work had been unfruitful "because of the poison of his spirit of personality." She cited an instance in which it seemed to her that Wright copied something she had designed. "I thought nothing of that till years later Wright began his publications claiming all the young Chicago architects as his disciples, which was far from the truth. I would grant that what one likes one can use—as in the growth of Gothic—but cannot claim."[38]

In one of her more scathing recollections Mahony Griffin wrote:

His [Wright's] first flat building was on the boards when I entered this office. The frieze was almost a direct copy from this building of Sullivan's [pictured on the opposing page] in whose office he had been trained. Throughout his practice it was he who followed others not they him. They were the creative ones. One wouldn't mind his taking up what inspired him but his claiming and publicity (made spicy by his scandals) stunned [sic] the movement, founded by Sullivan, in the United States for a quarter of a century.

He was quick on the uptake, naturally artistic but never an architect though he claimed the whole Chicago School of architects as his disciples. He spent most of his life writing articles making these claims and really was a blighting influence on the group of enthusiastic creative architects of his generation. Only a quarter of a century later has any creative architecture in the United States escaped the blight of his self-centered publicity.[39]

Marion Mahony Griffin returned to Chicago after her husband's death in 1937. In her remaining years she produced a few designs and was active in a quasi-religious movement known as anthroposophy. She died in Chicago in 1962, three years after Wright, at the age of ninety.

There were others who came to Frank Lloyd Wright's Studio in Oak Park, stayed for varying lengths of time, and made their own unique contributions before moving on. Yet, the ones treated here, particularly Byrne, Mahony, Griffin, and Drummond, are the architects who made the biggest marks while working for Wright or after their departure. As for Charles White, he practiced in the Chicago area and became a prolific writer. His most lasting work, however, may have been the record he left of life and work in Frank Lloyd Wright's studio.

From the entire ensemble we can conclude that this Wrightian community was a mixture of caring, indifference, excitement, and exploitation. Many who were there admired Frank Lloyd Wright's work but found dealing with him to be frustrating and at times unpleasant. Struggles in his personal life and his quest for identity, distinctiveness, and renown probably left him ill-equipped for leading a collection of talented men and women who were ambitious in their own right and who had limits as to what they would take from Wright, no matter his genius and reputation in the world outside the studio.

And yet, if Barry Byrne's assessment of the situation is right, all who worked with Wright in his studio were better for it, Mahony Griffin's assessment notwithstanding. In a letter to Mark Peisch, Byrne wrote, "Wright seldom worked on an idea without making it almost transcendentally better. The value of training under Wright lay in the matter of seeing top grade talent, or shall I say genius, function. There was no one around him that in any way approached him in ability."[40]

When Wright left for Europe, he wanted to make a clean break. That might have been devastating to his assistants, but the rather tentative relationship some of them had with him and his studio, as they came and went or took on jobs independently, no doubt softened the blow. Some had moved on and established their own careers before the studio closed. Griffin provides the best example. For some, such as Marion Mahony Griffin, Wright's departure brought new and enviable opportunities. In general, Brooks concludes, "[d]ifficulties were surmounted, the [Prairie School] movement did not collapse. Nor did it suffer depletion in its ranks. . . . Productivity increased, as did the quality of work. Wright's designs continued as a principal source of inspiration, but there was increasing independence and the beginnings of several strongly personal expressions." In fact, Wright's departure "strengthened the hand of those he left behind, taught them to stand alone, and prepared them for the final pre-war years—the most prosperous and prestigious years of all."[41] But they did not stand together as an alumni community of Frank Lloyd Wright's studio.

Whether the community in the Oak Park studio was a forerunner to the Taliesin Fellowship is, at best, debatable. In a way, though, it became that. As Paul Kruty has pointed out, "Wright's account of 1908 reflects a slowly evolving set of intentions, developed by the varied experiences of the previous decade. . . . While the description of office practice provided Wright with a blueprint for actual practice within the Taliesin Fellowship, the narrative concerning the ideal apprentice appears to describe Wright's experience with a single member of his Oak Park Studio, Barry Byrne. . . ."

Later in life, Kruty continued, "Wright routinely characterized all of his Oak Park draftsmen as pliable beginners—in effect, turned them all into Barry Byrne." The departure of Griffin in 1906 and the arrival of the younger, unmolded staff allowed Wright to envision "a new kind of practice in which he stood at the helm while hand-picked youngsters followed his commands." Ironically, he adds, Wright closed the studio within two years after arriving at that point and nearly a quarter of a century before he could test his hypotheses in the Fellowship.[42]

# 3 UNSETTLED YEARS

## *At Home and Abroad*

TALIESIN, OF COURSE, WAS TO BE AN ARCHITECT'S WORKSHOP, A DWELLING AS WELL, FOR YOUNG WORKERS WHO WOULD COME TO ASSIST. AND IT WAS A FARM COTTAGE FOR THE FARM HELP. AROUND A REAR COURT WERE TO BE FARM BUILDINGS, FOR TALIESIN WAS TO BE A COMPLETE LIVING UNIT GENUINE IN POINT OF COMFORT AND BEAUTY, YES, FROM PIG TO PROPRIETOR. THE PLACE WAS TO BE SELF-SUSTAINING IF NOT SELF-SUFFICIENT, AND WITH ITS DOMAIN OF TWO HUNDRED ACRES WAS TO BE SHELTER, FOOD, CLOTHES AND EVEN ENTERTAINMENT WITHIN ITSELF. IT HAD TO BE ITS OWN LIGHT-PLANT, FUEL YARD, TRANSPORTATION AND WATER SYSTEM.[1]

—**FRANK LLOYD WRIGHT**

The plan for Taliesin described so romantically by Wright in his autobiography may have been germinating vaguely in his mind when he abruptly closed his Oak Park studio in 1909 and left almost immediately for Europe. But if it was, he had to deal first with a more immediate matter. His mission was to meet with Ernest Wasmuth, the German publisher who planned to introduce Wright and his architecture to Europe through two portfolios of photographs and drawings. The portfolios would illustrate the buildings and projects Wright had completed in the sixteen years since he opened his practice. Historians frequently credit this work, titled *Ausgefürte Bauten und Entwürfe von Frank Lloyd Wright,* with spreading Wright's architectural influence in Europe, presumably giving his accomplishments greater impact there than in the United States.[2] Conventional understandings of the direction of architectural influence—America to Europe or Europe to America—have recently been challenged, however, as we shall see later in this chapter.

## MAMAH BORTHWICK CHENEY

Wright had someone in addition to Wasmuth on his mind, someone whose presence in his life had forced him to an agonizing but perhaps inevitable decision. That someone was Mamah Borthwick Cheney, the wife of Edwin Cheney. The Cheneys had been his clients in Oak Park. His poignant autobiographical reflections concerning this decision reveal that he did not simply run away, abandoning his family, his clients, and his assistants in the Oak Park studio. Rather, he deliberated over his course of action earnestly. On the brink of his fortieth year, he recalled, the "absorbing, consuming phase" of his experience as an architect had left him weary. He was losing his grip on his work, and even his interest in it. In the studio "every day of every week and far into the night of nearly every day, Sunday included," he had again and again "added tired to tired." Although this left him "continuously thrilled," he felt that he was up against a dead wall, with no way out. Knowing only that he wanted to go away, he asked, "Why not go to Germany and prepare the material for the Wasmuth Monograph? . . . I had looked longingly in that direction."[3]

He had tried to regain a grip on his work by getting away from it. One diversion was horseback riding, sometimes stopping to rest. Sometimes he would read Walt Whitman, his favorite. But to no avail. The intensity of effort and the unrelenting concentration his work required had done something troubling to him:

Everything, personal and otherwise, bore heavily down upon me. Domesticity most of all. What I wanted I did not know. I loved my children. I loved my home. A true home is the finest ideal of man, and yet—well, to gain freedom I asked for a divorce. It was, advisedly, refused. But these conditions were made: Were I to wait a year, a divorce would be granted. The year went by. Legal freedom still refused by Catherine and all concerned in the promise. There remained to me in the circumstances only one choice—to take the situation in hand and work out the best life possible for all concerned.[4]

Wright listed three "necessities that had emerged . . . as a means to an honest life": that "marriage not mutual is no better, but is worse than any other form of slavery"; that "only to the degree that marriage is mutual is it decent"; and that "the child is the pledge of good faith its parents give to the future of the race." This led him to conclude that, since marriage is but a civil contract between a man and a woman, it "is subject to the legal interpretations and enforcements of any other contract." Love, "so far as laws can go to protect it, is entitled to the benefit of hands-off and the benefit of the doubt." It "should be its own protection or its own defeat." As for children, they are entitled to "good shelter, good food, good treatment and an open door to growth of body and mind . . . in addition to the circumstances of birth may present to it—the most desirable thing of all being love." And love, he said, *"can be no concern of the laws."*[5]

So, after turning his clients' plans and his draftsmen over to Herman von Holst, whom he apparently scarcely knew, and making the best provisions possible for his family for one year, he broke with all family connections, "though never with such responsibilities as I felt to be mine . . . or that I felt I could discharge."

"Resolutely, with the same faith I'd had when leaving home and college, I took the train for Chicago. I went out into the unknown to test faith in freedom. Test my faith in life as I had already proved faith in my work. I faced the hazards of change and objective ruin inevitably involved with our society in every inner struggle for freedom."[6]

**SEPARATION ANXIETIES**

Now Wright was separated from the concentric circle of communities that had surrounded him: his family, the most intimate one; the coworkers in his studio; and the members of Chicago's architectural communities—his associates for more than two decades. The separations, according to Edgar Kaufmann, Jr., tested Wright's fiber as a man as well as an architect. His wife resolutely denied him a divorce. His six children "were deeply torn, those in their teens especially." Mr. Cheney agreed to his wife's separation, giving her partial custody of their two children.

Leaving his mother, Anna Lloyd Wright, who had been a dominant figure in his life and who had sent Wright's father away and ended her own marriage when the son was sixteen, could not have been unimportant. Wright had grown up with her, Kaufmann noted, had never separated from her, and still supported her emotionally and financially. Her imprint "was wide as well as deep." These facts and conjectures are worth reciting, Kaufmann contends, "because they indicate that Wright, in 1908–1909, which he called 'the miserable year of probation and demoralization,' acted from within a thick web of family feelings and precedents that extended beyond his twenty years of marriage, his children, and his unique career. If he reached his decisions as Frank Lloyd Wright the individual, he acted as a Lloyd-Jones at the same time."[7]

## LOOKING FOR EXPLANATIONS

The explanations for Wright's abandonment of his family and his architectural colleagues are no doubt more complex than those given in his autobiography, so biographers have speculated about them. Norris Kelly Smith, for example, rejects the popular notion that "Wright was a hurt and sensitive genius, driven by the indifference of his countrymen into the arms of appreciative foreigners," plausible though that may have seemed. As the architectural style he had pioneered gained popularity, Smith suggested, he was being "forced at last to confront the fact that architecture is the art of established institutions, and that there lay in the very fact of their establishment something that was inherently inimical to his Emersonian ideals. Somewhere he had miscalculated; and so now he found himself facing 'a dead wall.'" It must have seemed to him, Smith concluded, "that in the very act of defying law and custom he was breaking his way out of the trap of conventionality in which he felt himself to be caught, and was clearing the way for a new life that would now have to be built, whatever form it might take, upon the idea of the supremacy of individual freedom over social conformity."[8]

Neil Levine describes Wright's situation more broadly. After noting Wright's lack of fulfillment in his marriage, his love for another woman, and his bitterness over the failure of his critics to see the value of his work, he contends that Wright "needed time and distance to evaluate what he had accomplished and where it might lead." That, he says, points to the more positive aspects of Wright's decision to end his Oak Park practice. He needed to expand his horizons, to explore Europe, to assimilate ideas not found in his native land.[9]

## ON THE MOVE

With his newfound individual freedom, or at least what he regarded as freedom, Wright left Oak Park on September 20 and traveled to New York to meet Mamah Borthwick Cheney. From there they set sail for Europe, settling briefly in Berlin. On November 24, 1909, he signed a contract with Ernst Wasmuth Verlag for the publication of the monograph depicting his work.[10]

Tracing Wright's movements and relationships with others in the year that followed is difficult. He probably kept no records of the locations where he lived and worked, or with whom he worked, and if they ever existed they would have been destroyed in a fire at Taliesin in 1914. Such records as can be

Mamah Borthwick Cheney, Wright's companion from 1909 until 1914, when she was murdered at Taliesin. Courtesy of the Frank Lloyd Wright Foundation

Taylor Woolley, Wright's assistant
in Europe, shown here at Villino
Belvidere, where he worked as
a draftsman with Lloyd Wright.
Special Collections Dept., J. Willard
Marriott Library, University of Utah

pieced together from that year are scant and sometimes inconsistent one with another. In any case, there is no evidence that Wright attempted to form any kind of community beyond the one that included, in addition to himself, his companion, Mamah Borthwick Cheney; his son, Frank Lloyd Wright, Jr., known as Lloyd; and Taylor Woolley, a draftsman who had worked briefly in his Oak Park studio.

Drawing on fragmentary references in letters Wright sent and received and on other contemporary sources, Anthony Alofsin has reconstructed Wright's movements with this small community between his arrival in Berlin and his return to Oak Park late in 1910. The itinerary that follows is gleaned from his *Frank Lloyd Wright: The Lost Years, 1910–1922: A Study of Influence.*[11]

Wright and Cheney stayed initially in one of Berlin's newest buildings, the Hotel Adlon, where he could immerse himself in the city's rich culture and absorb ideas that later influenced his evolving career. Travels to the nearby city of Darmstadt, possibly in the late fall of 1909, enabled him to study the buildings of the late Joseph Maria Obrich, with whose work he was familiar. In January 1910, Wright visited Paris, where, he recalled years later, he heard a cellist play a madrigal that Lloyd had played on his cello and he had accompanied on the piano. This filled him with "interior anguish" and drove him out of the café into the streets. "It was not repentance," he continued. "It was despair that I could not achieve what I had undertaken as ideal."[12] Cheney was apparently not with him, having gone to Sweden to meet the prototypical feminist writer Ellen Key and become her official language translator.[13]

Wright may have gone directly from Paris to Florence, Italy, to begin preparing his drawings for publication by Wasmuth. His only assistant until his son Lloyd arrived appears to have been Taylor Woolley. Lloyd had been enrolled at the University of Wisconsin, but at his father's request and with his funds, he withdrew to travel to Italy. His main task, like Woolley's, was to assist Wright in preparing drawings for the Wasmuth portfolios.

## FLORENCE AND FIESOLE

The three men, working in the cold Villino "Fortuna," traced with quill pens all the drawings the senior Wright wished to have published. "It took high concentration," Lloyd recalled, as well as "time, and application of an intense order," as it involved "modifying, building up, correcting, simplifying, and converting all of the material into totally coordinated plates" for reproduction.[14]

Sometime in the spring of 1910 Wright moved to Fiesole, five miles northeast of Florence. Before long he went to Leipzig and returned with Mamah Borthwick Cheney. There, he recalled in his autobiography, he sought shelter "in companionship with her who, by force of rebellion as by way of love was then implicated with me." The romantic recollection of time spent with her in their modest dwelling, known as Villino Belvidere, continues:

Walking hand in hand together up the hill road from Firenze to the older town, all along the way in the sight and scent of roses, by day. Walking arm in arm up the same old road at night, listening to the nightingale in the deep shadows of the moonlit wood—trying hard to hear the song in the deeps of life. So many Pilgrimages we made to reach the small solid door framed in the solid white blank wall with the massive green door opening toward the Via Verdi itself. Entering, closing the medieval door on the world outside to find a wood fire burning in the small grate. . . .[15]

For Wright, making permanent this romantic life meant designing a studio-villa for himself and his companion. The design, according to Bruce Brooks Pfeiffer, "shows his thorough understanding of how to build in this Italian setting."[16] Realities intervened, however, before even the first steps could be taken to build it. Among them was the task of completing the drawings for the Wasmuth folios. More significant, though, was the decision he reported to his friend, British architect C. R. Ashbee, in a letter on July 8: "The fight has been fought—I am going back to Oak Park to pick up the thread of my work and in some degree of my life where I snapped it."[17]

## RETURNING TO OAK PARK AND FACING CONSEQUENCES

The Wasmuth work was not yet at a point, however, when Wright could leave Europe, and some matters remained unresolved three months later when he felt compelled to return to America. He arrived in Oak Park on October 8, 1910. Cheney remained in Europe for a time before returning to Oak Park, but she did not go back to her husband, who had filed for divorce on grounds of desertion. Wright moved in with his family again, but he left no doubt that he would soon be leaving again. To make that possible, he sought the assistance of wealthy friends, with whom he tried to justify his separation from Catherine and his affair with Cheney while at the same attempting to deny its continuation. For almost a year, Anthony Alofsin asserts, he led a double life, "a life of denying his love for Mamah Cheney while planning his future around her."[18]

Alofsin contends convincingly that, contrary to received wisdom, Wright's

Villino Belvidere, at Fiesole near Florence, Italy, where Wright lived briefly with Mamah Borthwick Cheney and where he and his draftsmen worked. Special Collections Dept., J. Willard Marriott Library, University of Utah

months in Europe had less to do with extending his influence there than with their impact on his architectural development. In addition to escaping from his troubled family situation, he says, the Wasmuth publication "allowed him to summarize in a systematic way his own architectural ideas." Although he had accomplished much with the Wasmuth effort and absorbed a great deal through his other experiences, Alofsin notes, his "'spiritual adventure' was incomplete. Before he could fully reveal how Europe had affected his work he had to face a return to his family, to translate his experience into his art, and to fit his principles into an unconventional life. His explorations of the lessons of Europe would take place in the midst of intense strife."[19]

At the center of that strife was the certainty that no good way existed for Wright to return to his family, even if he had wanted to. The press and the public treated his family abandonment and his sojourn in Europe with Cheney as a scandal ripe for exploitation. Exploit it they did, publishing and devouring front-page stories about it. His comportment and the treatment of it in the press made him an outcast in Oak Park. This neither surprised nor disturbed him. Rather, he rationalized the scandal as a self-justifying badge of honor.

In these circumstances there was no easy way for him to restart his architectural practice. Some of his prospective clients were offended by his conduct and turned to other architects. His antipathy toward Herman von Holst, who had taken over his practice when he left, was so intense that settlement of financial relationships between the two men required legal arbitration. But gradually he gained commissions and seemed pleased to be working again with clients.

Reestablishing his personal life was more problematical. In Europe he had been nomadic, and he continued to live similarly upon his return. For a time he stayed at his Oak Park home and studio, separately from Catherine, who refused to grant him a divorce. At some point he moved to a small apartment in a coach house at 25 Cedar Street.[20] In 1911 he returned briefly to Berlin to negotiate with Wasmuth for additional volumes of *Ausgeführte*. That year he also designed a four-story townhouse, intended to serve also as a studio, for a location on Goethe Street in Chicago, just four blocks from his Cedar Street apartment. Neil Levine remarks that the façade derives from Wright's design for Fiesole. Lack of funds as well as alternative desires evidently prevented him from building it.[21]

### BUILDING A HOUSE AND REBUILDING A PRACTICE

Indeed, his mind was concentrated on building something more important: a "cottage" for his mother at the home place of the Lloyd Jones family near Spring Green, Wisconsin, on property apparently acquired from her, possibly as a gift. The setting in the rolling hills of Wisconsin, on the south side of the beautiful Wisconsin River, was ideal for a person with Wright's aesthetic sensitivities. His concern for providing a home for his mother, Anna Lloyd Wright, is understandable. In Oak Park she lived next to Wright's home and studio, and after her son deserted his wife and children there, she was no doubt anxious to move away as well.[22] Moreover, he was accustomed to being his mother's project, even before she sent his father away nearly three decades earlier. His sister Maginel wrote that her mother "gathered all the strands of her yearning, wove them together, and fastened them once and for all to her son. He would accomplish what she and her husband could not. . . . Her every breath, every move, was for her little boy."[23]

As Wright's plans for the cottage took shape, the fiction that he was designing it for his mother soon gave way to real-life drama. On Christmas Day, 1911, Wright announced his true intentions: Taliesin, as he named it, would be his home to share with Mamah Borthwick; divorced, that is how she was known. This "Shining Brow" was to be their refuge, a retreat from the city. Levine describes it as "a direct outcome and logical extension of Wright's year in Europe. It was intended to be a 'transference' from Fiesole to Wisconsin of the new life he and Borthwick had begun in Italy."[24] The expanded studio at Taliesin enabled Wright to conduct at least part of his practice from there while also maintaining an office and studio in Orchestra Hall in Chicago.

Although his architectural productivity did not quickly return to the levels it had achieved before he left for Europe, his studios were busy. Fixing dates and numbers for Wright's projects (that is, unbuilt designs) and executed designs is not easy, but Edgar Kaufmann, Jr., gave doing so a try. In round numbers, as he calculated them, in the six-year period 1904–1909 Wright produced about twenty-five designs for public use, area plans, and service buildings; of these, 80 percent were built. In the same years he designed about eighty big houses and modest homes, with 60 percent of them being built. In the five years 1910–1914, he designed about twenty public-use structures, of which half were built. About half of the forty big houses and modest homes he designed were built in these years.[25] The most significant of these designs was one that has been called the greatest house in America, that is, Taliesin.

## WRIGHT'S COMMUNITY OF COWORKERS

As work continued in Wright's studios on projects in Wisconsin, the Chicago area, Michigan, Kansas, and Iowa during and after the design and construction of Midway Gardens, it is natural to wonder whether he tried to create anything resembling a community of coworkers—apprentices, collaborating artists, draftsmen, and builders—and to wonder about his relationship with them and theirs with each other.

On such matters there is only sketchy evidence. In his autobiography Wright mentions some of the men on whom he depended at Taliesin. Among them were "Father [Alfred] Larson, the old Norse stone mason" and "old Dad Signola," who was "the best of them until Philip Volk came along." Ben Davis was "commander of [the] forces at this time." William Weston, whose "nimble intelligence and swift sure hand was a gift to any architect," stayed with Wright for almost fourteen years. In the winter, these men would gather around open fireplaces, tossing on wood to keep warm. "All came to work from surrounding towns and had to be fed and bedded down on the place somewhere during the week. Saturday nights they went home with money for the week's work in pocket, or its equivalent in groceries and fixings from the village." Also working for him were several he brought from Chicago, including Johnnie Vaughn and Billy Little.[26]

One who came from beyond the local community to work at Taliesin was Antonin Raymond, accompanied by his wife, Noémi. "In the early spring of 1916," Raymond wrote in his autobiography, "we found ourselves all of a sudden at Taliesin. . . . One of the most remarkable happenings in our life was learning to know that most creative and courageous personality, Frank Lloyd Wright, in his own surroundings." Raymond mentions several of Wright's employees, including Dad Signola, the eighty-year-old stonemason, "a sturdy man with the build of an orangutan, long arms reaching almost to the ground." There was also a schoolmate of Wright's named Dan. A jack-of-all-trades, he was a heavy drinker who sometimes disappeared for days. Then Wright would find him and bring him back in a buggy. "Frank Lloyd Wright," Raymond continued, "was a most loyal person, and that made him lovable to all close to him."

Raymond and his wife lived in an apartment beneath the Wrights' living area and sometimes had dinner with the master in his part of the building. "He would start the meal in the usual way," Raymond recalled, "then get up all of a sudden, start walking around and exclaim with violence, 'Damn the thing, we have to do it over and over again.' He meant the process of eating." When Wright saw scenes of Taliesin that Noémi had painted, he insulted both of them. But they were pleased, subsequently, when Wright allowed them to restore part of a battered old house at Hillside and move into it. The privacy they found there, Raymond said, was "a relief from the proximity to the complexities of Wright's life." After a time, with scarcely any work being done in the studio, they returned to New York, "disenchanted but grateful for the [Taliesin] experience." Their disenchantment disappeared, however, and did not prevent them from accepting Wright's invitation several years later to accompany him to Tokyo to work on the Imperial Hotel.[27]

Frances Nemtin, who joined the Fellowship in 1945 and continued in it into the twenty-first century, compiled an account of others who worked for and with Wright at Taliesin through the years. She did so by drawing upon stories she heard as a member of the Fellowship, as well as on "memories of the descendants of the early workers, correspondence between them and Wright, firsthand accounts of apprentices, and *An Autobiography.*" Among those she identified as having been with him in the early days at Taliesin were Joseph Clary, a mason, and Petie Beaver, a mason's assistant, along with his brother John.[28] To what extent these men were part of a community that went beyond normal employer-employee relations is hard to say, although given their small number and the fact that some of them lived at Taliesin during the week, we might infer that these workers were in some respects precursors of the Taliesin Fellowship.

It is also possible to identify some of Wright's assistants beyond Taliesin. Wright called Taylor Woolley into service again in 1911, first in Chicago, then at Taliesin. Another to return was Harry Robinson, who in 1906 had invited Wright to speak to the Architectural Club at the University of Illinois, where he was pursuing a bachelor's degree in architectural engineering. In June of that year, at age twenty-two, Robinson began as a draftsman in Wright's Oak Park Studio. According to the biography written by his grandson, conditions in the studio deteriorated as a result of "Wright's cantankerous behavior, his continual neglect in paying salaries on time, and more importantly, because of Wright's very controversial extramarital relationship with Mrs. Cheney." He left Wright's studio in July 1908 and joined Walter Burley Griffin's, where he remained until October 1911.

Robinson then returned to serve Wright as the manager of Wright's office in Orchestra Hall. A letter from Wright dated October 18, 1911, suggested that he might be able to create a place for himself in Wright's business by satisfying the master's expectations:

I want your whole time and absolute loyalty, . . . True loyalty in business means to stand up for your own opinions before your employer and for your employer's opinions before the world. . . .

And everything for the good of the work. You will find that respect of others and power will come to you through submission to their proposition no matter how expedient it may sometimes seem to avoid them and take a short cut.

You can make yourself invaluable to me and win the real respect and confidence of clients by undisguised practice of these obvious but too often disregarded ethics—and have anything you want so your experience and intelligence develops.

I shall endeavour always to consider your family and treat you as a human being—developing you as fast as I can—there is no reason why our relations should not always be pleasant and inspiring.

Managing the office would seem to have been an imposing task in itself, but Robinson's biographer notes that while he was responsible for coordinating all the projects in the Chicago area, the design work for the larger projects, chiefly Midway Gardens and Taliesin itself, was carried out at Taliesin. Still, he was probably involved in some measure with notable projects executed during his tenure. "It is unfortunate," wrote his grandson, "that even to this day [he] has not been credited with the design of most, if not all of the smaller Chicago area commissions carried out by Wright's office from 1911–1916."

But Robinson left again "because of Wright's continual failure to pay wages and the apparent lack of clients, which had been compounded by the abrupt decline of the Prairie School design style. A very compelling reason for the decline in the number of clients was the antagonism of a majority of the public to Wright's personal life style." Personal difference no doubt also played a part in Robinson's decision. In an undated note, probably sent in late 1916, Wright responded testily to a sarcastic one he received from Robinson: "My office was run for four years chiefly for your benefit and you got all there was in it when it looked like folly to keep either you or Ethel [Robinson's wife and Wright's secretary]. You are not to blame for this—but when you are inclined to be sarcastic you might do something to realize the facts in the case." The same tone appears in the concluding paragraph: "I do not want to tie you down to me and my architectural misfortunes, Harry—and anytime you feel extra abused why fire me and hire a better Boss—you might appreciate me more than you do now."[29]

Alofsin identifies several other architects and draftsmen who worked for Wright briefly and apparently unremarkably. They included: Edward

Sanderson, whose letter to Darwin Martin, April 23, 1912, with a list of projects on which Wright was at work, suggests that he was an office manager; Wilhelm Bernhard, an architect who later entered a planning design in a competition for which Wright submitted an "hors concours," that is, a noncompetitive entry; William R. Gibb, a draftsman; and another draftsman named Fucher.[30] Whether Wright attempted to create anything resembling a creative community with these architects and draftsmen is unknown.

The picture is clearer concerning the design and construction of specific projects, such as Midway Gardens. Much of the design work was done at Taliesin, where Wright employed as draftsmen Emil Brodelle, an artist from Milwaukee, and Herbert Fritz, who had worked for various architects, including Walter Burley Griffin. Also in his employment were Thomas Brunker, a construction foreman; and David Lindblom, a landscape gardener. These individuals ate meals at Taliesin, and some lived there as well.[31] Another who worked for Wright was Russell Barr Williamson, his chief drafting room assistant in the Chicago office, beginning in 1914. During Wright's sojourn in Japan to work on the Imperial Hotel, Williamson supervised construction of the Emil C. Bogk Residence and the Munkwitz Duplex Apartments in Milwaukee and the Henry J. Allen Residence in Wichita, Kansas.[32]

The names of others who were involved in constructing Taliesin and other buildings Wright designed are recorded only in the memories of their descendants. Indeed, it might be said that most construction work is done by Anonymous. Similarly, in architectural practices past and present, the principals' names are on the drawings and recorded in history, but their draftsmen largely remain nameless. Nonetheless, without the labors of such persons unknown to those outside the firm or practice, the principals would themselves be unknown. So there is nothing extraordinary about the anonymous nature of Wright's coworkers, or about the fact that even when their names appear, little is known about them. The nature of Wright's interactions with all with whom he worked must be left largely to speculation, but given his transience in these years, it is unlikely that a sense of community developed anywhere but at Taliesin itself.

More is known about several men Wright brought in to assist him during these years: his sons, Lloyd Wright and John Lloyd Wright. Although exactly what they did with and for him, and when and where, is also ripe for speculation, it is possible to identify periods when they were with him and to describe their relationships. Lloyd had traveled to Europe to assist Wright in preparing drawings for the Wasmuth portfolios and was to work with him again in the 1920s. In this decade, though, it was John Lloyd Wright, the second son, on whom he depended for assistance.

### LLOYD WRIGHT

Not that Lloyd Wright was idle. In Europe he had been inspired by the landscape architecture he had seen, and upon returning he found employment briefly at the Harvard Herbarium. Next came another short stint in landscaping with the distinguished Boston landscape architecture firm of Olmsted and Olmsted. In the fall of 1911 he transferred to the Olmsteds' San Diego operation. When things did not work out there he turned to Irving Gill, a sometime colleague of his father in the studio of Louis Sullivan decades earlier. In Gill's firm he had opportunities to develop his apparently instinctive expertise as a landscape architect. Soon he formed a partnership with Paul Thiene, with whom he had worked in the Olmsted firm.[33]

Feeling good about his career progress, he wrote an optimistic letter to his father, expressing the wish that Wright might be able to free himself from the loads he seemed to enjoy piling upon his back so that they could work together as father and son. "I believe we could make them all sit up and enjoy us," Lloyd wrote, "and we'd have a glorious time doing it." And they would do it, he continued, "in a gloriously fine way too."

The partnership Lloyd Wright envisioned never materialized, but it may have laid the groundwork for the senior Wright's ventures in California at the turn of the next decade.[34] Indeed, along with his then-wife, actress Kirah Mirkham, Lloyd made connections in Los Angeles that served his father well a few years later. The most significant such connection was with Aline Barnsdall, a wealthy, aspiring theater producer and would-be builder. By 1916 the senior Wright was corresponding with Barnsdall, and some accounts have him doing initial sketches for a house and theater for her that year.[35]

With Frank Lloyd Wright's work in California remaining in the future and his son's career languishing, Lloyd and his wife enjoyed an extended visit at Taliesin and then moved to New York. When his marriage faltered, his yearnings for California and his sense that new opportunities would soon appear there prompted him to return, and that placed him in a position to collaborate with his father in 1919 and the years following.

## JOHN LLOYD WRIGHT

John Lloyd Wright, the second son of Frank Lloyd Wright, followed in the footsteps of both his father and his elder brother by enrolling at the University of Wisconsin and leaving prematurely, the victim of dismal grades. After working in low-level jobs in Portland, Oregon, and San Diego, he found the pull of architecture to be irresistible. A successful stint as a draftsman with the Pacific Building Company led to his being named chief designer. That induced him to look for a position in the Harrison Albright architectural firm. There he had an opportunity to design a home, based largely on one of his father's designs, and a workingman's hotel. Even so, he recognized the need for further training in architecture. When his father learned that he was seeking an apprenticeship with a renowned architect in Vienna, he invited him to join him in Chicago.

Late in 1913 Frank Lloyd Wright, who was moving back and forth between Chicago and Taliesin, placed John in charge of the Chicago office at Orchestra Hall. The big project then underway was Midway Gardens, an elaborately decorated complex on Chicago's south side that offered many possibilities for entertainment, among them an indoor restaurant and dance hall, a summer garden with a band shell and tavern, and a private club. John Lloyd Wright was soon engaged in preparing working drawings for it and acting as on-site superintendent, alongside another of Wright's long-time associates, Paul Mueller. Wright had first connected with Mueller in the office of Adler and Sullivan twenty-five years earlier. After building the Wright-designed Unity Temple in Oak Park, his construction company

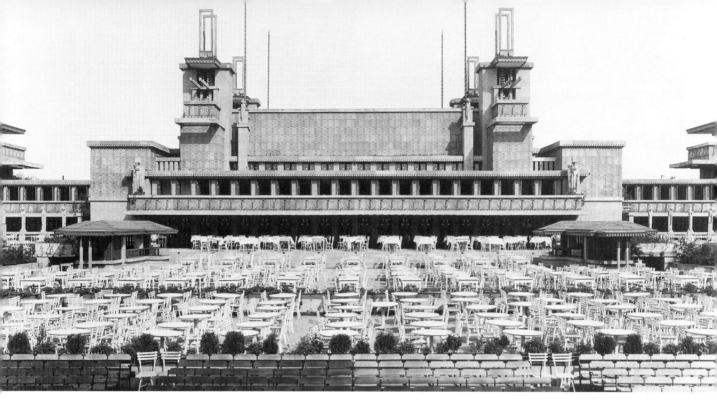

Midway Gardens, Chicago, the entertainment complex Wright designed in 1913. Courtesy of the Frank Lloyd Wright Foundation

failed, but he reestablished it after 1910 and was ready to be the contractor for Midway Gardens. Here, according to Andrew Saint, "Wright transfigured Mueller's role . . . into that of a noble slave-driver, pushing a complex project on from start to finish in four months. . . . On the technical side he relied upon Clarence Seipp, a Cornell-trained [civil] engineering graduate who specialized in reinforced concrete." Paul Kruty notes that Mueller "not only supervised the construction but also made crucial decisions about how to erect Wright's design." He and Seipp "made the calculations necessary to cast the floors and interior columns in concrete."[36]

The drawings had to be done swiftly, and the construction moved along at a rapid pace, with completion promised by the summer of 1914. Besides attending to his superintending duties, John Lloyd Wright took on the task of painting some of the murals his father designed, and he recruited a California acquaintance, Alfonso Iannelli, to work with Richard Bock in executing the many ornate sculptural designs for the Gardens.[37]

A tale recounted by the senior Wright in his autobiography reveals that Mueller found John Lloyd Wright's apparently aggressive presence troublesome:

"Look here, Wright," said the exasperated Mueller to me one day. "What's this you got here—this young bull-dog that he is. He follows me around and around. Every little while he sticks his teeth in the seat of my pants and I can't get away from him. Can I pull over everything that goes wrong in this work? Can I? Not if I get these Gardens finished up, already [sic] to open on time some day, I can't. Take him off me!"

But that sounded good to me and I didn't take him off. John was in it all up to his ears, and his teeth were serviceable.[38]

## DISASTERS AT TALIESIN

That summer, 1914, Frank Lloyd Wright and those close to him looked to the future with high hopes. Mamah Borthwick was living with him at Taliesin, and her children were there on an extended visit. In Chicago, although it was far from complete, Midway Gardens had opened, and the crews, with Wright in the midst of them, struggled busily and around the clock to complete many details. Then came an unspeakable disaster, shattering their hopes: On August 14, a startling phone call brought Wright this news: "Taliesin destroyed by fire." He and John, along with Edwin Cheney, Mamah's former husband and the father of her children, rushed to catch a train to Spring Green. Along the way they learned more, little by little, about what had happened. Julian Carleton, a recently hired house servant from Barbados, had locked the dining room door, poured a flammable liquid on the floor, set the room on fire, and waited by the lone exit to bludgeon with a hatchet those trying to escape. Mamah Borthwick and her two visiting children were killed instantly. Other victims were Emil Brodelle, whom Wright called "a talented apprentice," David Lindblom, Thomas Brunker, and Ernest Weston, the thirteen-year-old son of William Weston. Altogether, seven were murdered. William Weston himself escaped with serious injuries and Herbert Fritz with burns and other injuries.

When Wright arrived it fell to him, surrounded by members of his extended family who had rushed to Spring Green, to lead the recovery of what could be recovered. But his first concern, in shock, was to see to the burial of his beloved Mamah. Here is his autobiographical account:

A primitive burial ground of the family's chapel. Men from Taliesin dug the grave, deep, near Grandfather's and Grandmother's grave. Uncle Enos had come to say it would be all right. But I felt that a funeral service could only be mockery. The undertaker's offices—too, his vulgar casket—seemed to me profane. So I cut her garden down and with the flowers filled a strong, plain box of fresh, white pine to overflowing. I had my own carpenters make it.

My boy, John, coming to my side now, helped me to lift the body and we let it down to rest among the flowers that had grown and bloomed for her. The plain box lid was pressed down and fastened home. Then the plain strong box was lifted on the shoulders of my workmen and they placed it on our little spring-wagon, filled, too, with flowers—waiting, hitched behind the faithful Darby and Joan . . . We made the whole a mass of flowers. It helped a little. . . .

Walking alongside the wheels now I drove [the horses] along the road to the churchyard where no bell tolled. No people were waiting. John followed. Ralph and Orrin, two of my young Hillside cousins, were waiting at the chapel gate. Together we lowered the flower-filled and flower-covered pine box to the bottom of the new-made grave. Then I asked them to leave me there alone.

I wanted to fill the grave myself . . .

All I had left to show for the struggle for freedom of the five years past that had swept most of my former life away, had now been swept away.

Why mark the spot where desolation ended and began?[39]

One of humankind's greatest gifts is the capacity to recover from disappointment and loss, to overcome tragedy by intense, distracting work.

In time, Wright accomplished that, even as the community he was creating with Mamah Borthwick lay shattered and newspaper accounts brought renewed attention to the scandal that had piqued flurries of interest when he left for Europe with her almost five years earlier. Sometimes, as we shall see, he made unwise choices, but, sinking himself vigorously and creatively into his work, as is evidenced in the completion of Midway Gardens and other buildings and projects that flowed from his studio, he managed to continue his career.

Midway Gardens, in contrast, was not able to escape the effects of many adverse forces. Chicagoans initially supported Midway Gardens with enthusiasm, but that support soon moved elsewhere, and the spectacular entertainment center, renamed Edelweiss Gardens, descended rapidly to a sad demise. In his definitive account of the Midway Gardens' architecture and history, Kruty counters theories advanced through the years, including some by Wright, concerning the fate of this unique structure. "The fact remains," he contends, "that at any point in its history, a civic-minded, or culturally oriented, or eccentric-enough individual, with sufficient capital and a clever imagination could have saved Midway Gardens. Blaming the Germans, Chicagoans, Prohibition, Mrs. Palmer [an early patron who moved her upper-class social events elsewhere], or even Mr. Wright, just will not do. Midway Gardens simply disappeared by default."[40] Not to be overlooked, of course, is that the financing of the project was shaky from the outset.

With the tragedy at Taliesin and the completion and demise of Midway Gardens in the past, Wright had no choice but to begin again by reaching into new areas, with new associates in new communities.

# 4 UNSETTLED YEARS CONTINUE

## *Japan and Taliesin*

. . . SOME MONTHS LATER AN OFFICIAL INVITATION CAME BACK TO COME ON AT ONCE TO TOKIO. I WENT AS SOON AS I COULD. YES, I WAS EAGER TO GO, FOR AGAIN I WANTED TO GET AWAY FROM THE UNITED STATES. I STILL IMAGINED ONE MIGHT GET AWAY FROM HIMSELF THAT WAY—A LITTLE. IN SPITE OF ALL MY REASONING POWER AND RETURNING BALANCE I WAS CONTINUALLY EXPECTING SOME TERRIBLE BLOW TO STRIKE. THE SENSE OF IMPENDING DISASTER WOULD HANG OVER ME, WAKING OR DREAMING. THIS FITTED IN WELL ENOUGH WITH THE SENSE OF EARTHQUAKE, FROM THE ACTUALITY OF WHICH I SHOULD HAVE TO DEFEND THE NEW BUILDING. BUT AT THIS TIME I LOOKED FORWARD TO JAPAN AS A REFUGE AND RESCUE.[1]

— **FRANK LLOYD WRIGHT**

Frank Lloyd Wright's life, shattered by the murders at Taliesin, remained unsettled. He maintained his home and studio at Taliesin, but circumstances compelled him to leave his familiar surroundings for lengthy periods to pursue special, sometimes irresistible opportunities elsewhere.

Moving to new places meant leaving the communities of draftsmen and other assistants, tentative and temporary though they had been, for new ones yet to be formed. As these changes occurred, he also worked at rebuilding his personal life, an effort complicated by his ill-fated, decade-long liaison with Miriam Noel, who entered his life soon after the tragedies at Taliesin. As he dealt with these circumstances, he seems also to have been afflicted by the restlessness that sometimes seems to grip the minds of geniuses. His moves gave his creative powers fresh outlets.

Recounting Wright's experiences and accomplishments in all the places where he lived and practiced architecture during these years can be done only in sketchy terms, with elaboration at key points to establish contexts that reveal the circumstances of his life and work. Doing more would distract attention from this book's essential purpose, that is, to identify Wright's closest and most dependable associates, to discover the circumstances in which they worked, and to consider whether they functioned as effective contributors to his communities.

Because Wright kept few formal records of his activities and whereabouts, his routes and actions must again be reconstructed by examining his architectural record and his writings, as well as his correspondence with clients and friends. Recorded memories of his associates and observers and documents relating to his projects are also helpful. A number of scholars have traced his migrations, and we shall draw on their findings. Wright often had projects underway in several places, so constructing a precise year-by-year chronology would require the frequent use, implicitly or explicitly, of "meanwhile." Rather than attempting such a chronology, we will first follow him through his years in Japan, as he worked on the

Imperial Hotel and several other projects while maintaining his base at Taliesin. Only in passing will we note his overlapping work elsewhere, particularly in California; that will be the focus of the next chapter.

## THE JAPAN ATTRACTION

Looking for work in Japan came naturally to Wright, given his longstanding interest in Japanese art, architecture, and culture. Wright scholars typically acknowledge his insistence that all of his architectural work was original, not influenced at all by architecture in other cultures or by other architects, but few of them grant it plausibility. As for evidence of Japanese influence on his work, he claimed that it was not that nation's architecture that inspired him, but rather Japanese prints, of which he was an astute collector. Throughout his life he described how they intrigued and instructed him. In his autobiography, for example, he wrote:

The elimination of the insignificant, a process of simplification in art in which I was myself already engaged, beginning with my twenty-third year, found much collateral evidence in the [Japanese] print. And ever since I discovered the print Japan had appealed to me as the most romantic, artistic, nature-inspired country on earth. Later I found that Japanese art really did have organic character. . . .[2]

Two pages later in the autobiography, however, he describes what he learned from one kind of Japanese architecture: "I saw the native home in Japan as a supreme study in elimination—not only of dirt but the elimination of the insignificant." Fascinated by the Japanese house, he would spend hours "taking it all to pieces and putting it together again." He saw nothing meaningless in Japanese homes and "could find very little added in the way of ornament because all *ornament* as we call it, they get out of the way the necessary things are done or by bringing out and polishing the beauty of the simple materials they used in making the building."[3]

Architectural influence aside, Wright's collection of Japanese prints attests to the inspiration he found in them. Citing historic photographs displayed in Wright's home in the late 1890s, Bruce Brooks Pfeiffer suggests that his collecting may have begun not long after he opened his practice in 1893. By 1906 he had probably established associations, through the Art Institute of Chicago, with two prominent collectors, Clarence Buckingham and Frederick Gookin. In 1906 he provided the woodblock prints by Ando Hiroshige for an exhibition at the Art Institute of Chicago, and he wrote the text for an accompanying catalog. Two years later he and Gookin mounted a much larger exhibition there. In 1912 Wright published *The Japanese Print: An Interpretation,* and in 1917 he mounted another exhibition of Japanese prints, this time at the Fine Arts Club of Chicago.[4]

## COLLECTING PRINTS AND MAKING CONNECTIONS

Wright made his first trip to Japan in 1905, traveling with his wife Catherine and former clients Ward and Cecelia Willits. While in pursuit only of Japanese prints, he photographed landscaped gardens and buildings along the way. Margo Stipe, curator and registrar of collections in the

Frank Lloyd Wright Archives, in collaboration with Masami Tanigawa, a Japanese architectural historian, traced Wright's itinerary by identifying the locations of his photographs and gleaning information from documents in the Archives. Tanigawa also consulted hotel registers to help establish the route Wright had followed.[5] As Julia Meech points out in her definitive work, *Frank Lloyd Wright and the Art of Japan,* the album of carefully composed photographs Wright compiled reveals that his interests while traveling went beyond acquiring Japanese prints.[6]

Wright's passion for collecting Japanese prints prepared him for whatever opportunities involving Japan might come his way. Sometime in 1911, Frederick Gookin learned of plans to construct a new Imperial Hotel in Tokyo, and he asked Wright if he would be interested in being its architect. With his life and career in disarray, Wright would most likely have considered any large project appealing, but the prospect of finding one in Tokyo would be irresistible. So Gookin, enthusiastic about the chance for a Wright undertaking in Japan, wrote to the general manager of the hotel, Aisaku Hayashi, to propose his friend for favorable consideration. Correspondence between Wright and Hayashi in 1912 laid the groundwork for Wright's second visit to Japan.[7]

## THE IMPERIAL HOTEL COMMISSION

On January 10, 1913, Wright wrote to Darwin Martin, his friend and client in Buffalo, New York, to inform him that he would be seeking the commission to be the "consulting architect" for the new Imperial Hotel. If he got it, he told Martin, the commission on the seven-million-dollar structure would be forty or fifty thousand dollars and he would have several years of employment.

Traveling with Mamah Borthwick, Wright left the United States two days later. During his stay in Japan, Hayashi outlined the building requirements and Wright viewed the site where the hotel would be built, observed soil conditions, and considered building materials that might be used. He and Borthwick returned to the United States in May or June.[8]

With matters moving slowly in Japan, Wright was not idle at Taliesin. He concentrated on designing and building Midway Gardens and on mounting exhibitions of his recent work. The Chicago Architectural Club at the Art Institute of Chicago sponsored these exhibitions in 1913 and 1914, and they bear witness to the continuing appeal of Wright's work.[9] Also, after the murder of Mamah Borthwick and others in August 1914, he faced the challenge of rebuilding the Taliesin living quarters that had been destroyed in the fire set by Julian Carleton. He also designed other buildings during these years.

Not until late 1915 or early 1916 did Hayashi travel to the United States to meet with Wright. According to Kathryn Smith, his purpose was to view the best hotels in this country and consider questions surrounding the proposed hotel's design. Hayashi and his associates left for Japan on March 25, 1916. About nine months later, in January 1917, Wright and his new companion, Miriam Noel, along with his son John, arrived in Japan to begin a four-month sojourn. Wright's purpose on this occasion, as described by Smith, was "to begin preparations for construction—to examine the site thoroughly, make

Miriam Noel moved in with Wright at Taliesin in 1914. They were married in 1923 and divorced five months later after a bitter estrangement. Courtesy of the Frank Lloyd Wright Foundation

test borings, arrange for acquisition and manufacture of materials, and hire draftsmen to prepare working drawings."[10]

In subsequent years Wright traveled frequently to Japan. By Julia Meech's calculation, five sojourns there between 1917 and 1922 had ranged in length from two months to nearly a year, for a total of 34 months. Before beginning the actual on-site work in Tokyo, however, he had also been there in 1905 and 1913 for a combined seven months, bringing his total time in Japan to forty-one months.[11] Counting the days at sea at twelve each way, his time on ocean liners amounted to almost five additional months; moreover, he had to spend days at a time traveling to the seaports for his journeys. Given the lack of continuity in his presence in Japan, developing the kind of camaraderie that ordinarily characterizes well-functioning communities was difficult.

Miriam Noel, who accompanied Wright in 1916 and on some of the later travels to Japan, was a divorcée and self-described sculptress. She had entered Wright's lonesome and grieving life two years earlier by means of a consoling letter following the murder of Mamah Borthwick. Their relationship began, he recalled, in an after-hours meeting in his Orchestra Hall office. She appeared to be brilliant, sophisticated, and as having been very beautiful. Her health, she told him, had been broken by the tragedy of a luckless love affair, an experience he grasped as similar to his own. Looking back on that day, he wrote, "Drowning men—they say so—clutch at straws. Here was no straw but enlightened comradeship, help, more light than I had to see by. Salvation maybe from blackness—blindness. I did not know." Sadly, "here began the leading of the blind by the blind."[12] There is no evidence that Noel played a role in whatever attempts Wright might have made to create a spirit of camaraderie among his assistants.

### THE ARCHITECT AND PRINT COLLECTOR AT WORK

For more than a year after Wright's return to Taliesin in May 1917 he worked on drawings for the Imperial Hotel and other projects. He left John Lloyd Wright in Japan to represent him there. Arata Endo, a Japanese architect who later maintained a long association with Wright, and a Japanese draftsman named Kenjiro Fujikura assisted him, along with Vienna-born Rudolph H. Schindler, who was to play a greater role in Wright's work in California.

Meanwhile, his activities as a collector and dealer of Japanese prints continued. He invested heavily, selling some that he acquired and using others as collateral for loans from former clients, including Darwin Martin. He sold prints not only to individual collectors, but also to the Metropolitan Museum of Art in New York. Revenue he gained as a dealer kept him afloat financially, but at one point he fell victim to forgers, as occasionally did other dealers, and had to take costly measures to regain his credibility as a collector and dealer.[13]

As the project in Japan appeared ready to move ahead, Wright sailed from Seattle on October 30, 1918, arriving at Yokohama on November 17. Although he worked hard in the ensuing months, progress was slow. Illness for about three weeks in late July and early August, as well as the fact that construction was finally progressing, led him to return to the United States in September 1919.

His stay in the United States was brief and hectic. According to Smith, he stopped in Los Angeles and Seattle to meet with Aline Barnsdall, who was to become his client, but his primary concern was leaving for the East Coast to sell a large group of Japanese prints he had brought back.[14] While in New York he persuaded Antonin Raymond, who had worked for him at Taliesin, to come with him to Tokyo. Three months later, on December 16, 1919, Wright and Miriam Noel, along with Raymond and his wife Noémi, set sail for Yokahama.

## COMPLICATIONS AND DELAYS

Upon arrival on December 21, Wright learned that the Annex of the Imperial Hotel, built in 1890, had been destroyed by fire. Desperately in need of hotel rooms, the management decided to interrupt construction of the new building and to rebuild the Annex as a modern facility, with the design to be done by Wright. He and his men completed the drafting of plans for the new Annex in just ten days.

Here, Wright recalled, he built for himself "a modest little nook." It had "a small living room with a fireplace—fire always burning—a balcony filled with dwarf-trees and flowers, a bedroom with a balcony and bath, a small dining room where meals were served from the hotel." A narrow stairway led to "a commodious studio bedroom built as a penthouse," where he slept and set up his drawing board. His apartment had a small grand piano, and there, with Miriam Noel, he enjoyed, "for a time a peaceful, mutually helpful relationship," enlivened by recreation with a few friends and the presence of interesting people around him, including some charming Russians. But the peace was interrupted by Miriam Noel's "mystifying reactions [that] became more violent until something like a terrible struggle between two natures in her would seem to be going on within her all the time and be tearing her to pieces. Then peace again for some time and a charming life." The outbreaks became more destructive, however, and galling disturbances interfered with his work on the hotel.[15] Their tempestuous relationship notwithstanding, Wright and Noel stayed together. In November 1922, thirteen years after he had left Catherine, she finally succumbed to his demands for a divorce. A year later, almost nine years after Noel had moved in with him, the two were married, but the marriage failed to bring accord to their relationship.

The greatest complication for Wright, however, was that construction of the hotel was running far behind schedule. The necessity of his presence in Japan prevented him from meeting the demands of Aline Barnsdall. His assistants at Taliesin and in California could satisfy those demands for only so long. So he had to end his stay in Japan, return home near the end of June, and immediately give his attention to the Barnsdall project in California. Soon, however, he was again needed in Japan, and he sailed from Vancouver on December 16, 1920, arriving in Yokohama on December 28. The construction difficulties and delays at the Imperial Hotel became more worrisome. So did his health, and he began to feel the effects of his age. He admitted this in a letter to his daughter and son-in-law, Catherine and Kenneth Baxter: "Once upon a time I never could strike the bottom of my physical resources—but now I find that very grey hair and *fifty-three years*—

The Imperial Hotel in Tokyo, Wright's consuming project, 1916–1924. Courtesy of the Frank Lloyd Wright Foundation

indicate something that I will have to pay attention to—in this climate—which is the worst in the world I believe—."[16]

Nonetheless, he pressed on with the hotel. By late April 1921, the builder, Paul Mueller, who had also built Unity Temple in Oak Park, the Larkin Building in Buffalo, New York, and Midway Gardens in Chicago, reported that the main building and the north wing of the Imperial Hotel would be ready for the scheduled formal opening. He had 350 men at work, he said, and he expected that number to rise to 500.[17] That allowed Wright to return to California in late May and attend to the Barnsdall project. By early June he was back in Wisconsin. After spending two weeks in New York, presumably dealing in Japanese prints again, he traveled to Los Angeles, and on July 30, 1921, he and Miriam Noel were again on their way to Yokohama, arriving on August 15.

As November 3, the date set for opening the hotel, approached, it was not even nearing completion. Impatience among the architects, builders, and owners intensified. Tensions rose as Wright and the hotel management had to cope with rising costs and complaints about the design and the delays. These circumstances were bad enough, but Wright was also in the midst of a scandal involving his sale of revamped Japanese prints, for which he had to find a way to make good. A fire that destroyed the old Imperial Hotel in April 1922 made things even worse, putting pressure on Wright and the builders to complete the new one. Both Chairman of the Board Baron Kihachiro Okura and Manager Aisaku Hayashi, assuming responsibility for the losses caused by the fire, resigned and a new board was named, consisting principally of sons of the former members.

Then another force of nature struck on April 26, 1922, just ten days after the fire. Here is Wright's version of what happened:

It was nearly noon. The boys in the office, reduced to ten, were there, and workmen were about. Suddenly with no warning a gigantic jolt lifted the whole building, threw the boys down sprawling with their drawing boards. A moment's panic and hell broke loose as the wave motions began. The structure was literally in convulsions. I was knocked down by the rush of workmen and my own boys to save their own lives. . . . As I lay there I could clearly see the ground swell pass through the construction above as it heaved and groaned to hideous crushing and grinding noises. Several thunderous noises sickened me, but later these proved to be the falling of five tall chimneys of the old Imperial, left standing alone by the recent burning of that building.[18]

The new building survived what Wright called the worst quake in fifty-two years; he said it was undamaged. Work progressed, and the hotel opened in July 1922. So Wright, again accompanied by Miriam Noel, was free to

Wright's office force in the construction of the Imperial Hotel. He is at the far left, wearing a helmet. Next to him is Aisaku Hayashi, general manager of the Hotel; at Hayashi's left is Paul Mueller, the builder Wright brought to Tokyo from Chicago. Courtesy of the Frank Lloyd Wright Foundation

leave for the United States. Paul Mueller would continue to be the contractor and Arata Endo was placed in charge of completing the work.[19] With a few exceptions, those who continued working after his departure were men whose names he scarcely knew. As he departed the hotel it appeared to be deserted. That puzzled him, but at the entrance courts the scene was different. As he recalled in his autobiography, "there all the workmen were, crowding the spaces, watching and waiting. Already there had been gratifying evidence of appreciation—I thought—but here was the real thing. This could have happened nowhere but in Japan. Here was the spirit I had tried to compliment and respect in my work." As he came out "they crowded round, workmen of every rank from sweepers to foremen of 'the trades,' laughing, weeping, wanting awkwardly to shake hands—foreign fashion. They had learned 'aw-right' and mingled it now with 'arigato' and '*sayonara* Wrieto-San.' . . . ."

The dock at Yokohama was eighteen miles away. When he arrived there by train he found that "sixty of the foremen had paid their way down from Tokio to shout again and wave good-bye, while they faded from sight as the ship went down the bay. Such people! Where else in all the world would such touching warmth of kindness in faithfulness be probable or even possible?"[20]

We know little about the Japanese draftsmen and other hotel personnel who assisted him, although one can be identified as significant in Wright's community of workers: Arata Endo, who had been with him at Taliesin. Endo maintained close ties with Wright, and his son Raku enrolled in the Taliesin Fellowship in 1957 and later designed significant buildings in Japan.[21] Also with him in both Wisconsin and Tokyo, as well as California, was William Smith, a Canadian, who was his secretary and general assistant.

### JOHN LLOYD WRIGHT

John Lloyd Wright was one of only two of his coworkers who left substantial records of their experiences with Wright in Japan. Another who might have provided insights into his working relationship with Wright is Julius Floto, a structural engineer on the project. He wrote an article explaining how and why the Imperial Hotel survived the Great Kanto earthquake on September 1, 1923, the most destructive such event on record in Japan. However, he focused almost entirely on the technical aspects of the structure, noting Wright's disgruntlement over the structural requirements prescribed by law. Wright told him, he wrote, that his heavy-duty computations had been ignored and the design lightened. Floto regarded this as entirely logical. His only personal reference to Wright concerns a story he had recently heard Wright tell that "was as dramatic as it was interesting. The tale of the Imperial would rank with any in fiction. It is worthy of a pen like Kipling's." He chose not to repeat it.[22]

Floto's account of the Imperial Hotel's escaping damage in the earthquake and Wright's autobiographical suggestion that it was the only building in the region left standing are at odds with the facts. According to Masami Tanigawa, the report from the official government survey commission that the Imperial Hotel had sustained "earthquake damage but no fire damage." It was not the only building left standing, for many designed by Japanese architects also escaped serious damage.[23]

John Lloyd Wright recorded his recollections of experiences in Japan in *My Father Who Is on Earth,* published in 1946. On the day of its publication, March 29, John sent a copy to his father, who, being Frank Lloyd Wright, penciled comments in the margins of many pages and sent it back to John. The son then transcribed his father's notes in black pencil and answered them in red. Before sending that copy back to his father, John transcribed all the notes into a third copy. That version provided the basis for a republication of the work, with the notes, in 1994.[24]

The chapter on Japan begins with John's assertion that there was never a dull moment in working for his father, but there was one nagging trouble: trying to collect his salary. "That wasn't a trouble," he wrote, "it was an impossibility." His summary of Wright's financial method might have been written by dozens of the senior Wright's associates at points in their years with him: "He did not seem to regard money as having a value other than a quick exchange for what he wanted—and couldn't get without it. He carried his paper money crumpled in any pocket—trousers, vest, coat or overcoat. He would have to uncrumple a bill to see its denomination. He never counted his change. . . ."

John's arrangement for his work in Japan provided for a definite salary, but he soon learned that the figure he had been given meant nothing. Sometimes he would get a little for spending money, but that would be all. The first time he tried to talk to his father about being paid regularly, he says, "he looked at me with deep reproach, like some injured saint. He then proceeded to figure what I had cost him all during my life, including obstetrics." If he never received a salary for the rest of his life, John remarked, his father would still think that was too much. [His father's comment in the margin here: "Money seems to be the real subject of this chapter but—not fair John—not true."]

His father appreciated his assistance, John recalled, and even complimented him, something rare for him to do for a draftsman, "but paying for it in the coin of the realm seemed to be handled in a department not on earth." Raising the subject would lead to promises and promises broken. The Hotel Company provided for his expenses, but his father did not honor his part of the arrangement. John had brought his new wife with him, and that meant extra expenditures. But obligations meant nothing to Frank Lloyd Wright.

Father and son worked well together, solving problems, particularly those related to theories for earthquake-proof foundations, so the son "forgot to pester him." Perhaps he was too busy to do so, for in addition to his drafting and designing work for his father, he was also designing an educational toy known as Lincoln Logs. As the senior Wright's involvements in transactions involving prints increased, and as he picked up commissions for more architectural work in Japan, he left John in charge. Things went well for a while but John's work for his father ended abruptly. "I worked all the next day and night to complete the sketches for the layout Dad had left with me," he recalled, "delivered them to the Viscount the next day and collected two thousand dollars on account. After deducting twelve hundred dollars for salary due me, I cabled the remaining eight hundred to Dad." The next day a cable arrived: *"'You're fired! Take the next ship home. . . .'* Out went the lights! 'You selfish, ruthless tyrant,' I thought, 'to ask you for pay is all right if I don't get it, but sacrilege if I do. And I got it!'"

John Lloyd Wright assisted his father at Midway Gardens and in Japan. After Frank Lloyd Wright fired him, he returned to the United States and practiced architecture, first in Indiana, then in the San Diego area. Courtesy of The Frank Lloyd Wright Foundation and Elizabeth Wright Ingraham

So he booked passage for his return to the United States, ending his stay in Japan prematurely. His experiences with his father in Japan led him to conclude that "independence without luxury would be more suitable to me than luxury without independence." This awakening, he said, "made me bristle with a new-found self-respect and gave me whatever hope and cheer I could muster up."

Still, it hurt to be fired with a snap of his father's "royal fingers" after sixteen months on a project he wanted to see through. It was, he said, "no light lump to swallow." On his own back in the United States, John felt a lightening of responsibilities, as, one supposes, would anyone fired by Frank Lloyd Wright, but there was also a heavy sadness within him. For five years he had been at his father's side. Now the experiences and opportunities that had been provided were gone forever. "He had sired, hired, and fired me, but when I reached Chicago I learned that he had nursed his wrath by writing to Mother, accusing *her* of bringing up a thief. 'Confound him,' I thought, 'the rascal is like a king,' and I had exalted that king."

What next? One alternative would be to go to his father's office, where, "struck to the heart with remorse, he could forgive me for everything he had done, and then continue as before." He could "humor [his father's] whims, flatter his ego on all occasions until every vestige of individuality would die in me." That he could not do. Yet, "the break was too sudden—and the wound still open."

As usual, Frank Lloyd Wright tried to have the last word: He had only taken John to Tokyo because the Japanese hotel manager had asked him to. The Viscount Inouye episode, he said in his marginal comment, was incidental, not a principal factor. The principal factor, in his view, though he did not state it here, was acknowledged by John's daughter, Elizabeth Wright Ingraham, in her postscript to her father's memoir: "On his second trip to Japan, Dad had brought with him his new wife, Jeanette Winters, a dancer from Midway Gardens. It was a stormy marriage that adjusted poorly to Japanese culture. The manager of the Imperial Hotel . . . advised that Jeanette return home." This helps to explain Frank Lloyd Wright's comment: "But—John-boy your 'alibi' in this case amounts to a lie and is discreditable to you. Think it over son! Dad."[25]

John and his father never worked together again. That may explain why they maintained a reasonably good relationship over the next thirty-seven years and why, when Frank Lloyd Wright was in trouble with the law in 1926, in a case concocted by the embittered Miriam Noel, John "came down to get instructions about clearing up certain details of work at Taliesin."[26] The independence John prized enabled him to establish a successful but not lucrative career, first in Long Beach, Indiana, then in Del Mar, California. That independence, however, did not empower him to escape his father's shadow.

### ANTONIN RAYMOND

Antonin Raymond, the other assistant who left a record of working with Wright in Japan, was a Czech immigrant whose autobiography includes recollections of working with Wright and others at both Taliesin and in Japan.

He and his wife Noémi arrived in Yokohama with Wright on December 31, 1919. They were not the only "characters" living in the hotel. Paul Mueller was also there. He and his wife "were a typical Chicago German family, jolly and terre à terre." A good builder, Mueller was "able to get along with Wright in spite of the latter's habit of frequently changing his mind and tearing out work already accomplished." On the other hand, Mueller had a nervous temperament and "ran about instructing the workmen at the top of his lungs for better understanding."

Raymond's character sketches provide insights into the nature of the community in which he and his compatriots worked. Wright, he wrote, "had a well-developed sense of humour which saved many a difficult situation, although it was mixed on occasion with a biting sarcasm that expressed his contempt for the average mentality." Arata Endo "was the most amusing and able." He was a brilliant draftsman who had "such an admiration for his master that in dress he affected as near a duplication of Wright's attire as he could find, save of course that Wright's expensive deerskin suits and flowing mantle, capped with something like a Bruegel peasant cap set on top of his bushy white mane, were of the finest quality and workmanship." The closest to Endo was Kumazo Uchiyama, who, with the Raymonds and the stonemasons' foreman, was charged with inspecting quarries at Oya. They produced a greenish, porous stone filled with strange holes and debris that appealed to Wright's romantic nature. Raymond's principal responsibility at the temporary office they built upon their arrival was "to prepare detailed drawings and perspectives of the interiors and exteriors for the master's further study."

The plans for the hotel having largely been drawn at Taliesin, Raymond and others concentrated on their execution. Raymond said he found doing perspectives for presentation and a great deal of detailing laborious, and after a year of such work he became bored. The principal cause of this, he claimed, "was the endless repetition of Wright's mannerisms, his grammar, as he called it, to which I could add nothing and which seemed to me so devoid of content, particularly in Japan." Raymond felt that they had nothing to do with Japanese people and culture, but Wright did not perceive that, for his thoughts "were entirely concentrated on the expression of his own personal imaginings. The hotel finally turned out to be a monument to himself." This caused Raymond to consider leaving. Being witness to squabbles between Wright and Miriam Noel made both Raymonds uneasy, and that helped them decide that it was time to move on. Possibly, though, these judgments and his objections to Wright's personal life were contrived to justify his departure.

An opportunity came along for Raymond to form a partnership with a Princeton graduate named Slack, who had been designing undistinguished but serviceable schools and churches and other buildings, and a few days after meeting they both decided to quit their jobs and form an architectural design company. He informed Wright of his decision, promising to continue to work for him. However, what he produced no longer pleased Wright, who called him a traitor to the cause. They parted, with bitterness on Wright's part. He denounced him in a letter, calling his work disgusting and hopeless.

Taliesin Studio in 1925. From left: Frank Lloyd Wright, Kameki Tsuchiura, Richard Neutra, unidentified, and Nobu Tsuchiura. Copyright © 2009 the Frank Lloyd Wright Foundation, Taliesin West, Scottsdale, AZ

He would prefer Raymond's honest enmity, he said, "to any friendship you have or may profess for me or my work. You are now a gratuitous member of a guild that preys upon Architecture and Architect everywhere."[27] At age thirty-two, Raymond had worked with Wright in Japan for just over one year. He remained there and built an architectural practice that continued until the outbreak of World War II and resumed after the war.

As for the Imperial Hotel, while it survived the 1923 earthquake, "progress" in Japan proved to be too much for it. Olgivanna Lloyd Wright, the third wife of Frank Lloyd Wright, traveled to Tokyo in the Fall of 1967 in an effort to save it from demolition. But by then its fate was fixed. A carefully crafted campaign to sell the demolition to the Japanese public as an economic necessity had succeeded.[28]

## LIFE AT TALIESIN

Others besides John Lloyd Wright and Antonin Raymond recorded memories of experiences with Wright in this stage of his career, although not of working with him in Japan. One such was Kameki Tsuchiura, whom Wright met in Japan and who worked in Wright's studios from 1921 to 1925. His wife Nobuko assisted in drafting perspectives for Wright and putting his art collection in order. Aspiring to become an architect, she was in the studio every day. In 1923 Wright asked the Tsuchiuras and Will Smith to work in his temporary office in Los Angeles. Near the end of that year they moved to Taliesin to work with Wright there. Kameki recalled that Werner Moser and Richard Neutra were also assisting at that time.[29]

Richard and Dione Neutra visited Taliesin for the first time in July 1924. Richard had emigrated from Austria to the United States in the fall of 1923 and after a few months in New York made his way to Chicago. He met Frank Lloyd Wright in April 1924 at Louis Sullivan's funeral. In a letter to Dione, he said that Wright started to apologize that he had not been in touch with him, "because he was not yet settled, etc." Working for him, Neutra concluded, did not look promising. Wright looked about fifty-six, Neutra remarked, but he "is truly a child, but not a well-behaved one. God only knows. He is one in a million."

Dione Neutra had remained in Europe with their infant son, named Frank— for Frank Lloyd Wright—and Richard found work, first in New York, then in Chicago. In May she was able to join him, and in July the two of them accepted an invitation to visit Wright at Taliesin. In a letter to her mother, Dione provided a detailed account of the experiences she and her husband had with Wright on that visit. Werner Moser, son of Karl Moser, an architect with whom Neutra had studied briefly in Zurich, Switzerland, met them at the train station in Spring Green. As they approached the "one-story house, quite low, winding around a hill like a snake, becoming higher only on top of the hill," she experienced "immense astonishment." The interior of the house, too, she found to be "more beautiful than anything [she] had seen before." The simple dinner was delightful. After dinner they were introduced to Kameki and Nobuko Tsuchiura, and also to Will Smith. They also met Moser's wife Sylva, whose baby was due that day. Mrs. Neutra also mentioned "a German who has an eight-month-old child in Los Angeles and whose wife had died."

When Albert M. Johnson arrived, accompanied by his wife, daughter, and son-in-law, Dione told her mother, the air "was charged with electricity." Wright was hoping to design a skyscraper for Johnson. For weeks they had prepared for his visit, enlarging the office and adding space for twenty draftsmen. Wright called the young people into the living room to meet Mr. Johnson, the president of the National Life Insurance Company of Chicago. Dione Neutra's observation of the Johnson family inspired this sketch: "Mr. Johnson is an elderly, harmless, benevolent, little, dull-looking man. One would never suspect him to be a millionaire. His very amiable, gracious wife seems to be very superficial, their adopted daughter a powdered, pallid, dull-looking female with a doll-like beauty. Her husband had black hair, laughed and smiled, and looked like a nincompoop." As for Wright, she found it painful "to see such an outstanding man humbling himself by being amiable, offering hospitality in order to get a commission."

Then the music began. Playing an out-of-tune Steinway grand piano, Dione sang Bach and Italian arias and accompanied Moser, who played the violin. While the music was appreciated, the main thing was that they "helped Wright out of a great embarrassment because even the best entertainer finds it difficult to entertain these society people in the long run." In the afternoon Wright drove the Neutras around the countryside. "The estate," Dione observed, "is like a fairyland." Hearing Wright speak in a "winning, agreeably self-conscious manner," left her with the feeling that "he loves this, his native country, very deeply."[30]

The Neutras' visit lasted only two days, but Wright invited them to return, and in early November that year they moved to Taliesin, where Richard assisted Wright. He was thirty-two years old and Dione was twenty-three. They stayed at Taliesin until early the next February, when they moved to Los Angeles. During their stay, Richard, Werner, and Kameki were kept busy working on three projects, the building for Albert Johnson's National Life Insurance Company, a desert guest house for Johnson, and the Nakoma Country Club, a design for Madison, Wisconsin; none of the three was executed.

Kameki Tsuchiura recalled a delightful visit by Erich Mendelsohn, a young German architect, when Wright gathered the Neutras and others around him in the Taliesin living room: "Mrs. Neutra played Bach on her violoncello and Mendelsohn drew sketches of the Einstein Tower on many sheets of paper again and again, so fast."[31] Mendelsohn also recalled his days at Taliesin with Wright, "two days in the marvelous current, expectant and giving, tensed and relaxed." Despite their twenty-year age difference, and although he thought the fifty-seven-year old Wright was sixty-five, they "were friends at once, bewitched by space, holding out our hands to one another in space; the same road, the same goal, the same life, I believe."[32]

While there were many moments such as this, beneath the surface the Tsuchiuras, at least, were restless. In letters to Martin Feller, with whom they had worked in Japan and California, both Kameki and Nobu wrote of their strong desires to leave Taliesin, to find jobs in Chicago, to travel to Europe, and eventually to return to Japan. Their desires were fueled by the dearth of creative work in Wright's studio, Wright's practice of making changes again and again in work they had done, and ambition mixed with impatience. The lack of funds to do what they wanted to do also troubled them, as did the uncertainty of being paid, the cold weather, and the wearing thin of Taliesin routines.

When the Neutras left, probably for some of the same reasons, Kameki and Nobu were lonesome, and so was Wright. So Wright called them to his living room, Kameki wrote to Feller on February 2, 1925, "We must go soon to make him gay. But as you know, I'm not very much talented to make others gay. Anyway this is Taliesin." Eleven days later Kameki's frustration continued: "These days we are quite often called to Mr. Wright's room to hear music or dance by his order. These are disgusting hours. I decided not to go there everytime."

Soon after the Neutras' departure, the Mosers moved to Chicago, and shortly after that, on April 20, a second fire destroyed Taliesin, but not the drafting room or Wright's collection of Japanese prints. Here is Kameki's account of the fire, written the next day:

Fire started in Mr. Wright's bed room, 6:30 p.m. April 20th.

We were eating supper and when we came down, his room was all in flame. We carried water in buckets but how helpless, we were only Mr. Wright, I and Nobu, Mrs. Ohlson and Jack and chauffeur. Mr. Ohlson was in Madison and Smith was in Town. We connected the hose to the water pipe and firemen came, but too late. His apartment and all the guest apartments were burning. Strong wind blew from east to west. Such a smoke and flame no one could get in the house to bring anything out. We could cut the roof connecting Mr. Wright's kitchen and studio and prevent the fire from spreading west. After 9 o'clock, wind changed, rain started to drop. And what a sight we had till midnight, fire, thunderstorm, lightning, and more fire.

We moved from downstairs to Mr. Moser's room on Sunday, 19th, just one day before. So we are all right. But Mr. Wright lost all the previous things except those in the safe.

His apartment and guest apartments and all rooms in downstairs are ashes. (Nobody was hurt.)

Stone piers and stone chimneys are standing high from the ashes, where we can find sometimes heads and other pieces of stone figures of Orient.

Mr. Wright will move in the summer house in Hillside and start to rebuild from tomorrow.

A musical gathering at Taliesin, 1925. From left: Frank Lloyd Wright, Richard Neutra, Sylva Moser with baby Lorenz, Kameki Tsuchiura, Nobu Tsuchiura, W. Moser, and Dione Neutra. Courtesy of the Frank Lloyd Wright Foundation

Tsuchiura and Smith worked on drawings for reconstructing Taliesin, their last job before leaving in November 1925.[33]

Dione Neutra's letter (cited above) offers glimpses into Wright's manner of dealing with his young assistants and the possibilities he may have envisioned for developing a working community there. So does Wright's autobiographical recollection of his experiences with them, written in the years following their departure:

While I was alone at Taliesin after coming back from Japan, I had three wives, Sylva, Dione, and Nobu, looking in on me and keeping my spirits up. But they were not mine. They were the wives respectively of Werner (Moser), Richard (Neutra), and Kameki (Tsuchiura)—apprentices from Zurich, Vienna, and Tokio. But I can't imagine what I would have done without them at the time. On the rocks mentally, morally, emotionally.

We had music in the Living Room. . . . We occasionally drove about the countryside. Werner (Werner played the violin) and Sylva had a fine little boy, Lorenz. I liked to hold Lorenz sometimes. I loved to have him around. He was a beautiful boy. Richard and Dione had a small son, too (named for me before leaving Vienna); Kameki and Nobu were only just married. Together with Major Will (Smith) they were all my immediate family. A happy one because they were all good to what was left of me at that bad time. The boys kept my mind on my work; the girls kept kind attentions and flowers all through the house. While they did make me feel less lonely, they only made me feel all the more need of "the woman in my life" in these several pre-Olgivanna years. . . . I guess the happiness of these young couples pushed me gently over the precipice of divorce and marriage to really live again.[34]

And maybe working with them in his home and adjoining studio at Taliesin encouraged him to consider an idea that led, within a decade, to the creation of the Taliesin Fellowship.

# 5 TRANSITION IN CALIFORNIA

SO, WHEN CALLED UPON BY ALINE
BARNSDALL . . . TO BUILD A HOME
FOR HER IN HOLLYWOOD, WHY
NOT MAKE ARCHITECTURE STAND
UP AND SHOW ITSELF ON HER
NEW GROUND, OLIVE HILL, AS
CALIFORNIA ROMANCE?[1]
— FRANK LLOYD WRIGHT

Frank Lloyd Wright designed more than fifty buildings for clients in California. Twenty-four were executed, the first of them a Prairie Style residence for Emily and George C. Stewart, built at Montecito in 1909, as Wright was closing his Oak Park studio. While he was designing the Imperial Hotel and overseeing its construction, he had California on his mind again. Perhaps it was a place for developing new styles and using new materials. Fortunately for him, his first client was receptive to the innovations he proposed.

That client was Aline Barnsdall, a wealthy heiress to entrepreneurs in petroleum and related industries, who had studied theater in Europe.[2] When she returned to the United States she affiliated herself with an experimental theater company in Chicago. Determined to put her wealth to creative uses, she selected Wright to design a new theater for that company. He began to do so in 1915, but in what became the Barnsdall fashion, she changed her mind before Wright's preliminary plans progressed to a design stage.

The new theater should be built, she decided, in California. Her quest for land in Los Angeles led to the purchase in June 1919 of a site known as Olive Hill. By then Wright had begun sketching a home for her. In early 1920, juggling this new project with his work in Japan, he moved the plans along as time and assistance permitted, striving to satisfy Barnsdall's expanding wishes. With her residence, called Hollyhock, at the center of the Olive Hill plans, there would also be an art complex featuring several theaters, shops, a restaurant, lodging places for artists and staff members, and gardens open to the public. Lawns, pools, and fountains would surround the house itself, located in the most prominent place on a commanding hill.

The distinctive design of the Hollyhock House and the associated structures, as well as the potential for the landscape, posed new challenges for Wright's assistants and the builders. Critics' analyses of the design reveal what they faced. David Gebhard, in *Romanza,* contends that by drawing upon Mayan sources, Wright produced "a historical form associated with Mexico, and by implication with the Hispanic sections of the American Southwest and Southern California." This image "gave an appearance of being natural and 'organic' to the place; it represented a historically logical response to the physical and climatic environment of California and the Southwest."

Aline Barnsdall, Wright's client for the Hollyhock House in Los Angeles, with her daughter Betty (called Sugartop by her mother), who joined the Fellowship for two years, 1936–1938. Security Pacific Collection / Los Angeles Public Library

"Wright's recourse to the pre-Columbian," he continued, "also accommodated his participation in the open romanticism so prevalent in the then fashionable Period Revival architecture." Although Wright always insisted that his architecture was original, "his borrowings were as intense and as varied as any of his contemporaries. The difference, though, between Wright and other architects of his time has to do with the way in which he transformed borrowed forms and absorbed them into his own architectural language."[3] Wright's assistants bore responsibility for helping translate that language into architectural realities.

Kathryn Smith, author of the most substantial work on the Hollyhock House, also sees Mayan influence in it, although less directly than Gebhard. She cautions against assuming that Wright's designs were intended to give the Barnsdall buildings "local roots," as his assistant, Rudolph Schindler, asserted. Not only did he use the same imagery in such wide-ranging locations as Wisconsin, Japan, and Arizona, but he also made the initial drawings before Barnsdall had selected Los Angeles as the location for her projects.

In the 1910s and 1920s, Smith continues, Wright sought "a more expressive architecture" and "took the risk of creating a series of unresolved compositions to move beyond the convention of the Prairie house toward a greater evocation of nature." He was moving, she contends, from decoration to geometric abstraction and "from the locally referential to the universal in metaphor." Accordingly, to him "the Mayan temple represented a symbolic mountain, and in Oriental art, mountains are perceived as cosmic pillars, shafts connecting heaven and earth. It is likely that Wright was searching for a metaphor for this vital connection between the dualities of nature."[4] That search created problems for assistants charged with giving that metaphor material, tangible meaning.

Also to be mastered by Wright's assistants were strategies for keeping the Hollyhock project moving while serving a largely absentee architect and a peripatetic client, who had her own assistants. Wright spent part of each year in Japan between 1916 and 1922, and his returns to the United States were typically brief and his schedules hectic. Barnsdall was also on the move, but her sometimes impetuous, sometimes imperious demands kept coming.

Wright's relations with Barnsdall reached a crisis point in October 1920 when, according to Smith, chaotic circumstances at Olive Hill shut down construction. Wright had to return to Los Angeles to meet with his client before sailing for Japan in mid-December. In turn, unpleasantly demanding situations in Tokyo no doubt made him eager to return to the United States, as he did in May 1921. While he had been away, his assistant, R. M. Schindler (as he was known), had supervised construction, and Barnsdall, having gone to Europe, left her business manager in charge. "She had grown highly suspicious and distrustful of Wright," according to Smith, "and as a result, she had left a check with strict instructions that it would be the last. The buildings had to be completed with the agreed-upon amount."[5]

In Japan, as we have noted, Wright's working communities were temporary and ephemeral in character. In California the situation could hardly have been different, especially because he spent a fair amount of his time while in the United States attempting to improve his financial circumstances by dealing in Japanese prints.

Two assistants, Schindler and Lloyd Wright, figured most prominently in the story of the building of the Hollyhock House. Kameki Tsuchiura, who had been with Wright in Japan and at Taliesin, was also in California in 1923; his photographs of construction sites are an important part of the record of Wright's accomplishments that year. Also there was Wright's secretary, Will Smith.

Schindler was an Austrian-born architect who came to America aspiring to work with Frank Lloyd Wright. Although Wright was always reluctant to grant credit to his assistants, it is clear that Schindler played a significant part in his work. As Judith Sheine notes in her biography of Schindler, he started working for Wright in February 1918, and in the next several years Wright left him in charge of his Chicago and Los Angeles offices while he was in Japan.[6] He had done this only once previously, with Walter Burley Griffin in 1905. Consistent with his usual claims, however, he later denied ever having given anyone, especially Schindler, such a responsibility. Indeed, in a 1931 letter to Schindler he denounced him, as he had earlier scolded Harry Robinson, for having said he had been in charge of his office:

Get this: Where I am my office is. My office is *me*. Frank Lloyd Wright has no other office, never had one, and never will have one. You know it damned well. . . . I should have bawled out your 'under-hand' or turned you over to the authorities long ago and have broken the pus-bag of treachery and dis-affection in Los Angeles. . . . I want no more communication with you. Anything from you will go back unopened. Lloyd is near enough to take this up.[7]

But Sheine contends that the two architects had a special relationship in the early 1920s, and she thinks it strange that Wright barely mentioned him, even in connection with the Barnsdall project. Most writers, she says, accept Wright's version of the facts.

However, a recent discovery by Maureen Mary, archivist of the Schindler family, of correspondence between Wright and Schindler from 1914 to 1929, the majority of which covers the years from 1918 to 1922 during which Schindler was in charge of Wright's office, has provided revealing evidence that casts new light on both Schindler and Wright. It confirms Schindler's version of the events, especially concerning the 1931 dispute with Wright that erupted over Schindler's claim, which appeared in a flyer announcing his lectures at the Chouinard School of Art, that he had been in charge of Wright's office.[8]

The animosity evident in Wright's letter to Schindler over this incident, and in Schindler's response, reflects the legacy of lingering differences between them. Wright had accused Schindler, as well as Richard Neutra, who had worked with him briefly at Taliesin, of exploitation and "a cheap attempt to magnify [themselves] at the expense of those who were both generous and kind" to them at their own expense. "No sincere or honest aid," he continued, "have either of you given to me in my work nor to the cause of organic architecture."[9]

Concerning the circular in question, Schindler replied that he had asked that it be sent to Wright, "although I know of your inability to sympathise

Lloyd Wright, Frank Lloyd Wright's eldest son, assisted his father in Europe and California on his way to establishing his own practice in Los Angeles. Copyright Eric Lloyd Wright—Architect

with anybodys efforts, the stupidity of your mudslinging answere is unexpected. I was in charge of your office and I can prove it."[10]

In charge of Wright's office or not, not only did Schindler have to do a great deal of design work during Wright's long absences from Taliesin, but the correspondence cited by Sheine shows that he also tended to some of Wright's personal affairs, such as the rental of the Oak Park studio.[11] Moreover, Wright's pique with Schindler is puzzling, for in 1929 he had described Schindler's work positively in drafts of letters to the Board of Architecture in Southern California in support of his application for a license to practice architecture in California; he asked Schindler to select the one to be sent. Later the ill feelings of 1931 seem to have subsided. When Wright learned from Pauline Schindler in 1953 that her former husband was terminally ill, he immediately wrote him a sensitive note, recalling that he had been served well by Schindler's talents.[12]

In her volume on the Olive Hill projects, Kathryn Smith credits Schindler with having done the drawings for one of the proposed structures, the unbuilt Director's House, and notes that Wright based his scheme for several of the Barnsdall structures on plans developed by Schindler during his absence. Schindler's involvement began in Wright's Chicago studio and at Taliesin in the project's early stages and continued in Wright's Los Angeles office and as on-site construction supervisor. He revised drawings, negotiated with suppliers of materials and contractors, kept construction moving, dealt with Barnsdall's designated representatives, and communicated with both Wright and Barnsdall. Problems relating to changes demanded by the client or proposed by the architect persisted during the life of the project.[13]

Lloyd Wright, the other principal assistant at the Hollyhock construction sites, had been asked by his father to go to Los Angeles in 1919 to represent him as superintendent of the Hollyhock project. Despite the notoriously testy relationship between the father, age 52, and the son, age 29, Lloyd served effectively in that role, at least for a while. While assisting as a technical advisor and drafter of presentation drawings, he was in charge of construction supervision until Wright asked Schindler to take over in mid-1920. He continued thereafter as landscape designer, a considerable responsibility, given the large tract of land where construction was occurring.[14] Whatever his role, Lloyd encountered problems similar to Schindler's. Even as he gave his father optimistic reports, Barnsdall was raising questions, making explicit demands concerning design details, protesting delays, setting deadlines, second-guessing landscaping plans, and threatening to abandon the project. Lloyd Wright and Schindler had responsibilities that required interaction with one another, and that posed severe challenges for both men.

The circumstances in which they worked together were far from ideal. Schindler's wife, Pauline, described what things were like at 522 Homer Laughlin Building, Wright's office in October 1919: "At present, RMS [Schindler], Lloyd Wright (who is at least six feet tall), two draftsmen and an office boy are all crowded into two small office rooms, which are otherwise already overflowing with huge drafting tables and desks," and "on TOP of them, various stenographers coming in to bring rush copy of contracts, while burly contractors stand about looking crafty and expensive."[15]

When the construction of the Hollyhock House and other buildings at Olive Hill drew to a close, Schindler continued to work for Aline Barnsdall. First, though, he needed "a vacation to restore [his] equilibrium." He informed Wright in September 1921 that he hoped to be able "to think about something else besides patches, leaks and contracts."[16] The next month he left for Yosemite. Wright and Barnsdall reached out-of-court settlements on issues raised in the design and construction years.

Lloyd Wright was no doubt happy to see Schindler leave, for in a letter to his father he had questioned Schindler's usefulness. His father responded:

I know R.M.S's faults—He is doing his best—but his attitude has always been what it is. He means neither harm nor disrespect really—It is not that he respects Wright less but values his hope of Schindler rather more in the secret recesses of his soul. It is the artist in him characteristically seducing and soothing his innermost Ego. . . . I ought probably not depend on him—but I will put you together to see what the mix is like for the next three weeks. I need the son's loyalty and help as far as he can go.

In the same letter Wright chastised Lloyd for *his* many faults: He was not reliable. He would say a thing was so when he only thought it was so. He made promises he did not keep. He would buy when he could not pay. He was sentimental but not kind. That he had no personal culture, that he was not really at heart a gentleman "owing either to ignorance or bad-fibre— or a little of both." And so on, for four handwritten pages.[17] Nonetheless, Lloyd continued to work for his father and attempted to help him establish a practice in Los Angeles.

In *An Autobiography* Wright reflected on his Hollyhock experiences with Barnsdall and others. When called upon by Aline Barnsdall to build a home for her in Hollywood, he mused, "why not make architecture stand up and show itself on her new ground, Olive Hill, as California Romance?" Miss Barnsdall, he wrote, "wanted no ordinary home, for she was no ordinary woman."

If she could have denied she was one at all, she might have done so. But the fact claimed and got her continually, much to her distress and the confusion of her large aims. If any woman ever hitched her wagon to a star, Aline Barnsdall hitched hers thereto. And so . . . she chose her architect as that bright and particular star.

. . . .

Miss Barnsdall turned this beautiful site, Olive Hill, over to me as a basis on which we were to go to work *together* to build under the serene canopy of California blue.

Wright went to work, but he soon found that his client had ideas of her own. A restless spirit "as she traveled over the face of the globe, she would drop suggestions as a war-plane drops bombs and sails away into the blue. One never knew where or from where the bombs would drop—but they dropped."

Acknowledging that his obligations in Japan complicated his relationship with Miss Barnsdall, Wright cited specific problems encountered at Olive Hill. For example, his "untried amateur superintendent Schindler," he said, "was too smooth a party ever to learn how to be serious." That was one reason he liked him. "But," he continued, "that was bad for the house." Additionally there were problems with the contractor and Miss Barnsdall's insurers. Notwithstanding, he "consented to hang on by way of my affable superintendent Schindler and my son Lloyd, plainly seeing nevertheless that I would have to take the consequences of [Barnsdall's] insurance brigade and eventually of the usual conspiracy. Now this on my part was due to utter weariness, or else was utter cowardice." Continuing:

Nevertheless from out this confusion, from this welter of misunderstanding and misapplied heat and fury . . . a shape appeared, inviolate. A strangely beautiful "form" crept inexorably into view. Even the quarreling pack began to see and be impressed by it. Something had held all this shifty diversity of administration together enough to enable a new significance to come out and adorn that hill crown. Was it the marks on paper that this quarreling was all about, these traces of a design that, no matter how abused, would show itself in spite of friction, waste, and slip? Of course.

But rather, and *somehow*, by way of the downright brutality, insolence and persistence of the architect and the client's desire, too, though both architect and client were torn to tatters—"Form" got into the building in spite of all the folly.

This it is that seems to me the miracle as I saw Hollyhock House on its hill now on returning from Tokio. And it is a miracle to this day.[18]

If form took shape in the building, there are no indications that Wright's wrangles with his client contributed to the forming of a community among the workers on whom he depended. He relied on Schindler more than he wished to acknowledge, then and later, and the work done by Lloyd Wright was indispensable to him. But the character of these individuals and circumstances in which they worked, particularly with Wright having been absent while much of the work was being done, evidently prevented the development of good relations among them.

While Schindler continued to work independently for Aline Barnsdall, Lloyd Wright remained a loyal assistant to his father when the senior Wright returned to Los Angeles in 1923. Robert L. Sweeney, author of *Wright in Hollywood: Visions of a New Architecture,* acknowledges that "little is known of the circumstances that caused [the senior] Wright to return with such determination, though his practice was to respond to major new opportunity [*sic*]." Moreover, there was some evidence, Sweeney continues, that "he was attracted by vast tracts of land that were then being subdivided and offered for sale." An article in a local newspaper announced that "he planned to develop the foothill properties between Hollywood and the sea."

Sweeney notes further that in March 1923 Wright had rented a modest house at 1284 Harper Avenue in Hollywood and that a sign posted on the door indicated plans to build a permanent studio in Beverly Hills.[19] According to Lloyd, "F.L.W. was trying very hard to get started on the West Coast, and he had all kinds of projects going on out there, but somehow he could not get the people to play ball with him. He spent considerable time with the Chandlers and General Sherman, trying to interest them in his architectural schemes—they were very amused and entertained by F.L.W., but were unreceptive."[20]

Nobu Tsuchiura, who, with her husband Kameki, assisted Wright at Taliesin and in Los Angeles, is seated between Will Smith, Wright's draftsman, and an aspiring actor named Harry, in Wright's temporary studio at 1284 Harper Avenue, Los Angeles. Courtesy of T. Nakamura. Photo by Kameki Tsuchiura.

In any event, Lloyd's continuing to work with his father meant that these would be times of testing: Together they tested the realities of building in Los Angeles; together they tested new construction possibilities; and together they tested each other's patience. Lloyd had worked with textile block construction earlier, and his father drew him into fresh efforts in building with it on four houses. The first was a home and bookshop for Mrs. Alice Millard, designed in 1923. Also designed that year, almost simultaneously, were the John Storer Residence, the Samuel Freeman Residence, and the Charles Ennis Residence.

Lloyd Wright supervised the construction and designed the landscaping for all four of these residences. The design work was apparently done in the Harper Avenue studio, but there is no official record as to who, in addition to Lloyd Wright, worked as draftsmen or apprentices. According to Kameki Tsuchiura, however, Wright had asked him in 1923 to work in his temporary office in Los Angeles, on the Doheny Ranch project and the Boat House at Lake Tahoe. He recalled that he, his wife, and Will Smith were Wright's only assistants there, while Lloyd Wright worked as a partner. In December 1923 he and Smith returned to Taliesin to work with Wright there.[21]

In addition to supervising construction, Lloyd Wright offered technical advice on textile-block construction, prepared presentation drawings, and designed the landscapes. As Robert Sweeney points out, the correspondence between them, along with the construction photographs Lloyd Wright preserved, "reveal the challenge of translating the concept into reality and the compromises that were made."[22]

Lloyd Wright's involvement with the textile-block houses and other projects continued.[23] In 1926 he designed a studio for the Millard House, located to the side of the ravine below it; Mrs. Millard did not like it, nor did Frank Lloyd Wright, although he had approved the design.[24] Even later Lloyd was involved in dealing with these buildings' lingering problems, particularly the Ennis House. In the 1940s Lloyd worked with its second owner, John Nesbitt, to correct some of these problems—a number of them created by changes the Ennises had made—and to integrate alterations designed by the senior Wright. In 1974 Lloyd Wright and his son, Eric Lloyd Wright, directed an extensive restoration of the Hollyhock House, and Eric was the architect for the restoration of the Storer House in the 1980s.[25]

While the California years represented a transition in Wright's career, there were transitions also in his personal life. In November 1923 he married Miriam Noel, who had been his companion in a tempestuous relationship since 1914. In 1924 he apparently abandoned plans to maintain a studio in Los Angeles and returned permanently to Taliesin, although in an October 18, 1923, interview with his friend William T. Evjue of the *Capital Times,* he stated that he expected to have studios in Chicago, Hollywood, and Tokyo.[26]

Also in 1924 Miriam Noel, by then a morphine addict, left Wright, and he met Olgivanna Lazovich Hinzenburg at a ballet in Chicago. The next year she moved in with him at Taliesin and divorced her husband. Rebuilding costs following another fire at Taliesin and legal fees involving his divorce from Miriam Noel added weight to his chronically burdensome debt.

If experiences like those described earlier, particularly the ones with young people at Taliesin, inspired him to think about creating a genuine community of architects, draftsmen, apprentices, other assistants, and kinfolk, hitting bottom most likely impelled him to take a life-changing course of action. From these circumstances, in just half a dozen years, emerged the Taliesin Fellowship.

# 6 THE FELLOWSHIP

## *Distinctive by Design*

The founding of the Taliesin Fellowship occurred in a context congenial to such ventures, and there were precedents that Frank and Olgivanna Wright might have followed as its founders. But the melding of ideas rooted in experiences each had had in earlier times made it a singular institution—that is, one like no other. Its design was distinctively their own.

## EARLIER INTENTIONAL COMMUNITIES

Comparisons with earlier intentional communities confirm the Taliesin Fellowship's distinctiveness. For example, the Shakers, members of America's longest-lasting such communities, were renowned for their simple furniture designs and their disciplined communal lives, but their religious convictions and their practice of celibacy meant that their communities, distinctive in their own right, were no models for emulation. Another, the Society of True Inspiration, had prospered in the Amana colonies in central Iowa from the 1850s until the 1920s. The members produced distinctive furniture and lived simple, religious, communal lives, but in 1932 its members concluded that the forces of change surrounding them were irresistible and voted to become shareholders in a capitalist organization. In the 1840s the charismatic John Humphrey Noyes drew followers together around his unorthodox teachings about sex and marriage, first in Putney, Vermont, then in Oneida, New York, where in 1848 they established a utopian community. Life there, with its controversial practices, flourished before going into decline and dissolving in 1881. Like Amana, it became a joint stock company, led until 1961 by descendants of Noyes, in the making of fine silver products and china.

Not in any of these utopian communities, nor anywhere else in a long list of America's experiments with communal living, could the Wrights have found a model for what they wished to create. "Utopian" simply does not fit with the nature, purpose, and history of the Taliesin Fellowship. Rather, the Fellowship was a pragmatic creation designed to provide Wright with capable hands and eager minds and to enable him to be a productive architect. Besides, he and Mrs. Wright desperately needed the money the apprentices paid to be his "volunteers." The stimulation provided by the arrangement they conceived ran both to and from Frank Lloyd Wright, and in the process he trained young people for careers in architecture themselves.

**THE ARTS AND CRAFTS MOVEMENT**

Nor did the communal inclinations of the secular Arts and Crafts movement in England and the United States offer guidance or inspiration to the Fellowship's founders, even though Wright and other Chicago architects had relations of one sort or another with the Chicago Arts and Crafts Society, founded in 1897.[2] Indeed, Wright presented one of his most notable lectures, "The Art and Craft of the Machine," to that society at the Jane Addams' Hull House in March 1901.[3]

Wright no doubt knew of the work of Elbert Hubbard, who had established the Roycroft Press in East Aurora, New York, in 1895. Several years later Hubbard founded an artists' colony there, consistent with the practice established in England by the most notable figure in the Arts and Crafts Movement, William Morris. The emphasis at Roycroft, in addition to printing, was on handcrafting furniture. Hubbard, before deciding to concentrate on writing, publishing, and other ventures, had been a part owner of the Larkin Company in Buffalo, New York. His successor at that company, Darwin Martin, may have suggested Frank Lloyd as the architect for the three-story furniture shop at Roycroft, for at that time Wright was designing the Larkin Administration Building and homes for Martin and Larkin's attorney, William R. Heath, Hubbard's brother-in-law. Wright, however, did not design Roycroft.[4]

Hubbard's Roycroft attracted artists from various fields, and according to architectural historian Jack Quinan, his industry was conducted "in the spirit of a summer camp." In its prime years Hubbard's dormitory housed about 500 artists, craftsmen, and other workers, but Roycroft did not become an intentional community of the kind that Wright later conceived. Nonetheless, Hubbard had a number of things in common with Wright. For example, in addition to demonstrating appreciation for the finest in artisanship, they both nurtured antipathies toward the kind of experiences colleges and universities offered. Hubbard had dropped out of Harvard to pursue a career as a writer. Also, they both had a penchant for pithy aphorisms. Carved into doors around Roycroft, which functions as an inn yet today, are these examples: "The love you liberate in your work is the love you keep." "Blessed is that man who has found his work." "Produce great people—the rest follows."[5] Any possibility that Wright and Hubbard might collaborate in some way ended when, on May 17, 1915, Hubbard and almost 1,200 others perished in the sinking of the famed British ship *Lusitania* by the German navy.

When the Wrights were creating the Taliesin Fellowship, they certainly knew that Gustav Stickley, an Arts and Crafts designer and builder of furniture, had been producing furniture for years that borrowed from Wright's designs. That may have been why Wright apparently thought it appropriate for clients who could not afford his custom-designed furnishings to use those produced by Gustav's brothers, L. and J. G. Stickley.[6] Gustav Stickley made no references to Wright in his writings, and no articles by Wright appeared in his magazine, *The Craftsman*.

It is plausible to surmise, however, that Wright was aware that in 1908–1910 Gustav Stickley, also a native of Wisconsin, had established Craftsman Farms in New Jersey's Morris County. There Stickley attempted to create a community that would reflect the ideals of the Arts and Crafts movement. It would be a place, he said, "for the definite working out of the theory I have so long held of reviving practical and profitable handicrafts in connection with small farming carried out by modern methods of intensive agriculture."[7]

Life at Craftsman Farms would be simple. Stickley's apprentices would learn to design and build in the tradition of manual training fostered by the movement. The school for boys at the Farms was to be self-sufficient. Its orchards, vegetable gardens, dairy cows, and chickens were to be sufficiently productive to sustain a community of about one hundred that Stickley anticipated. Because he never managed to open the school, Stickley used the farm surplus produced by his family and others in the Manhattan restaurant he opened in 1913.[8]

At the Farms, he designed and built the large, solid structure known as the "clubhouse," using logs and stone found on the property. It served initially, however, as his family's home. He also built three cottages for his apprentices and a number of buildings to support the Farms' operations. According to Mark Alan Hewitt, it appeared that "Stickley intended to rule as a kind of headmaster, craftsman, and farmer over his utopia—the 'Master's House' was the unrealized evidence of that dream." The idea of combining an estate with a school, Hewitt continues, "was neither original nor particularly beneficent—Stickley simply did not possess the wealth to accomplish his dream."[9]

In 1915 Stickley, once an ambitious, proud, and successful furniture designer, architect, writer, and publisher, filed for bankruptcy. Despite the similarity of Stickley's and Wright's ideals, Craftsman Farms provided the Wrights no model for translating their vision for a learning-by-doing community into reality.

## THE CRANBROOK ACADEMY AND ELIEL SAARINEN

Also in the larger context of movements bearing some similarity to the Taliesin Fellowship is the Cranbrook Academy of Art, founded around the same time near Bloomfield Hills, Michigan. The founders were George and Ellen Booth, who had amassed a fortune, initially through ownership of the *Detroit Evening News* and later through Booth Newspapers, Inc. Ellen Booth was the daughter and heir of Harriet and James Scripps, founders of the *Evening News,* and George Booth and his brothers built a prosperous chain of small-city newspapers in Michigan.

George and Ellen Booth were near-contemporaries of Frank Lloyd Wright, but unlike the always-destitute Wright, they had money to spare. Some they gave to philanthropic causes, but early in the twentieth century their interest began to focus on developing public-service opportunities on farmland near the community of Bloomfield Hills. They named their newly acquired land Cranbrook in honor of the village in Kent County, England, where George Booth's father had been born. By 1908 they were able to move into their home at Cranbrook, designed by Albert Kahn, the renowned architect of factories for the Ford Motor Company in Detroit, and they made their property a beautifully landscaped country estate.

Always committed to serving interests that reached far beyond their family, the Booths looked for ways to commit their land to public purposes. After visiting the American Academy in Rome in 1922, they were determined that what had by then become the Cranbrook Foundation should develop a comparable institution. Before long they built a meeting-house, several schools, and an Episcopal church. Recognizing the need for an architect for all these ventures, they engaged Eliel Saarinen, an immigrant from Finland who was a visiting professor at the University of Michigan. George Booth was sufficiently impressed by Saarinen's work to ask him to provide architectural leadership in instruction in the arts.[10]

In 1932 the Cranbrook Foundation officially established the Cranbrook Academy of Art, with Saarinen as president. He remained in this role for more than a decade, and despite hardships resulting from the Great Depression, Cranbrook attracted distinguished artists to its faculty. According to the 1932 prospectus, the Cranbrook Academy was "established to afford talented students the opportunity to study in a favorable environment under the leadership of artists of high standing" and to "influence the development of contemporary design into an art form which will be a true reflection of our times."[11]

Thus, as at Taliesin, the emphasis was on informal learning in a small community, but the differences between Cranbrook and the Taliesin Fellowship are more striking than their similarities. Taliesin did not award degrees until the 1980s, and the Fellowship remained much less institutionalized than the Cranbrook Academy. Furthermore, the Cranbrook plan called for offering studies in arts in addition to architecture, such as design, drawing, painting, sculpture, landscape design, weaving and textile designing, cabinet work, metal work, pottery, and book printing and binding. There would be residencies by visiting artists from various parts of the country, who would bring "freshness and new impulses to the institution," and help its participants achieve "a richer and closer understanding of contemporary movement in various minds and in various countries."[12] This sounds very much like the Wrights' initial plans for the Taliesin Fellowship.

To a much greater degree than at Cranbrook, the Taliesin apprentices had intimate interactions with their community's leaders. If the apprentices were to learn architecture by doing, they were expected also to learn about life by living together in a community, and that meant taking responsibility for cooking, farming, building, and everything else essential in communal living.

Frank Lloyd Wright and Eliel Saarinen knew one another, and Wright visited Cranbrook on at least two occasions.[13] Saarinen's biographer, Albert Christ-Janer, records a remark by Wright to Saarinen as he walked with him through the corridors of Kingwood School on the Cranbrook campus. Saarinen, he says, "was amused to hear his visitor exclaim: 'You always have the luck to work with good materials, while I seem always to have to work with lesser ones.'"[14] Wright expressed similar sentiments in his autobiography. Recalling having traveled with Saarinen to Rio de Janeiro in October 1930, he wrote that he "had always resented Saarinen a little, regarding him as our most accomplished foreign eclectic—a little jealous too of his easy berth, bestowed by the hand of American riches, while I had to wait and work and scrape for mine, the hard way." But, he says, they became fast friends "and had no basis for disagreement on anything whatsoever."[15]

Edgar Tafel, a Taliesin apprentice from 1932 to 1941 who recorded recollections of his experiences at Taliesin, recalled that Cranbrook was completely different. "[Saarinen] ran a postgraduate workshop—we called it the country club. Young architects stayed there for a year or two and went off again to practice. In no sense was it a commune. Saarinen's place had a swimming pool, tennis courts, well-kept lawns, maids and waitresses."[16]

## THE BAUHAUS, WALTER GROPIUS, AND LUDWIG MIES VAN DER ROHE

The Bauhaus, a school of architecture established in Weimar, Germany, is a contemporaneous institution that influenced Wright's plans for the Taliesin Fellowship. He was determined to counter what he believed to be the misguided ideals and practices of this most renowned architecture school in the first half of the twentieth century. As at Taliesin, the students in the Bauhaus were called "apprentices," and they were expected to master the crafts, materials, and processes of building. However, the Bauhaus apprentices were taught by a number of "masters," while at Taliesin there was only one— and he was *the* master.

Architect Walter Gropius founded the Bauhaus in 1919 and served as its leader until 1928. Ludwig Mies van der Rohe assumed the leadership in 1930, by which time political and cultural circumstances had compelled it to move from Weimar to Dessau. He served in this role in 1932, when it was forced to move to Berlin and stayed with it until the Nazi government closed it in 1933. As the situation in Germany deteriorated, Gropius moved to London and, in 1937, to the United States. Here he established the Architects Collaborative, a firm that carried into practice his belief about the importance of collaboration among architects, and between them and other artists. Almost immediately upon his arrival, Gropius was appointed to a professorship in architecture at Harvard, where he served from 1938 until 1952 as chairman of the architecture department. Mies van der Rohe also came to the United States in 1937 and continued his practice while serving as the director of the architecture department at the Armour Institute of Chicago. When that institution was transformed in 1940 into the Illinois Institute of Technology, through a merger with the Lewis Institute, he not only headed its school of architecture, but he also designed the new campus and its buildings.

Gropius and others of the Bauhaus school who established practices in the United States and who believed in collaboration involving architects and other artists took exception to Wright's emphasis on individualism. Mies van der Rohe, for example, acknowledging that there was no question about Wright's genius, said, ". . . I think he cannot have real followers. In order to do the things as he does it, you need a lot of fantasy, and, if you have fantasy you will do it differently. I am quite sure it is an individualistic approach, and I don't go this way. I go a different way. I am trying to go on an objective way." Gropius was candid in expressing his differences with Wright:

I saw a lot of things of Frank Lloyd Wright, who interested me very much. Of course, in the philosophy of architecture I am on another limb than he is. He is very strongly an individualist whereas I am very much in favor of teamwork. I think that the field we have to see today is so large that it is impossible to have everything in one head. I dare say that even a genius, if he understands how to develop teams around himself and lead these teams, that the spark that he can give can come more to the fore. It can be used better when he has many team helpers than when he is all alone in an ivory tower by himself.[17]

Taliesin, Gropius asserted, was an "example of an autocratically-run architectural school of fame."

. . . Recently I visited his school, which his widow valiantly carries on after his death. I saw the work of several scores of students, who were without exception turning out designs in the vocabulary of their great master. No independent approach could be found. This experience assured me again that such a method of education cannot be called creative, for it invites imitation and results in training assistants, not independent artists in their own right. Certainly the contact of the student with a great radiating artistic personality like Frank Lloyd Wright . . . is an invaluable and unforgettable human experience, but here I am trying to compare educational *methods* and *goals,* which must not be confounded with the artistic potency of the teacher. A great artist is not offhand a great educator.[18]

From the International Style of architecture, so labeled by Henry-Russell Hitchcock, emerged what is sometimes known as the functional architecture of the Bauhaus school and its practitioners, reflecting their commitment to rationalism. Wright generally treated the Bauhaus practitioners respectfully in personal terms, but not always, as he had difficulty in separating them as individuals from the International Style, which he repeatedly denounced. Edgar Tafel recalled an instance when Walter Gropius was in Madison to give a lecture and someone called on his behalf to arrange a visit to Taliesin and to meet Wright. The response was brusque: "I'm very sorry. I'm quite busy and I have no desire to meet or entertain Herr Gropius. What he stands for and what I stand for are poles apart. Our ideas could never merge. In a sense, we're professional enemies—but he's an outside enemy. At least I'm staying in my own country." Later that day, in a chance encounter at the Jacobs House in Madison, Wright again treated Gropius rudely.[19]

In *Apollo in the Democracy: The Cultural Obligations of the Architect* (1968), Gropius recalls that when Wright came to Boston in 1940 to deliver a lecture, he accepted an invitation to Gropius's home in Lincoln, Massachusetts. They had, wrote Gropius, "a few undisturbed hours of free conversation, during which he complained bitterly about the treatment he had received in his own country." Particularly disturbing to Wright, according to Gropius, was the fact that he had been made chairman of the department of architecture at Harvard, while Wright had never been offered such an influential position when he was younger. He believed that Gropius "had been given every advantage and every opportunity in [his] life and career that anybody could wish for." Gropius found Wright's self-

centeredness "irritating and at the same time disarming, for he was hiding his hurt feelings behind a mask of haughty arrogance which gradually became his second nature."

Although Wright distanced himself also from the approach to architectural education practiced by Mies van der Rohe, he treated him more cordially than he treated Gropius, at least for a while. By his own account, he and Mies had always been fond of each other, and he thought of Mies as "a sincere man as well as an architect."[20] His warm feelings were evident on a number of occasions, but particularly when an invitation by Wright, prompted by several young Chicago architects, resulted in a four-day stay by Mies at Taliesin in 1937. They talked about Broadacre City, with the text of Mr. Wright's comments published in the first issue of a Taliesin magazine several years later, under the title "Mr. Wright Talks on Broadacre City: To Ludwig Mies van der Rohe." Wright sent a copy to Mies, who replied that the journal "recalled vividly the enjoyment of my first visit with you."[21]

Edgar Tafel drove Mies and Wright back to Chicago by way of Racine to see the Johnson Wax Building. Later, discussing with other apprentices the contrast between the two men, Tafel and the others concluded that Mies was dedicated to finding, refining, and purifying one style, whereas Wright "kept

This snapshot was taken when Mies van der Rohe visited Taliesin for several days in 1937. With Mies in the Taliesin tea circle are Mr. and Mrs. Wright, Wright's sister Maginel Barney, and apprentice Hulda Drake. The man in the foreground may be an interpreter, as Mies was not conversant in English and Wright spoke no German. Behind the tree is apprentice John Lautner. Chicago History Museum. Photographer— Hedrich-Blessing. HB-25942A.

evolving, growing, developing new styles. He was never locked into one design establishment, which bore out his favorite phrase: 'What we did yesterday, we won't do today.' . . . By the time architectural copyists had caught on to an idea of Mr. Wright's, he was already on to something new. Mies's credo was just the opposite: 'You don't start a new style each Monday.'"[22]

Mies asked Wright to speak at a dinner in a Palmer House ballroom on October 18, 1938, celebrating the beginning of Mies's tenure as director of the architecture department at Armour Institute in Chicago. He recalled the occasion in *An Autobiography:*

It was all superficial blah or labored lip service, so when I rose I put my arm across Mies' shoulders . . . , and simply said, "Ladies and gentlemen, I give you Mies Van der Rohe. But for me there would have been no Mies—certainly none here tonight. I admire him as an architect and respect and love him as a man. Armour Institute, I give you Mies Van der Rohe. You treat him well and love him as I do." I abruptly stepped down and walked out.[23]

Henry Heald, the president of Armour Institute, wrote later that Wright had concluded his introduction with "God knows you need him." Why he left abruptly, with some followers, he did not explain. Some witnesses considered his departure a deliberate act of upstaging. His colleagues said he had a pressing out-of-town engagement, a claim refuted by Heald, who says he found him in a bar, where he had been waiting out the rest of the program.

Had he stayed, he would have heard Mies's address, delivered in German and badly botched in translation, advancing arguments about architectural education similar to those propounded by Wright. Moreover, he would also have heard an extemporaneous tribute paid to him by Mies. Peter Blake wrote that there is no record of that tribute, but that two years later Mies said this about him: "Wright resembles a giant tree in a wide landscape which, year after year, attains a more noble crown." If Wright had listened to Mies's inaugural address at the Armour Institute a month later, he would have heard a clear statement of Mies's educational philosophy. Although elements of Bauhaus principles were evident in it, and the architectural program that he advanced was more rigid than what Wright had formulated at Taliesin, Wright may have found reason to endorse Mies's closing lines:

The idealistic principle of order, however, with its overemphasis on the ideal and the formal, satisfies neither our interest in simple reality nor our practical sense.

So we shall emphasize the organic principle of order as a means of achieving the successful relationship of the parts to each other and to the whole. And here we take our stand.

. . . .

Nothing can express the aim and meaning of our work better than the profound words of St. Augustine: "Beauty is the splendor of Truth."[24]

The warmth Wright and Mies felt toward each other gradually chilled. In April 1953, *House Beautiful,* a magazine with a long association with Wright, published an attack by editor Elizabeth Gordon on Mies's Farnsworth House

Mies van der Rohe at the dinner celebrating his appointment as director of the architecture department at the Armour Institute, October 18, 1938. President Henry T. Heald is at Mies's right, James Cunningham at his left. Courtesy of the Illinois Institute of Technology

in Illinois and extended it into a broadside against the International Style. Her sentiments reflected Wright's, who said, "These Bauhaus architects ran from political totalitarianism in Germany to what is now made by specious promotion to seem their own totalitarianism in art here in America." Mies did not answer him, nor did he ever communicate with him again.[25] Indeed, throughout this dispute, according to Martin Pawley, "Mies did nothing. He did not defend himself, neither did he attack his opponents. He retired to the sparsely furnished apartment in Chicago which he had occupied since his arrival in America and busied himself with other projects."[26] Although he was wounded by Wright's attacks on him and the International Style, he continued to admire Wright's work.[27]

Concerning connections between Wright's Taliesin Fellowship and Mies van der Rohe's architecture department at the Armour Institute and later at the Illinois Institute of Technology, there were none. Nor is there much to compare. Mies's operation was too formal, too academic, to appeal to Wright. Mies had disciples on whom he relied and who served his interests, but he made no effort to meld them into a community where learning by doing was the overriding principle and learning about life was as essential as learning architecture.

This brief glimpse at utopian and other architectural communities confirms that Frank and Olgivanna Lloyd Wright's design for the Taliesin Fellowship was indeed distinctive. Translating their ideas into plans and their plans into action was an awesome but inviting challenge.

# 7 A HOME AT TALIESIN AND HOPE IN THE DESERT

FOR MORE THAN EIGHTEEN
YEARS, THE PERFECT MISTRESS,
OLGIVANNA, AND I HAVE LIVED
AND WORKED, IN LUCK AND OUT
OF LUCK AT TALIESIN, CONSTANTLY
TOGETHER IN ANY CASE. AND
THIS IN SICKNESS AND IN HEALTH.
MOSTLY HEALTH. NO FAIR-WEATHER
FRIEND WAS OLGIVANNA. THERE
WAS GREAT WORK TO BE DONE
THERE AS WELL AS A FULL LIFE TO
BE LIVED. BUT ONE THAT WOULD
HAVE DESTROYED ANY HUMAN
BEING LESS WELL TRAINED FOR THE
STRUGGLE FOR THE BETTER THING,
AND LESS INSPIRED BY NATURAL
GIFTS, MUTUAL LOVE
AND UNDERSTANDING FOR
THAT HIGH STRUGGLE.

JUST TO BE WITH HER UPLIFTS MY
HEART AND STRENGTHENS MY
SPIRIT WHEN THE GOING GETS
HARD OR WHEN THE GOING IS
GOOD.[1]

— FRANK LLOYD WRIGHT

Frank Lloyd Wright always worked in the company of others. As he grew older, many of his associates were younger than he, sometimes by a generation and more. These young persons, Henry-Russell Hitchcock observed, "could share, as in no other architectural office, in a broad educational experience." At Taliesin in the years 1919–1924 their experience came in what Hitchcock called "a sort of minor version of the Fellowship."[2] As they learned from Wright, so also he learned from them.

Earlier, Wright's experiences with young men and women in the Oak Park studio no doubt helped shape his plans for the Fellowship. These young persons, he said, came to him "almost wholly unformed" and had to be "patiently nursed for years in the atmosphere of work itself, until, saturated by intimate association, at an impressionable age" they became helpful.[3] His interactions with the younger assistants in the studio were evidently more satisfying to him than with those who had architectural training and university degrees. He seems to have considered them too fully formed. Lacking university training himself, he may also have seen them as potential challengers to his stature as an architect.

## THE PARTNERSHIP—FRANK LLOYD WRIGHT AND OLGA IVANOVNA HINZENBERG

In 1924, with his marriage to Miriam Noel beyond repair, Wright found a new partner, Olga Ivanovna Hinzenberg, known as Olgivanna. The following year she moved to Taliesin, and in 1928, when divorces had freed both of them to marry, she became Olgivanna Lloyd Wright. Although thirty-one years younger than her husband, she brought a valuable array of experiences to their collaboration, and she played an essential partnership role in the creation of the Taliesin Fellowship.

In her unpublished autobiography, Olgivanna, as we shall identify her here, recounted experiences from early in her life. She was the daughter of Iovan Lazovich, chief justice of the Supreme Court in Montenegro. Her father, who, she said, had the laws of jurisprudence imprinted in his memory, continued working on the court even though he had been struck blind at age thirty-five. Olgivanna read the morning paper to him daily, column after column, as well as books written in Russian and French. She had to translate as she read, for her father did not understand those languages.[4]

Her mother, Militza, was an imposing figure, "of regal bearing and imperious in manner." She would walk "straight and proud and with great dignity," Olgivanna recalled, "in full possession not merely of the city but of the world. . . . Strong, beautiful, despotic, with flashing black eyes, she belonged to the sort of women who inherit the strength of ruling in society, not to mention their families."[5]

Olgivanna remembered vividly a transforming moment in her life: a visit to a fortune-teller with a friend named Milotchka:

The fortune teller came in from another room and asked us to sit down. She was a thin, pale blonde woman about thirty who looked very tired. She first talked to me while looking into the crystal ball. "You have a choice of two lives," she frowned with intense concentration. "You may marry a man early in your youth. You will have a most unhappy life. But for some reason this is not certain. Someone keeps interfering. I don't know who it is." She hesitated and said thoughtfully, "You will be given a chance to change your life. If you do, you will marry a very famous man. I think he has something to do with geometry. That is it. I see lots of triangles, circles and squares."

She was getting paler now. "Maybe he is a professor. You will be happy. You will have the respect and admiration of both men and women. You are destined for a most wonderful life. That is, if you overcome something. I don't know. I am tired. I must rest." She almost collapsed in the chair. I was intense, never expecting such an unusual séance, nor such cultivated language.

After a short rest she spoke then to my friend. "Your destiny is to be harsh," she said. "Much work, a big family, an unhappy marriage." She told her, "You will have to exercise much strength in order to carry a very difficult life. I see no change in your future." Then she looked compassionately at my friend, and said softly, "I am sorry."

We paid two rubles each and walked out silently. I impulsively kissed Milotchka. "None of this is going to happen to either of us," I said. "How can she foresee the future in a crystal ball? This is all nonsense." But both of us were strongly affected by the experience.
And it happened as she predicted. . . .[6]

Olgivanna Lloyd Wright on her visit to Taliesin, 1924. Courtesy of the Frank Lloyd Wright Foundation

At age sixteen Olgivanna met Vladimir Hinzenburg, a thirty-one-year-old architect, who flattered her by his attention. During their courtship she met his parents, and when his mother was dying she asked Olgivanna to promise that she would marry her son. She so promised, and they were married;

she cried, she recalled, throughout the ceremony. Although he was a good man and gave her a nice apartment, they found nothing to talk about, for he had no interest in philosophy, nor was he creative. He bought a sunny, large modern apartment for them in Moscow, but she was disappointed in his architecture. She had other concerns, too: "[S]omething strange began to broil in Moscow. Here and there bread lines were forming." Her husband, concerned with her safety, told her decisively that she should go to the home of her sister, where she had lived since she was eleven, in Batum (or Batumi), Montenegro. She left immediately, on the last train out of Moscow. Things were quiet at home, and she reestablished relationships with her friends.[7]

"Then," however, "the news broke." The Bolshevik Revolution had begun. Reports from Russia told of blood flowing "like autumn rains." That brought confusion and worse. "Life was shaky; the government fell apart; money lost its worth; food was scarce." In Montenegro, though, life went on without major disruptions, at least for a while. Her daughter Svetlana was born, and her husband, known as Volodia, was present for the birth. He soon undertook a number of architectural projects. Meanwhile she fell in love with a friend from her childhood, Luigi Valazzi, and she performed in some theatrical scenes with him. His father forced an end to their romance. She recalled this as a "first, pure, innocent love of childhood into youth which took many years to subdue," but years later she understood it to be wrong for both of them.[8]

Before long, hardship reached Montenegro. Olgivanna, by then living in Tiflis (the capital of Georgia, known today as Tbilisi), had to stand in line to get bread for Svetlana, "very black bread with straw in it. . . . Everything was rationed." Feeling duty-bound to her husband, she tried to make the marriage work. Describing herself as having been "brooding, questioning, looking for something beyond the limits of my senses," she had a happy, bubbling friend, Valya Valechevska, who was the very opposite.

One day her friend, feeling sorry for her, burst into her room and said, "I have met a wonderful man who teaches dances based on philosophy just along your line. His name is Georgi Ivanovitch Gurdjieff. I know you would be interested to meet him. I want you to come with me." After protests and pleadings, she made her way, led by her friend, to the home of Gurdjieff. In an upstairs room she saw a small group surrounding a buffet. In the midst of this, she recalled, she instantly saw the remarkable man her friend had brought her to meet.

Gurdjieff did indeed look remarkable. He had a beautiful, closely shaven head and classic features, with a fine nose and strong jaws; his eyes were dark and luminous. It was a noble face, with the traditional oriental black moustache which seemed natural on his face. His expression was of profound strength and great compassion. He was part Greek and part Armenian.

After they observed five women do exercises in intricate geometric patterns that "could even be called a 'dance,'" her friend introduced her to Gurdjieff, the man who had created them.[9] Her autobiography continues with detailed recollections of her initial experiences with Gurdjieff and the profound transformation those experiences caused in her life. So profound were they, she remarked, that the "need of Gurdjieff's presence in my life became ardent." The most important thing to her was "to be where he was."[10]

Soon Olgivanna joined Gurdjieff's company of followers, and after moving to various cities, she and others eventually settled with him in Fontainebleau, near Paris. There it became apparent to her that the "world inside and world outside were at odds." With Gurdjieff and others in his Institute for the Harmonious Development of Man, she had a wide array of experiences, including responsibility for managing the Institute.[11] She even participated in "movement" performances in Carnegie Hall, Orchestra Hall in Chicago, and in Boston and other cities. She took Svetlana, who had been living with an aunt and uncle in New York, with her when she returned to Europe.[12]

Not long after their return, and following an automobile accident in which he had been badly injured, Gurdjieff told Olgivanna she was ready to go to America. The Institute was going to stop functioning. It was time for her to start a new life, so he arranged for her departure for New York and paid for her passage. From New York she went to Chicago. In her new world, she wrote, she had prayed, "God help me find a man some day whom I can love and respect and create life with deep content, full of the rich experiences of working together, thinking and feeling together."[13]

Her first encounter with Frank Lloyd Wright was at a Russian ballet performance at Orchestra Hall, where she found herself in a seat by him. As they watched the performance, he remarked to her, she recalled, that the dancers and the audience were well matched, for both were dead. "And he smiled, looking at me with unconcealed admiration. . . . I knew then that this was to be."[14]

After being introduced by a mutual acquaintance, the two of them left the performance at intermission and had tea at the Congress Hotel. Wright told her of his life, his struggles, about Catherine and Mamah and his unbearable family life, and about his travels in Europe. He recounted in some detail his relationship with Mamah Borthwick, explaining that being separated from their families had aggravated the relationship; that his image of his wife and children kept interfering constantly with his "complete fusion" with her; that she also missed her family. He described the tragedy that took her life, how alone he felt, how he established his relationship with Miriam Noel and why it failed, and how alone he felt again after she left Taliesin.[15]

Wright then asked Olgivanna to tell him about herself, so she described Gurdjieff's Institute and its emphasis on the necessity of harmonizing emotion, intellect, and sex. She came to America, she said, because she "liked the idea of equality in a democracy." As their conversation continued, "deep communion occurred," and the "world around them no longer existed." They danced to a Strauss waltz and both expressed the desire to be together always. Olgivanna gave him her address and phone number. He told her he was leaving for New York and that he would call her when he returned.[16]

By then she was ready to leave her husband, she wrote, because she "longed for an exchange of ideas along the line of inner achievement while attending in full to life's responsibilities." The gap between Olgivanna and her husband had widened, and "now that I had met and instantly fused

# GEORGI IVANOVITCH GURDJIEFF

■   Michel de Salzmann, one of Gurdjieff's
followers, said that those who knew him regarded
him as "an incomparable 'awakener' of men"
who brought to the West "a comprehensive
model of esoteric knowledge and left behind
him a school embodying a specific methodology
for the development of consciousness." Such
consciousness required a "harmonious blending
of the distinctive energies of mind, feeling,
and body." His teachings, no doubt made more
appealing to some by his exceptional personal
character and demeanor, attracted leading artists
and intellectuals to the Institute, located at
Fontainbleau after moving from Russia because of
the revolution there. Gurdjieff had a genius, says
de Salzmann, for "using every circumstance of life
as a means for helping his pupils feel the whole
truth about themselves."

   Gurdjieff was a prolific writer and lecturer,
as well as a designer of dances. He was also a
composer, in collaboration with Thomas de
Hartman, and much of his music was used to
accompany the dances. According to de Salzmann,
misleading accounts of his work "overshadowed
the integrity of his ideas, . . . [but his] teaching
has emerged out of this background of rumor and
innuendo to be recognized as one of the most
penetrating spiritual teachings of modern times."
Foundations and societies perpetuate his work in
many cities around the world.[17]

   The Taliesin Fellowship is associated with
none of them, and there are no references to the
Wrights or Taliesin in Gurdjieff's writings. In the
Fellowship, however, during Mrs. Wright's lifetime
and beyond, Gurdjieff's influence was present,
to be—by their choice—absorbed, ignored, or
rejected by its members. But the choices had
consequences.[18]

Georgi Ivanovitch Gurdjieff, Mrs.
Wright's mentor in Europe who
visited both Taliesin and Taliesin
West. Courtesy of the Frank Lloyd
Wright Foundation

my whole being with a man with whom I had spent only a few hours—the realization of the hopelessness of my marriage to Volodia became a truth. Within me it was ended. I talked to him about it and he agreed that our life together had been, for a long time, coming to an end. Realizing this, some last weight of burden was lifted from my heart, and my expectation and faith that Frank was coming back was unshakable."[19]

When Wright returned to Chicago, he brought fruit and again they talked. He invited her to Taliesin, as he recalled in his autobiography, "to have her meet Sylva, Dione, and Nobu, and their clever husbands. Olgivanna and 'the merry wives of Taliesin' had much in common all being European." He left again, "as breezily as he came," Olgivanna recalled, but he sent fruit and flowers and, on another visit to Chicago, again invited her to come to Taliesin, and made this promise: "From now on you won't be seen for the dust."[20]

## DRAWING EXPERIENCES TOGETHER

At some point in their relationship they began to assimilate their separate experiences into visions and plans for a new future together. He drew upon what he had learned in his communities of architects. Her studies with Georgi Ivanovitch Gurdjieff, particularly his remarkable training methods, provided her with resources for new ventures. Recasting in his own terms what Olgivanna told him, he said that Gurdjieff "took unrhythmical neurotic human beings in all the social stratas, took them apart, and put them together again better correlated, happier, more alive and useful to themselves and others." Olgivanna had been one of his "star leaders."[21]

## TIMES OF TRAVAIL

When Frank Lloyd Wright and his new partner began living together, and particularly after their baby was born, travails pursued them. Persecution through legal maneuvers by Miriam Noel, even after her marriage to Wright was dissolved, made them targets of aggressive prosecutors, law enforcers, and the press. Fleeing to Minnesota, they were jailed briefly and suffered humiliation and threats to Olgivanna's immigration status that made it seem she might have to leave the country.

All of these troubles complicated Wright's financial woes. Both he and Taliesin were brought back from the risk of disaster by the willingness of his siblings, clients, and friends to raise enough money to incorporate him. The terms of the incorporation provided that no debts or obligations were to be incurred unless authorized in writing by an officer of the Corporation; that no obligation was to be incurred unless there was money in the bank to honor it; that Wright and the principals were to meet from time to time to agree upon what expenditures were necessary and the maximum amount to be expended for any of them; that there were to be no charge accounts, with all payments to be made in cash; and that Wright was to submit monthly statements of cash disbursed. All of the income of Frank Lloyd Wright the man, meager as it was given the lack of architectural commissions he faced, went to Frank Lloyd Wright Incorporated. The man was forced to depend on allowances granted by the members of the corporation.[22]

No doubt Frank Lloyd Wright and Olgivanna found in all this not only the inspiration for creating something new, but also the necessity for doing so. They knew better, of course, than to think that they could jump from financial hardship to prosperity without frustration and stumbles. They had learned how to adapt to circumstances and then take control of them.

## A PLACE IN WISCONSIN

The place where the act of creation was to be played out had come to them from Frank Lloyd Wright's forebears. The story of the Taliesin Fellowship must be traced back to that place and to a specific year, 1886. In that year, Wright's aunts, Jane and Ellen Lloyd Jones, known as Aunt Jennie and Aunt Nell, opened their Hillside Home School on land they inherited from their father in the Wisconsin River Valley near Spring Green, Wisconsin. The aunts created the School primarily for their nephews and nieces and other kinfolk who lived in the Valley, about forty of them, but others were welcome, including city-bred youngsters who would benefit from country living and learning. Maginel Wright Barney, Frank Lloyd Wright's sister, called it the first coeducational boarding school in the country.

The boarding students lived in what was called the Home building, designed by Wright in 1887. The adjacent building, built in 1902, held classrooms, a gymnasium, and an assembly room. Now known simply as "Hillside," it became the center of the School's activities. The students' experiences in the Hillside Home School were not confined to its buildings and classrooms, for the Lloyd Jones sisters practiced what educators in those years called "Progressive education." They gave their youngsters ample opportunities for dances, nature walks, picnics, outdoor games, and farm activities.[23]

In 1915, with one of Wright's aunts approaching age seventy and the other already having passed that age, the Hillside Home School closed. Wright acquired the land, honoring his promise not to let it fall out of the family, while also protecting his home and studio, named Taliesin, located on the brow of a hill a short distance away. Newspaper accounts, bank records, and family correspondence, according to biographer Robert Twombly, show that Wright failed to honor the terms of the purchase agreement. Nor did he provide the aunts the monthly support that was part of the bargain.[24]

Consequently, Aunt Nell and Aunt Jennie, who had lived in California for several years after closing the school, were strapped for money and returned to live at Taliesin. One day in 1917, according to Wright's sister Maginel, Jennie "went back to the school, now desolate and deserted. She crept back into the great, echoing, empty building that had been her home, and up to her old room. She died there, alone." Nell, the elder sister, lived in the guest room at Taliesin until she died in 1919.[25]

After the closing of the School, and probably even before then, the Hillside buildings deteriorated from lack of maintenance. In his autobiography, Wright described the physical environment as it existed in 1927: Taliesin, he said, had been "stripped to join the destitution of Hillside." Plundered by the bank and abused by curiosity, as had been also the Hillside Home School building, it was defaced and "all but destroyed." Water had come through the decayed and broken roofs at Hillside, and the entire place was

Jane and Nell Lloyd Jones, Wright's aunts, founders of the Hillside Home School, shown here in 1896 when Romeo and Juliet was built. Courtesy of the Frank Lloyd Wright Foundation

rapidly becoming a ruin. Bank-rented fields were grown up with weeds. The buildings needed repair, but "the next move, even the next meal," was becoming a problem to be solved somehow without money, and of that there was "less than none." Of his assistants, he wrote, they "had gone on to other fields, there was no one working with me here now that I was, at last, free to work. Denied work and what Freedom have you?"[26]

## A PLACE IN THE DESERT OF ARIZONA

Necessity and ambition drove Wright to explore possibilities for resurrecting his career and establishing a new life. In early 1928 he, Olgivanna, their daughter Iovanna (born in December 1925), and Svetlana, Olgivanna's daughter from her previous marriage, traveled to Phoenix, Arizona. There, in exile, as he characterized it, Wright served as a design consultant to Albert McArthur, the architect for the Arizona Biltmore Hotel. Later that year he moved to California, where he and Olgivanna were married on August 25. Before long he adopted her daughter Svetlana. Soon the family returned to Phoenix to work behind the scenes with McArthur, apparently in a role he had played earlier with the nominal architect of the Biltmore.

While in Phoenix, Wright met Dr. Alexander Chandler. Formerly a veterinarian, now a hotel owner and real estate developer, Chandler owned several hundred acres of desert near his town, fittingly named Chandler. In that town, located about twenty miles southeast of Phoenix, he also owned "the pleasant, aristocratic Hotel San Marcos," where he and Wright could discuss plans for a project he had proposed: a resort to be called San Marcos in the Desert. Chandler's dream, Wright noted in *An Autobiography*, seemed to be "an undefiled-by-irrigation desert resort for wintering certain jaded eastern millionaires who preferred dry desert to green, wet fields." He said, according to Wright, that he had delayed planning for the resort "because he knew no one who could give him what he wanted, unless, I could."

This ambitious project held great promise for the financially and professionally destitute Wright. "[T]here could be nothing more inspiring to an architect on this earth," he continued, "than that spot in the pure desert of Arizona he took me to see, so I believe. At last here was the time, the place, and here was, in Dr. Chandler, the man."[27]

Frank Lloyd Wright, Mrs. Wright, and daughters Svetlana and Iovanna, at Ocatilla, 1928. Courtesy of the Frank Lloyd Wright Foundation

In a cold vacant office in the little town, he drew the plans for the camp. Using drawing boards on boxes, the entire Wright party pitched in—a good way to build not only buildings for a community, but to build spirit in that community, too. The next morning, with the plans in hand, they began to build on desert land Chandler had given them. Wright recalled that they made so much progress that day that one of his "boys," Donald Walker, "slept that night outside on a pile of lumber, rolled up in blankets." By the next night they had set up the first "box-bottom" of the tent tops and put cots in it for three more boys. The next day there was room for all to sleep except for him and his family of three. They returned reluctantly to Mesa to the hotel in Mesa, but they came back for an early breakfast in that "wonderful dining-room sixty miles wide, as long and tall as the universe. We were shivering, oh, yes. But we were all singing happy in that clear cold sunrise. A great prospect." The sound constitution of any entity, he continued, "is pregnant with graceful reflexes. . . . Now by the way of an architect's work-camp comes fresh adventure in the desert. We called the camp: 'OCATILLO.'[28]

The camp was so named, Mrs. Wright recalled, for the cactus that was all around. It soon consisted, she wrote, of "fifteen cabins of wood and white canvas wings that looked like little ships in the desert. We took long horseback rides and walks over the sharp paths made by the Indians." As they studied the "magnificent structural inventiveness" of the "sparse and abstract desert," the community found the experience to be new and exciting.[29] As Wright saw

Six of Wright's draftsmen at Taliesin traveled with him to Ocatilla. Four appear in this photograph, taken at Taliesin in 1928. From left: George Kastner, Henry Klumb, an unidentified visitor, Cyril Jahnke, and Vladimir Karfik. Courtesy of the Frank Lloyd Wright Foundation it, the desert plants' remarkable growth showed scientific building economy in their construction. The stalks especially, he believed, taught anyone "modest and intelligent to apply for lessons." After expounding further on such instructional points, he expressed his delight in his construction project, remarking that a "human gaiety in the Desert is underway."[30]

Then in Wright's account comes a sense of the community he was building as the board walls and canvas roofs of the physical structures found their place in the desert. He names the draftsmen he brought with him: Heinrich Klumb, Donald Walker, George Kastner, Frank Sullivan, Vladimir, Cy, and Will Weston.[31] Weston had worked as a carpenter in the building of Taliesin and was there in 1914 when the infamous murders occurred. As chief carpenter, he brought his wife, a daughter, and son Marcus with him to Arizona to help build Ocatillo. Mrs. Weston cooked for the group, and the two Weston children were to be companions of Mr. and Mrs. Wright's daughters.[32]

Ocatilla served the community's purposes well and was a handsome place, as pictures bear witness.[33] From its near-completion on January 19, 1928, until the middle of June, Wright and his draftsmen worked on plans and a model for the San Marcos in the Desert resort. In *An Autobiography*, Wright recounted with pride the results of the community's efforts, and his own, and he exuded enthusiasm about the desert as "the architect's workshop." The resort, he asserted, proved that indigenous architecture "is not only possible but that it is here."[34]

San Marcos in the Desert, however, was a dream not to be realized. Dr. Chandler could not raise the money to build it, and the Great Depression ruined any chance that he might be able to do so. For Wright that not only meant the loss of a $40,000 fee, but it left him with a deficit of $19,000. With the already-mounting debt at Taliesin and only $2,500 on hand, the situation was desperate. Or perhaps it was not. The project might be lost to an uncooperative economy, and Ocatilla might very soon fall victim to vandals and the harsh desert weather, but that is not the end of the story. "Never mind," Wright remarked in his autobiography. "Something had started that was not stopping thus. Later you will see the consequences."[35]

The evolution of ideas, tested and nourished by Ocatilla, was to continue in Wisconsin and be tested and nourished further when Wright and his assistants returned to Arizona in 1935. And again and again thereafter.

# 8 DREAMS AND REALITIES

WELL, TALIESIN BELIEVES THE DAY HAS COME FOR ART IN THIS MORE SIMPLE ORGANIC SENSE TO TAKE THE LEAD IN THIS THING WE MISCALL "EDUCATION"; BELIEVES THE TIME OVER-RIPE FOR A REJECTION OF THE TOO MANY MINOR TRADITIONS IN FAVOR OF [THE] GREAT ELEMENTAL TRADITION THAT IS DECENTRALIZATION; SEES A GOING FORWARD IN NEW SPIRIT TO THE GROUND AS THE BASIS FOR A GOOD LIFE THAT SETS THE HUMAN SOUL FREE ABOVE ARTIFICIAL ANXIETIES AND ALL VICARIOUS POWERS, ABLE AND WILLING TO WORK AGAIN AS THE FIRST CONDITION OF TRUE GENTILITY.[1]

—**FRANK LLOYD WRIGHT**

Upon returning to Wisconsin with the idea of creating a community of young men and women aspiring to become architects, Frank Lloyd Wright and his wife embarked on an ambitious venture. A brochure published in October 1931 provides details of their vision for this venture. A cursory examination of its contents reveals why they soon concluded that their plans were too complicated. Yet, those plans convey a vivid sense of what they had in mind when, almost exactly a year later, they founded the Taliesin Fellowship on a more realistic scale.

## THE HILLSIDE HOME SCHOOL OF THE ALLIED ARTS

The brochure, written by Wright, began by explaining why they wanted to create this new school. America had provided innumerable schools for educating its children, he explained, and there was good reason to be proud of the results they produced. But "a minority report" was needed, and it was "high time to plan for the super-structure" that would provide for the development of culture beyond "the matters of behavior, commerce, industry, politics and an unsure taste for objets d'art" in which the schools specialized.

Wright asserted that European countries had recently shown Americans many things they had expropriated that were in fact America's very own cultural features. Why not take hold of what we have, he wondered, and "gradually build with it a Nation where no commodity can hope for success except it contributes not only to the ease and wealth of the Nation, but contributes as well to the integrity of the Nation considered as created for the spirit of Man—not merely for men." This was the age of the machine, and the machine should be put "into young hands . . . in a practical and inspirational way." This would of course be a school, but it should not be part of the present educational system. Raising funds to establish and maintain this new kind of school, Wright recognized, would be essential, and he himself had few to contribute.[2]

In the next part, Wright described the school they envisioned. Naturally, it would be an art school, but it would be a "hive of industry in which all the arts, having by nature an architectural background, and so allied to industry would be at work." Architecture, allied with landscape and decorative arts, would be one division. There would be divisions also for painting, sculpture, music, drama, and dance, all grouped under architecture. Architecture in this School would be "that practical expression of contemporary life in terms of building best suited to each and every material, true to purpose, environment and materials."

Additionally, there would be studies in glass making, pottery, textiles, the forge, casting in all materials, woodworking, and sheetmetal-working. There would be incentives for the seven industries that produce these materials "to contribute the equivalent of $150,000 in machinery and plant for experimental purposes." They would have the first right to purchase from the School any design or process that would originate in their particular branch of industry and the first right to draft a competent worker, if approved by the School director, who was developed by the School. The School could also serve as a research organization for manufacturers.[3]

The location, of course, would be that of the former Hillside Home School, at a price of $25,000 for the building and ten acres. The central building alone, Wright said, was "a piece of modern architecture . . . worth five times the sum." With the building and grounds would come Wright's architectural services "in making plans and superintending the completing of the plant proposed according to the accompanying design or one to be approved by the school organization."

Frank Lloyd Wright's design for the Hillside Home School of the Allied Arts. The initial building, in the foreground, and Romeo and Juliet, in the upper right, were in place when this was drawn; the other proposed structures were never built. Copyright © 2009 the Frank Lloyd Wright Foundation, Taliesin West, Scottsdale, AZ

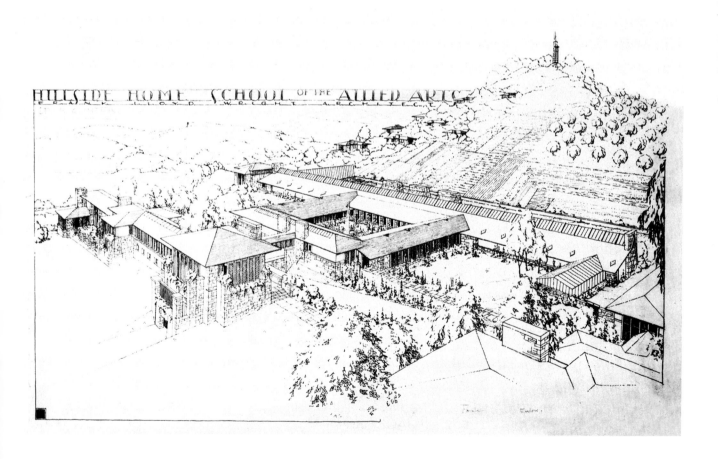

Getting started would require $90,000 for rehabilitation and new construction; $7,000 for farm equipment, stock, machinery, refrigeration, and tools; $3,500 for materials to use in the first year's work; and $1,500 for the first year's fuel and light. To meet these costs, industry would be expected to contribute $140,000 for buildings and equipment, and they were also to provide actual machinery, furnaces, and other equipment. Workers would need to be paid, and that would cost an unspecified sum. A revenue-producing endowment of about $250,000 would be needed to cover first-year salaries and operating costs. Beyond this, the School would "produce articles easily worth fifty thousand dollars a year above cost."[4]

So productive would the workers be, Wright claimed, that only $3,500 would be needed for simple, temporary furnishings. Moreover, the workers would design and build all the furnishings and additions to the buildings and take care of repairs and plantings around the buildings—all this in two hours each day. Altogether there might be sixty students and a resident group of paid workers, possibly fourteen of them, as well as two more to be in direct charge of the student body and the farm and a reasonable number of persons in the families of the paid workers, maybe as many as forty-eight.

The Hillside Home School, Spring Green, Wisconsin, designed by Wright, 1902. Courtesy of the Frank Lloyd Wright Foundation

With everyone except family members working an additional seven hours each day, six days of every week, there would be "a large well directed **creative power** with modern machinery to produce superior articles of every kind in the crafts, articles to be sold and exhibited."[5] This list of beautifully useful or usefully beautiful things reveals the expansiveness of Wright's thinking: stuffs, tapestries, table linens, new cotton fabrics, batique (with special emphasis on tapestries), table glassware, glass flower holders, lighting devices of glass, glass dishes of all sorts, ashtrays, windowglass and glass mosaics, necklaces, decorative beads and objects of glass, well designed modern furniture, wrought iron screens, light standards, light fixtures, gates, fire irons and tools, light decorative forms in beaten metal to be enameled as jewelry and in which precious stones might be set, enameled iron for decorative purposes, cast iron and concrete sculpture, special hardware, outdoor furniture, gates and doors, sheet-metal objects in copper, silver, tin (also enameled in color for ornaments), flowerpots, water jars, pottery, decorative drawings and paintings in free modern spirit, and sculpture.

Additionally, there would be an orchestra, "available for paid concerts as propaganda for progress in music." Plays, after given at the school, might be repeated at the nearer universities. There would be dancers, sets for cinema, and newly published music, as well as designs for the theater, farmhouses, farm buildings, gardens, town-cottages, towns and villages, industrial towns, gas stations, country homes, factories of various sorts for the crafts, landscape designs for various locations and regions, and plans for typical plantings. The School's presses would print illustrations of all these things for distribution.

The School, again called "a hive of industry," with the seventy-six or more workers in the community, would be "advised and inspired by . . . great artists, as would be their guests from time to time by invitation." All this would have a "tremendous effect on Industry in these United States within a few years and might swing the tide of production toward new and genuine significance in all design-forms of American Industrial production." Exhibiting and marketing the products would be another feature of the School's work.[6]

Wright's vision for the new school revealed a frequent theme in his writings: simultaneous disdain for universities and hope that he might be able to achieve his goals by collaborating with at least one of them, the University of Wisconsin.

Now this school could be no university where thousands must be herded or cradled and handled together. It would have to remain small, capacity, say, at most sixty students. Of necessity it would be isolated, mobile, sensitive, specialized and free. But it could serve mass-production well as antenna for proper methods of teaching and might provide desirable teachers.

As an alcove, or adjunct, or experimental station in connection with university or art institute courses in the allied arts, it would be [an] ideal resource.[7]

As any worker showed special ability and marked competence in any line of the industrial arts, that worker would be available for a position in an industrial factory as a designer. Manufacturers who contributed to the School should have first choice of such students at all times, or they might be supplied as teachers at similar schools, of which, Wright believed, there soon would be many more.

Concerning the school's operations, Wright explained that the resident director should be an architect chosen for his association with the crafts, meaning that he would have to be found in Europe. He had an ideal candidate in mind: "Heer Wijdeveld of Amsterdam, Holland, a member of the Royal Academy, whom Holland has made a Knight of the House of Orange . . . and whom France has made chevalier of the Legion d'Honneur. He is editor of *Wendingen,* the famous European Fine Art Publication and is himself a tireless worker in the Arts."

The director, Wright proposed, should live in a cottage at Hillside and be paid $5,500 annually. He should be surrounded by a group consisting of "an architect, a sculptor, a painter, a musician, a teacher of rhythm as practiced by D'Alcrose, at Hellerau, or by Gurdjieff at Fontainebleau, France." All their needs, including travel expenses, should be provided for. Seven resident foremen of experience in their particular lines would assist this inner group. Their material needs, too, had to be met. And there should be another guest system of visitation, providing for consultations with experts.

The providers of the endowment fund, Wright continued, should elect the president for the Hillside Home School of the Allied Arts. That person should administer all the funds. Everyone who worked in the school would ultimately be responsible to the president, who would also have direct charge of all architecture. Wright himself would be chairman of the board, and Taliesin, "just over the hill from the school would be available as a tributary atelier."[8]

The brochure offered a list of men and women who might be called upon as visiting artists. The best-known among them, at least in the first third of the twentieth century, were European architects Erich Mendelsohn, J. P. Oud, and Le Corbusier; writer Carl Sandburg; literary critic Alexander Woollcott; landscape architect Jens Jensen[9]; painter Joseph Stella; composers Ernest Bloch and Igor Stravinsky; cellist Pablo Casals; conductor Leopold Stokowski; playwrights and critics Eugene O'Neill and Somerset Maugham; and for clergy representation, William Norman Guthrie, rector of St. Mark's in the Bowerie.[10]

In the brochure's concluding pages Wright asserted that, consistent with the traditions of the Hillside Home School, the new institution should probably be coeducational, with entry open to boys and girls aged eleven to twenty-one. Students should be empowered to expel or punish a fellow student by unanimous vote, approved by the director. There might also be a "small Kindergarten of day-pupils three to nine years of age."[11]

The final section presents again the argument that art should be at the center of education, that creativity must be encouraged, and that democracy means that "Man should be himself, too modest or ashamed to try to be someone else."[12]

## EXPLORING OTHER POSSIBILITIES

Before long Wright recognized that these plans were too ambitious. Sensing that something else was needed, he began to explore other possibilities, several of them simultaneously. One involved establishing a connection with the University of Wisconsin, an idea he proposed privately to professors there as early as 1928. In the fashion of academe, talks and negotiations continued for a year, as the professors deliberated over aspects of Wright's proposal and considered alternatives. Scholars who have studied the proposal and the faculty members' deliberations have concluded that financial considerations and practical arrangements—particularly Wright's insistence that the program he envisioned had to be based at Hillside, near Spring Green—rather than the nature of the undertaking, caused negotiations to collapse. An angry letter to the president of the University brought the matter to an end.[13]

Integral to Wright's plan was his hope that Alexander Meiklejohn, who headed an experimental college at the University of Wisconsin, would assume leadership of the school he hoped to establish. His friend and correspondent, Lewis Mumford, reported on a recent lectureship he had had in Meiklejohn's college. It was, Mumford wrote in a letter sent on May 12, 1929, "the real thing: a complete break with cram and drill and routine. The experience first throws the students off their feet: it is a shocking change for them: but when they get back [on their feet] again they are on the way to knowing what an education and intellectual responsibility are." However, Mumford remarked, the University was hostile to Meiklejohn, for should he be successful the faculty would be routed out of their old habits. That Meiklejohn was using his unique methods at the University rather than at Taliesin caused him to mourn.[14]

### ON AND OFF WITH H. TH. WIJDEVELD

In a letter written almost two years later, April 7, 1931, Wright informed Mumford that Meiklejohn was out at the University. In the next sentence came another possibility: such a school as he hoped to establish at Taliesin loomed in Chicago. He had reason to believe, he said, that this new venture was severing its hasty connection with the Art Institute "to go along with me."[15] In fact, the day before he had sent a letter to H. Th. Wijdeveld, dealing first with matters related to the catalog for an exhibition in the Netherlands,[16] then reporting that a school was forming in Chicago, known as Allied Arts and Industries, similar to the plan he had in mind, "with an endowment of 2 1/2 Million Dollars." They wanted him to take direction, he told Mumford, "but I suggested you—with me as Chairman of the board. Salary $10,000 per year,—contract for ten years. Would you come? Next September or October the thing is to begin. Let me know if this tempts you and I'll send particulars."[17]

On April 16, 1931, a telegram arrived from Wijdeveld, announcing that he accepted the directorship and that he was willing to come immediately to settle matters. The coincidence, he added, was marvelous, for he had sent a letter on April 11 suggesting cooperation on School plans at Taliesin.

Almost four months later, Wright responded: He could at last report progress on the school matter, although he was in a precarious position. He had lined up someone to help in Chicago, but he thought he should be chairman of the board, with Wijdeveld serving as director of the School. "I want to practice Architecture for fifteen years more," he continued, expressing the wish to shape the School's policy and his intention to see the freedom of the School maintained as well as his own. But "I should have a deciding voice from 'behind the throne' for some years. Then I should probably not be needed."

But he cautioned Wijdeveld that all would not go smoothly: "Times are bad here. Disappointments will be many. You may be disappointed in me. I am unused to working *with* anyone. But I have always wished to do so and believe the time has come in my lifetime when I should. And I believe too that the understanding of life and work that makes us comrades in arms will make us good yoke-fellows."[18]

On September 5, Wijdeveld informed Wright by telegram that he was ready to cross the ocean, first alone for a short stay, to meet with Wright and settle matters thoroughly; his family would come later. He asked Wright to respond at his earliest convenience. Two months later, on November 4, Wijdeveld sent another telegram to Wright, informing him that he had arrived in New York and wanted to see some of the United States before coming to Taliesin. He planned to reach Taliesin by way of Boston, arriving around the middle of November.

H. Theodore Wijdeveld, the Dutch architect and writer whom Wright considered for a leadership role in the venture that became the Taliesin Fellowship. Courtesy of the Frank Lloyd Wright Foundation

The talks at Taliesin produced the draft of an agreement for the "founding and conduct of the proposed TALIESIN FELLOWSHIP—by and between Frank Lloyd Wright and H. Th. Wijdeveld." It provided, among other things, for Wijdeveld "to come to Taliesin before April 15, 1932, with Mrs. Wijdeveld and their three children and establish himself in quarters provided by Frank Lloyd Wright until a suitable cottage can be provided in connection with the FELLOWSHIP on the present Hillside Home-School grounds."

The Widjevelds were to give all their time to the "upbuilding and conduct" of the Fellowship along the lines already agreed upon. In the spirit of that agreement, Wright was to be consulted and his wishes were to be respected on matters of policy or expenditures for construction and equipment during the preliminary stage. The enterprises of the Fellowship and collateral enterprises growing out of them were to be subject to mutual agreement between the two principals, and Wijdeveld or the Fellowship might accept outside commissions that had to be agreed upon by Wright. Moreover, "All questions affecting the growth, stability or character of the FELLOWSHIP will be discussed and decided by agreement between the founders of the FELLOWSHIP, Wright and Wijdeveld, for the period of three years covered by this instrument."

Further provisions of the agreement involved such matters as the financial investment to be required of Wijdeveld, the provision of land for the School (to be separated from Taliesin), the conveyance of property rights and responsibilities to Wijdeveld, the financial investment Wright himself would make, the sharing of income derived from the School (two-thirds to Wijdeveld and one-third to Wright), the renting of the 140-acre Taliesin farm to the Fellowship, the furnishing of farm machinery for the first year, and the apportioning and disposition of contributions to the School. This was to be an agreement for a three-year probationary period, with a reevaluation of the physical property and a new agreement made on the matters cited in this one. The agreement provided for arbitration in the event of differences between the founder and the leader, and if that failed, dissolution of the partnership. It concluded with a summary of additional financial terms of the arrangement.

Both Wright and Wijdeveld signed this agreement in November 1931, but for reasons left unexplained, it was never put into effect. Wijdeveld apparently inquired about its status, and on January 1, 1932, Wright replied that he had not responded to Wijdeveld's cablegram because the news he had to convey required a letter, reading in part thus: "To have you join me in Wisconsin to work in the proposed school would be a dream realized. But the Wisconsin University can do nothing within years,—if at all. The University is a ponderous State-affair ruled by the State-legislature,—and that Legislature cares nothing about Art." Meanwhile, he continued, the proposed school had aroused considerable interest, but for it to begin the school would need "patrons who will give enough money—say $100,000 to get the affair set up for a beginning with proper equipment." There would be plenty of "pupils" who would be "keen" to come. All he had was ground and the building—a beautiful building that would cost $200,000 to build that was going to "rack and ruin for lack of occupancy."

## SECOND THOUGHTS

But there was more to it than that. Despite the enthusiasm Wright had expressed in his correspondence with Wijdeveld, he had had second thoughts about the proposed working relationship. On February 1, 1932, he wrote to Mumford about several things, with this line slipped in: "Would you be interested to lead the Taliesin Fellowship, with Mrs. Mumford according to the prospectus enclosed?" By then, he said, the strength of the rumor that the school he had in mind would open had resulted in approximately 25–35 applications from young men and women who were interested in coming.

Apparently anticipating a negative response from Mumford, Wright wrote to him again the next day. With that letter he enclosed a copy of the proposed contract with Wijdeveld, asking him to scan it and to consider Wijdeveld's reactions to the proposition. "To tell the truth," Wright continued, "if I could keep the fellowship primarily on our own ground I would like it better. I am growing suspicious of 'internationalism.' . . . Can't we manage a group of our own somehow?" If Wijdeveld wanted to come as one of the associates Wright would take him as architect and his wife as a musician, but he didn't welcome the responsibility he would face were Wijdeveld's family to come with him.

Just four days later Mumford responded. Although he was "warmed by the honor and confidence and all that they imply," and although he would like to be near Wright and to work with him, the job was beyond his range and powers. He was compelled to say no. Wijdeveld's rightness for the job, that was another matter. He had had only a few hours with him in New York, and although he seemed to have plenty of intelligence and understanding, he had no notion as to how he would wear. The leader, Mumford thought, should probably be an American, for several reasons. And so, "If you have any doubts at all about Wijdeveld I think that the fairest thing, even at this late stage of your relations, would be to call it off. Unless you yourself can close your eyes and say Go Ahead both your position and the leader's would be too delicate a one to remain in stable equilibrium any length of time." Too much of the leadership burden, he believed, would fall on Wright.[19]

That was not quite the end of Wright's dealings with Wijdeveld, for on March 10, 1933, after the Fellowship had been established, Wright wrote a friendly note to "Dear Dutchy." He enclosed a brochure and invited him to come to Taliesin: "If you would be still interested in coming to America there is still a place for you with me in that work although the basis would be somewhat changed as I have changed the plan I at first had in mind. We might now work out something better for both of us—on a less risky basis."[20]

That did not happen. Instead, plans for the Fellowship emerged gradually, reflecting the ongoing evolution of Wright's ideas and vision.

## A NEW BEGINNING FOR THE WRIGHTS AND THEIR ARRIVING APPRENTICES

In the summer or fall of 1932 Wright announced his plans through a brochure distributed to friends and acquaintances. Stylistically, it lacks coherence, its contents are redundant, and the writing falls short of Wright's usual standards. But many who read it apparently found that it addressed their needs and hopes. Wright himself evidently was not satisfied with it, for on January 1, 1933, he published a more polished version. Yet, it makes sense to review here the contents and purposes of the initial brochure, for it contains the information the very first apprentices had when they decided to apply for enrollment in the Fellowship.[21]

The brochure's heading and first paragraph stated Wright's intentions:

THE TALIESIN FELLOWSHIP AN EXTENSION OF THE WORK AT TALIESIN
TO INCLUDE SEVENTY APPRENTICES

Frank Lloyd Wright, together with a competent leader, . . . will be in residence with the apprentices and be in direct charge of the work of the Fellowship.

a group of three resident associates; a sculptor, a painter and a musician;

a group of seventy qualified apprentices, carefully chosen for the work to be done;

a group of seven honor apprentices who will have the status of senior apprentices and three technical advisers trained in industry. This group will constitute the Fellowship.

Leaders in the thought of many countries will come to assist and share for a time in our activities, perhaps reside here temporarily.

After contending that "any rational attempt to integrate art and industry should correlate both with every day life" and that the future of American civilization will be erected on organic architecture, the brochure asserts that "the qualities most worth while in philosophy, sculpture, painting, music and the industrial crafts are, fundamentally, architecture." Those who worked at Taliesin could have spontaneous recourse to modern shop and working conditions, while also benefiting from the "inspirational Fellowship of the genuinely creative artist" and constant contact with nature. With the city being a "dead or dying expression," the Taliesin Fellowship was designed to live and work in the country, forty miles from Madison and four miles from the nearest village.

Building on the work in architecture during the previous thirty years, the Taliesin Fellowship would expand from ten apprentices to seventy. Direct personal contact with the modern currents of thought would give aspiring young artists the means "to uplift spiritual forces that guaranteed a lifework in the architecture of the arts as a natural fulfillment belonging to ourselves." To accomplish this, home life would be simple; meals would be in common; hours for work, recreation, and sleep would be fixed. Each individual would have a room for study and rest, and suitable toilet accommodations would be convenient for all rooms. Entertainment would be a feature of the home life, with plays, musical events, cinema, and evening conferences; musicians, literary men, artists, and scientists would be invited, and sometimes the public, as well. "The beautiful region," the brochures stated, "is, itself, a never failing source of recreation."

There would be no age limit for the apprentices, "but the qualifications of each applicant for entrance will be decided finally by the leader of the fellowship [should that be someone other than Wright] and Mr. Wright after a month's trial in the Fellowship work." A primary requirement would be the ability to draw well. Although studios and demonstrating rooms were already built or being built, laboratories and machine workshops were not yet ready. Eventually they would be planted next to the living quarters.

Essential to Wright's plan is this affirmation: "The Fellowship work in all its manifold branches will emanate directly from the organic philosophy of an organic architecture for modern life as we are living that life at the present time, with some sense of the future." Also essential was Wright's plan for funding the new enterprise. Initially, revenue would come from tuition and fees amounting to $675 per year, and the apprentices would be required to contribute three hours of labor daily. Additionally, Wright hoped that compensation might also come in return for services rendered, from publications to be printed by the Fellowship, and from contributions of money and equipment by "Friends of the Fellowship," consisting of those who believed in its work and were willing to "add scope to its usefulness" as the Fellowship grew.[22]

The content of the second brochure, dated January 1, 1933, was generally the same, although it was more coherent and there were differences in emphases and details. The number of apprentices anticipated remained at seventy, "carefully chosen for the work to be done," but in the new plan there would be seven "honor apprentices," selected by the Fellowship for qualifications of leadership, who would pay no tuition. The list of charter apprentices in the brochure ran to forty, although notes about some of them make this figure misleading.[23] The "new Fellowship," the brochure continued, would enable the apprentices "to be immersed in the many-sided activities of Architecture in all its phases." The annual tuition remained at $675, but the daily hours of required work was to be increased from three to four.[24]

In December 1933, with the Fellowship proving itself, Wright published an elaborate, visually appealing brochure. Loose-leaf in design, printed in red ink on white sheets of paper, it included: drawings on the back and the inside of both the front and back covers; a four-page statement titled "Our

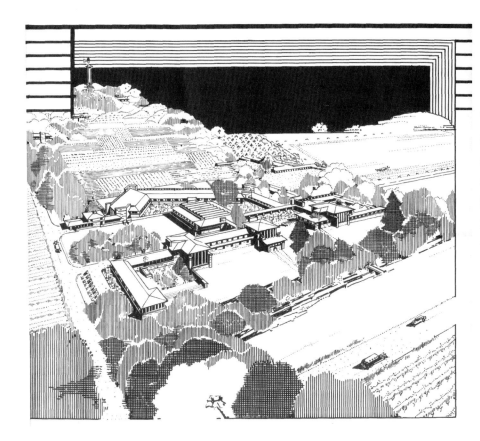

This drawing of Wright's plans for the Fellowship appeared in an elaborate brochure, 1934. None of the proposed new structures was built. Copyright © 2009 the Frank Lloyd Wright Foundation, Taliesin West, Scottsdale, AZ

Cause"; a three-page statement titled "Our Plan," preceded by a drawing of the projected complex of buildings designed to house the Fellowship; a two-page sheet with a picture of apprentices working, and a summary of the Fellowship's intentions and operations, along with the "Application for Fellowship"; and a tri-fold sheet, twenty-four inches in length, with an aerial photograph of Taliesin on one side, and on the other, lists of 56 Fellows (and a footnote showing the 31 institutions attended previously by the Fellows) and more than 140 Friends of the Fellowship on the other.[25] The substance of this brochure was similar to that found in the first two.

This brochure defined the Fellowship's organic character by attacking academic institutions, including schools of architecture that Wright judged to be inorganic, incapable of producing men of vision, men of deep feeling, men equipped to create life anew. "Textbook and classroom education by way of 'credits' and 'degrees' has inflated utterly commonplace intelligences far beyond their merits." As a result, the salt and savor of life that is the joy of work soon runs stale in any academic formula whatsoever or in any attempt at 'institution.' A stale sap is the consequence." Continuing:

. . . Taliesin sees work itself where there is something growing and living in it as not only the salt and savor of existence but as the opportunity for bringing "heaven" decently back to Earth where it belongs. Taliesin sees art as no less than ever the expression of a way of life in this machine age if its civilization is to live.

As for the young men and women who were voluntary apprentices, Wright recalled an occasion when, as he was watching them work, "several apparently well educated people came up and, all together, asked: 'Can you tell us what they are building here?'" "Yes," he replied, "they are building a refuge from the universities. There is now no place to lay one's head." He walked away to let them figure out what that meant, supposing "the impertinence does come to something like that. A group of volunteers: no courses, no credits, no examinations, no teaching." This, he continued was "a work in progress" and many refugees from "Education" were doing all they could "to help it forward wherever the work lies and whatever it may be."[26]

A fourth variation of the text used in establishing the Fellowship appears in a revision of Wright's autobiography, published in 1943. He introduces it under the heading: "A STATION FOR THE FLIGHT OF THE SOUL." Many times, Wright remarked, in desperate circumstances he came up with ideas, some of them bad ones. But not this time. "No buildings to build at the harrowing moment but, capitalizing thirty-five years of past experience, why not build the builders of buildings against the time when buildings might again be built?" So he, the son of Wisconsin Welsh pioneers, and Mrs. Wright, a daughter of Montenegrin dignitaries, "aiming to be educators, composed and sent out during the summer of 1932" a circular letter to a small list of friends.[27]

The circular letter in the autobiography is similar to its predecessors, although its tone is slightly more philosophical and its emphasis on apprenticeship as opposed to scholarship is more sharply defined. Wright also states that he and Mrs. Wright thought it wiser to stick to what they already had than "to go too far institutional or 'educational.'" Taking stock of their individual and collective capacities, they simplified their plans and reduced the possible membership to twenty-three from the seventy initially proposed.

The brochures and other publicity about the Fellowship had the desired effect: "Twenty-three young men and women," Wright recounted in his autobiography, "brought twenty-three times six hundred and fifty dollars"— one year each—to work it out at Taliesin. This "fair cross-section of Young America" assembled at Taliesin on October 1, 1932, "eager to go to work at something—ill prepared for anything except academic study of some sort. Least of all for the Freedom Taliesin had to offer."[28]

Wright was candid in acknowledging that the results, at least initially, were mixed: "As the plan for the Taliesin Fellowship unfolded itself," he wrote, "I had hoped that apprentices—like the fingers on my hands—would increase not only my own interest and enthusiasm for my work as an architect, but would also widen my capacity to apply it in the field. The first came true. But the second, as yet, is a temporarily frustrated hope. We somewhat overshot the mark. But I have not yet given up hope. We are steadily improving."[29]

Wright's intentions were clear. The Fellowship had been created. How his intentions were realized is in the story yet to unfold.

# 9 FELLOWSHIP DISCOVERIES

Many discoveries awaited the twenty-three adventurers who joined the Wrights' new community in October 1932. The newcomers could see instantly that they had come to an uncommon place to be part of an uncommon company. Mr. and Mrs. Wright made it that, of course, as did the men and women who had been working for them, but the newcomers also brought a rich mixture of fresh ideas and ambitions, and they were entering a setting where exchanging ideas and pursuing ambitions were part of the daily fare.

## THE APPRENTICES' UNCOMMON COMPANY

Some of the new community members brought perspectives shaped by having lived in one or more of at least thirteen states. Foreign countries represented in the mix were China, Denmark, France, Germany, Poland, and Switzerland. Among them were curious and determined adventurers. Yen Liang, for example, emigrated to the United States after graduating from Tsing Hua College in Beijing, China, to study architecture. Disappointed by his experiences at the University of Pennsylvania, he enrolled for a summer at Cornell University. That too was disappointing, so he took additional summer work at MIT before transferring to Yale. There he completed a five-year course in three years and enrolled at Harvard for further study, but he "still felt no closer to understanding architecture." Moonlighting in a Boston office was also unsatisfying. His awakening, bringing with it a sense of ecstasy, came with the reading of Wright's *An Autobiography,* and that compelled him to join the Fellowship.[2]

About a dozen of the newcomers reported having college or university degrees; some fifteen more indicated that they had attended an institution of higher education; three were high school graduates. William Wesley Peters, the first apprentice to arrive at Taliesin, said the group included "some terribly good fellows with wonderful spirit, and two or three extreme bohemian types." He characterized one newcomer as being "a type of professional liberal" and another as "a kind of a professional communist." Some, he said, came to satisfy their curiosity, some for the prestige attached to the name of Frank Lloyd Wright. But "still others came because of a genuine wish to participate in a great work under the leadership of Frank Lloyd Wright."[3] The youngest in the group was seventeen, the eldest thirty-one.

Edgar Tafel and Yen Liang, new apprentices whose Fellowship activities included performing—Tafel on the piano, Liang on the violin. Courtesy of Robert Silman on behalf of Edgar Tafel

Particulars concerning most of the original twenty-three are sketchy, at best, for the records about the initial years, compiled decades later, are incomplete and not convincingly accurate. By now memories of their lives in the Fellowship are gone except in letters and journals they wrote, and they are probably dimmed even among those to whom they passed those memories along. But we know that those who came were adventurers or possibly malcontents or restless misfits in a conventional culture. Taliesin provided them with a creative alternative to that culture.

The stated number of "twenty-three" new arrivals is itself uncertain. Perhaps that number derived from the realization by the Wrights that that is how many they could actually house. Never mind the count, however, for membership in the Fellowship has always been fluid. From the outset, comings and goings have been a normal part of the operation, and in the early years, particularly, the members were not tracked closely, nor was the duration of residencies in the Fellowship ever clearly or firmly established. Moreover, as women in the Fellowship married, their names sometimes changed, and that complicates recording their membership.[4]

According to Bruce Brooks Pfeiffer, Wright discovered that a husband's studying at Taliesin while separated from his wife lessened the husband's ability to learn and work, so through the years he admitted many married couples as apprentices. William and Geraldine Deknatel and their young child were among the first to join. He was a graduate of Princeton, she of a school of design in New York; both had studied in Paris. Alden Dow, already an architect with a degree from Columbia University when he applied, initially asked to be permitted to commute to Taliesin from Madison, forty miles away. But Wright said that in such a circumstance he could not see him as an integral member of the Fellowship, so he and his wife both became members. Wright welcomed Stanhope Ficke to the Fellowship with the understanding that his bride-to-be, Sally Stevens, would join him later, "for better or for worse." Because they would be sharing a room, he charged her an entrance fee, but not tuition. Stanhope Ficke had studied at Harvard and the University of Michigan, and post-Taliesin he attended the Massachusetts Institute of Technology. George and Ruth Dutton were a fourth married couple.

Pfeiffer noted that from the very beginning "an absolute sense of equality between men and women was established, and Fellowship wives learned to mix concrete, make architectural renderings, and participate in construction work even as the men learned to cook and bake and take care of the household."[5] The commitment to equality became a hallmark of the Fellowship.

In the brochure dated January 1, 1933, Wright listed forty "charter applicants." Of these, seven were "Taliesin men," that is, men who had been working at Taliesin before the founding of the Fellowship was announced and would continue for a time thereafter.[6] One was the wife of a Taliesin man, another, Svetlana, the daughter of Olgivanna Wright, who had been adopted by Frank Lloyd Wright.[7] One of the individuals listed apparently did not appear at Taliesin and information about another could not be located.[8] One was a frequent guest but never a member.[9] Three were apparently honorary members of the Fellowship; perhaps they were the "honor fellows" Wright mentioned in his brochure announcing the formation of the Fellowship. If so, they paid no tuition.[10]

Ten of the so-called charter applicants apparently stayed with the Fellowship for not much more than one year, although some of these may have maintained contact with Wright and the Fellowship longer.[11] Their reasons for leaving are not recorded, but it is safe to surmise that some, as the Great Depression deepened, ran out of money or were needed at home. Perhaps others concluded that they were unsuited for communal living, or that the Fellowship's insularity and isolation made them uncomfortable, or that they could not tolerate the Wrights' autocratic leadership. There was practically nothing to do in the drafting room, and those who came to become architects may have decided that they could not wait for work to arrive. Romantic relationships that had been tested by separation may have drawn some away. Others no doubt believed, as did many of their successors through the years, that they had accomplished their purposes in studying with Wright and that it was time to move on.

Some were asked to leave. Wright wrote to Willets Burnham's mother that her son, a nephew of Chicago's renowned architect Daniel Burnham, was

**CHARTER APPLICANTS** for Fellowship accepted and at work in temporary quarters at Taliesin October 25th 1932. All are taking part in the construction of the Fellowship buildings under the direct leadership of Frank Lloyd Wright.

■ Meantime the studio for architecture and private studios for the men, the studios for sculpture and painting, the little theatre, living rooms and conference rooms, private studios for women, water and sewer system; barns and servants building, the directors house and farmers cottage are either completed or well under way. The foundations are in for the kitchen and dining rooms. The buildings for shop work will be begun next spring, also the several cottages for associates. Garages and filling station will be built.

■ Meantime the following apprentices are sharing in the making of the Fellowship plant and working on plans and models for the buildings for the Broadacre City.

| | | | |
|---|---|---|---|
| Stephen Arneson -A.I.T. Chicago | Architecture | Else Klumb -Cologne-T.L.S. Bonn | Crafts |
| Elizabeth Bauer-Vassar (B.A.) | Architecture | Yuan Hsi Kuo-Shanghai-U.of Penn. | Architecture |
| William A. Bernoudy-Washington U. | Architecture | ..Michael Kostanecki- T.H. Danzig | Architecture |
| Robert Bishop -Swarthmore (B.A.) | Architecture | Fred.L.Langhorst-Cornell (B.A.) | Architecture |
| Visscher Boyd - U.of Penn | Architecture | Yen Liang - Pekin - U.of Penn. (B.A.) | Architecture |
| Christel Tessa Brey -Vassar | Architecture | .Rudolph Mock-Basel-E.T.H.Zurich | Architecture |
| Willets Burnham -Winnetka H.S. | Architecture | Chandler Montgomery -Ohio State U.(B.A.) | Sculpture |
| William Deknatel-Paris Beaux Arts | Architecture | Charles L.Morgan - U.of Illinois | Architecture |
| Geraldine Deknatel-Paris Beaux Arts | Architecture | Robert K. Mosher-U.of Mich. (B.S.) | Architecture |
| Abe Dombar - U.of Cincinnati | Architecture | .Isamu Noguchi-Guggenheim Fellowship | Sculpture |
| James Drought-U.of Wisconsin | Landscape | ..Takehiko Okami-Tokyo-Imperial U. | Architecture |
| Robert B.Ebert - U.of Wisconsin | Architecture | William Wesley Peters - M.I.T. | Architecture |
| Chas. Edman, Jr.-Northwestern U. | Architecture | Louise Dees-Porch -Wellesley-Antioch | Architecture |
| William Beye Fyfe-Yale | Architecture | .Samuel Ratensky - U.of Penn. | Architecture |
| ◦Mendel Glickman-Tri State U. | Civil Engineering | ◦Manuel Sandoval -Nicaragua | Crafts |
| •Robert Goodall-U.of Illinois | Architecture | Irving Shaw - U.of Minn.-U.of Chicago | Architecture |
| Phillip Holliday -U.of Wisconsin(B.S.) | Painting | Lewis E. Stevens - U.of Michigan | Architecture |
| John H. Howe -Evanston H.S. | Architecture | Edgar A.Tafel - New York U. | Architecture |
| •Karl E.Jensen-Copenhagen, Denmark | Architecture | Elizabeth Weber -Chicago Art Ins. | Architecture |
| •Heinrich Klumb-Cologne, S.H.B. | Architecture | Svetlana Wright -Hillcrest H.S. | Painting |

◦Honor Fellowships    •Taliesin Men    +Returned to Poland    •Returned to Tokyo

This list of charter members in the Fellowship reveals different forms of membership. Courtesy of the Frank Lloyd Wright Foundation

Wes Peters with Olgivanna Wright's daughter Svetlana, whom Frank Lloyd Wright had adopted and whom Peters married in 1935. She and one of their sons died in a tragic accident in 1946. Courtesy of Robert Silman on behalf of Edgar Tafel

"something of a problem here." Among other things, according to Wright, he was a restless promulgator of his own ideas, utterly lacked any sense of responsibility, didn't follow through on tasks, got dead drunk and messed the place up, wanted to grow a beard, roamed around whistling early in the morning instead of tending fireplaces in the studio, and left the truck he had driven to stand undrained overnight at zero degrees, resulting in a cracked engine block. At age twenty-one, Wright observed, Willets was an adolescent in his behavior. Moreover, "So far as I can see he can only be ruled by his affections for he has no respect for any living creature more than another and though conceited enough he has not enough real respect for Willets himself." This kind of conduct, Wright continued, had two goals: "one the insane asylum and the other jail." He would be welcome to return, Wright suggested, when he had discipline "coming from an ideal *within*."[12] This young man was not the last to be exiled.

Eleven of the early members were in the Fellowship for several years.[13] Robert Mosher and Edgar Tafel stayed for about a decade, John Howe was there for more than three decades, and William Wesley Peters remained with the Fellowship for almost sixty years, until his death in 1991.

Who on Wright's list of forty failed to appear at Taliesin in October 1932 remains unknown. But never mind that, for Wright's brochure published in December 1933 lists fifty-six Fellows. Here five names that were on the January list disappear, thirty-five continue, and twenty-one are added.[14] As with those whose names appeared in the first list, many stayed only a year or two, or occasionally three. Three who remained longer than three years were Alfred Bush, until 1940; John Lautner, until 1938; and Eugene Masselink, who became Wright's secretary, until his premature death in 1962.

Reconstructed records, even though they are incomplete and sometimes inaccurate, provide credible information about some of those who arrived in 1932 and many who joined in later years. Most deserving of recognition for reconstructing the records is Elizabeth Bauer Kassler, one of the initial apprentices. In March 1979, inspired by a visit to Taliesin West, she began to compile information by whatever means would produce it—correspondence, interviews, examination of such records as existed, and surveys returned by former members. Her "immodest ambition," as she described her effort, produced "a modest result": a publication titled "The Taliesin Fellowship: 1932–1982: A Directory of Members." Kassler called the Directory an unofficial publication, for Taliesin had not reviewed it. It was in some respects, however, "an in-house document," as it was not intended for the general public or for scholars, but rather for "Fellowship members early and late as encouragement to renew old ties and to consider in our maturity the nature and meaning of the Fellowship as we individually experienced it."

As the first attempt to record names, current addresses, and vital statistics of the hundreds of persons who were at one time or another affiliated with the Fellowship, the Directory's contents are uneven. Some of the entries contain only names and membership dates. Others include such information as dates and places of birth, deaths, marriages, names of spouses, and divorces. Some list individuals' AIA registration and the nature and location of their architectural practices and accomplishments.[15] Its deficiencies notwithstanding, the Kassler publication provides a glimpse into the lives of the first apprentices and some who joined later.

## MR. AND MRS. WRIGHT'S FINANCIAL STRAITS

In addition to discovering interesting compatriots in the Taliesin adventure, the initial twenty-three young men and women soon made another significant discovery: that Mr. and Mrs. Wright desperately needed the "twenty-three times six hundred and fifty dollars" they brought for the privilege of being there. Wright had no architectural work, nor had he had any since designing a home in Tulsa for his cousin, Richard Lloyd Jones, in 1929. He may even have lacked a place for his drawing board. Although his prodigious writing about architecture brought him an indeterminate amount of earnings, his income fell far short of what he needed to care for his young wife and daughters or to rebuild the home that had been twice ravaged by fire, and then, for a while, taken away by creditors.[16] Bruce Brooks Pfeiffer, who is intimately familiar with the Wrights' lives, recalled that Mrs. Wright was grateful to Mr. Wright's sister for sending her a used wool coat. She had not had a new coat for three years.[17]

In material terms, therefore, creating the Taliesin Fellowship required making something out of nothing. The $14,950 brought by the adventurers who had arrived that October, assuming they all paid the required amount, provided only temporary relief, perhaps not much more than was required to provide the newcomers with food and shelter. For sustaining their own lives and building the physical setting for the community they envisioned, Mr. and Mrs. Wright needed more than the new apprentices' dollars—they needed commissions. But the nationwide depression appeared to dash any hope they might have had for such commissions or for other possibilities for improving their economic circumstances.

Evidence of the consequences of Wright's financial straits appeared in dramatic fashion shortly after the new members of the Fellowship arrived. His departing employees, no longer needed, were angered by his inability to pay them—a chronic situation. When they left Taliesin they demanded payment of the amounts in arrears. Day after day they came, Wright said, asking for money that he believed they were entitled to only when they had kept their word and met the requirements of their "partnership agreement." In his autobiography Wright described how they kept coming, even though they were on federal government relief. Getting such relief when wages are due was illegal, but Wright did not want to inform authorities about this. As for paying the men, Wright wrote, "We kept the promises just as well as we could, all the while looking and hoping for miracles." The miracles, he continued, would be "'work'—buildings to build."

One day Jones, a "troublesome ringleader" of the angry men, desperate for the money owed him, attacked Wright in the studio, trying to choke him. Henry Klumb jumped at the attacker, yelling so loudly that Jones released his grip. This frightened Wright's secretary, Karl Jensen, who had played a part in another frightening incident involving Wright in Madison about a week after most apprentices arrived. A man named C. S. Secrest, who, with his wife, had been employed by Wright, assaulted him on the street over $282 in unpaid wages. In the bloody ensuing fight, Wright was kicked on the bridge of his nose. That evening five of Wright's men broke into Secrest's home and horsewhipped him; he chased them out with a butcher knife. Secrest's wife and daughter called the police, who arrested him and the five young men. Wright's five— Jensen, Rudolf Mock, Sam Ratensky, William Beye Fyfe, and William Wesley Peters—spent several nights in jail. The first four were eventually fined $150 and costs. Peters, who had been a bystander, was fined $50. Secrest remained in jail as he awaited a trial and eventually left the state.

"The Taliesin Fellowship," Wright wrote, "had got off to a very bad start. Indeed."[18]

**RESPONSES TO THE GREAT DEPRESSION**

While some succumbed to the effects of the Great Depression, or rolled with its punches, others, like Wright, sought creative ways to deal with it. Similarly, it stirred desires in some young men and women to engage in creative adventures. What did they have to lose? Or perhaps they asked what they might gain by joining Wright's community; if they and their parents could come up with $650, they could at least buy time for their economic prospects to improve while learning from the Wrights at Taliesin. Some who wished to apply explained that paying the required tuition would be impossible. Wright responded that waiving the tuition requirement was likewise impossible. Nonetheless, some applicants benefited from his willingness to suggest the prospect of exceptions. To Abe Dombar, for example, he wrote, "For boys like you there should be a scholarship. After the first year I hope to be able to manage this. But the first year unless we collect the tuition in full, we can't carry on."[19] Others, too, were told that they were deserving of scholarships. To Charles Edman, whose family's circumstances had been impaired by the freezing of their bank accounts, he wrote, "I am inclined to tell you to come along anyway and pay us when your money comes loose. I hate to think of your frustration in this regard and the Fellowship will do what it can to help you."[20]

Edgar Tafel, who gained prominence as a member of the initial group, recalled that his parents could afford to pay the $450 tuition fee at New York University but not the $675 Mr. Wright required. When he submitted his application, he explained that he could not afford to pay the full amount. In his book, *Years with Frank Lloyd Wright: Apprentice to Genius,* Tafel reproduces the telegram he received in response, dated September 22, 1932:

BELIEVE WE CAN MANAGE A FELLOWSHIP FOR YOU IF YOU PAY ALL YOU CAN NOW STOP YOU MAY COME NOW INTO TEMPORARY QUARTERS IF YOU LIKE . . . . FRANK LLOYD WRIGHT[21]

In an interview conducted years later by Edgar Tafel, John Howe remarked that when he had told Wright that he wanted to come but had only $350 for the fee payment, Wright said he would be welcome if he kept the fireplaces and boilers going. The only fuel available being wood, Howe was kept busy. When Wright passed a fireplace that was not burning, he let Howe know about it.[22]

## WRIGHT'S CELEBRITY STATUS

The young people's reasons for coming were as varied as the comers themselves, but all no doubt found the prospect of working with Frank Lloyd Wright to be compelling. For three decades Wright had been a celebrity, and it is useful to consider how a principal contributor to his celebrity status—the publication of *An Autobiography*—occurred.

The impetus for writing *An Autobiography,* published months before the founding of the Fellowship, had come from Mrs. Wright six years earlier. The Wrights were then in Minnesota, seeking to evade harassment by Mr. Wright's embittered former wife, Miriam Noel. Among other things, she was apparently behind efforts to have Wright charged with violation of the Mann Act, an act that made it a crime for a man to transport a woman across state lines for "immoral purposes." At the same time, the Bank of Wisconsin foreclosed on a mortgage on Taliesin and took his Japanese prints and other personal property as security.

In the midst of this turmoil, Olgivanna Lloyd Wright believed that the story of her husband's extraordinary life needed to be told, that no one could tell it better than he, that his already-published articles could be adapted for inclusion in the new work, and that with his architectural career at a standstill, he needed an outlet for his creativity. With her editorial guidance and encouragement, and with the assistance of a typist, he produced a publishable manuscript. He also designed the book and its cover.[23] After seventy-five years, reprints continue to find a place on booksellers' shelves.[24]

While the contents of *An Autobiography* are as truthful as poetry is truthful and as factually accurate as such writing allows, its author was a romantic genius with a knack for recalling things the way he would like for them to have been. Near the end of his autobiographical romance he acknowledges that all autobiography is written "between the lines," concluding, "As I remember, the best of life is a becoming. And so I record the barren lines and leave the rest to go the way of life."[25]

Donald Leslie Johnson speculates that Wright was driven, as are many other autobiographers, by an ego that believes other people would be interested in his stories. He may also have wanted "to set records straight," to explain past conduct, to philosophize, and to affirm his belief that his views were correct. Further, he may have wanted to live again the events of the 1920s, giving them the judgments he wanted others to make, and, perhaps most important, to let the world know that he was "ready to accept any and all invitations."[26] That does not diminish the book's value, however, for one finds in it the Frank Lloyd Wright that the writer wanted readers to find.

Whatever Wright's motivations, *An Autobiography* clearly enhanced his status as an imposing figure. The book was reviewed widely and favorably within months of its publication. In *The Architectural Record,* for example, Fiske Kimball recalled some of Wright's architectural innovations and concluded, "In Wright . . . we have a master who has not escaped inherent tragedy, but has enriched us with the only gifts which art can bring, the individual creations of the inspired artist."[27]

An unidentified reviewer in the *New York Times Book Review,* acknowledging implicitly the widely known scandals that had haunted Wright for two decades, wrote, "It is inevitable and right that the architect should justify and explain himself as a man, though the ethics of Frank Lloyd Wright's domestic life are no part of his ethics as an architect. The domestic story he has told simply and unequivocally, so that no open-minded person will fail to understand. It has been unfortunate and tragic. But the passion of the man was needed to support the passion of the architect and the end, architecturally and humanly, has been happy."[28]

Some of the young men and women who arrived at Taliesin in October 1932 had read *An Autobiography*. Edgar Tafel, for example, wrote that he read it and that he had earlier "stumbled onto other writings of [Wright] in libraries," sparking his interest in the master architect.[29] In any event, Wright was so well known that an announcement of plans for another bold new venture would surely attract attention.

## THE NEWCOMERS' THIRD DISCOVERY

Another discovery of the new apprentices may have been the most daunting, though it should not have been a surprise. In the 1932 circular Wright stated, "LABORATORIES AND MACHINE workshops are not yet ready but, eventually, will be planted, as planned, next to the living quarters. Studios and demonstrating rooms are already built or are now being built. The first experimental units to be put to work are those of architectural construction and design. . . ." The task of restoring the dilapidated buildings already there, particularly the Hillside Home School buildings and the house and Wright's studio a short distance away, and building new ones, fell to the members of the Fellowship. They were also called upon for farm and garden work and to help with other things that needed to be done.

According to John Howe, "All work was considered to be creative, not menial, whether one was working in the drafting room or in the kitchen." Mr. Wright set the example for this by often sweeping the walks early in the morning.[30] The apprentices were not expected to do all the work by themselves, of course, for Wright had a crew described by Howe as "various devoted retainers." In addition to farm workers, there were carpenters, masons, a plumber, and others ready to help with whatever project was at hand. Howe described Wright's centrality in the work:

Mr. Wright was a dynamo of creative ability. We were drawn ever closer into his orbit by this magnetic force and felt privileged to share his exciting life. He was our center of inspiration, the master, and we apprentices were his followers. Life in the Taliesin Fellowship was similar to that of a large family. Mr. Wright was the patriarch, with Mrs. Wright at his side to keep things running as smoothly as possible. Ours was a communal life in which we all shared. Work was done by rotation, by means of weekly lists. All work was considered creative, none merely menial. . . . Mr. Wright was an early riser and was often riding the road grader before breakfast. He personally directed all work whether it was at the quarry, limekiln, sawmill, threshing operations, corn shocking, or a multitude of construction and reconstruction projects that were continually in progress.[31]

Howe saw Mrs. Wright's role in all this work as crucial: "I think Mr. Wright might have terminated the Fellowship before the first year was out if it hadn't been for Mrs. Wright's steadying hand. Mrs. Wright brought serenity and stimulation to Mr. Wright's life, and was his intellectual equal. She established an atmosphere conducive to a creative life after so many years of upheaval."[32]

It took more than dynamism and serenity and stimulation, however, to make the new enterprise work, and that was diligent and determined labor. That is what the new apprentices were expected to provide. In the 1943 edition of his autobiography, after a half dozen pages of romantic musings, Wright returns to the mundane:

. . . Tough as the going mostly was, there was continual accomplishment. Both inside and outside, this thing we wanted most, a suitable characteristic place to work and play in, grew in integrity, beauty and usefulness, kept on growing up on the hillside at 'Hillside' as though it belonged there. It did belong there. We saw now ideas familiar on paper becoming useful and beautiful features of life and important effects that stood on the ground and would live long.

We worked, we sang, we played with the enthusiasm of youth undiminished. Loves' creative labor well spent.[33]

# 10 GETTING STARTED

With winter approaching, the need for sleeping and dining quarters was urgent. Also urgent were the need for a studio, lest the apprentices conclude that the promise of a Taliesin education in architecture was a false one, and for indoor places for community activities. Frank Lloyd Wright wanted his new apprentices to have all this and more. But neither they nor he had much to work with.

Funds for new buildings were nonexistent, so what had been built at Taliesin years earlier had to be salvaged. With his aunts gone from the Hillside Home School, Wright wrote in his autobiography, "their 'property' vanished into the surrounding air." Apart from Hillside I and Hillside II, designed by Wright in 1887 and 1902, the old buildings were of no value. The dormitory and servants' buildings, carpenter-built with no design, were in such sad shape that it seemed best to demolish them, for they spoiled the buildings that still expressed his aunts' spirit.[2]

Acknowledging that he had made many promises in his life, always intending to keep them, he envisioned a "corner of hell" paved with those promises that turned out to be only intentions. But one promise would not let him go: a promise "to see [his aunts'] educational work go on at beloved Hillside on the site of the pioneer homestead." That promise went with him everywhere. If he lived, he was sure to keep the promise whether he wanted to or not. He had become "an Instrument of Fate."

Reflecting on this in the early 1940s, when he updated and expanded his autobiography, he recalled memories of the economic breakdown of the nation's economy in 1929. Workers in nearby areas were starving, needing work, while he watched the shingle roofs of the Hillside Home School building falling in for the lack of the labor these men might have provided. The buildings and the unemployed laborers, he observed, were "rotting away." Roofs leaked, waxed sand-finish walls were "completely scribbled over with proper names like some provincial privy, desecrated by this ever devastating passerby whose better name is Curiosity." These buildings could not go through one more winter in such an agonizing condition. There was no money to pay long-standing debts. Except as he and his few faithful workers could raise it themselves, there was no food.[3]

Wright's meager earnings from architectural commissions and sales of Japanese prints were gone, and any credit he might ever have had was also gone. Outside Taliesin's door a "motley horde of outstretched hands" had come frequently, in all-too-familiar guises: "legal 'repossessions,' press interviews, duns, more repossessions, more threats. He had faced private blackmail, private and public 'adverse examinations' by shyster lawyers, long-distance telephone duns, duns by friends, duns by relatives, duns by employees," as well as threats and more threats, all "lit by the sinister flares of interior treachery."

My trouble too is, I know, that I yearn to be on good terms with myself and have never yet succeeded in getting rid of this deep-seated, inherited, tragic ancestral plague—the desire to stand well with my kind—to win the esteem and affection of my fellows. . . . I have always been ready and willing—I still am—to do without the Necessaries of Life if only I may have the Luxuries. This has seemed the only way to do "the things that are more excellent" while the Criterion—Money—secretly calls the turn.[4]

## "A STATION FOR THE FLIGHT OF THE SOUL"

What Wright needed in these moments of despair was "a station for the flight of the soul." In the 1943 edition of his autobiography he recounted the plans for the Fellowship he and Mrs. Wright had conceived earlier. Now they and the Fellowship's members were creating that station, and stations for their bodies as well as their souls. Work for that purpose had begun before they announced the opening of the Fellowship. They were compelled to do it not only by seeing the surrounding deterioration, but also by their experiences in showing the place to their friend H. Th. Wijdeveld when he was under consideration to lead the school the Wrights planned to establish. The pitiful state of Hillside, with its ceilings and floors caving in, Mrs. Wright recalled, caused the Dutch architect's spirit to collapse within him. Judging the place to be too far gone, Wijdeveld remarked, "You can do nothing to save it. It will take enormous capital to restore these buildings and far too much work." Mrs. Wright agreed: a superhuman effort would be required to bring Hillside back to life.

The experience with Wijdeveld seems to have inspired the Wrights to begin that superhuman effort. Mrs. Wright described what they did:

. . . Mr. Wright and I began to clean the buildings with our own hands—making order out of chaos. Every day we walked over to Hillside and attacked the work with more zest than ever. His spirit was indomitable and I raced fast to keep up with him. With hammer and nails almost constantly in his hands, he nailed the splitting boards together, repairing, patching, reorganizing, redesigning, changing the old gymnasium into a theater, the carpenter shop into a dining room and working on and on, until an opportunity came to employ a few workmen to help in the resurrection of Hillside. Somehow or other with that small handful of men, we managed to prepare the Hillside dining room and kitchen, but it was impossible to build any rooms yet.

But Wright was undaunted: "I know what we'll do," he said.

We can still open our school; we will call it the Taliesin Fellowship and we will make our thesis for the apprentices the building of the drafting room. We'll start from the

Foundation up. We'll send the boys [and as it turned out, the girls] to get sand from the river banks; we'll send them to cut green lumber and quarry and haul rocks. . . . They will learn to be better architects than anywhere else in the world.

Mrs. Wright wondered where the newcomers would sleep. That didn't matter, her husband responded. They could be crowded in at first. That very afternoon they sat down to make plans for the rooms and discovered they could house twenty-three people, and even then, said Mrs. Wright, they began to distribute the invisible students to not-yet-existing rooms. To attack their seemingly insurmountable challenges they turned to their "faithful old carpenters," William and Ralph Reilly, and their masons Charlie Curtis and Allan Brunker.

With solutions to logistical matters on the horizon, the Wrights turned to outlining the "complete education of an architect." That would include the kinds of experiences envisioned in Wright's plans for the Hillside Home School for the Allied Arts—in music, choir, drama, and dance. The apprentices would be expected to develop abilities in speaking and writing, making them capable of describing an idea clearly and concisely, and to understand theater and literature, as well, "all to become a part of his life."

## WELCOMING RECRUITS TO THE GREAT ADVENTURE

Now came the time to send out the circulars, inviting young men and women to join them in a great adventure. "Neither of us," wrote Mrs. Wright, "expected more than fifteen or so to respond, if that many to begin with." But in mid-September 1932, cars bearing prospective apprentices seeking interviews began to arrive. Among the prospects was one who stood shyly to the side. That was Edgar Tafel, about whom, after the interview, Wright remarked, "That young man is very good looking, isn't he? Like a curly-headed cherub." "Yes," she replied, "very nice looking indeed." But they found out later that "the shy cherub was in reality an incorrigible prankster."[5]

In the next day or two that curly-headed cherub found that "Taliesin shoved us at once into the reality of the world of building." His first job on the first day found him whitewashing bathrooms. They used whitewash rather than paint because it was cheaper. Everything had to be done on the cheap; everything was labor-intensive. The second day, Tafel recalled, he "got to help a real carpenter install partitions, toe-nailing the studs, cross-bracing, nailing up the wood lath." Next came helping a construction worker mix sand and lime and lugging the resulting mud to a plasterer, who taught him how to slather it on the lath. Wright liked the plaster to have a "sand-float" finish, created by placing a piece of carpet over a "float" or trowel and running it over the plaster in circular sweeps. He also learned from Wright, who was "always coming by," how he put colors into the final coat, thus avoiding paint. Tafel and others were having their first experiences in "learning by doing—the Taliesin way—and by listening."

When more apprentices arrived they regarded Tafel as an old hand, believing he had been there for years. He taught them what he had learned: how to set studs, nail lath, mix mud, and float. Before long they were engaged in the same kinds of activities.[6] Necessarily so, for so much needed to be done, and so much more remained to be learned.

## THE WORK—REBUILDING AND BUILDING

Speaking to apprentices in a seminar led by Vernon Swaback in 1967, Wes Peters, Wright's first apprentice and the husband of the Wrights' daughter Svetlana, provided an account of the building and rebuilding activities at Taliesin as the Fellowship was taking shape. Peters was a robust, commanding, hard-working presence in the Fellowship for so long that his richly textured recollections have a special place in reconstructing the Taliesin story. That his colleagues held him in singular esteem is not surprising. At his funeral on July 20, 1991, Aaron Green, a former apprentice who had known him for fifty-one of Peters's fifty-nine years in the Fellowship, spoke for many when he referred to him as a combination of giant and saint.

No other person . . . led a more uncompromising life in the spirit of Frank Lloyd Wright. By his love of life, of people, his great generosity, his sense of fun, his continuous striving for excellence, his great sense of integrity, he has enriched all of our lives. How providential that he existed when Mr. Wright died! A tower of strength and ability to assist Mrs. Wright, and someone the world could recognize and respect.[7]

In the seminar, Peters began by mentioning the buildings in the area of Hillside when he arrived. Included were the old original home building, Frank Lloyd Wright's first built structure; the original cottage built by Wright's grandfather, known as the East Cottage; a little two-story house that stood west of the present drafting room; a long laundry building that served as a cookhouse and dining room and provided lodging for Wright's workers; and a great octagonal barn with a wood silo, built in the 1870s, possibly the first in the state. Some of the structures that remain today had different functions then: the place where models were shown (in 1967, when he spoke) was originally the Manual Training room, with a laboratory at the upper end. The Dana Gallery and the Roberts Room were chemistry and physics laboratories. The current drafting room was not there at all. Peters continued:

Mr. Wright had somehow optimistically hoped, with these 50 workmen and the apprentices, to finish all these buildings by the winter of 1932. This became an obvious impossibility since there was no money with which to purchase materials. We . . . had virtually nothing but our own ability to produce. We received a couple of gifts from the Pittsburgh Plate Glass Co. . . . Also the American Radiator Co. gave us some radiators and two boilers. But apart from that we had to make everything ourselves.

Elizabeth Wright Gillam (Wright's niece, known as Bitsy), and apprentices William (Beye) Fyfe and Bill Bernoudy have fun doing Fellowship maintenance chores, 1934. Courtesy of the Frank Lloyd Wright Foundation

Frank Lloyd Wright with Wes Peters, one of his first apprentices, whom Wright later called his "right bower." Courtesy of Robert Silman on behalf of Edgar Tafel

Edgar Tafel working at the Taliesin lime kiln. Courtesy of Robert Silman on behalf of Edgar Tafel

We had no cement or lime. We had to go out and burn the lime. We also went up to cut down the trees to saw the wood, and then topped the trees out and hauled them down to use as fuel to fire the lime kiln and for heating boilers at Taliesin. We took big logs down to Taliesin. There was a sawmill set up at the end of where the drafting room is now. It was a sawmill with an old steam tractor running it. One of the heaviest jobs was hauling away the oak slabs after they were sawed. They were extremely heavy and had to be stacked and sawed for use as fuel. All during the winter we felled these big trees and sawed up the tops and the slabs in order to provide the firewood for the boiler. That first winter at Hillside they just had stoves. . . . It turned out to be a very early winter and a very severe one.

Firing the lime kiln, Peters said, "was a real pleasure." The kiln was perhaps seventy-five to one hundred years old. They made lime in the primitive way, building a great arc of lime rock hauled to the area and firing the kiln continuously for two or three days. Working in continuous shifts, three or four apprentices ran the whole thing, taking turns sleeping by the kiln. "It was pleasant to lie out in the hills" that September and October, Peters said, as they produced "tons and tons" of lime of very good quality. The lime mortar used in the original Hillside buildings, he said, held up amazingly well.

All this required supervision, of course, and Wright was fortunate in having one of his former assistants, Mendel Glickman, return that Fall. Glickman, an engineer, had been in Stalingrad, sent there by the United States government to advise builders of a tractor factory. Wright made him the field boss at

Taliesin. Besides the apprentices, there were other workers to be supervised, and from them the new apprentices learned the building arts. Peters described them to the 1967 apprentices:

We had an old professional quarryman by the name of Alan Brunker, a marvelous worker. . . . We had some fine men, along with occasional riffraff among the workers. There were a few marvelous characters. Some were the old strain, such as Charlie Curtis, a magnificent old mason, an old Cornish mason who for years and years worked for Mr. Wright. To work with Charlie Curtis was an education in itself. For a while Bill Weston came back to work—he was a skilled carpenter, the father of Marcus Weston [later an apprentice]. Bill Schwanke, from Spring Green, was a fine-looking fellow with white hair, another skilled carpenter. He was the carpenter foreman in charge at Hillside.[8]

Charley Curtis, a Cornish mason, worked for Wright at Taliesin for many years and trained a number of apprentices in masonry. Courtesy of the Frank Lloyd Wright Foundation

An especially important part of the apprentices' work in their first winter at Taliesin concerned finding ways to keep warm. Some of the newcomers, at least, had been warned to expect cold weather. For example, Karl Jensen, Wright's secretary, reminded Bill Bernoudy, a St. Louisan soon to arrive as an apprentice, that the weather would likely be cold and that warm sports clothes would be the most comfortable to wear "here in the country." He should also bring overshoes and warm underclothing, drawing instruments ("a t-square, triangles, and such other equipment as you may have"), and a pair of blankets and a comforter for his bed.[9]

While Peters, other apprentices, and Wright's employees were working outdoors, Wright himself was usually in the studio, mainly working on the drawings for the Hillside renovation and construction. That was his only architectural work until late 1933. But as Tafel noted, he was often on the move around Taliesin, sometimes on horseback, keeping things going.

**EMPLOYEES**

Searching for workers while the Fellowship was forming, Wright posted a notice in the Hillside kitchen on October 1, 1932, inviting men to partnerships that provided suitable board and lodging and one-third of agreed-upon wages to be paid in cash weekly. The balances were to be paid when the buildings under construction were completed and ready for occupancy and increased apprenticeship fees could be obtained. Each workman was asked to sign a contract with these provisions. The men were appreciative, Wright believed, and soon he had forty men as partners in working to save the Hillside Home School buildings. They fixed up the old laundry building and equipped it with hot and cold running water, installed tables and benches, and made it seem inviting and homey. So, Wright concluded, "We had man-power. About forty men."[10]

Only two among the forty are mentioned in Wright's autobiography, but thanks to an article by Herbert Fritz, Jr., some of those not mentioned can be identified. Fritz came from a family that lived near Taliesin and interacted frequently with the Wrights. When he was a sophomore in high school, before the Fellowship was formed, he asked Wright if he could work for him during the summer vacation, an inquiry that pleased Wright. Although he worked on the farm, where he came to feel at home with Bill Slaney and Ed Carmody, he also became acquainted with Wright's assistants in the studio: Rudolph Mock, Won Hsi Kuo, Henry Klumb, Sam Ratensky, Yvonne Bannelier, and Karl Jensen, who came, respectively, from Switzerland, China, Germany, New York, France, and Denmark.[11]

The most significant of them for Wright was Klumb, who was born in Cologne, Germany in 1905. He earned a degree in architecture, with honors, from the Technological Institute of Cologne in 1926. Shortly he came to Taliesin, where Wright engaged him in general architectural and shop work, model making, building construction, gardening, and farming. In 1932, moved by his desire to grow individually as an architect, Klumb began to distance himself from the new Taliesin Fellowship. Wright offered him a position as senior apprentice, but Klumb declined, in part because he believed that Wright was unable to acknowledge the existence in young people of an urge to grow. Rather, he believed that Wright wanted his apprentices to surrender absolutely and to blindly devote their lives to his ideas without attempting to create their own things.[12]

In the summer of 1932, Herb Fritz returned to work on the farm at Taliesin, but with restoration work begun on the dilapidated Hillside buildings, he began to lose interest in farm work. So he asked Wright if he could change jobs and work on the foundation ditches for the new studio. This role put him among other Wright workers, men and women whose presence at Taliesin was essential in the construction process and in helping the apprentices learn by doing. Fritz recalled masons (Allie Hemstock, Hiram Stuart, Paul Holmes, and, of course, Charlie Curtis), carpenters (Ole Anderson and Bill Schwanke), a cabinetmaker (Manuel Sandoval), quarry workers (Allen Brunker and Dude Carmody, brother of Ed), and cooks (including Mabel Larson, his aunt).

He had other strong family connections with Wright and Taliesin. His maternal grandfather was Alfred Larson, an immigrant from Norway who farmed near Taliesin and worked as a stonemason for Wright. Fritz's father, born into a German immigrant family, became a professional draftsman when he was fourteen and began working for Wright as a draftsman in 1912, three years before the birth of Herbert, Jr. He was one of the survivors when Mamah Borthwick and her children, as well as four others, were murdered at Taliesin in 1914. Subsequently, many members of Fritz's extended family worked for Wright at Taliesin. Without these persons and those working with them, the Fellowship would most likely have had a fate less happy than what it experienced.[13]

Working alongside other apprentices, Fritz helped not only with the Hillside projects, but also with rebuilding the dam and replacing old wire fences between the fields and pastures with electric fences. If that didn't keep the apprentices busy, there was always farm and garden work to be done. In its first several decades, apprentice labor produced the fruit, grains, and vegetables for hungry men and women at the Taliesin tables.

Cold weather was a constant theme in the recollections of Taliesin's apprentices. According to Wes Peters, when winter came they were busy almost all the time "just making it possible to live." Many times they would have to "take a gang into the woods early in the dark winter mornings and prime the Caterpillar with ether to start it." They would then start the power-saw to saw up the wood and spend a day getting two or three loads of wood down to keep the boilers going. "Mr. Wright," he said, "was working right along with it. He led everywhere. He worked on everything. We practically had to restrain Mr. Wright to prevent him from going daily to the woods. [He] endured unbelievable hardships in those early winters."

Speaking to the apprentices about harvesting wood, Peters recalled a humorous incident: Wright had rented woods from Herb Schoenemann, a nearby farmer, and to haul it out they had to cross his fields. That worked when the ground was frozen, but in the spring the ground began to thaw while Taliesin still needed wood. Mendel Glickman helped organize the hauling, and they decided it would be all right to do it at night when the ground was again frozen solid. One morning around one or two o'clock Glickman started toward the woods in the lead truck, a Model T or a Model A. Peters was behind him and when he arrived he saw a light, "and there was Herb Schoenemann standing out with one of his sons with a shotgun leveled off on Mendel. Mendel had his hands up in the air. . . . Schoenemann was absolutely livid with anger. Contrary to our plan, Herb didn't realize we were trying to save his land but thought we were trying to pull a march on him; but we calmed him down before he shot Mendel."[14]

Farming, harvesting trees, rebuilding existing structures and adding new ones, working in gardens and kitchen—these activities dominated Fellowship life in the early years. The Wrights were in the middle of all of them. The lack of commissions made it difficult, however, for Wright to give the apprentices what they most wanted, that is, studio experiences. The best he could do was to have some of them trace his drawings, thus learning how to be draftsmen and to better comprehend what it would mean to work with him as an architect.

As for the rebuilding of Taliesin, that was a never-ending, always challenging task. John de Koven Hill, recalling his arrival as an apprentice in 1937, said, "[Taliesin] was so beautiful; I felt as though I had come home. I had no idea anything like that was in the world. It had all the loveliness of the Georgian mossy brick and all of that, plus something. It was ageless. It was falling down in places, but it was really . . . it's a place designed for the soul and the emotions, not for comfort. I cried. I just couldn't believe what I had gotten into."[15]

Others, too, many of them, found it to be a place designed for the soul.

Jim Charlton, Leonard Meyer, and Fred Benedict help with haying at Taliesin. Photograph © Pedro E. Guerrero

# 11 BEYOND SCHOOLING

AND AGAIN WE READ ANOTHER
NEWSPAPER ARTICLE—FROM
PHOENIX THIS TIME—ABOUT THE
"STUDIES" OF THE "STUDENTS"
OF THE TALIESIN "SCHOOL"
UNDER THE "TUTELAGE" OF FRANK
LLOYD WRIGHT, WELL KNOWN
"DESIGNER."
IT MAKES ME SICK TO REPEATEDLY
SEE SUCH ONE-TRACKED
STUPIDITY THAT WORSHIPS
"SCHOOL" AS SUCH AND WILL
NOT UNDERSTAND—IF IT COULD—
ANYTHING THAT ATTEMPTS TO GO
FAR BEYOND MERE SCHOOLING.
THIS LATEST ARTICLE SMEARS A
FULL COLUMN AND DOESN'T
CONTAIN A LINE OF TRUTH.

—JOHN HENRY HOWE III

For more than two years, Jack Howe, as he was familiarly known, and other apprentices had been telling newspaper readers in Madison, Wisconsin, and nearby communities about working, living, and learning with Frank Lloyd Wright and with one another at Taliesin in Spring Green, Wisconsin. With Wright's encouragement and under his editorial direction, they had begun to write short articles under the heading "At Taliesin." Their commitments to Wright and to the ideals of the Fellowship compelled them to spread the word on the true character and intentions of the Fellowship, and they did so with wit, insight, and verve.[1]

## GLIMPSING THE FELLOWSHIP'S EARLY YEARS

By the time Howe's piece appeared, more than 165 "At Taliesin" columns had been published. That some of their readers, along with other observers of the Fellowship, seemed unable or unwilling to grasp the substance and spirit of the Fellowship experience and the nature of their community pushed Howe's patience beyond its limits:

When will people—who protest their real interest—learn the few simple main facts about us: that we have no "studies," believing in "study" only as applied to actual work; that we are not "students," but apprentices to Frank Lloyd Wright, having abandoned as hopeless the "student" and the university through which he glides getting at the roots of nothing; that Wright is not a noted "tutor" as the last article would have it—to see him in action would completely wipe out that illusion—and Wright is not a "designer." He is a builder. He is an architect, and as anyone should know before he ever attempted to write an article for publication, the designs of Wright's buildings are the result of construction in the nature of materials, site, purpose, climate, etc. But this, mind you, is never an end in itself. And this is the principle of architecture which differentiates organic architecture—in which we are working under Wright—from the buildings which surround us in America . . . .

So, God deliver the American people from dilettante writers like this one, and deliver us from people who faithfully believe in them. . . .[2]

Howe was not the only apprentice exasperated by outsiders' mistaken impressions of the Fellowship. Fred Langhorst, for one, responded to a letter from a reader of earlier columns who was convinced by what he had read that visiting Taliesin would be a waste of time. Regardless of its intention, he asserted, Taliesin had "degenerated into a rural edition of the phoney post-Greenwich village 'art' colony—the 'village' which remained when the real artists moved out." The critic's letter, Langhorst wrote, "is a verbal dose which has been vigorously administered in the wrong place. . . . Actually, it is merely popular abuse of [an] uncomprehended endeavor." However, the letter gave him an opportunity to make more clear the root ideas of his essays and those of his fellow apprentices:

First—an explanation of the who and why behind these articles might clarify their intentionally kaleidoscopic nature. Because the work of Frank Lloyd Wright at Taliesin stands advanced in the field of creative art, *The Capital Times* has generously given this space for furthering the understanding and appreciation of his work. Mr. Wright encourages his apprentices to contribute to this column because he believes the expression of an idea in literary form as well as in all other forms is essentially architecture.[3]

John Howe, at Wright's side, served as the studio's chief draftsman from the 1930s until he left the Fellowship in 1964. Courtesy of Lu Howe (Mrs. John Howe). Photo by John Amarantides

Apprentices accounted for more than two hundred "At Taliesin" columns published irregularly from January 11, 1934, to early 1938, mainly in Madison's *Capital Times* and the *Wisconsin State Journal,* but also in four other southern Wisconsin newspapers.[4] More than seven decades later, the apprentices' writings continue to provide a window for glimpsing into the Fellowship's early years, enabling us to understand the experiment founded and directed by Frank and Olgivanna Lloyd Wright and to gain an intimate sense of what it was like to have been there.

## JOINING THE FELLOWSHIP

Frank Lloyd Wright's apprentices joined the Fellowship because they saw it as the right place for them to be at that time. They understood, as Bob

Bishop wrote, that the Taliesin Fellowship would be a very odd school, if it meant to be a school at all. But that was not its purpose, nor was it to be "Mr. Wright's school." Rather, the Fellowship's resources, products, and ideas all belonged to a philosophy of life called "organic." It was the members' desire for an organic life that moved them to join. They saw Wright's life and work as outstanding examples of an organic life.

That, Bishop continued, was not an abstruse idea. An organic life meant "a simpler, more natural life, closer to the soil and to the things which always have and always will give men and women greatest peace and satisfaction," such as nature, beauty, honesty, sincerity, love, and common sense. All this mattered more than material success. And so, Bishop wrote, they were working instead of studying. They did study, of course, "to learn to work effectively, but the study is a means rather than an end."[5]

That the Taliesin Fellowship was not an "institution" was an implicit theme in the "At Taliesin" columns. Nor was it an art colony, although all its members aspired to be artists by "at present and forever doing 'whatever befitteth a man.'" It was difficult to recall past labors that contributed to their growth, according to Nicholas Ray, but they were growing through the concentrated activities the Fellowship offered.[6]

Some who joined the Fellowship found the appeal in its striving to correlate art, industry, and agriculture. As Hank Schubart understood it, there were to be master apprentices for painting, music, and philosophy, but architecture was and always would be "the center line of all work and the source from which subjects radiate since it involves the structural principles of organic growth." The Fellowship program, he wrote, would always be in line with personal freedom and growth. "Led by a great architect, the group itself is richly endowed with the attributes of the artist and perhaps—who knows—of genius." Of principal importance was the fact that those who were forming the Fellowship were volunteers. Many of them had already been educated by universities, and thus had a sense of the importance of what they were experiencing at Taliesin. The Fellowship, Schubart continued, was "attacking the obvious fallacies of our educational system," and the apprentices were there to help it grow, and by so doing, grow themselves.[7]

Unsatisfying experiences in schools of architecture impelled some of the apprentices to join the Fellowship. One such was Burton Goodrich, who wrote a column in the form of a letter to the architecture department at the University of New Hampshire, where he had been a student. They would be surprised, he said, to learn that he was in Wisconsin, studying architecture with Frank Lloyd Wright, rather than continuing toward his university degree. While at the university he had questioned the professors' claims that they were teaching students to design "real, honest architecture." They could not accomplish this when "the real aim of the student has to become—'to please the jury'—in order to be recognized as being good in design." When the Beaux Arts method "not only advocates but practically demands that its students go to plates and books for inspiration," he continued, it results in the imitation of details composed into something which must look different. After giving examples of this practice, he asserted that he "found the Beaux Arts system destroying the very seeds of creative architecture." They knew him well enough, he remarked, to know that he had neither the habit nor the desire to injure others in any way, but when he saw the harm done to thousands of young men by the Beaux Arts method of training he could not, and believed he should not, restrain himself from sending the letter.[8]

Paul Beidler recalled that he had ostensibly been doing well in the architectural school he attended, but somehow architecture, as it was fed to him and his classmates, lacked vitality. There was something wrong. "What was it? Our school had an established reputation. We had the best imported professors. The Beaux Arts Institute awarded us many medals. . . . There was much pride and spirit. Much cheering for Dear Old Penn. . . . But some of us couldn't feel the exuberance. Something was wrong." His professors had taught him and his colleagues to imitate, so imitate they did. But they imitated the wrong things and received deservedly low marks. Then:

In a dark, dusty corner of the library one of our small "radical" group unearthed a short article by Frank Lloyd Wright with a few illustrations of his work. We devoured it voraciously and eagerly looked for more but more was not found in that library. The scent was getting warm and we spoke of Frank Lloyd Wright to our professors. "Tsz, tsz, tsz," said the professors, "lay off that guy, steer clear of him, he's dangerous, he'll put bad ideas into your heads. He is silly enough to think that America can have an architecture of her own and zat, you [know] is empooseebal." So zat was zat.

We lined up lock step in appropriate gowns, sang raw, raw [rah, rah?] songs, and took our exquisitely engraved diplomas.

What next? Where? How?

Being American, Beidler wrote, he looked abroad. In Germany and Holland he noticed vaguely familiar forms. Suddenly he remembered Frank Lloyd Wright's work. The modern Dutch architects asked why he had come there seeking architecture, telling him, "We got all our stuff from Frank Lloyd Wright." So he bought and read Frank Lloyd Wright's autobiography in Amsterdam. "Irony. At last. Journey's end. I quit my job, broke all ties and hotbooted for Taliesin, Spring Green, Wis., U.S.A."[9]

Another whose dissatisfaction with a school of architecture prompted her to join the Taliesin Fellowship was Cornelia Brierly. When she arrived at Taliesin in 1934, she said, Mr. Wright asked her where she had been going to school. She told him she had left Carnegie Tech because of the "uncreative classical Beaux Arts system taught there." Failing to dissuade her, the faculty wrote her off as a "young radical embarking on a complete misadventure." Mr. Wright was pleased to learn that she had rebelled against the stultifying situation existing at Carnegie Tech.[10]

The next year, she wrote in "At Taliesin," she returned to that institution to visit, but was dismayed by "the cramped concepts of the so-called 'crits' system" in an entire architectural program. The students were limited by the stagnation of Beaux Arts competition. Responding to her criticisms, the head of the architecture department explained that extraordinary leaders like Wright may have left the scope of the average mentality of the mass, and they have followers like the apprentices, but "it is the duty of architectural schools to educate their students only to the level of the mass mind so that

Cornelia Brierly joined the Fellowship in 1934. Farmhand Ed Carmody, admiring her hard work, called her "the million-dollar lady." Mrs. Wright took this picture in 1935. Courtesy of the Frank Lloyd Wright Foundation and Cornelia Brierly

their architectural knowledge serves the mass in the thing it wants and can comprehend." She considered this to be a "stupid outlook or goal for any educational institution." It seemed to her that it was the duty as well as a privilege "for an educated person to give the inexperienced mass something that it has been unable to attain for itself." Considering what transpired to be a "fruitless argument," she left the office of that "great high chief of the architectural department." He placed upon her the stamp of "young reformer," a title "not to be scoffed at."[11]

## DAILY LIFE IN THE FELLOWSHIP

Many of the "At Taliesin" columns reveal that the apprentices spent their days as workers. On occasion, particularly in chapel services, they even sang about joy in working, to the tune of Johann Sebastian Bach's chorale, "Jesu, Joy of Man's Desiring." Wright called it the Fellowship's "for he's a jolly good fellow" song.

> Joy in work is man's desiring,
> Holy wisdom. Love most bright;
> Drawn by hope our souls aspiring,
> Soar to uncreated light,
> Nature's love our strength that fashioned
> With the fire of life impassioned,
> Striving still to Truths unknown,
> Working, striving, though alone,
> Through the way where Hope is guiding,
> Hark what inspiration rings,
> Where the man in life confiding,
> Drinks to joy from deathless springs,
> Ours is wisdom's greatest treasure,
> Nature ever lead her own,
> In the love of Joys unknown.[12]

Apprentices Earl Friar and Cary Caraway wrote about the Fellowship's philosophy of work. Work, they said, was not simply something to be endured, or a device for earning a living, or a means to an end. Rather, at Taliesin working gave them a sense of the connection between work and life. The spirit in which the work was done—with willingness, spontaneity, and wholeheartedness—was different. The laggard, they said, "gradually catches this feeling and once experiencing the joy in accomplishment, the true reward of work, he no longer needs urging."

At Taliesin we don't work to earn money—we work for the joy of working with a share in a great cause and good living assured. The more creative the work we can do the greater the joy, for work represents translation of thought into action. . . . Work which involves no great mental activity naturally brings proportionately less joy of work, however, drudgery is unavoidable in any walk of life. We should welcome a certain amount of it as a means of self-discipline. Work is an important part of life at Taliesin, but of no greater importance than design, rather it is complimentary to designing—serving as a means to derive the greatest benefit from designing—thought and action working in unison.[13]

Another who mused on work at Taliesin, reflecting the concerns that the nature of the apprentices' work inspired, was Everett Burgess Baker. Calling the apprentices "a mixed crew from all walks of life," he wondered whether they subscribed to Taliesin ideals because they were "a cross-section of young American Society above the hum-drum average." Some among them, he observed, "have come to Taliesin with the sincere desire to join in a great work, others, perhaps, for more selfish reasons." Or some may have a greater capacity for giving than others. How, then, was the group affecting "this thing called work." Was the work they were doing significant? Was the tempo or rate of doing the work in proportion to the immensity of their task or fast enough for their personal satisfaction?[14] Such questions were no doubt on the minds of many of the apprentices.

In 1934, George Beal, an engineer and professor in the School of Engineering and Architecture at the University of Kansas, and his wife Helen were summer visitors at Taliesin. Beal found it refreshing to see activities "directed as joy in itself and work valued for its contribution to the whole rather than for pay and profits." This, he observed, provides a basis for growth in character, craftsmanship, and the realization of the nature of things. Further, he saw it as the background for action in music, gardening, painting, weaving, carpentry, sculpturing, swimming, saving of stones, sleeping, washing dishes, exchanges of ideas and ideals—the things that give life its problems and make it worthwhile to be alive. Beal realized that at Taliesin, facing these problems was complicated by the lack of good tools, but apprentices would, in time, realize the importance of owning such tools, all in the process of growth. In the meantime, fixation on the finality of material things should not be seen as a part of the spirit of growth through organic change.[15]

Marybud Roberts Lautner noted that visitors at Taliesin often doubted that the method of learning there was practical, thus implying that the Fellowship was not a good alternative to attending college. She and others, she wrote, had been to college, and the reason they were at Taliesin was that college did not give them what they wanted. More significantly, she pointed out that the most obvious difference between university students and the Taliesin apprentices become evident by comparing girls in the different settings. All the work girls did at Taliesin, she asserted, would be of value for the rest of their lives. Although they did not do the heaviest work in building, all the other work was done with no distinction between boys and girls—in the kitchen, in gardening, in maintaining living quarters, and even in the doing of architecture, or music, or various crafts. For all, work was an integral part of their lives at Taliesin.[16]

That girls did not do the heaviest work, at least when it came to sawing wood for the fireplaces and boilers, was not entirely true. An anonymous apprentice reported on November 15, 1934, that the wood-sawing crew brought back a forest of bittersweet, and that Cornelia Brierly, who had arrived recently, was hailed by Ed Carmody "as worth one million dollars after he had seen her five and a half hours of work."[17]

Gene Masselink, Mr. Wright's secretary, described how the work at Taliesin was organized. During the day it was conducted in spontaneous fashion under the supervision of the "chief of the fortnight." It was done outdoors, weather permitting, until tea time by the fire in the studio. Between then and dinner at 7:00, everyone worked in the studio, engaged in drafting, building models, painting, and drawing. After dinner came relaxation, with lights out at 10:00. However, there was no set routine of work, as the apprentices were free to maintain their individuality.[18]

### ROUTINE TASKS

Philip Holliday provided an account of apprentices at work, in this instance, on an "ear-nipping" day of winter. The day began at 6:00. After a breakfast of buckwheat cakes, bacon, prunes, and coffee, they cleaned their rooms and then appeared in the studio. However, because there were sixteen fireplaces and three boilers at Taliesin, some of them spent at least part of each day bringing wood from nearby farms, sawing it, and keeping the fires going. Everything else, he said, was a part of the "planned objective in a creative sense." That meant working with Wright and other apprentices on drawings and a model of a Fellowship complex (a structure that was never completed), repairing models damaged by traveling and by visitors in many exhibitions, and making working drawings for the house Wright had designed for Malcolm and Nancy Willey.

Apprentices at lunch at Taliesin, 1936. Facing the camera, from left: Jack Howe, Hans Koch, Noverre Musson, and Hulda Drake (Cornelia Brierly's sister). Courtesy of the Frank Lloyd Wright Foundation

At noon the call of the dinner bell left the studio deserted, but if Wright was at his drawing board, there were "few who wouldn't rather watch Mr. Wright draw than eat." Back at work, one apprentice was designing a poster for the roadside billboard of the theater, another was weaving a necktie—hurriedly, because a rug-weaving project was waiting. Half a dozen apprentices rehearsed a play one of them had written; set designing would come next. Tea at four o'clock, featuring lemon and apple cake or cinnamon toast, provided time for rest and "renewed stimulation of tired minds." Then three hours remained for apprentices to do as they chose, "learning to draw before all else." The supper bell, Holiday said, ended the day.[19]

It ended the day, that is, except for those serving in the never-ending cycle of accumulating the food products for the meals, cooking and baking, serving the diners, washing dishes, and readying the kitchen for use by those who would prepare the next meal. In her memoir, *Tales of Taliesin,* Cornelia Brierly described what went on in the kitchen:

The kitchen was the heart of Taliesin family life. In those early years, a large black iron stove dominated the ample space. The stove kept every cook busy stoking it with kindling wood, from four in the morning until the evening dinner. With no such things as thermostats or even oven thermometers, the cooks learned to hand-test the heat in order to turn out legions of loaves of bread, pies, cakes, roasts, and stews. In the winter this friendly beneficent stove made the kitchen a cozy gathering place, but in the hot, humid Wisconsin summers an apprentice could not find a steamier, more torrid work place.[20]

Cornelia also recalled that when she arrived in 1934 the construction underway was paralleled by intensive farm and garden work. Given the economic circumstances of the times, that was a necessity. Working alongside the apprentices, the Wrights taught them to garden, shuck corn, make hay, and thresh grain. The Taliesin farm, striving for self-sufficiency, produced milk and milk products, eggs, beef and pork, and an abundance of fruit and vegetables. If a surplus of garden produce remained after some was canned and stored in the root cellar, they marketed it. Brierly's description of how the apprentices worked together in food production reveals the character of the place:

Work proceeded with gusto and camaraderie and often with a spirit of competition, such as who could produce the largest pumpkin for the county fair. Everyone went to the fair, and we were sometimes rewarded with prizes for our produce. We earned prizes for a fat, milk-fed pumpkin, for a branch heavily laden with crab apples, our strawberry preserves, apple butter, cider, and for our superior animals.

The routine tasks of feeding the members of the Fellowship and Wright's other assistants required careful planning. An unsigned "At Taliesin" column described how garden planning was done in the same way as building planning: "Using a large map of the farm and a box of colored pencils, the entire garden layout is planted in straight, parallel rows of red, yellow, green, and blue. In this way the various crops are put in their places before the actual sowing begins."[21]

The apprentices had to take two-week turns in the kitchen, subscribing willingly or reluctantly to Wright's belief that an architect must know what goes on in kitchens, and the best way to find out is to work in them. Noverre Musson mused on kitchen work at Taliesin. Some apprentices, he wrote, despised it, regarding it as the hardest work of all. Others did not mind it so much and enjoyed "the coordination required and [got] a kick out of the last-minute excitement, ringing the bell, and seeing everyone hurry in to clamor for the fruits of their morning's scullery service." A few kitchen workers, he wrote, "take real pleasure in experimenting with foods, flavors, season and occasionally evolve new ways of preparing familiar dishes, or proudly repeating those with which they have formerly had success." Of course, kitchen duties did not end with preparing and serving the meals. Alas, the dishes and pots and pans demanded time and attention. "Well—it must be."[22]

Bennie Dombar brought good humor to his account of kitchen work. "Mention of the word 'scullery,'" he wrote, "causes my nose to crinkle and my thoughts to dwell on murky things. But recalling my year of work in the kitchen, I think the word is a perfect onomatopoeic description of the work itself." Successive dishwashers had disliked certain pots and pans that were especially difficult to clean. For Blaine Drake it was the orange squeezer and for Jim the burnt oatmeal pan. Pie tins raised his own blood pressure, but their contents were ample compensation. Some had a pet aversion for muffin tins. All kitchen workers, according to Bennie, were unanimous on one issue: "they would rather dig trenches, mix concrete or saw wood than labor with the dishes and pans."[23]

Mabel Morgan found challenges, drudgery, amusement, and delight in kitchen duties. Wright provided amusement at one Saturday night cookout: Each person was given a pan, vegetables, and things for making "sukiyaki." All were responsible for cooking their own meals over one of the five fires. Wright added soy sauce here or mushrooms there. Then came considerable laughter as they struggled to drop the chopsticks' morsels into their mouths and lost them at the point of entry. That caused them to resort to cups and fingers. She enjoyed other times in the kitchen:

Easter is an exceptionally merry time in our kitchen for it is then that Mrs. Wright's Baba and Pascha cheese is to be made, something like 140 eggs broken, much beating and mixing, then several hours later we watch her taking huge round yellow loaves from the oven, carefully placing them on pillows and rocking them to and fro until cool.

To make delightful dishes from France, Germany, Russia, and Poland such as Brioche, Borscht, Chiarpchichi, Shashlick, Vsvar, Golubisi, Colivo and many others under the personal supervision of Mrs. Wright has been my unique experience at Taliesin.[24]

Mabel Morgan, daughter of a Taliesin employee, worked with apprentices in the kitchen, both in preparing daily fare and serving guests. Courtesy of the Frank Lloyd Wright Foundation

## SPECIAL EFFORTS FOR SPECIAL TASKS

Apprentices were frequently given special tasks requiring special effort, and not only in the kitchen. With spring arriving in 1934, a flood of water caused a breach in the dam below Taliesin. To apprentices that meant work and more work. "But," wrote apprentice Alfred Bush, "we must work! That is part of our life and the best part of it. None of your city regimentation and theory. We work. And we like it."[25] In 1935 the dam needed reconstruction again. According to Gene Masselink, that required a week or more of intensive hauling and digging for the new spillway to take shape and for the dam to be recapped. The water then filled to the brim and over it, so the turbine could once again supply power for the lights at Taliesin.[26]

Some projects were completed quickly, such as the building of a room in Taliesin for eight-year-old Iovanna. This was accomplished by lowering the ceiling in the loggia and raising the roof above it, thus creating "the most playful room in the house." The work, including the building of furniture, was done by several new apprentices, aided by two carpenters, using Wright's sketch on a shingle for the plan. Women in the Fellowship made the curtains. To celebrate its completion the builders threw a "room-warming party" as a surprise for Iovanna. Apprentices sat around the fireplace and told her fairy stories. It would be up to Iovanna to carry in the wood for the fireplace and keep the room in order. This, wrote Abe Dombar, "will develop her sense of responsibility, a valuable trait that few grown-ups seem to have."[27]

The same week construction of the Playhouse, a remodeled space that had been a gymnasium in the Hillside Home School, took a step closer to completion. On November 1, 1933, Mary York, a writer for the *Capital Times,* had reported on its opening, scheduled for that evening. She explained that the apprentices had "felled the trees, sawed them into lumber, quarried rock, and burned lime to lay the rock in the wall." Apprentices, too, had done all the finishing work.

Taking York on a tour, Wright led her backstage, where apprentices were singing as they worked. "They are happy because they are doing what they want to," he told his guest, "and they have an ideal. We live what we do here." He also showed her a large fireplace at the rear of the room that would keep the place warm.[28]

But not warm enough. On February 9, 1934, Abe Dombar described a learning-by-doing experience: "A group of apprentices with overalls and wrenches in their hands are seen talking to Scotty, the master steam fitter. He explains to them a few fundamentals, then points out a radiator for them to connect up. They know just what to do and why. They cut the threads on the end of a pipe and screw on the nipple. It's all recreation to them . . . . Relaxation to these fellows merely means changing to a different job."[29]

While leading Mary York on the tour of the Playhouse, Wright pointed to other work in progress, most notably the drafting studio, where the apprentices would work under his guidance. He told her that there were 18,000 square feet of wood used in the room, all of it hewed from the forest. However, work on the studio progressed slowly, and records of who did what are sparse. By September 1937, we learn from an unsigned "At Taliesin" column, attention had been focused on this project and that John Lautner took charge as chief. He encouraged the apprentices to carry out the work of finally completing the drafting room.

Apprentices built the Hillside drafting room, extending north from the Hillside living room; it took more than seven years to complete. Courtesy of the Frank Lloyd Wright Foundation and Cornelia Brierly

For four years we have looked forward to the time when the big drafting room would be an alive and active workroom surpassed by none, and we need the working space. For a long while for various reasons it was just outside our grasp—unfinished and empty: filled with strong clear light from the north, perfect for the work we anticipate doing there. We would walk through it regretful, waiting for the day when we could be at work on it.

Now we are entering into what we hope to be the final phase of construction and the end of a long waiting. Two months of continual and concentrated group activity by the Fellowship should announce the fact that our principal workroom—an abstract forest in oak timber and sandstone—is in order. Then watch our dust![30]

The abstract forest in oak timber was long in coming. Wes Peters, one of its builders, explained one of the complications to Vern Swaback's seminar with apprentices. The trusses supporting the roof had to be modified. They had been erected when the oak timber was green and unseasoned; that was the only kind Wright could afford to buy. For the first three or four years they were in place, Peters said, "they shrunk and twisted and moved around and bent and warped. The diagonal members and quite a few other additions to the trusses were made subsequently when they were straightened out and rebuilt." That had to be done to correct the warping and twisting. Asked whether they had initially been submitted to analysis, his answer was No. "They weren't engineered before they were built. They were simply built up as we went along and constructed in that manner." They were an example, Peters remarked, "of Mr. Wright's intuitive engineering analysis."[31]

According to Jack Howe, the drafting room was not sufficiently completed for occupation until 1942. For nine years, he said, the oak trusses had been raised, but a number of setbacks like the ones Peters described, as well as the welcome necessity of concentrating on Wright's architectural work, had brought work to a standstill.[32] Curtis Besinger, who joined the Fellowship in the Fall of 1939, said that the drafting room was finished and ready for use then. His preenrollment interview had occurred in the Taliesin studio, but when he arrived in September of that year, he and other apprentices began to work in the Hillside drafting room.[33]

Perhaps it is not the datings of the two men that are at odds; rather, their perception of what "finished" meant may have differed. As with most things at Taliesin, the drafting room was probably "in progress" year after year. Indeed, as Howe remarked, at Taliesin "no project was ever 'finished'; all was in a state of constant change. Change was sought and embraced, stagnation abhorred."[34]

# 12 REACHING IN ALL DIRECTIONS

IN THIS BUILDING OF A
FELLOWSHIP, BOTH IN EQUIPMENT
AND PERSONNEL, WE DO NOT
FACE ON SEPARATE FRONTS,
ONE PHYSICAL FRONT, PLUS
ONE MENTAL FRONT, PLUS ONE
SPIRITUAL FRONT, BUT [WE BUILD]
WITH A MASTER WHO BELIEVES
ONLY WORK DONE WILLINGLY
AND EAGERLY [ON ALL FRONTS], IS
WORTH CONTEMPLATING
AS CREATIVE.

— **FRED LANGHORST,
APPRENTICE**

Work on the physical front was clearly an essential element in the apprentices' lives at Taliesin, as the two previous chapters confirm, but as Fred Langhorst insisted, work on mental and spiritual fronts was equally essential. He might also have mentioned the social and artistic fronts, for social interaction and experiences in the arts were key elements in the daily life of the Fellowship. To gain a sense of what it was like to have been there requires considering the community's creative activities, all of them integral to Fellowship life. Langhorst helps with this:

We strive to reach out in all directions, planning, designing, farming, road and dam building, drawing, weaving, carving, making models of organic buildings, writing these articles expressing our reactions, views and aims and characteristic incidents, making posters and signs for our playhouse, editing and illustrating a monograph of our own work, "Taliesin"—soon to appear—criticizing our movie programs, refreshing our guests with tea and coffee as well as entertainment, when they reach us from the city, brightening our chapel with foliage as well as lifting up our own voices together in music and seeking from our varied guest-speakers such enlightenment as their rich experience may bring to our own.[1]

By sampling their interactions with one another and their participation in conversations and activities with the outsiders, whose presence was an ongoing part of the life of the Fellowship, one sees how they, along with Mr. and Mrs. Wright, faced the physical, mental, spiritual, social, and artistic fronts they encountered.

## VISITORS AND GUESTS

The Fellowship distinguished between Taliesin's "visitors" and its "guests." The visitors were welcomed, paid fifty cents, signed a register, and were guided through the workshops and gardens. The fee was inaugurated, wrote Jack Howe sardonically, "as a substitute for three 'positively no trespassing' signs and a good, though rickety, revolver." It kept away "the idly curious and the curiously idle" and helped raise funds to pay for gasoline. It also made it possible "for the really interested people to see what we were doing while it kept the others (not willing to gamble 50 cents) away."

Thanks to the fee, the apprentices had in their charge many really fine people, "the cream of the crop," who knew what the score was, so to speak. To show them around Taliesin was almost a pastime and more than compensated for the others," that is, those "not so interested and the 'dregs.'" The apprentices gained insights from the interested visitors and valued their criticism as well as their praise.[2]

The Fellowship's guests were there for more specific reasons. Some came for educational and cultural purposes. In January and February 1934, for example, a former member of Congress, Thomas R. Amlie, led a discussion on economists' views of the future; Alice Williams, soon to be a faculty member at Skidmore College, exhibited her portfolio of watercolors; Alexius Bass, from Carroll College, gave a song recital of Schubert Lieder; Franz Aust, of the landscape department at the University of Wisconsin, gave an illustrated lecture on "Beautiful Wisconsin," assisted by an apprentice, James Drought, who showed Aust's slides; two young ladies from Liverpool, England, portrayed a Victorian matrimonial situation in pantomime; and puppeteer Everett Baker "introduced the English players and followed their act with a request performance of his impersonation of a speaker before the Tuesday afternoon Ladies Club." Some guests, such as Rabbi Max Kadushin and his friends from Madison, came simply to visit. In preceding months, around the fireplace at Taliesin the apprentices viewed several films made by Rockwell Kent, a painter, and heard presentations by Baker Brownell, a professor of philosophy at Northwestern University, and Ferdinand Scheville, a University of Chicago historian.[3]

In the following month, Dean C. L. Cristensen of the University of Wisconsin College of Agriculture joined the Fellowship for a fireside discussion about the condition of agriculture in America. Cristensen was concerned about the farm being a slave to industry and in danger of being run to death by the city.[4] In October farm issues remained a concern, as the apprentices spent a Sunday evening with Dr. Asher Hobson, head of agricultural economics at the University of Wisconsin, who gave an appraisal of the New Deal program, the Farmers Emergency Relief Act, designed to raise prices by curtailing production.[5]

Typically the guests at Taliesin were friends of the Wrights. One such was Paul Frankl, a well-known interior decorator from New York, who during his visit of several weeks presented lectures to the Fellowship and held impromptu classes on various drawing techniques intended to make drawing easier. He also made a present for Wright: a beautiful reed reclining chair he had designed. The chair posed one disadvantage, however, for students stood in line for hours to recline in it. Frankl left his twelve-year-old son Peter to be a member of the Fellowship.[6]

William Evjue, editor and publisher of the *Capital Times,* was at Taliesin a number of times, and he, like other guests, contributed to the apprentices' learning. One Sunday evening Evjue and Ernest Meyer, a columnist in the *Capital Times* and a poet, were there for supper. "Together," Bob Bishop remarked, they "made a complete evening. Fast conversation and exciting tales. Then together we all listened to the usual music—piano, violin, and singing. Outside contacts like this are valuable and stimulating and good fun."[7] Nicholas Ray noted that Meyer, having caught the spirit of the evening, transferred it to a column in the newspaper.[8]

Mr. and Mrs. George Parker, from Janesville, Wisconsin, were among Wright's favorite guests. World travelers, they regaled the Fellowship with tales of their trip up the Yangtze River, and on one occasion they hosted the Fellowship at their impressive pen factory and their home. For the first time, wrote Edgar Tafel, "the Fellowship was out en-mass on a new type of activity. It was being entertained. Instead of receiving week-enders it was itself a weekender." The next day the apprentices marveled at the efficiency of assembly-line production in Parker's factory. After dinner and ready to return to Taliesin, the Fellowship "fizzed out" trying to sing its chorale without accompaniment.[9]

In an "At Taliesin" piece about a Parker visit at Taliesin, Wright remarked, "It is upon the character and vision of such men as George Parker that the Fellowship bases its hope for a more creative future." Parker, "he who made a quality pen outsell a cheap one and leads the field in consequence," was a Wright client as well as a friend.[10] However, he died in July 1937 before the garage Wright designed for him could be built. Wright eulogized Parker in an "At Taliesin" column on July 30, 1937, describing him as "so warm in spirit that people seemed to love him automatically."[11]

Another couple, Mr. and Mrs. Edgar Kaufmann, from Pittsburgh, also counted among Wright's favorites. They were guests at Taliesin in November 1934 when the Parkers were also present. After those in attendance that Sunday evening "had got safely back from the Yangtze with the Parkers," Wright remarked, Mr. Kaufmann gave a talk that "showed that romance has not dropped out of merchandising . . . and gave us the most encouraging view we have had of the hand the enlightened merchant is taking in improving the product he sells."[12] Kaufmann soon came to play a major role in the revival of Wright's career, first for his sponsorship of the building of a model for Broadacre City, illustrating Wright's urban and suburban planning ideas, and then as the client for whom Wright designed Fallingwater near Pittsburgh.[13]

Another of the Taliesin guests, Jens Jensen, inspired Cornelia Brierly to describe his memorable visit lyrically:

Despite the unceasing flow of energy that manifests itself in human lives there is one energy, that cosmic spark, that the Universal Spirit reserves for great men. Two such great men have just met at Taliesin—our master, Frank Lloyd Wright and the poetic naturalist, Jens Jensen. With different words these two strong men sing a freedom song for the beauty of America. We apprentices are at Taliesin to build our master's song into our lives. Jens Jensen offered to our score a new theme to aid in the building. This Dane, with all the strength of his powerful vitality, is trying to help Americans be Americans by conserving their regional foliage and intelligently replanting where men have scarred the landscape. . . .

Jens Jensen is of Danish virility. Erect, ruddy, whitehaired. . . . [H]is flow of pictorial speech is interspersed by a firmly accented, "By Jove!" His experiences are to the listener as fresh as ice crystals on pine boughs. He tells us that when the leaves of the lupine begin to unfold they are tinged with pastel colors and have the appeal of a baby's palm. And, he says, the most touchingly beautiful sign in nature is to see that leaf with a drop of dew upon it.[14]

Almost three months later Jensen visited the Fellowship again, this time during its first sojourn in Arizona. Calling him a "true friend of the Fellowship," Bennie Dombar wrote that "Jensen and the saguaro, their strength and character, the principle of their structure gave us cause to think, the desert breeze sweeping across our faces. . . . The desert—each flower, each plant—will always bring him back to us."[15]

Occasionally guests came to Taliesin on a specific mission. John Gloag, a writer from London, spent several days there in December 1934 gathering material for an article to be published in *The Architectural Review*. Bob Mosher remarked that he brought them all "very close to the London scene." But what he took away mattered more. In his article, he described meeting Frank Lloyd Wright: In the inner room at Taliesin to which he was led, "there, standing before a wood fire that snapped away in a stone fireplace, was an old man with the carriage of a youth; a robust figure, obviously in splendid health. He had a kindly, furrowed bronzed face—a cloud of silver hair; an unforgettable dignity of movement and manner, and friendly dark eyes." Quickly the visitor knew why young men almost worship him: "it is because he is eternally young—a youth with a touch of wise malice, and a gift for reducing problems to their simple elements."[16]

"The Taliesin Fellowship," Gloag discovered, "is not an 'art colony.' It is not an 'escapist school.' . . . It is training designers as they have certainly never been trained before, to accept responsibilities for civic and national planning, for architectural and industrial design." Further:

In the theater they have built, those fortunate young men and women at Taliesin are studying film technique, and in no narrow national sense either. Painting, drawing, sculpture and music are among their studies, and when the Fellowship begins to work outside its own immediate territory, when its activities spread beyond the completion and perfecting of its own buildings, its influence may be far greater than anybody at Taliesin yet suspects.

"Save for a few discerning architects, writers and critics," Gloag concluded about Wright, "he is unknown and unhonoured among people who make loud public noises in America. He made me feel humble, ignorant and encouraged; and he made me feel ashamed for the great country that knows so little of his work and understands nothing of his greatness."[17]

Guests were frequently called upon to speak to the Fellowship and the Wrights. One such was Gareth Jones, from London like Gloag, and also there in December 1934. "Mr. Jones afforded us joyful entertainment with dramatized stories in dialect of his experiences in Russia, England, and Wales," a columnist reported. "Being in the employ of David Lloyd George, he gave us a fine character study of this important and famous Welshman. Welsh characteristics were brought to light in humorous, quick-witted dialogue." Perhaps awareness of Wright's Welsh heritage made the humor more delightful. Also guests that evening were Mr. and Mrs. Stanley Marcus, who were acquiring wealth through their Neiman-Marcus department store in Dallas. They commissioned Wright to build a house for them, but it was not built.[18]

Sometimes the guests at Taliesin came in groups. On June 2, 1934, for example, the Fellowship entertained the Technical Club of Madison. Its members toured Taliesin, then the Fellowship buildings, the Playhouse, the drafting room, and a painting exhibit. The dinner served to the more than one hundred and fifty guests was a typical evening dinner—"baked ham, scalloped potatoes, coleslaw, cakes, and coffee, with plenty of ice water." After dinner Wright spoke to the guests assembled in the Playhouse, telling them that the Fellowship was not a "back-to-the-soil" movement. Rather, "we are living a very busy but greatly simplified life here—we derive our pleasure and happiness from things that really count—from doing things; a combination of action and appreciation." Always eager to create favorable impressions of his community, Wright invited questions and chose various apprentices to respond to them. The evening continued, as usual, with music—four songs sung by Gene Masselink, accompanied by Ernest Brooks, and piano works by Scarlatti, Bach, Chopin, Brahms, Debussy, Prokofiev, and Schumann performed by artist-in-residence Glen Sherman. The showing of *The Fall of the House of Usher* followed.[19]

This photograph, taken in 1937, is a typical one of the Fellowship, with apprentices gathered around their master. Front row, from left: Benjamin Dombar, Kevin Lynch, Wright, James Thomson, Wes Peters, Robert Mosher. Gathered behind them: Cary Caraway, John Lautner, John Howe, Eugene Masselink, Blaine Drake, Ellis Jacobs, E. Brookins, Herbert Fritz, Burton Goodrich, Edgar Tafel. Chicago History Museum. Photographer—Bill Hedrich, Hedrich-Blessing. HB-04414-H.

## WRIGHT'S KINFOLK

In a letter to Richard Carney, written in 1992, a family visitor revealed insights into the Fellowship's early days by recalling visits he had made sixty years earlier. That visitor was Jenkin Lloyd Jones—the son of Richard Lloyd Jones, Wright's cousin and editor of the *Tulsa Tribune*—for whom Wright designed a home in 1928. Carney had joined the Fellowship as an apprentice in 1948 and became the CEO of the Frank Lloyd Wright Foundation when Mrs. Wright died in 1985. Jenkin succeeded his father as the editor of the *Tribune*.

I was a senior at the University of Wisconsin, Madison, in the fall of '32 when Wright started his school. But, as Frank's second cousin, I was a frequent moocher at Sunday night suppers at Taliesin from the fall of '29 until my graduation.

When I understood what Wright proposed, I was sure it couldn't last. Slave labor has been outlawed in the United States since 1863, and here was slave labor with refinements undreamed of by Simon Legree. Not only were the young laborers paid nothing for growing food crops and restoring buildings in advanced states of decay but they were charged for the privilege. I shamefully underestimated the magic of Frank and Olgivanna. I watched the peasants labor in a drafting room made of green lumber because Frank couldn't afford kiln-dried. I saw them eagerly consume concentration camp cuisine. In spite of gross exploitation they gathered worshipfully around their two gurus, male and female, and the talk was not only stratospheric but often incomprehensible to me. Here was Plato. Here was Joan of Arc. No matter that Frank was far overdue on payments for his front-wheel-drive Cord automobile. No matter that the Sunday supplement scribblers were still nipping at his heels. There was a spurious opulence in the midst of near-starvation. Bittersweet and pussy willows, gathered in the bog across the road, adorned the living room. Apples from the orchard overflowed the bowls.

Oscar Wilde once sniffed a rose and said, "I have had my dinner." A pragmatic Oklahoma college kid was amazed at the power of style. Wes Peters, an Indiana editor's son, was one of the first disciples. He never left. There may have been nothing on the table but soup and dark brown bread, but Olgivanna would trot out a jar of Montenegren plum jam which she called pavidla and we all feasted.

It was my personal privilege to see Frank Lloyd Wright at the nadir of his fortunes and live to die at the height of his fame and fortune. It was no tribute to my intelligence, back in 1932, that, when I watched a handful of my contemporaries hammering, sawing, whitewashing under conditions of a Spartan camp, I couldn't imagine what held them together.[20]

Some of Frank Lloyd Wright's kinfolk not only interacted with the Fellowship, but they lived in its midst. In 1907 Wright designed a home called Tan-y-deri near Hillside for his sister Jane and her husband Andrew Porter. This was their family residence from 1908 to 1917, and Andrew Porter served as business manager of the Hillside Home School from 1908 until it closed in 1915. The Porters moved to the home of Anna Lloyd Wright in Oak Park in 1917, and from then until 1934 Tan-y-deri was their vacation retreat.

When they prepared to return to their home in Oak Park in October 1934, an "At Taliesin" contributor wrote appreciatively of the parties the Porters had held for them every Thursday night at Tan-y-deri, giving them the chance to enjoy singing and dancing. The apprentices threw a party, with cider and doughnuts, to thank Mrs. Porter for all that she had done, "but she got even with us and at the end of the evening presented the Fellowship with her records of the dance music so that we could enjoy them all winter." Tan-y-deri served as the Porters' retirement home from 1935 to 1954, and for decades, beginning in 1955, it provided "overflow housing" space for apprentices, whose number had grown substantially.[21]

## GEORGI GURDJIEFF

A guest whose philosophy played a part in shaping the practices of the Taliesin Fellowship was Georgi Gurdjieff. Mrs. Wright had been one of his disciples for seven years in Europe, particularly in France, before she emigrated to the United States, and his influence on her leadership role in the Fellowship was long-lasting. In the early years, however, that influence was scarcely considered in the "At Taliesin" columns, perhaps because the writers mention Mrs. Wright only in passing. If she was less assertive in those years of the Fellowship it may have been because she was still a young woman, not much older than some of the apprentices.[22] Yet, they gave Gurdjieff limited but interested attention. A column on July 26, 1934, reported on a Gurdjieff visit:

Taliesin was much honored last night by the visit of Georg Gurdjieff, the noted philosopher and leader of the famous work at the Prieure Fontainbleau, France. In the evening we heard some of his music, and the introduction to the vast series of books which he has written. His powerful personality affects all strangely. It seemed as though we had an oriental Buddha come to life in our midst.

About two weeks later a writer alluded to Gurdjieff's visit as he recalled a gathering of a few apprentices—one of those occasions when "conversation flows and dies." In this one Wright participated. With one topic suggesting another, it turned to Gurdjieff. A difference of opinion quickened the tempo and led to a debate over the relation of the disciple to the master, "of Orage to Gurdjieff, Saint Paul to Jesus." Shortly the group gathered itself up and slowly dispersed. Although it was early, the tomorrow would start early too.[23]

Three weeks after Gurdjieff's visit, Wright mused on the occasion in his usual elliptical manner. Beginning with the notion that "real men who are real forces for an organic culture of the individual" are so rare that "one might count them on the fingers of one hand with the thumb to spare—unless the thumb were to go to George Gurdjieff," he asserted that there was only one Gurdjieff. Having roamed around Asia and western Europe in search of the temple rituals of oriental culture, Wright remarked, Gurdjieff has, "by the way of the genius that is his, developed new rhythms in the dance and new music so designed as to integrate human faculties and prepare the man for a more harmonious development than any we can show by way of our current ideas of education."

After referring to Gurdjieff's ingenuity as a composer and writer and to his enormous ego, Wright noted that Gurdjieff had affected the Fellowship "strangely as though some oriental Buddha had come alive in our midst with perfect unconsciousness of self." Wright's conclusion: "Notwithstanding super-abundance or personal idiosyncrasy Georgi Gurdjieff seems to have the stuff in him of which genuine prophets are made."[24]

Guests like these no doubt kept life at Taliesin from becoming tedious, but if it became so in the winter, wrote Philip Holliday, even as he insisted it had not, "we have many pleasant things to anticipate. The garden, the building and painting—relaxation such as swimming, picnicking, drawing outdoors." Winter, he continued, "is not a dreaded word here. It implies that the work goes on inside instead of outside, that is about all."[25] The work on the inside had to do with the mental or intellectual front.

## SUNDAY CHAPEL SERVICES

On that front, as well as on the spiritual and artistic, the Sunday morning chapel services satisfied many wants and needs. A sampling of speakers and topics reveals the nonsectarian character of the chapel experiences. On February 23, 1934, Harold Groves, a professor at the University of Wisconsin, spoke about the close relationship of economics to religious life. This, wrote Beye Fyfe, "was a truly inspirational meeting—the talk itself, the sun streaming in the windows, the bell ringing overhead. There is something in the atmosphere of that little building which makes it doubly significant as a place of worship."[26] The next Sunday the apprentices heard a sermon by a Baptist minister from the University, the Reverend "Shorty" Collins. Towering over the congregation at "six foot six," Bob Mosher reported, he spoke "sensibly and persuasively about the Fellowship of Man."[27]

The next week Wright was the speaker. He began by quoting Oswald Spengler's definition of religion: "Religion is that which the soul of the faithful is." He then read a few of Walt Whitman's poems and commented on "the close relationship between the philosophy of Walt Whitman and what we are doing in the Fellowship."[28] Reverend Rupert Holloway from Madison, speaking on architecture and art in the field of spirit religion, presented religion as a simple, sincere, honest way of life. It was thus, wrote Alfred Bush, "the solution for a good life well lived—as much as an organic architecture is the solution of a full honest life in America."[29] Another Sunday his topic was "Why I am a Unitarian," prompting a writer to remark, "Why anyone should want to be other than Unitarian in the sense he gave the word—none present could say."[30] On a third Sunday, Holloway brought many from his Madison congregation. His sermon was a strong one, an apprentice observed, but addressing two audiences, "it lacked the peculiar force and character of his previous talks as applied to us because of the divided attention. We like our lectures straight."[31] The Fellowship and Holloway's congregants picnicked in the chapel yard after that service.

Between Holloway's sermons the Fellowship heard one by Rabbi Max Kadushin, whose remarks were based on "a few suggestive comments made by Mr. Wright while walking into the chapel." He followed, according to Fred Langhorst, the Welsh theme of the Lloyd Joneses, and therefore of Wright himself: "Truth Against the World." The Rabbi remarked that it had taken him three weeks to read Wright's "An Autobiography," three weeks to digest it, and three weeks to formulate a plan of his own inspired by it. "Our experiment in bringing all faiths to the platform of this little chapel,"

Langhorst concluded, "is showing that at bottom all great faith is one." Another speaker was an Episcopalian minister, Reverend Francis Bloodgood, who spoke on "The Spirit of God." He was an impressive figure, noted Edgar Tafel, and the apprentices all liked him immensely.[32] Another Sunday morning Mrs. Max Kadushin, substituting for her rabbi husband, spoke of the new movement toward Palestine. Her sermon, wrote Gene Masselink, was judged to be magnificent.[33]

One Sunday a misunderstanding somewhere along the way meant that no member of "the 'brethren of the cloth'" was present, so they had a "Quaker Sabbath." Each person who was moved to share his or her thoughts was invited to do so. Additionally, a request for Mr. Wright to read the Lamentations of Jeremiah, "which gives a fine treatise on the sins and artificialities of the modern city," was cheerfully granted.[34] Another Sunday four apprentices spoke: John Lautner "told of a way of life as simple living by way of the cooperation of intuition and intellect"; Gene Masselink read Robert Frost poems; Fred Langhorst read poems by Edward Arlington Robinson; and Karl Jensen read from Nietzsche.[35] This was a "homemade" service, but as on other occasions, they found that when they stood up and spoke out, as John Lautner noted, their meetings were "neither dull nor commonplace."[36] The appearance of Karl Bogholt, a philosopher at the University of Wisconsin,

Unity Chapel in 2008 is little changed from when Wright helped build it in 1886 and when it served as a gathering place for the Fellowship in the 1930s. Photo by Myron Marty

led to a debate with Mr. Wright over whether the "good life" is circumscribed by habit. The professor's belief that it is, had only one defender: Bisser Lloyd Jones, Wright's cousin.[37]

As the end of 1934 approached, the apprentices decided that although they had heard fine Sunday sermons by many of Madison's "brethren of the Cloth and University personages," to whom they were grateful, they had become too dependent on the performances of others, "becoming too much the 'much and mediocre' congregation." So in the future, "each in his turn and all in time," would be "both congregation and pulpiteer." The designated apprentices were to preach sermons on assigned topics having to do with an aspect of human character, with the "particular assignment going to who most needs the specific knowledge derived from it." In other words, they were to address areas in which they were perceived to be deficient. The topics on which they spoke provide clear evidence as to what it meant to work in a community led by Frank Lloyd Wright.

Gene Masselink, the first, spoke on "the first shall be last."[38] A columnist the next day called it a "fine, thoughtful, and sincere sermon of a quality which would be quite enviable among many church leaders." They closed the service with the singing of the Fellowship's Work Song and had dinner at the chapel.[39]

Another designated speaker was John Lautner, who expounded on "energy," concluding that "talking about energy is like talking on what makes the world go around. If anyone thinks they know—I would like to learn."[40] Burton Goodrich, whom Cornelia Brierly characterized as quiet and retiring, spoke on "self-expression." In previous environments, he said, he had been "guided by unnatural ideals and stifled and stunted by the overbearing common mold of custom and tradition." Associating with the lame, he limped, but now, at Taliesin, he was inspired to stand up and walk.[41]

Abe Dombar, recalling his Jewish tradition and beliefs, said he would like to have his brother Bennie join him in chanting passages from the Torah. Then would come the sermon, but he acknowledged that he had a problem: "I am forced to discuss the quality of 'Persistence,' about which I know nothing." Anyway, he said that the most beautiful parts of the services were the sweet organ music and voices and the sweet silence just before the sermon, and the absolute silence immediately after it. He regarded these "moments of infinity" as deeply religious, with the sermon nothing more than the filler in between. So his filler was in the form of a story about changes in the Wisconsin River. It ended with "To Be Continued." This was the last chapel service before the Fellowship embarked on its journey to Arizona, and there is no record of the sermon's continuation.[42]

Upon the Fellowship's return, chapel services resumed, but only for a while. Cornelia Brierly spoke on "prudence," as assigned, and summarized her remarks in an "At Taliesin" column on June 1, 1935. She acknowledged that she was not prudent, for though she recognized intellectual values, her reading was "niggardly" and her conversation was "too often of trifles." And although she understood the physical needs of her body, she sacrificed its care in her enthusiasm for other pleasures.[43] Next came Blaine Drake, speaking on "intellect." Then Don Thompson spoke on "relaxation," a concept that could be condensed in three words: "change of work." "Sleep if necessary," he advised them, but "never sit, just for the sake of sitting."[44]

The assigned topic for Bennie Dombar was "self-assertion," on which he was to assert his true self. In a sense he continued the sermon on persistence begun but left unfinished by his brother Abe months earlier. Work and art, he said, provide opportunities for self-assertion. Then, in an astute comment on what apprenticing with Wright meant, he explained that at Taliesin the apprentices are "free to grow and develop in enriched soil, free to assert themselves. . . ." Masters of old, on the other hand, "had a craft or a procedure which they inherited and which they, in turn, transferred to their apprentices, individuality not wanted nor respected."[45]

In what might well have served as a chapel talk, Marybud Lautner offered a further perspective on being an apprentice at Taliesin. She had been away for a spell, and her encounters with practices and values outside the Fellowship led her to say that those at Taliesin "should be forever grateful to Mr. Wright for the privilege of belonging to the Fellowship." Being an apprentice, she said, puts things into the right perspective, for at Taliesin life "is really life, with no chance of stagnation." Yet, having been at Taliesin for nearly two years, she felt that she had been only an apprentice to being an apprentice, that she and others had not yet attained the idea of the Fellowship. A real apprentice, she said, "is one who is able to put selfish interests aside for the good of the whole because he has learned to see life as a whole, one who gives of the best there is in him rather than give way to emotions about his petty feelings. . . . So there are sacrifices to be made and hardships to be endured, but they are of such a nature that are a challenge and exhilarating rather than depressing defeats." Indeed, "to be an apprentice to Mr. Wright is worth any amount of sacrifice because everything done is worth doing."[46]

The chapel service led by Bennie Dombar was the last one reported in "At Taliesin." There are stories about other Sunday activities, but no mention of sermons and other morning events at the chapel. The freshness of what had occurred in the chapel most likely wore off, and more important, the apprentices, having begun to play a larger role in Wright's studio as commissions began to come in, had less time for them.[47]

## FELLOWSHIP CRISES

Had Jack Howe been asked for a "postscript sermon," he might have delivered one on "Crisis." That was the subject of his "At Taliesin" piece in early 1936, a piece that captures the essence of the Fellowship in the mid-1930s. He began by stating that if he were ever to write the story of the Fellowship that would be the title, for the Fellowship was born due to a crisis and ever since it had been in a series of crises. But those facts accounted for the "fresh, radical (of the root) pioneering group" that they were. Without the continual crises caused by emergencies, they might have become "merely academic and, therefore, just another educational institution."

The crisis that caused the Fellowship's being, Howe said, "was America's need for indigenous culture; the youth of America are beginning to realize that culture comes first by way of the natural scheme of things and that otherwise we are merely automatons, machines or encyclopedias." The crisis, as we have seen, brought disillusioned university students to Taliesin "to work with the architect of the machine age where architecture has a new and broader meaning, and we speak of 'architecture' as life itself."

Concerning emergencies, the most obvious but least important included "pushing cars up the icy front drive, pulling wells, hauling wood, draining radiators, cooking and catching chickens." The apprentices, Howe said, were their own heating and lighting system, transportation system, water and sewer system, church, theater, and entertainment. There was always the need for wood, coal, kerosene, gasoline; for painting, staining, roofing, waxing, washing, sweeping, firing, plowing, cutting, cooking, cleaning, hauling, and pumping—always pumping. But these were not the important crises.

The really important crises, and certainly the most interesting, are such things as finishing the theater in time for the first performance . . . ; quickly building interesting rooms to house the new apprentices who are to come in a few days; spring plowing and planting; perpetual anti-weed wars; building the new spillway and repairing the dam, washed out last spring (a real engineering job); staying up nights to finish house plans for a frantic client; and last but not least came the big emergency for 1935—building Broadacre City for the Industrial Art Exposition in New York City. On all these emergencies we concentrate all of our effort as a kind of symphony orchestra, with Mr. Wright at the helm (or as conductor, if we must have complete parallel).

In short, everything that catapults us out of the ever-present menace of routine, keeping our minds alert and fresh and ready to tackle each new situation clearly—this is the crisis welcomed at Taliesin.[48]

# 13 EACH DAY AN EXCITEMENT

AT TALIESIN THE MOON IS CAUGHT NAPPING. IN ANOTHER HOUR WORK BEGINS ON THE ROAD, IN THE FIELDS, AND IN THE STUDIO. THIRTY OR MORE APPRENTICES AT TALIESIN WHO ARE PART OF THE FELLOWSHIP UNDER THE LEADERSHIP OF FRANK LLOYD WRIGHT (YES, HE IS ALSO BREAKFASTING AT THE SAME TIME) HAVE WIPED SLEEP FROM THEIR EYES AND ARE ABOUT THEIR BUSINESS WHILE CITY FOLK ARE STILL DREAMING.

DURING THE DAY WORK IS CONDUCTED IN SPONTANEOUS FASHION UNDER THE SUPERVISION OF THE "CHIEF OF THE FORTNIGHT." . . . THERE IS NO ROUTINE OF WORK. EACH DAY IS AN EXCITEMENT, AN INDIVIDUALITY ITSELF.

**—EUGENE MASSELINK**

The weekly chapel services may have ended, perhaps unceremoniously, but that did not mean the end of the Fellowship's mental, spiritual, and social activities. Indeed, they flourished, for, as Gene Masselink explained, "the idea of culture and belief in organic architecture . . . [were] the central line upon which the Taliesin Fellowship is built." That central line inspired a variety of activities.[1]

## THE TALIESIN PLAYHOUSE

The only events open to the public were presented in the Taliesin Playhouse on Sunday afternoons, where residents from surrounding communities joined the apprentices, the Wrights, and Taliesin employees for programs planned by the apprentices. The programs might include a screening of "Pathe News, a Walt Disney 'animation,' and some famous feature pictures, selected with discrimination from the best the movie world, not only in America but in Europe, has to offer." The playing of good music and an interpretive talk by some chosen member of the Fellowship would round out the afternoon.[2]

Movies played a singular role in the cultural lives of the apprentices. In addition to showings open to the public, they were frequently shown for the apprentices also on Saturday evenings. Almost every "At Taliesin" column concluded with an announcement of forthcoming films as a way of inviting members of the community to attend. Randolph Henning lists 113 different ones in the Film Index in his book, and the number mentioned in the columns but not included in that book no doubt matched or exceeded that number.[3]

The apprentices were proud of the place that films played in their lives. One of them noted that at the end of the first year of showings in the Playhouse they had seen films from Russia, France, Germany, England, Japan, and Norway.

And of course from Hollywood, but Hollywood seems rather shallow after seeing the Russian films. Most of the foreign films have been beautiful, particularly the Russian. Instead of lavish, rococo extravaganzas—or fool-proof stories—guaranteed to rouse every emotion of every individual until his or her emotions are numb—

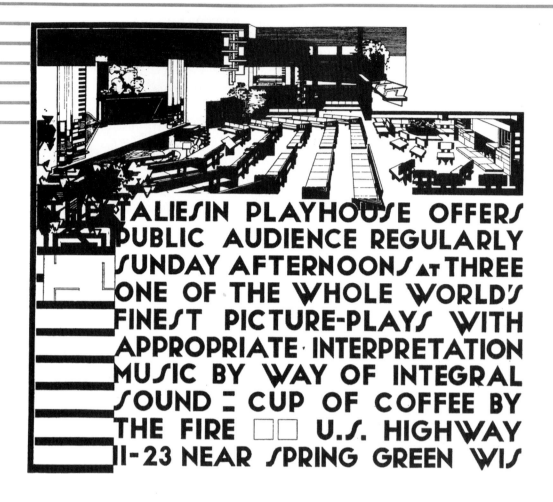

TALIE/IN PLAYHOU/E OFFER/
PUBLIC AUDIENCE REGULARLY
/UNDAY AFTERNOON/ at THREE
ONE OF THE WHOLE WORLD/
FINE/T PICTURE-PLAY/ WITH
APPROPRIATE · INTERPRETATION
MU/IC BY WAY OF INTEGRAL
/OUND = CUP OF COFFEE BY
THE FIRE □□ U./. HIGHWAY
II-23 NEAR /PRING GREEN WI/

This advertisement appeared in the *Capital Times* and on a three-foot-square panel at Taliesin. Courtesy of the Frank Lloyd Wright Foundation

however dumb—we have beautiful pictures sensitively made, charming, subtle and always concerned with real life . . . . And so we have learned more of the life of other countries from these interpretations than we could have learned in less than a lifetime of residence there.[4]

Almost two years later Gene Masselink recalled how two months of work had transformed the gymnasium of the Hillside Home School into the Taliesin Playhouse. That this was the first building completed at Hillside bears witness to Frank Lloyd Wright's concern for the cultural growth of his apprentices, as well as his own interest in the cinema and his desire to reach out to the communities surrounding Taliesin.

In the winters of 1934 and 1935, the Playhouse had been closed while the apprentices were in Arizona, but when it reopened the crowds increased as anticipation of what was showing grew. Sweden, Japan, Ireland, and Czechoslovakia were added as sources for the films. The apprentices and their guests from nearby places became observers and critics of the work of Sergei Eisenstein (Russian), Alexander Korda (British), Carl Dreyer (German), and other notable directors.[5]

## MUSIC

While visitors were welcomed and appreciated, the apprentices themselves played notable roles in enriching and illuminating the cultural life in the Fellowship. For example, Ernest Brooks, an accomplished pianist, thrived in his role as Taliesin's musician-in-residence. He collaborated with another apprentice, violinist Yen Liang, in performing Beethoven sonatas.[6] To add to the appeal of his performances, he and others planned a series of musical evenings to illustrate the work of great composers through history, to be presented at two-week intervals.[7] Brooks's performances could be lighthearted and highly entertaining, as he described in this column:

Last Sunday I perpetrated a bit of fun . . . playing Edward Ballantyne's piano variations on the tune "Mary Had a Little Lamb," in the styles of several "representative" composers, namely, Mozart, Beethoven, Schubert, Chopin, Wagner, Tchaikovsky, Grieg, and MacDowell.

I listed the compositions contrary to the order of playing so the audience might judge the composer's styles independently and mark their choices. . . .

A tabulation of correct judgments . . . turns up the information that there were two perfect scores of 25. Eighteen were correct on Schubert, Wagner, and Grieg; 15 on Chopin, 14 on Tschaikovsky; 12 on Mozart and MacDowell; 11 on Beethoven.[8]

Edgar Tafel, a fellow apprentice reported, returned from New York with some lovely new piano music by Schubert,[9] and Tafel himself wrote about playing at a chapel service, at which "Ernest Brooks came alive and surprised everybody by playing—beautifully—a Bach organ prelude and fugue. . . ." Tafel noted that there is "an almost endless amount of fine church music that is available for the more stereotyped and solemn service," but that the Fellowship had been trying to have a more varied musical program "suited to the spirit of the Chapel gatherings."[10] Yet Brooks's performances of Bach were appreciated. Philip Holliday observed that he not only played preludes and fugues by Bach, one or two each Sunday, but that he gave his fellow apprentices a rich perspective on them.[11]

Although Brooks left Taliesin several months later and references to music appear less frequently in "At Taliesin" pieces, other apprentices, such as Tafel, and later, Curtis Besinger, Bruce Brooks Pfeiffer, John Amarantides, Susan Jacobs Lockhart, and Effi Casey, among others, maintained the place of music in the life of the Fellowship. From time to time, guest artists performed, and occasionally musicians would be identified as "in-residence" for periods of time. On July 4, 1935, for example, the Fellowship welcomed a trio from New York City as artists-in-residence, led by pianist Anton Rovinksy, "well known as soloist in orchestras in many large cities," who would take charge of activities in music that summer. He brought with him "some ancient instruments such as the spinet and gamba d'amour," to be used at Sunday programs in the playhouse.[12]

Several weeks later an "At Taliesin" contributor, possibly Frank Lloyd Wright, stressed the importance of music in the life of the Fellowship:

The Fellowship has, more than ever, been hearing great music this summer, not only in concert in the living room at Taliesin and in the Playhouse, but in rehearsal when music comes up from beneath the eaves or through the vines and walls that enclose it within the spaces of Taliesin. Music makes the life within those spaces more completely an enriched unity and Taliesin plans to continue and develop its relation to the finest chamber of music by its own performances.

The life expressed in music has a depth of form and line and even patterned surface by way of the movement that the walls and roofs of Taliesin make with the hill and the buildings at Hillside as well as upon their gentler slopes. Music in graphic terms is made also by way of the many plans and the drawings and models of executed buildings and buildings being designed in the studio. . . .

Taliesin's walls sing. They speak naturally. Great music belongs to them as organically and intrinsically as the more humble materials of which they are built.[13]

In the summer of 1937, Wright invited Wesley LaViolette, a composer in the School of Music at DePaul University, to spend a month at Taliesin; with him were George Perlman, a pianist-composer, and a string quartet from Chicago. They performed at teatime and on Saturday and Sunday evenings. Although they played works from the standard chamber-music repertoire, they also read manuscript compositions and presented new works.[14]

**THEATER**

Theater, an art form that thrives on collaboration as a genuine communal activity, was another favorite among the apprentices. When Paul Beidler wrote a short play it was produced under the direction of Nicholas Ray.[15] Gene Masselink wrote about apprentices writing the script and the accompanying music for *Piranesi Calico*. Apprentices built the sets and rehearsed it for production in the playhouse.[16] While the theater claimed significant portions of apprentices' time, one might conclude from the newspaper columns that, in a larger sense, Taliesin was a stage, that the shaping of the Fellowship was a grand theater production, that Frank Lloyd Wright was the director, and that the apprentices were the technicians, designers, producers, and performers.

**VISUAL ARTS**

Specific references to the visual arts are less frequent in the columns, but given architecture's predominant place at Taliesin they were certainly not slighted. Occasionally guests would exhibit their art at Taliesin, but the apprentices themselves were artists as well, engaged in painting, sculpture, and weaving. Many of their experiences in the visual arts, as well as in the literary arts and in discussions of current issues, occurred at teatime or at the Sunday suppers with the Wrights. They looked forward to these occasions as "a time when mutual appreciation and understanding of great works of art may continue from yesterday's tea or new creative endeavors may be brought into discussion. One day it is the Japanese prints of Hiroshige or Hokusai that draw our interest," wrote Charles Edman "and perhaps 16th century Momoyama Japanese silks are brought out to keep company with the prints."[17]

In October 1934, Gene Masselink reported that a large group of visitors, along with the Fellowship, had seen an exhibition of Japanese prints hung in the Charles E. Roberts room by Bob Mosher and Jimmy Drought under the supervision of Mr. Wright. The prints, he continued, "looked splendid on the freshly-painted walls and were hung in groups of three according to their series. . . . If exhibits like this which will appear from time to time are worth a trip from Madison to see (some forty people thought so last Sunday) certainly our close neighbors in Spring Green should take advantage of the opportunity. . . ."[18]

Japanese prints made a profound impression on some of the apprentices. Burton Goodrich, for example, wrote about having worked as a steamfitter in ragged clothes during the day and in the evening reading Mr. Wright's *The Japanese Print*. It is a short book, and he read it through. When the lights went out he lay awake with thoughts provoked by what he had just read and pondered what a "real civilization" meant for him and others and where the evidence exists for such a civilization.[19]

In 1936 a distinguished visitor, Marya Lilien, arrived at Taliesin. A practicing architect in Poland, she quickly integrated herself into the life of the Fellowship and was persuaded to stay for a while. She saw that in the working community Wright had created, his young charges learned not only from him, but also from each other. The beauty of Japanese prints captivated Marya Lilien as it had others, but there was beauty also in other experiences. After describing the feast they had enjoyed on Thanksgiving and Mrs. Wright's role in making the celebratory event true to Taliesin tradition, she continued:

And in this beautiful atmosphere among pine branches and chrysanthemums as if growing out of interior architecture—there came to us the romance of Japanese prints—told by our Master. Mr. Wright has this wonderful manner of giving his most profound thoughts in a conversational tone. They seem so natural—in fact, I think every great thought is natural, only it takes a great mind and creative imagination to formulate it and show it to people.

But this story told how the great collections of Japanese prints, being now the nucleus of various great American collections were mostly gathered by Mr. Wright while he was building the Imperial Hotel in Tokyo. . . . Early in his work Mr. Wright was impressed by the skillful simplifications, by the depths of its vegetable colors and profound knowledge of rhythmic expressive line. . . .

And in the low beautiful Fellowship dining room with pine branches overhead and yellow chrysanthemums [around us], dramatic and picturesque scenes, past and present, passed before our eyes; each of them seeming to have itself the colors and designs of a Japanese print, as Mr. Wright was telling how the hoarded cases and boxes in Japanese court circles finally got open after centuries to show their contents and to tell him and the world their illuminating story. And [thanks to Wright's work] find a final resting place in the great museums of the world.[20]

## LEARNING FROM LECTURES

In the evening of the day that the Japanese prints exhibition opened, the Fellowship gathered in the Dana gallery for an event Wright called a "potpourri." First the apprentices listened to Wright discuss his Hollyhock house in Los Angeles and crowded around him to see "unnumberable photographs." Shortly, though, after a brief reminiscence of the romantic dream embodied in that house, Wright discussed criticism and critics, intending to give his listeners "a better conception of what constitutes valid criticism and authentic critics" than they had had before. He also promised four sermons for chapel services on modern commandments: Love, Sincerity, Determination, and Courage.[21]

In early August 1934 Wright spoke to apprentices on the interrelation of space and structure. After commenting on abstract drawings apprentices had given him that week, he turned to the design of the Unity Temple in Oak Park and its distinctive spatial features. Gene Masselink summarized the points Wright had made and concluded, "A little more discussion and the splendid lecture was summed up with the great principle of Louis Sullivan, [Wright's] Lieber Meister: 'form follows function.' Taliesin goes further to say, 'form follows function—out of the nature of materials.'"[22]

The following September Wright spoke to the apprentices about two unbuilt projects in California, the Doheny ranch and the Lake Tahoe cabins. After describing the projects and explaining the rationale behind each, Wright said that an architect's projects are never built, and that a half-finished, nearly ready drawing is always immediately built. "Each building is during the actual process of construction, an education in itself for that particular building, so that when it is finished, the architect knows how it should be done—not always the way it was completed."[23]

In October, responding to the apprentices' request, Wright talked about steel, reminding them of the properties that distinguish it from all other metals: "its ductability, rigidity, continuity, adaptability in welding, and, above all, its great strength." Also that there are problems in building with steel that have not been solved, including that combining it with glass doesn't work because of their different coefficients of expansion. Rust is a soluble problem, he said, but stainless steel is expensive because patent laws allow ideas that led to its development to be held from the public.[24]

Another Tuesday evening Wright lectured in the Dana Gallery, this time on glass, "a wonderful material medium in the hands of the sympathetic and organic architect." In his hands, wrote the columnist, "glass is the recessed and seeing eye of the shelter built for men—whether you see from within or without."[25]

## LEARNING BY OBSERVING

As important as these lectures were in the apprentices' learning, they learned also from observing Wright at work and experiencing life in his presence. Apprentices were aware that impressions beyond Taliesin were that they spent more time on agriculture than on architecture. Alfie Bush attempted to explain that they were trying to correlate their two lines of work: "[I]n our plowing and cultivating and raising of hogs and chicks we look at various forms, but not only that, we constantly study their forms and relationships by coming into constant contact with them." In that way, he continued, "we have a better conception of how to build for the country and . . . we can apply new forms and create new forms, based on nature's geometric patters as we find them in agriculture." Where else on earth, he asked, "would there be a better place to carry on form-research, and where else do they even consider this worthwhile? That is the difference between any architect of today and Mr. Wright."[26]

Responsibilities of daily life sometimes intruded on endeavors in architecture and the arts, as when muddy roads required apprentices to give vehicles a push. Here, as in so many things, Wright joins in the effort. Courtesy of the Frank Lloyd Wright Foundation

Hulda Drake is engaged in a typical apprentice activity: working on a model. Courtesy of the Frank Lloyd Wright Foundation

Some of the learning came in the making of models. Burton Goodrich observed that when visitors were shown into the model studio, they scrutinized and commented on any model that happened to be in the process of construction, but the nature of their remarks was frustrating, for it was the craftsmanship that held their attention rather than the architectural ideas. "This is so," he wrote, "in spite of the effort of the guide to stress the architectural and living side of the exhibit." That they saw and appreciated craftsmanship did not bother him, but he wondered whether they also saw the significance of the model and the craftsmanship it represented.[27]

With his architectural practice having been dry since 1928, Wright had little studio work for the apprentices to do. A few of them assisted him in drawing the designs for projects at Taliesin, such as the transformation of the Hillside gymnasium into the playhouse and the construction of the Hillside studio. Some apprentices were most likely engaged in assisting Wright in designing about a dozen structures based on the Broadacre City project. In early 1934 that began to change, slowly at first, but every sign of change created excitement among the apprentices.

### THE WILLEY HOUSE

On February 1 that year a writer reported that plans for the Willey House in Minneapolis were nearing completion. Three weeks later, on February 22, 1934, came word that "Mrs. Malcolm M. Willey is expected at Taliesin to confer with Mr. Wright on the final drawings for her house which is to be built this spring in Minneapolis." The ownership of the apprentices in this project is evident in a comment made a week later by Bob Mosher. He wrote that she had returned home with her new house plans and that "these drawings would later form part of an exhibition for theater patrons. This exhibition of our work is underway and is our leading activity at the present time."[28]

By May 3, Gene Masselink's model of the Willey House, the result of his "unfailing perseverance," was nearing completion. Apparently this was a collaborative effort, for on March 8, Hank Schubart had remarked on Bob Bishop's finishing the model for "Willey House Number One": "It is a beautiful little house and Bob's workmanship on the model is as his work generally is, splendid. Every detail has been handled with care, even to the lighting fixtures in the living room. 'Drama' it is and complete to the end of the last act."

"At Taliesin" columns continued to report on the Willey House: On June 28 "Three cheers filled the studio when a telegram was received telling of the breaking of the ground for Mr. Wright's design, the Willey House in Minneapolis. Dean and Mrs. Willey are to have a unique house mainly because of its utter simplicity and use of local materials. Brick comprises the major portion of the structure, used for interior walls and floors, as well as exterior walls. . . . Until the union saw the plans for the house we were afraid the building strike would cause considerable trouble. They then backed out shyly and the strike settled itself." On December 9, 1934, Bob Mosher conveyed good news from Minneapolis: "'Moved in yesterday. You have made another masterpiece. Thrilling beyond word!' came the wire from

Dean and Mrs. Willey. . . . This long low simple-lined dwelling is the latest completed work of the Taliesin studio. Complete, too, furniture and all. To Mrs. Willey go the laurels of the world's best client."

**MORE PROJECTS**—MORE WORK FOR APPRENTICES

In the next several years there were more projects and more clients. One was speculative in nature, as Wright prepared plans for small houses to appear in the inaugural issue of the Fellowship's own publication, referred to as a monograph and titled "Taliesin." An "At Taliesin" column dated August 30, 1934, summarizes Wright's intent with these houses and states that within them there must be inexpensive units for a kitchen, bath, and heating. The column also stated, "These units can be shipped to the building site at low cost. Around this the house is designed. The materials are brick, concrete, or prefabricated composition."

Involvement in the design of such structures no doubt appealed to the apprentices assisting Wright, but it also suggested a problem that Wright addressed in *Taliesin,* the Fellowship's magazine: "There is a bogey man, or bugaboo of small minds," he said, "that gets in the way of our Fellowship here and causes annoyances from the outside. It is the idea, wholly gratuitous, that the apprentice may become a little imitator of his master."

Some do say that a dominant personality like myself (thus I plead guilty to the soft impeachment) would oppress or repress the individuality of others: that unconsciously they would take on the Frank Lloyd Wright "Style" and that eventually a flock of little F.LL.W's would issue to plague the great superindividualities that now compose creative American Society.

Well, I repeat that I have long observed that those who had least individuality were those who worried most about it and, of course, needing it so much were most contented to have ever so little just so they could see it and feel it as their very own.

In the next place there can be no "little Frank Lloyd Wrights." They can't be made.[29]

Although in Wright's mind there was no reason to worry, the worry persisted in others throughout his years as leader of the Fellowship and beyond.

Eventually there were real projects to work on, and as the apprentices found themselves engaged in them there was apparently less desire, and no doubt less time, to write about Fellowship life. None of the larger, more impressive projects of the mid-1930s garnered as much attention as did the Willey house, but they did not escape notice either, particularly the Jacobs house.

In late November 1936, one of the apprentices assembled a "series of unconnected notes" on a lecture Wright had given to the Fellowship on the Jacobs house to be built in Madison. The Jacobs house, he said, was an effort "to build a small compact house with a modern sense of space or the sense of space that seems to me modern." The Fellowship, he said, was "endeavoring to face this reality called life, out of which must come a new 'pattern for living'—a term we can justly use for the organic dwelling place."[30]

Two months later Gene Masselink cited letters inspired by a short notice about plans to build the Jacobs house that appeared in newspapers across America. The letters came from New York, Connecticut, North Carolina,

Texas, Florida, Indiana, California, Pennsylvania, and Ohio, and one from Montevideo, Uruguay. If the apprentices wondered whether Wright's architecture was moving in the right direction, such letters as these must have been reassuring.[31]

Musing on the Jacobs house several months later, Bennie Dombar remarked that the idea for such a house had apparently been slowly growing for many years—an idea for room planning, for construction, for family growth, and for combining all of these into one. Because simplicity seems effortless and undeliberate, "the Jacobs House will at first appear to be nothing to write home about. . . . Just too simple, I suppose." But this house was "a great step with even greater possibilities."[32]

The roles of Bob Mosher, Edgar Tafel, Jack Howe, and Wes Peters in the building of Fallingwater, the house Wright designed for E. J. Kaufmann, are described in the next chapter. Here we simply note that upon Mosher's return to Taliesin he provided a succinct account of the siting and construction process on January 22, 1937. He portrayed the growth of the house, "as something in nature, a series of low cantilevered concrete shelves projecting out from the cliff-bank and projecting far over the waterfall itself." To the layman, Mosher wrote, "the Kaufmann house must be something strange, because it does not resemble any other kind of house, but like the boulders, streams and trees, the logic behind its conception is its reason for being."[33]

Earlier, Jack Howe offered a fascinating description of another Wright design: "God alone knows why the bees make up their honeycomb on the hexagon, but we do know why the Dr. Hanna house, Leland Stanford University at Palo Alto, is built by Mr. Wright on the hexagon unit and why any house might well be built on the same hexagonal unit." The reason: the use of the hexagon in a building eliminates sharp corners and creates a sense of spaciousness. The furniture also followed the honeycomb pattern. Howe concluded by asserting that, when finished, the Hanna House will not only be the most beautiful house yet, but also the most comfortable.[34]

This house was also the subject of much discussion among apprentices. In a January 31, 1937, column, Cornelia Brierly explained why bees found the hexagonal design of their hives to be essential: "The sociological structure of the bee hive demands a unit that is proportionately adaptable to the tremendous growth, expansion, and activity that flows on from one generation of bees to another, and so the bee selects a hexagon as its workable unit, a plastic unit with opportunity for continuity that is infinite and economy that is complete." After expounding on the virtues of the design, she concluded, "Because of the clarity of the conception which so well relates this California honey-comb house to the climate, locality and to the human activity of the Hannas, this home will inspire a great simplicity and freedom in living for its alert little family."[35]

Not surprisingly, the Roberts house, near Marquette, Michigan, also attracted attention. Known as Deertrack, the house was designed for Abby Beecher Roberts, Marybud Lautner's mother; her son-in-law, John Lautner, supervised its construction. Like all of Wright's houses, this was not a type house, nor a style house, wrote Lautner, but it was "an individual house in the country: designed and built for one woman with two servants. There is no house in the world anything like it." The primary aim was "to see what a beautiful living condition could be made for the individual on this particular site," a site that included a sand hill, a view of low hills crowned by cedars, and Lake Superior in the distance. The house, he remarked "unfolds out of the hills into a rhythmic, light, free space for living. . . . It is organic architecture, growing and living. Not existing in spite of, but because of a beautiful circumstance to live with a joy giving atmosphere that would enrich anyone's life." The house was planned, he noted, so that Mrs. Roberts could close it when she traveled, leaving a caretaker living in two rooms and the kitchen.[36]

## BETTER TIMES, BIGGER PROJECTS

As the nation's economy began to improve and as Frank Lloyd Wright's career continued its rebound, another big commission came his way: The Johnson Wax Company Administration Building in Racine, Wisconsin. On March 5, 1937, in his only known contribution to "At Taliesin," Wes Peters provided an account of its progress in terms that were surely instructional for his fellow apprentices. He began with a description of Wright's 1903 Larkin building in Buffalo, New York, and called the Johnson Wax building its lineal descendant. The Johnson building, Peters wrote, would probably never surpass the Larkin building, but "the two represent wonderful growth and development." The Larkin building was "primitive in its directness and straightforward strength: primitive in the sense of the radical—the 'root.' the stem, the spring whence starts the river." In contrast, "the Johnson building is civilization, civilization with all the beautiful significance that the word could—should—have. . . . No less strong for all its grace."

Peters was intimately acquainted with the building's structural details, and he describes them well, but his rapturous concluding paragraphs reveal his enchantment with the aesthetic appeal of the building:

Wonderful experience it is to see a great building like this grow. A building where once again after years of virtual disuse all the varying crafts known to man are called upon to really exert themselves in order to preserve a vast simplicity. Once again the master-builder is in control. Once again the various craftsmen look to him for direction in the weaving of a great fabric. . . .

Enough. Impossible to describe the infinite ramifications of simplicity inherent in this design. The significant fact in regard to the linking of the Larkin and Johnson buildings is this:

Were there but one we should have a remarkable building. With the two we have a "line"—a flowering of the one from the root of the other—the essential linking with the past, the prophesy of the future that is inherent in natural growth.[37]

## WRIGHT, THE APPRENTICES, AND THE ARCHITECTURAL FORUM

In late 1937 the members of the Fellowship had a new experience in working with Frank Lloyd Wright, as they helped him compile materials for the January 1938 issue of the *Architectural Forum*. Reports six years earlier of his demise as an architect were, in a phrase made famous by Mark Twain, "greatly exaggerated." Despite the distressing hiatus in his work in the late 1920s and early 1930s, Wright was producing again, and the *Architectural Forum* decided to devote a full issue to his new and unpublished work. Randolph Henning notes that of the thirty projects represented in the 1938 issue, fifteen were post-1930 projects. This publication, designed and written by Wright with the assistance of the Fellowship, he continues, "helped greatly to reintroduce Wright's emergence as the preeminent leader in the architectural world."[38]

The apprentices recognized that this issue of the *Forum,* as the first collection of Wright's recent work, was of signal importance. In addition to reviving interest in his architecture, it tacitly demonstrated the importance of the Fellowship in making his productivity possible. Every effort, wrote William Cheaney, "was devoted to making it as complete and significant as possible." Consequently, "Every apprentice was busy at his table in the studio, preparing plans, perspectives and elevations of buildings which Wright has designed in the last few years." The materials to work with were removed from filing cases and prepared for reproduction. Two secretaries worked long hours in typing the written material, and professional photographers "scurried over several states to get pictures of the houses and also did much work at Taliesin." Two young editors, he continued, who were sent to help Wright were worn to a frazzle. Telegrams and airmail communications came and went frequently.

According to Cheaney, Wright supervised and organized the effort "with characteristic energy and artistry." This included revising the usual format of the magazine, introducing constructive changes, and individualizing the number of the magazine by designing both front and back covers. The way he "tossed aside" publication difficulties "left the two young editors white at the gills." Wanting the issue to be more than a graphic presentation of his latest work, he gave it "a resounding foreword and sprinkled it with apropos quotations from Thoreau and Whitman" and included articles describing the houses shown and the principles working in them.

Besides doing these things, Cheaney continued, "Mr. Wright was ever busy in the studio—showing apprentices how to clarify drawings, doing decorations and revisions himself. He trekked over Taliesin in bitter weather to supervise the photographers." At a "breathless last moment" he managed to secure from custom officials plans and photographs of his work he had taken to the Soviet Union the previous summer. While Cheaney was writing about the work done by apprentices, Wright was in New York "checking up on the issue before it goes to press."[39]

Frank Lloyd Wright was never shy about self-promotion. At his elbow and in his shadow, his apprentices did not seem to mind.

# 14 BROADACRE ADVENTURES

For the last three decades of his life, Frank Lloyd Wright, moved by such sentiments as this, sustained his passion for a concept embodied in a project he called Broadacre City. His intent was to change the American landscape and, in so doing, to change the citizenry's ways of living and to save America. Although his architecture and writings had revealed the direction in which he was moving, Wright gave that passion its first full play in *The Disappearing City,* a manifesto denouncing the ills of cities and extolling the beauties of decentralized, small-town living. During these decades, British historian Lionel March observed, "Wright and his clients were building Broadacre City whenever and wherever the opportunity arose."[2]

## BROADACRE CITY—THE FELLOWSHIP'S PARALLEL CREATION

Wright published *The Disappearing City* in 1932, almost simultaneously with *An Autobiography* and preceding by only a few months the founding of the Taliesin Fellowship. Thereafter, Wright's parallel creations—Broadacre City and the Taliesin Fellowship—were marked by paradoxes. He acknowledged the Broadacre City paradox in *An Autobiography* with this enigmatic line: "The new city will be nowhere, yet everywhere." Decentralized but integrated by great arterial highways, this would be the "great metropolis of the future."[3] Of the Taliesin Fellowship paradox, he might have said, "The new community will be somewhere, yet everywhere." If he had had the resources, Wright mused, he and the young workers arriving at Taliesin to form the Fellowship "might have started Broadacre City right then and there, ourselves."[4] Those young workers, paradoxically, paid a substantial fee to be—as they saw themselves—the master's volunteers.[5]

## THE BROADACRE IDEA

Broadacre City was not a fantastic utopian scheme. Rather, it grew out of Wright's experiences in the 1920s and even earlier, and inspired him to conceive a better way of life for America.[6] Having been much on the move in the 1920s, frequently in automobiles for long excursions, Wright gained insights into the nature and vastness of the American landscape, coast to coast. Given his agrarian roots, it is not surprising that crowded cities were repugnant to him, as he grasped their inhuman character and judged them to be places where individuals could not flourish. There was in the city, he wrote, a "parasite of the spirit," a "whirling dervish in a whirling vortex."[7]

Wright's prototypical conception of Broadacre City called for communities four square miles in size, populated by 1,400 families. Everything in each city—the buildings, highways, parks, and roads, as well as its management and control—was designed to provide convenience and safety in all the resident families' activities of leisure and work. Everything was to be coordinated with everything else. All social institutions, including schools, would be decentralized. Warehouses would be conveniently located and housing costs kept low. Low-cost factories, farm cooperatives, and artists' centers would be essential to the communities' operations. Controlled traffic systems, using highways and flying machines Wright called "aerotors," would make it all possible.

Broadacre City families were to own an automobile and to have an acre of land to build and live on. There was a strong political and social emphasis in Wright's idea, but he insisted this would not be socialism. There would be no upper class, no proletariat. Enlightened democratic citizens would be directed by the only aristocrat: the architect.[8] They would live according to slogans such as those displayed on posters in the 1935 Broadacre exhibition. Stated as negations, these slogans included, among others:

| | |
|---|---|
| NO LANDLORD | NO TENANT |
| NO POLITICIANS | NO ACADEMICIANS |
| NO TRAFFIC PROBLEM | |
| NO POLES | NO WIRES IN SIGHT |
| NO DITCHES ALONGSIDE ROAD | |
| NO SMOKE | |
| NO RADIO OR BILLBOARD ADVERTISING | |
| NO SLUM | NO SCUM |
| NO RAILROADS | NO STREETCARS |
| NO PUBLIC OWNERSHIP OF PRIVATE NEEDS | NO PRIVATE OWNERSHIP OF PUBLIC NEEDS[9] |

## BUILDING THE BROADACRE MODEL

Even though the principles remained constant, the Broadacre City concept evolved through the years, as it played an important role in Wright's desire to develop his new building design, that is, Usonian houses. Its suffusion into the life of the Fellowship contributed to its evolution. Part of its moving into maturity in its third year of existence involved building a model of Broadacre City. Work on the model began in November and continued intensely until its unveiling in April 1935 at the Industrial Arts Exposition at Rockefeller Center in New York. The work had begun at Taliesin and was completed at La Hacienda, the desert resort at Chandler, Arizona, owned by Alexander Chandler, the man for whom Wright had expected to design San Marcos in the Desert.

The first mention of the model in an "At Taliesin" column was on December 9, 1934. Bob Mosher asserted that Wright's treatise on the decentralization of cities had become extremely vital, and Washington was slowly realizing its importance. Early in 1935, he continued, an important exhibition in New York would present "Taliesin's pattern for a New America in the form of [a model for] Broadacre City." Attempting such a project, that is, building the model, in less than a year's time would be futile, "were it not for the fact that much already has been designed—contained in most of Mr. Wright's work in recent years." Broadacre City, he insisted, "is not dreaming nor is it planning ahead of the times. If America were up to the times, the times wouldn't be going down hill."[10] The next day an anonymous columnist wrote:

Daylight gave us Wisconsin in a sharp pattern of black and white, ushering in nature's rest time, winter. Forced inside and drawn closer to the great fireplaces we gather to work each day in the studio on the Broadacre City model. An imaginary landscape is taking shape in plywood. The courses of rivers and the forming of lakes which were first determined by the sweep of a pencil in hand are now being cut by the band saw. Plans and elevations in the flat are taking on physical form in balsa wood and cardboard yielding to the straight edge and sharp blades.[11]

On January 22, 1935, Bob Bishop wrote, "All Taliesin is humming with Broadacre activity," and he offered a detailed description of the model and the ways it demonstrated Wright's design and convictions.[12]

## TRAVELING TO ARIZONA

Early in 1935 the Fellowship was ready to forsake the beauty and the cold of Wisconsin to embark on a great adventure. The apprentices' anticipation had grown since the previous summer, when Wright first proposed a move to Arizona as a possibility. It heightened as snow arrived and persisted despite frequently frustrated plans. Starting thirty people in one direction, all at once, and keeping them going over ice and through mountains for almost 2,300 miles would surely test their mettle and determination.[13] "Even Ulysses and the children of Israel," someone wrote, "could not have left home and most of their possessions with more preparation, more excitement, and more prayerful anticipation than the Taliesin Fellowship when it leaves . . . for Arizona and the desert." A truck was loaded with canned fruit and vegetables, drafting tables, beds and bedding, tracing paper and drawing instruments— and barrels of sauerkraut.[14] After the truck's departure, according to the migration plan, ten cars would follow: "the Cord or Ford leading and then the various denominations: Fords, Plymouth, Hudson, Graham-Paige (Egyptian gray) and maybe one or two thrown in for good measure."[15] The date was January 23, 1935, with arrival at Chandler set for January 29.

The journey to Arizona was an adventure, made the more so by the Fellowship's skimpy travel budget. That budget, of course, would have been far skimpier if Wright's friend and soon-to-be client E. J. Kauffman, the department store magnate, had not underwritten the cost of constructing the model with

The first of the Fellowship's migrations to Arizona began on January 23, 1935. Here the travelers gather at the Parson & Hocking Meat Market in Dodgeville to load provisions. Kneeling in front of Mrs. Etta Hocking, her mother, and Mr. Hocking are Bennie Dombar, Iovanna Wright, and Jim Thomson. Next to the Hockings is Bob Mosher, and behind him are Mrs. Wright and Mr. Wright (wearing a beret). Courtesy of the Frank Lloyd Wright Foundation

a check for $1,000. On the way west, one of the cars broke down in Iowa, and those who stayed with it had to spend the night in "a sort of 'flop house.'" They dined along the way in Lawrence, Kansas, with George and Helen Beal, who had been residents at Taliesin the previous summer. They were treated to a sumptuous luncheon at the home of Wright's friends Mr. and Mrs. William Allen White in Emporia; White was one of the most renowned journalists at the time. In Wichita, Mr. and Mrs. Henry J. Allen served them dinner in a prairie-style home designed by Wright about two decades earlier; Allen was a newspaper publisher and former governor of Kansas. The next stop was in Tulsa, where Richard Lloyd Jones, Wright's cousin, allowed them to spread sleeping bags and blankets on the floors of his 10,000 square-foot textile and glass-block home, Wright's last design before his architectural career dried up.

Traveling on winding roads, they were awestruck when they entered the purple mountains. Excitement heightened as they approached their destination. Gene Masselink described it as a "garden like none had ever seen" and a "desert like something [he] had never dreamed." After a quick stop in Mesa, eight miles from Chandler, all the cars of the caravan caught up with them, "with startling theatrical rapidity and there the truck which had proceeded was waiting."[16]

## WORK ON THE MODEL CONTINUES

Their new home, a resort called La Hacienda, was a rambling spacious building ideally suited for the work-life they were entering. The rooms, twenty-eight of them, faced an open patio and included a living room with piano, a large dining room, a kitchen, bathrooms and showers. There was an automobile court and a large patio. The nascent Broadacre model was set up in the center of the covered section of the patio. Drafting tables and workbenches surrounded it, and there the apprentices would work all day long, out of doors, in and out of the sun, "wearing shorts as if it were the hottest summer in Wisconsin."[17] A letter to the *Baraboo Weekly* by W. C. Schwanke, a carpenter from Spring Green who was to be "an advisor on construction," listed the twenty-five apprentices in Wright's traveling company; Mrs. Schwanke was also part of it.[18]

La Hacienda, at Chandler, Arizona, where the Fellowship lived and worked in the winters of 1935 and 1936. Courtesy of the Frank Lloyd Wright Foundation

Soon the apprentices were immersed in model work again. In an "At Taliesin" column dated February 24, 1935, Cornelia Brierly described the enterprise that brought them to Arizona and learning-by-doing experiences they enjoyed there:

In the courtyard of our Hacienda the master and his apprentices are working on the model of Broadacre City. . . . Because of the scale of the city (75 feet to the inch) we have learned to create methods of presenting flowers, vegetable gardens, wood lots. When the model is given to the public, the abstracted forms such as those of the wood lots can't mean so much to them as to the apprentice who evolved them. It is an exciting experience to create a landscape—to determine its orchards, fields of blooming clover, tennis courts, swimming pools, its reservoirs, its forests. We live in this future city. Speed in the shady lanes of its super-highway. Know the repose of its floating lake-cabins and when our backs ache and our eyes smart from bending over this finely detailed work we loose our pent up energies by romping in the grass of the courtyard.[19]

While work on the model was intense, the Fellowship found opportunities to interact with Mr. Wright, most interestingly on an automobile journey to Los Angeles to see his textile block houses built there a decade earlier and to delight in the always-changing scenery along the travel route. They also enjoyed picnics, overnight camping trips, and other excursions in the desert. Good times like those they had had in Wisconsin continued. For one of the apprentices, however, the good times did not last. According to Cornelia Brierly, Fred Langhorst, a charter apprentice, "could absolutely never get up [in the morning]."

And the reason was that he would stay up very late at night reading and drinking; . . . So Mr. Wright would always say, "Call Fred," and they'd call Fred. Well, one morning he got kind of disgusted. He said, "Go and get Fred and bring him in here." This was

(above) Apprentices gathered around the Broadacre City model. From left: Burton Goodrich, Edgar Kaufman, Jr., Blaine Drake, Benjamin Dombar, Abe Dombar, John Lautner, Jim Thomson, Edgar Tafel, Alfie Bush, Bruce Richards, Jack Howe, Karl Monrad, Wright, Will Schwanke (a Taliesin builder who accompanied the Fellowship), Gene Masselink, Bob Bishop, Bill Bernoudy. Courtesy of the Frank Lloyd Wright Foundation

(right) Edgar Kaufman, Jr., and Bill Bernoudy, looking at part of the Broadacre model, with Mr. Wright. Courtesy of the Frank Lloyd Wright Foundation

about 11 o'clock in the morning. So Fred came in and said, "You wanted to see me, Mr. Wright?" And Mr. Wright said, "Yes, Fred, you're wasting your time around here." "For Christ's sake!" Fred said, "Why didn't you tell me that a year ago!"

So then he put his chaps on and his Stetson hat and his whole paraphernalia, and his Indian blankets; and he got his dogs and got in his station wagon and left![20]

## RETURNING TO WISCONSIN AND EXHIBITING THE MODEL

On April 18, 1935, Gene Masselink reported that the Fellowship was preparing to return to Wisconsin and that "the Broadacre's model was declared complete on the last day of March." It was loaded on the truck and sent to New York City in the custody of three apprentices, to be exhibited, according to plan, from April 15 through May 15 at the Industrial Arts Exposition in the Rockefeller Center. There, according to *The New York Times,* 40,000 persons saw the model and the explanatory material during the month-long display. Next the model was exhibited in a gallery at the State Historical Society of Wisconsin for nine days.[21]

Blaine Drake and Bob Mosher load the truck for the return to Wisconsin; Hulda Drake is in the foreground. Courtesy of the Frank Lloyd Wright Foundation

From Wisconsin the model traveled to Kaufmann's Department Store in Pittsburgh, the hometown of Cornelia Brierly. Sent there by Wright to interpret the model and the ideas it illustrated, she later recalled that she had spoken to thousands of visitors every day and tried her best to explain Wright's ideas for decentralization, "which he felt was bound to happen with the increasing numbers of cars and trucks." This increase, he believed, made it necessary to start some long-range planning. After the Pittsburgh exhibition closed, Wright drove Brierly to the Corcoran Gallery for the model's next stop.[22] This exhibition was made possible with financial assistance from Mrs. Avery Coonley, for whom Wright had designed a house in Riverside, Illinois, almost two decades earlier.

In an interview in 1990 with Charles Aguar, a landscape architect and city planner, Brierly said that at the Corcoran visitors came by invitation only and included department heads, congressmen, and other government officials. They took their time and asked many questions. Engineers and transportation people, she said, seemed especially interested in Mr. Wright's highway proposals, for at the time most roads were narrow and unpaved. The interest these visitors showed and the notes they took led her to believe that the model "had a tremendous effect on the development of the later interstate highway system—even if what was built was not as far-reaching as Mr. Wright's ideas of separate lanes for cars and trucks, with a monorail in the center."

Aguar noted that planning for the interstate highway system had begun earlier, but that "Brierly was correct in crediting these exhibitions as having influenced the direction of development far into the future." Indeed, he continued, "no planning proposal has ever had as much exposure or influence as Wright's Broadacre City, due in large measure to the articulation crafted into the models and the quantity and quality of publicity generated through their exhibition."[23]

## BROADACRE INFLUENCE

The Broadacre influence was evident most clearly in Wright's own architectural work. As he applied the principles of Broadacre City in the designing and building of Usonian homes, he relied on members of the Fellowship to translate his ideas and drawings into concrete results. Moreover, the apprentices' involvement helped prepare them for careers in architecture, should they decide to leave the Fellowship.

In the meantime, though, there was another close-to-home consequence of the Fellowship's involvement in Wright's Usonian and Broadacre commitments. Writing in 1942, architecture critic Henry-Russell Hitchcock noted that as more and more commissions came to Wright after 1935, work on buildings at Taliesin slowed down. It is "an ironic indication of the success of the Fellowship that its own buildings are unfinished. For Wright has kept the members of the Fellowship so busy as real apprentices on major architectural commissions of all sorts that this remodeling on which they set to work in the dull years of the early thirties has properly been neglected."[24]

## BROADACRE CONTROVERSIES

The Broadacre City idea—and it must be called that, for Wright never considered it to be a plan—provoked controversy immediately. Some critics attacked it sharply, and others saw in it a valuable contribution to planning and building. The controversies lasted for decades, but as they continued, Wright developed further Broadacre ideas and principles in his work. Contributors to *Frank Lloyd Wright and the Living City,* edited by David De Long, provide evidence of this as they cite Broadacre influences in many of his built and unbuilt designs from the 1930s through the 1950s. Similarly, De Long and others find influences in the model for Broadacre City in Wright's unbuilt projects of the 1920s. "It would be naïve to claim Wright's unbuilt schemes of the 1920s as perfect," according to De Long, "or even as fully workable," but he considered it fair to identify Wright "as the first major architect to address issues of suburbanization and the automobile with such detailed proposals." Moreover, that he "grasped their larger potential became clear near the end of the decade, when he more fully confronted larger questions of the American city." Perhaps living in Los Angeles, De Long surmises, stimulated his attention.[25]

Vernon Swaback, who lived and worked in Wright's communities from 1957 to 1979, first as an apprentice, then as a senior fellow, refers to Taliesin and Taliesin West as Wright's "micro-communities." They served as places for his "exploration and commitment to his own expression of the Broadacre City ideal." Wright's critics, Swaback says,

dismiss Broadacre City as being too simplistic to be worthy of consideration, and his followers inflict unintended harm by focusing on its details rather than seeing it for the deeper exploration of relationships between democracy, nature and habitation that Wright intended. The unhelpful believers are those who offer a literal interpretation for every model and sketch. This does nothing but prompt others to criticize what they see as lacking in cultural or ecological diversity or point out that the model shows inadequate parking, which leads them to judge that Wright greatly underestimated today's traffic volumes.[26]

Another former apprentice, Paolo Soleri, whose tenure was much shorter than Swaback's—about eighteen months in 1947–1948—and who was expelled from the Fellowship by Wright, brought the perspective of an unbeliever to questions about Broadacre City in a 1992 interview:

That's the big, big, big, failure of Frank Lloyd Wright. . . . That's a tragedy, more than a failure. That's my position there. Well, because it encouraged, it glamorized the notion of the single home. The single home, the family home. And the spread out, the two-dimensional spread out, and consumerism. There's nothing as consuming as suburbia. It's an engine for consumption, colossal engine for consumption. So—I'm sure that if Mr. Wright was alive now he would have changed his rationale about Broadacre City.[27]

### ON THE BRINK OF NEW EXPERIENCES

The Taliesin Fellowship, having matured further through the Broadacre experiences, caravanned to Arizona again in January 1936, making some of the same stops as in 1935 and, by rising early and traveling late, traversing over 2,200 miles in four days. Again they stayed at La Hacienda. Their assignment this time was to produce models of what the interiors of Broadacre City houses would be like.[28] By the end of April, with no major accomplishments to their credit, they returned to Wisconsin. There the Fellowship continued to evolve as Wright gained two career-saving commissions—and perhaps those commissions also made possible the continuation of the Fellowship.

The "At Taliesin" columns appeared less frequently and, with the excitement over life in the new community supplanted by experiences that did not lend themselves to the kind of revelations that gave the earlier columns their luster, it was allowed to expire without mourning or fanfare. The last column, December 24, 1937, was a review of *Architecture and Modern Life,* by Wright and Baker Brownell, a Northwestern University professor. The reviewer, Charles Poore, who wrote the review for the *New York Times,* had no connection with the Fellowship.

Frank Lloyd Wright's new work allowed him to loosen Taliesin's hold on him, at least physically. Additionally, fearing that another bout of pneumonia like he had suffered the previous winter would recur, he honored his doctor's orders and left for Arizona on Christmas Eve, 1937. Plans were underway for the Fellowship to follow early in 1938. This migration had long-lasting consequences. Another chapter in the Fellowship's history had begun.

### FRANK LLOYD WRIGHT'S PUBLICATIONS ON BROADACRE CITY

■ Scholars trace the roots of Wright's idea for Broadacre City to his article, "Plan by Frank Lloyd Wright," *City Residential Development: Studies in Planning* (University of Chicago Press, May 1916). It began to take fuller shape in six lectures, "Modern Architecture, Being the Kahn Lectures," given at Princeton University in 1930 (Princeton University, 1931).

Wright's first full treatise on Broadacre City, *The Disappearing City* (New York: William Farquhar Payson), appeared in 1932. His article "Broadacre City" [*American Architect* 146 (May 1935): 55–62] consisted almost entirely of pictures of the large model and separate ones of buildings designed for Broadacre City. Elaborations on the Broadacre idea are found in *Architecture and Modern Life,* written collaboratively with Baker Brownell (New York and London: Harper and Brothers, 1937).

In the next decade Wright self-published explanations of Broadacre City in "The New Frontier: Broadacre City" (*Taliesin* 1, no. 1. Mineral Point, Wisc.: Democrat-Tribune Press, 1940), and *An Autobiography: Book Six: Broadacre City* (Spring Green, Wis.: A Taliesin Publication). The latter, containing a clear expression of Wright's political and economic ideas, was written for inclusion in his 1943 edition of *An Autobiography,* but the publisher decided not to include it. Also in the 1940s he published *When Democracy Builds* (Chicago: University of Chicago Press, 1945), an enlarged version of *The Disappearing City* (from 91 to 131 pages, with photographs of the 1935 Broadacre City model).

In 1958, a year before his death, Wright published *The Living City* (New York: Horizon Press), yet another revised and expanded version of *When Democracy Builds.* The text is included in Bruce Brooks Pfeiffer, ed., *Frank Lloyd Wright: Collected Writings,* vol. 5 (New York: Rizzoli International Publications, 1995), 252–343.

# 15 LANDMARK BUILDINGS

WHEN WE WERE BUILDING EDGAR KAUFMANN'S HOUSE AT BEAR RUN, I HAD ONE OF MY ENTHUSIASTIC, FAITHFUL BOYS, BOB, "LITTLE SUNSHINE," ON IT ON THE USUAL APPRENTICE ARRANGEMENT MADE WITH EVERY CLIENT. "TAKE HIM AWAY," SAID E. J. IN DESPAIR AT AN EARLY STAGE OF THE PROCEEDINGS. "HIS BLUNDERS WILL COST ME MONEY. TAKE HIM AWAY!"

"NO, E. J.," I SAID, "NOT YET. BE PATIENT. HE MAY BE, AND HE IS, COSTING US BOTH A LITTLE MONEY, BUT NOT MUCH. YOU GAVE ME A THOUSAND DOLLARS TO HELP MAKE THE MODELS OF BROADACRE CITY. WELL, IT'S ONLY FAIR FOR YOU TO PAY YOUR SMALL SHARE OF THE EDUCATION OF THESE YOUNG FELLOWS–AMERICA'S FUTURE ARCHITECTS. IT IS FAIR, IF FOR NO OTHER REASON THAN JUST BECAUSE THEY ARE GIVING YOU AND ME, WHERE YOUR OPUS IS CONCERNED, SOMETHING NO MONEY CAN BUY: AN ALIVE AND ENTHUSIASTIC INTEREST IN OUR WORK AND THE EAGER COOPERATION THAT GOES WITH IT TOO, AS WELL AS THEY CAN."[1]

— FRANK LLOYD WRIGHT

Frank Lloyd Wright's career had been in a slump for almost a decade when a glimmer of hope for its revival appeared in 1933. The design of the house in Minneapolis for Malcolm and Nancy Willey provided that glimmer, but he waited in vain for phone calls or letters from additional prospective clients. He continued an active life, however, and garnered meager income as a writer and lecturer. More important, he devoted himself mainly to designing and renovating buildings at Taliesin and Hillside, and both he and Mrs. Wright were deeply engaged in sustaining the Fellowship's operations and shaping its purposes.

## E. J. KAUFMANN—CLIENT AND FRIEND

Wright's wait for a client ended splendidly in 1935, when E. J. Kaufmann, a department store magnate and civic leader in Pittsburgh, began talking with him about building a country home on land he and Mrs. Kaufmann owned about fifty miles southeast of the city. Kaufmann had a lifelong interest in architecture, and Wright and his work would be well known to anyone with such an interest. Moreover, his 24-year-old son, Edgar J. Kaufmann, Jr., having been captivated by Wright's autobiography while studying painting in New York, had begun a six-month apprenticeship in the Taliesin Fellowship in October 1934. He did not intend to become an architect, but he wanted to experience communal living and observe Wright close at hand. [Note: As in common parlance then, the father is identified here as E. J., or Kaufmann, his son as Edgar.]

While Edgar was apprenticing, his parents visited Taliesin, Wright's only home at the time. There the Kaufmanns began a friendship with the Wrights and may have conceived ideas for the country home they planned to build. Always financially impoverished, Wright never hesitated to pluck fruit from trees of friendship when he had the chance to do so, and Kaufmann had his first experience at being plucked when Wright asked him to support the building of the architectural models for Broadacre City, his big idea for saving American cities. Kaufmann obliged.

Stories abound about how it happened that the Pittsburgh merchant asked the Wisconsin architect to design his new home, as they do also about the relationship between the two men. A number of historians have collected the stories in fascinating books, and rare is the book on Wright that fails to give considerable attention to the house he named Fallingwater.[2] Franklin Toker, a historian of art and architecture at the University of Pittsburgh, published what aspired to be a definitive account of the building of Fallingwater, but Edgar Tafel and other apprentices who played a part in the designing and building of the house have challenged portions of it. Sorting through the conflicting versions of the Fallingwater story lies beyond the scope of this book, as does attempting to describe the building's distinctive architectural features. Moreover, the essence of Toker's account lies in the relationship between the principals, Wright and Kaufmann, summarized thus:

Over a period of twenty years E. J. Kaufmann and Frank Lloyd Wright seduced each other, loved each other, hated each other, and betrayed each other, now with one getting the upper hand and now the other. It is hard to imagine the often-buffoonish Kaufmann as the prime client of Frank Lloyd Wright's career, and still harder to take in what Kaufmann's support did to launch Wright on one of the great comebacks in art history. That comeback was remarkable not only for its chronological precision— exactly the five years that Wright prophesied from his humiliation at MoMA in 1932 to his triumph at Fallingwater—but even more for its completeness. The 1938 reviews of Fallingwater in *Time, The New Yorker,* and elsewhere conceded to Wright nothing less than the title of greatest architect of the century.[3]

## WRIGHT'S APPRENTICES AND FALLINGWATER

Looking back at the demands and threats issued by Wright and countered by Kaufmann, and at the delays and the problems with contractors, engineers, and consultants at the building site, one wonders how the project avoided being scuttled at some point along the way.[4] But both men were determined to keep it going, and Wright's apprentices played a large part in making that possible. They demonstrated that the Fellowship really was a working community, even though much of what they did was done offstage, so to speak, and therefore in anonymity.

There is nothing particularly unusual about that, for yet today architects employ assistants whose work attracts attention only when it is defective and whose names are typically not publicly associated with the designs they help produce. But there is a difference: Wright's apprentices, at least those who persisted in the Fellowship, saw themselves as members of his extended family. His conduct with them was in many ways paternalistic, and he thought of the Fellowship as his family, but unlike proud fathers in bloodline families, he was disinclined to grant credit publicly for the assistance they offered. Yet, the work done by Wright's apprentices can be well understood by reviewing the course of events resulting in the design and construction of Fallingwater.

With the rapport established at Taliesin in November 1934, and with the ideas for projects they had discussed in mind, it seemed natural for Wright to visit Kaufmann in Pittsburgh. That he did on his return to Taliesin from a mission in New York. After discussing the possibility of having Wright design an office for him in his store, Kaufmann took his friend to Bear Run, the site he had in mind for his country home. Wright had a remarkable capacity for absorption, and he left Bear Run with images of the setting fixed in his mind. But he needed something tangible, as well, so he asked Kaufmann to send him a contour map of the site, locating every boulder and large tree. At this point, Donald Hoffmann remarks, "Kaufmann had become more than a client. He was a patron."[5]

## BROADACRE MODELS AGAIN

Meanwhile, Wright and his apprentices were engaged with the exhibition of the Broadacre models in New York. At Wright's request, Kaufmann paid for transporting them there. Using a small convertible that belonged to Kaufmann and a Taliesin-owned truck, Kaufmann's son, along with apprentices Edgar Tafel and Bob Mosher, took turns driving as they carried the models across the country. Characteristically, Wright sought both publicity and clients in New York. When the exhibition in New York closed, the models traveled to Wisconsin, but the senior Kaufmann arranged for them to be displayed in an exposition called "New Homes for Old" on the eleventh floor of his department store in Pittsburgh. The exposition was open from June 18 to June 29. His son was one of the Broadacres' interpreters. Kaufmann was delighted by the response to the exhibition: "Howling success. Miners, mill workers, white-collar workers deeply interested; few architects during the first week; few of the upper crust. Second week—more architects, plenty of upper crust. Exhibit closed in a blaze of glory."[6]

## PLANS AND PROGRESS ON FALLINGWATER

In subsequent months Kaufmann and Wright jousted, through the mail, over when Wright would produce drawings for the Kaufmann office and sketches for the country home. Mixed in were questions over fee schedules and projected costs for construction of the home, and when construction work could begin. Wright's answers were, at best, hazy. Engaging a local contractor who would be acceptable to both Wright and Kaufmann required frequent back-and-forth consultations.

Wright worked fastest and best when there were forces concentrating his mind on work to be done. A critical force presented itself on August 26, 1935, when Kaufmann notified Wright that he would be in Milwaukee on business the following month and that he intended to come to Taliesin from there. Various apprentices differ on precisely when Wright began making definite drawings for the house that became Fallingwater. Blaine Drake recalled that it was immediately after they returned from Bear Run in June; he had been Wright's driver on that visit. Cornelia Brierly remembered that Wright made sketches early in the morning of September 22, 1935, before Kaufmann called to say he was leaving Milwaukee and would arrive in Spring Green within hours.[7] Edgar Tafel and Bob Mosher believed that Wright did not begin to make the drawings until he received Kaufmann's phone call.[8] The facts of the moment make little difference, for what Kaufmann saw, Donald Hoffmann has written, "proved to be a remarkably complete presentation of the house as it was built." Wright, he continued, had "conceived the house with an awe-inspiring finality," for "behind the pencil in his hand stood imagination as disciplined as it was free. . . . He sometimes spoke of Fallingwater as if it had been inevitable, and almost easy."[9]

Also inevitable was the fact that Tafel and Mosher would sketch more elevations while Wright and Kaufmann were at lunch. Kaufmann returned home excited about what he had seen and, according to his son, spent "quite some time at Bear Run showing just where the various rooms would be . . . and we are all anxious to see just what the house really will look like."[10] For Tafel and Mosher, their experiences with Fallingwater that morning foreshadowed what was to come. Along the way, other apprentices joined in Fallingwater tasks. For example, Blaine Drake worked on some of the drawings, and Mendel Glickman (who was not an apprentice but a longtime participant in Fellowship activities) and Wes Peters played important roles in making structural calculations and preparing blueprints and construction specifications.

With Wright at a drafting table are three apprentices who played key roles at Fallingwater: Bob Mosher, Edgar Tafel, and Wes Peters. Behind Wright is John Lautner. Chicago History Museum. Photographer— Bill Hedrich, Hedrich-Blessing. HB-04414-W

## CONSTRUCTION, COMPLICATIONS, AND CONTENTIOUSNESS

Initially, Abe Dombar, who had recently left the Fellowship and was working at Kaufmann's store, was to oversee construction of the house. When that arrangement did not work out, Wright selected Bob Mosher, who had earned a degree in architecture at the University of Michigan, to replace him. His journey to Bear Run began in the company of Wright and Edgar Tafel at the end of May, several days after the Fallingwater drawings were completed. Also with them was Manuel Sandoval, a master craftsman from Nicaragua who was to execute Wright's design for Kaufmann's office. They arrived in Pittsburgh on June 5, after driving first to Buffalo, New York, to see the Larkin building and the house Wright had built for Darwin D. Martin.[11]

As the resident supervisor, Mosher encountered one complication after another as building progressed. Some involved matters of design; some had to do with site and construction details, some of them calling for redesigns and correcting construction errors; some concerned managing the contractor and workers and dealing with experts in engineering Kaufmann consulted, regarded by Wright with dismay as an unwarranted intrusion; and some resulted from the understandable intrusion of E. J. Kaufmann and Edgar at points along the way and the resulting conflicts with Wright. Although Mosher handled many of the complications effectively and gained a sense of exhilaration from doing so, he was compelled to make some decisions that lay beyond his authority or competence. That meant seemingly countless letters and telegrams to and from Wright.

Exchanges between Wright and Kaufmann were frequent and contentious. In one of them Wright mentioned that Bob Mosher was working under his direction on the details necessary to complete the work and that he would work with Hall, the builder. Further, Wright admonished Kaufmann that Mosher was not there "to adjudicate between owner and architect. He has no such power. He is there to interpret the architect's details and explain their intent and help get them executed. Any objection raised by the owner against these details come to the architect."[12]

Frustration in Wright built to the point that he sent a sharply worded telegram to Mosher:

DROP WORK AND COME BACK IMMEDIATELY WE ARE THROUGH UNTIL KAUFMANN AND I ARRIVE AT SOME BASIS OF MUTUAL RESPECT. YOU ARE NEEDED HERE. DO NOT DELAY ONE HOUR AND BRING ALL PLANS YOU CAN GET. IF YOU HAVE NO MONEY DRAW ON ME FARMERS STATE BANK.[13]

Although Kaufmann expressed regret that Mosher was being called back, he acknowledged that Wright's action was beyond his control. Kaufmann recalled Mosher's departure in poignant terms: "Bob, with the help of the family, packed his two shirts, his one pair of work pants, two sweaters—we could not find his socks and his work shoes—and reluctantly put on his first Pittsburgh outfit for traveling back home. We all stood at the gate and waved him goodbye. It was not an easy moment. . . ."[14]

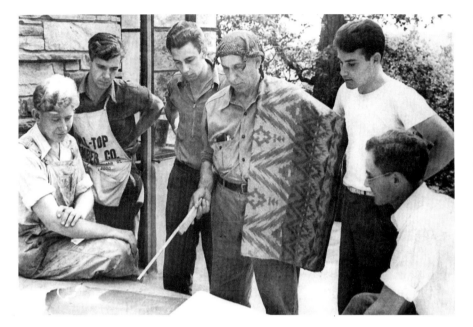

Walter J. Hall, Fallingwater's builder, with members of his crew. His grandson believes the Indian blanket over his shoulder mimicked the cape Wright frequently wore. Courtesy of the Art Institute of Chicago and Ray Hall

More exchanges between Wright and Kaufmann, and several involving the contracting builder, Walter Hall, about whom Wright had learned from an apprentice, followed. Work continued without a replacement for Mosher, even as Mosher had worked earlier without a builder. With the work falling far behind schedule, Wright sent Edgar Tafel to take charge. He arrived at Bear Run on October 7. Later that month Wright came to evaluate the construction progress and to bring Tafel back to Taliesin. However, having observed several cracks in the structure, he returned without Tafel, allowing him to stay at Fallingwater until the end of November. The cracks were an early indication of more severe ones to come, and dealing with them multiplied the complications for the builder and particularly for the architect, who had been stricken by a serious case of pneumonia.

When Wright recovered sufficiently to involve himself in problem solving, he had more conflicts with Kaufmann. By the end of 1936, Hoffmann noted, "the shell of the new house on Bear Run languished under a palpable shadow of doubts. It had been a long, hard year." But despite the trouble, Hoffmann continued, "all the mistakes, delays, lapses in communication, angry outbreaks and ominous signs of structural distress, Kaufmann sustained an extraordinary optimism, somehow greater even than Wright's."[15]

## WRIGHT AND FALLINGWATER IN THE NATION'S SPOTLIGHT

On its own merits, but also because of Wright's remarkable power to attract attention to his work, Fallingwater gained national attention. In March 1937, before the building was completed, the *St. Louis Post-Dispatch* published a portrait of Wright, with Jack Howe standing at his side, and Wright's rendering of his masterwork, in color. The house itself was completed that year, and the January 17, 1938, issue of *Time* magazine featured Wright in its cover story; Fallingwater provided the background for the cover portrait of Wright. *The Architectural Forum* devoted its January 1938 issue to a third Wright retrospective, which included pictures of Fallingwater. (For the apprentices' role in assembling and editing this issue, see Chapter 13.)

## COSTS AND FEES

Many finishing touches, including those related to furnishings, remained to be done. The servants' wing and guest suite were built on the hillside behind the house in 1939. Another finishing touch of interest to readers in the twenty-first century concerns the cost of building and furnishing such a distinctive house. For the house the total came to nearly $75,000 by the end of 1937. In the next four years completing various details and making changes in hardware and lighting added $22,000, and the servants' wing and guest quarters yet another $50,000. For all this, Wright's fees came to $8,000.[16]

## CLIENTS AND ANOTHER SIDE OF WRIGHT

The apprentices working with Wright, whether at Bear Run or in Spring Green, saw one side of Frank Lloyd Wright as an architect and as a person. E. J. Kaufmann learned much about another side of Wright that earlier clients already knew, described by Hoffmann:

Wright would be slow to send drawings of sufficient detail, stingy in supervision, prone to make minor changes, loath to accept blame for mistakes, slippery in promising solutions, quick to take offense, and even quicker to give it. He also would be shameless in pressing for additional fees, whether or not any were due, and in soliciting outright gifts of cash. But in defending the integrity of his imagination, of what he called "the honor of the work," Wright would attain magnificent stature. The building as a work of art, conceived in rebellion against disorder and all that was mediocre, meant everything.[17]

## A NEW CLIENT—THE S.C. JOHNSON & SON COMPANY

As Fallingwater progressed, another big project arrived in Wright's studio: designing and building a new administration building for the S.C. Johnson & Son Company, manufacturers of wax and paint, located in Racine, Wisconsin. Herbert F. Johnson, known as Hib (his given name was Hibbert before he changed it), was the president and the grandson of the company's founder, Samuel Curtis Johnson. Although he had no particular design in mind for a new building, he wanted something significant as his company approached its fiftieth year of operation that reflected its completely American image.

For Wright, the story of the Johnson Wax project was as dramatic as the story of Fallingwater. It required collaboration between the 37-year-old Johnson, who presided over a well-established family company, and the 69-year-old Wright. In his autobiography, Wright described how it came to be: "When the sky at Taliesin was dark and the days there gloomy, . . . Hib and Jack were the ones who came out to Taliesin to see about that new building. They came, you might say, like messengers riding on the white steeds trumpeting glad tidings." Jack was Jack Ramsey, the company's general manager, and "that new building" was the one the company needed as a result of its growth. Also present was William Connolly, the company's advertising manager.

Ramsay had been skeptical about engaging Wright, but he changed his mind after hearing what a key person in a group of art directors who had recently visited Taliesin had to say. E. Willis Jones, who was working for a Chicago advertising firm in which Johnson's brother-in-law was a partner, urged them to consider Wright to be the architect for the new building. A young architect named Howard Raftery, Wright recalled, had "put up a sacrificial fight for Taliesin." That led to an official visit by Johnson and his compatriots in July 1936. When word of the impending visit spread, Edgar Tafel recalled, the "apprentices went to work: windows were washed, the grounds raked, floors cleaned and waxed, the vases were filled with foliage." When the visitors arrived, Wright showed them around and the apprentices served them an elegant lunch.[18]

The visit was successful. Wright called it a "gratifying annunciation." The "occasion," he continued, "was pleasant all around."

Next day came a note from Hib enclosing a retainer (one thousand dollars) testifying to his appreciation of what he saw on that occasion. And, the pie thus opened, the birds began to sing again below the house at Taliesin; dry grass on the hillside turned green, and the hollyhocks went gaily into a second blooming. The orchard decided to come in with a heavy crop of big red harvest apples and the whole landscape seemed to have more color; Iovanna rode more fiercely through the Valley; and both Olgivanna's responsibilities and mine were doubled—with smiles. Work was incessant. Taliesin galvanized into fresh activity.

## REALIZING THE "GRATIFYING ANNUNCIATION"

Johnson abandoned the plans already drawn up by a local architect and gave the commission to Wright, who described himself as "an architect held back outside the current of building for seven years." He was on the road back to architectural work and exulting in being there:

So I now look back upon that visit—July 20, 1936—with a deep and pleasant satisfaction, never ceasing to be glad that I have for friends the two men who came to see me that day.

What a release of pent-up creative energy—the making of those plans! Ideas came tumbling up and out onto paper to be thrown back in heaps—for careful scrutiny and selection. But, at once, I knew the scheme I wanted to try. I had it in mind when I drew the paper plant at Salem, Oregon, for Editor George Putnam, which he had been unable to build. A great simplicity.[19]

When Wright was given the commission his apprentices were elated. This was their first "big, solid commercial project!" It meant work for them and justified their confidence in Wright. Several days later, according to Tafel, some of the apprentices drove to Racine to meet the Johnson Wax staff and see the plant. Johnson and Wright, he observed, "seemed headed for a close friendship and working relationship." Back at Taliesin, Wright and the apprentices worked night and day for ten days preparing the sketches. When they returned to Racine, Tafel put the roll of plans under his arm, planning to follow Mr. Wright into the building. But Wright, he said, "took the roll from me and said, 'The architect carries his own plans.'"[20] As the project developed, Johnson no doubt became a familiar figure to the apprentices.

The apprentices recognized that building the Johnson Wax Administration Building was particularly important for Wright, as it gave him the opportunity to move beyond building houses; the income the project provided also meant much to them. That an advertising executive was in on the planning at this early point meant that Wright's building would be extensively and well publicized—and it was.

Wright was less contentious in dealing with Johnson than with E. J. Kaufmann, concurrently his other major client. The good beginning no doubt helps to account for that. In an August 18, 1936, letter dealing with construction details and costs, Johnson added a reassuring note: "I am completely sold on you as an architect. Your work is tremendous. Can I show the plans to people? I already have shown them to a few."

**PROGRESS AND IMPASSES**

If some saw Wright as hard to get along with, what they meant, he wrote, "was hard to *go* along with." But for Johnson and his coworkers, he was "never too much for these boys," even as the cost went up with features added to the design. Ongoing dealings were smoother, as well, given the relative ease with which Wright could go to Racine and Johnson to Taliesin. Wright estimated that over a period of two years, in all kinds of weather, he made about 132 automobile trips to Racine, a distance from Taliesin of 165 miles. His purpose: to get the building built the way he wanted it to be built. Accomplishing that was attributable in large part to the builder, Ben Wiltscheck, whose good work Wright valued highly.[21]

That does not mean that construction of the building was without complications. They came principally from having to deal with strong unions in Racine and rigid Wisconsin building codes, but there were also maddening delays. One of them resulted from an impasse with the Wisconsin Industrial Commission, which, according to Wright, would not say yes to the plans and did not say no. The impasse was broken when Wright and Johnson agreed to conduct tests as the building progressed.[22]

At issue were the dendriform columns designed to support the ceiling, roof, and mezzanine. As designed, they were expected to support twelve tons each. The commission estimated the maximum weight they could bear would be five tons. In a well-publicized demonstration, Wright had one of the columns built, and on June 4, 1937, about one week after the concrete for it had been poured, workmen began to place bags of sand in a wooden ring on the top. At twelve tons the inspectors were satisfied, but with a large crowd on hand, including reporters, photographers, and two carloads of apprentices from Taliesin, Wright ordered more weight to be added. At sixty tons the column began to show cracks, and Wright called for it to be pulled down. When the top of it landed, it broke a drainpipe ten feet underground. The Industrial Commission granted permission for construction to proceed.[23]

## MAJOR ROLES FOR WRIGHT'S APPRENTICES

The good progress notwithstanding, toward the end a case of pneumonia suffered by Wright threatened to slow things down. That is when his apprentices, who had been in on the project from the beginning, proved to be invaluable. Many worked behind the scenes, some of them no doubt assisting with the drafting of the plans, but three, in particular, played major roles: Jack Howe was the chief draftsman, charged with taking Wright's sketches and turning them into elevations, presentation drawings, perspectives, and working plans. Others probably assisted him, with the final touch always being his—subject, of course, to erasures and redrawings by Wright. Wes Peters was the structural engineer, working closely with Mendel Glickman. In these days of computer-assisted design, it is good to be reminded that their instrument for calculating everything was a slide rule. Peters made weekly trips to Racine. Edgar Tafel, the on-site supervisor, lived there temporarily. His role was especially important in seeing that things were done right. On one occasion, while Wright was recuperating from pneumonia in Arizona, Tafel traveled by train to meet with him out there.

Others were also directly involved. Bob Mosher, having been recalled by Wright from Fallingwater, replaced Tafel when Tafel was sent to take his place at Bear Run. Hulda and Blaine Drake and Gene Masselink built a large, detailed model of the Johnson building that could be separated into two parts, allowing observers to peer into the workroom it encased. Johnson initially seemed to want such a model but, concerned about the additional cost, said, "never mind." Wright wrote back, ". . . we will mind about the model." According to Jonathan Lipman, the model was valuable to Wright for refining the design.[24]

Wes Peters, Frank Lloyd Wright, and Herbert F. Johnson at the construction site of the S.C. Johnson Administration Building. Courtesy of the Frank Lloyd Wright Foundation

As construction progressed, the architect and builders and their clients faced a string of vexing problems relating to such matters as wiring, heating, cooling, lighting, and furniture design. The unusual nature of the building meant that they could not refer to precedents in solving them. Costs, too, were a concern. Calculated on a cost-plus basis, the cost of the building came to about $450,000, in addition to the architect's fee of $30,000.[25] But the building was built to Johnson's satisfaction, so much so that in 1937 he asked Wright to design a home for him—Wright named it Wingspread—and in 1944 the Johnson Research Tower. The apprentices' role in constructing these buildings was no doubt a continuation of their involvement in the earlier projects. When the Research Tower opened in 1949, Jack Howe, Gene Masselink, and Wes Peters were still playing key roles. Tafel, Mosher, and the Drakes had moved on, and new apprentices assumed responsibilities they had had. However, it is unlikely that the excitement that came with the Kaufmann and Johnson projects could be sustained. Besides, they had other projects requiring attention.

## INTERNATIONAL FOCUS ON THE JOHNSON BUILDINGS

As for the Johnson buildings, not only did they serve the company well, but they also accomplished the public relations purposes Hib Johnson had in mind when he asked Wright to be his architect. In 1979, Sam Johnson, the namesake of the company's founder, had succeeded his father as president. He explained what the building meant for the company. They became a different company, he said, "the day it opened. We achieved international attention because that building represented and symbolized the quality of everything we did in terms of products, people, the working environment within the building, the community relations and—most important—our ability to recruit creative people."[26]

## FLORIDA SOUTHERN COLLEGE

Wright and the Fellowship had additional extraordinary projects waiting for them in the 1930s. One with great long-term potential was hatched in the mind of Ludd Spivey, the new and aggressive president of a faltering college in Lakeland, Florida. On a trip to Europe, he had been inspired by a war memorial and returned to the United States with a vision: He would construct a campus for Florida Southern College in the orange groves of South Florida. He, like many others, was moved to action by reading Wright's *An Autobiography*. Apart from what he learned there, he knew little about Wright.

On April 1, 1938, he sent a telegram to Wright: "DESIRE CONFERENCE WITH YOU CONCERNING PLANS FOR GREAT EDUCATION TEMPLE IN FLORIDA STOP WIRE CONTRACT WHEN AND WHERE I CAN SEE YOU." Wright responded: "CAN YOU COME TO TALIESIN, SPRING GREEN, WISCONSIN FOR CONFERENCE. ARRIVING THERE APRIL 20TH."

When the two men met, a remark by Spivey revealed that he had something in common with Wright: "I have no money with which to build the modern American campus, but if you'll design the buildings, I'll work night and day to raise the means." Wright needed the money such a project would bring, and his respect for Spivey prompted him to visit Spivey's orange grove. There, he said, the buildings would rise "out of the ground, into the light and into the sun." Consciously or unconsciously honoring architect Daniel Burnham's dictum, "make no small plans," he developed a master plan calling for eighteen buildings, to be built of steel, sand (native to Florida), and glass (to bring God's outdoors into man's indoors). Work was soon underway, with groundbreaking for the hexagonal Annie Pfeiffer Chapel occurring on May 24, 1938. This building, with a seating capacity of 800, was dedicated on March 9, 1941.[27] Thereafter, building occurred only intermittently, as funds became available.

## PLEAS FOR PAYMENTS AND GRADUAL PROGRESS

One can imagine that through the years apprentices were as fully involved in the creation of these buildings as they had been in earlier ones, but it must have been hard for them to maintain enthusiasm for endeavors that were so far away and so often delayed for lack of funds. That lack of funds is evident in Wright's letters to Spivey, as he tried to find different ways to beseech him for payment. June 16, 1939: "And now my dear man—the disagreeable matter of money. Couldn't you manage to clean up the payment agreed

Kenn Lockhart was Wright's construction supervisor at Florida Southern College. To his left, facing FSC's president, Ludd Spivey, are Wright and Polly Lockhart. Courtesy of the Frank Lloyd Wright Foundation

upon in the signed contract for preliminary services?" March 29, 1941: "I hope you realize the significance to our work of your promise to send us $500.00 each month. The going is specially tough just now." July 30, 1941: "It distresses me to remind you of the fact but, as you are doubtless aware, we are many months behind schedule on payments of back fees . . ." January 15, 1942: "We are desperately hard up this winter and if you could borrow $500.00 more it would help us no end."

To this Spivey responded, January 20, 1942: "I am sorry to tell you that it is not possible for this college to send you any more money at this time. I do not even have the money to pay my teachers. . . . Just as soon as I possibly can I shall send you more money." Wright's response, February 5, 1942: "Cheer up! We are working on your plans and good luck to us meantime." But the beseeching resumed months later: August 31, 1942: "I can't and needn't tell you how we need money. And I am sure the small sum you sent represents much more in your situation than we realize."

In the meantime more buildings gradually followed: three seminar units (designed 1940, completed 1941); the E.T. Roux Library (1941, 1946); the Industrial Arts Building (1942, 1952); the Watson/Fine Administration Building (1945, 1949); the Waterdome (1945, 1949); the Minor Chapel (1954, 1955); the Science and Cosmography Building (1953, 1958); and the Esplanades, connecting the Wright-designed buildings (1946, with various completion dates).[28] In the initial stages Spivey tried to use students in construction roles, but that was ineffective. In 1946 Wright sent Wes Peters, along with newlyweds Kenn and Polly Lockhart, to oversee construction. The Lockharts were at Florida Southern until 1949, long enough for both of their children to be born there. At one point in these years Wright called them back to Taliesin, a maneuver to compel Spivey to pay what he owed, as construction could not proceed in Kenn Lockhart's absence.[29] As the above dates indicate, however, construction continued long after this, with only intermittent supervision by Wright's apprentices.

Ludd Spivey died in 1962. Since then, as Bruce Brooks Pfeiffer has noted, "the light has somewhat gone out of his architectural dream for Florida Southern. Many of the proposed buildings in the Frank Lloyd Wright master plan were not built, and most of the built ones were renamed and remodeled for other uses. Architects "unsympathetic to the rhythm and fabric of Mr. Wright's overall design" designed some new buildings on the campus. The harmony he envisioned in a group of homogeneous buildings was only partially and temporarily achieved.[30]

## APPRENTICES' PERSPECTIVE ON WRIGHT

In these years, while occupied with building Taliesin West and the major works described above, Wright also designed noteworthy residences for other clients. Although most of the work by apprentices on these projects was done in the shadow of Wright's formidable persona, it is possible to identify apprentice participation in some of them. For example, Bennie Dombar and James Thomson, who witnessed the signing of the handwritten contract for the Herbert and Katherine Jacobs Residence in Madison, Wisconsin, were designated by Wright to superintend the construction of the house and perhaps help with it. However, according to the owners, "Wright became so interested in the house that he virtually took over the supervision himself," adding that for some of the later houses Wright charged his clients a fee for the apprentices' superintending services and required that they be provided room and board.[31]

Among the many caricatures of Frank Lloyd Wright, one has him treating his apprentices and clients in a cavalier manner, sometimes even abusively. Many former apprentices and clients recall his conduct differently. He could be brusque at times, but at others he was delightfully considerate, and he often enjoyed having good times with them. For example, at the first in an annual succession of Taliesin parties at the Jacobs Residence, in early November 1938, Mr. and Mrs. Jacobs recalled, "the fellowship chorus produced roars of laughter from Wright with a parody of 'On, Wisconsin,'" which began, "Taliesin, Taliesin, good old shining brow. Run the pencil round the paper, try to please Jack Howe." They were aware that Howe was the leader of a group of apprentices who worked long hours "to transform Wright's brilliant imaginings into the complicated drawings and perspective for which [he] was so widely acclaimed."[32]

### APPRENTICES IN WRIGHT'S EXPANDING PRACTICE

Apprentices' work with other projects in these years was essential to Wright's practice. While some, such as Jack Howe, labored mainly in his studio, others have been identified as construction supervisors for residences he designed for clients in California, Michigan, Wisconsin, Illinois, Arizona, and Alabama.[33] As construction supervisor for the Rosenbaum Residence in Florence, Alabama, Burton Goodrich's role was distinctive, but so were the roles played by other apprentices in other locations. In all instances, the clients brought unique concerns and styles to working with the apprentices.

### THE ROSENBAUM RESIDENCE

A review of Goodrich's interactions with the Rosenbaums and Wright provides insights into the way the apprentice-supervisor system worked. In sociological terms, Goodrich's experiences in Florence can be seen as a case study, representative of the kinds of experiences other supervising apprentices encountered.[34]

Consider first Wright's practice of providing minimal details in the working drawings. For the Rosenbaum Residence the details ran to five pages, double-spaced. He wanted builders capable of grasping the nature of the structure and adept at discovering the details as the building went up. Work began on the house before Goodrich arrived, and the builder immediately encountered problems: The house was to have a heating system fueled by oil, but oil could not be acquired in Florence; some of the construction materials the plans called for were not available locally; the working drawings were not completed until late November; and by the time Goodrich arrived in early December the mild-weather season had ended.

Goodrich, who would be working closely with the Rosenbaums, had to learn how to deal sensitively with them and their interests. Because Stanley Rosenbaum's father was a local businessman—he operated the downtown

Burton Goodrich's infamous Bantam parked near the under-construction Rosenbaum House in Florence, Alabama. Courtesy of the Frank Lloyd Wright Foundation

theater—they wanted to use local union labor and buy materials in Florence; Goodrich thought the wages and prices were too high. To complicate matters, the Bantam automobile Wright provided for Goodrich had one operational problem after another. Even though he had been in Florence only a short time and in adverse circumstances, Goodrich was under pressure to move things along. Wright wanted him to drive to Milwaukee to take delivery on a Lincoln Zephyr, drive it to Des Moines, pick up the Dinky Diner—a small chuck wagon, a toy of Wright's—that had been abandoned there when the car towing it had broken down, and tow it over snowy and icy roads in the Midwest and on to Phoenix. Goodrich extricated himself from that assignment, but Wright told him to leave the job when he felt he was no longer absolutely needed in Florence.

In his first month Goodrich made little progress. The bids for construction were too high: $10,500. He got them reduced to $9,000. By the time Rosenbaum decided he would prefer electric heat to an oil-fired boiler, oil suddenly became available.[35] The weather turned bad. Goodrich's girlfriend left him for another apprentice. His heart dropped at this news. Whether it helped to have Wright say to him that the girl "is no loss" who had been taken into the Fellowship only for his sake, and that "she is really a dumb Dora where anything you are vitally interested in (above the upper region of your pantaloons) is concerned" is hard to judge.[36]

He spent weeks taking bids and working on contracts for materials, and when they found three days to get a crew to work, the temperature dropped again. The footings and retaining walls were not underway until mid-February, by which time Goodrich had been there for ten weeks. The Rosenbaums had already paid Wright $250 for his services. Half of that was to go to Wright, the other half for his living expenses. Goodrich tried to negotiate the weekly fee downward, but Wright would not bend. If Rosenbaum was honoring his part of the bargain, Wright said he would let up on him from February 15th forward, but, he wrote, "we cannot afford to deduct a membership for more than eight or ten weeks to get one little house built, Burt."

The authors of the book on the building of the Rosenbaum Residence offer this appraisal of the situation:

Wright could be imperious and blunt. His students lived for his praise and agonized under his criticism. The young apprentice [he was 28 years old, had been in the Fellowship five years, and held an architecture degree from the University of New Hampshire], evidently stung by the master's tone, confided in the client. Rosenbaum quickly wrote to Wright in support of Goodrich. "My wife and I both like Burt very much and we would certainly dislike losing him with the work scarcely begun. We would greatly appreciate it if you could see your way clear to let him stay here until he can see the thing through."[37]

Soon, though, Goodrich said he was preparing to leave, but before he could do that he had to take care of problems with the Wright-owned Bantam: replace a tire and install new piston rings. Without new rings it would burn forty quarts of oil in the 2,000-mile drive to Taliesin West. Before long the crankshaft broke and the main bearings had to be replaced. These matters aside, he was most disappointed that "this greatly desired experience of building [a house] is to be once again put off into the future." Realizing Goodrich's demoralization, Wright sent a response by telegram: "TELL ROSENBAUM WILLING YOU SHOULD STAY ANOTHER MONTH TO PUSH THINGS ALONG."

But progress continued to be slow, and Goodrich persisted in trying to solve problems, such as finding hardware that Wright specified and dealing with leaks that appeared during a period of heavy rain. As his departure approached, he was under continued pressure to send Wright "$12.50 each week," prompting him to remark, "No one is getting rich on this venture unless it is I, in experience." Not until late August was he able to say farewell to the Rosenbaums and their house, shortly after they had moved into it. The Bantam died in Terre Haute, Indiana.

Considering the many houses designed by Frank Lloyd Wright in these years, built and unbuilt, and the several other projects described here, it is natural to ask once again how he could produce so much. The Fellowship provides the answer: It was rewarding him—and its members—with big dividends.

# 16 THE DESERT CAMP

OUR ARIZONA CAMP IS SOME-
THING ONE CAN'T DESCRIBE AND
JUST DOESN'T CARE TO TALK MUCH
ABOUT—SOMETHING LIKE GOD IN
THAT RESPECT?

AND HOW OUR BOYS WORKED!
TALK ABOUT HARDENING UP FOR
A SOLDIER. WHY, THAT BUNCH OF
LADS COULD MAKE ANY SOLDIER
LOOK LIKE A STICK. THEY WEREN'T
KILLING ANYTHING EITHER, EXCEPT
A RATTLESNAKE, A TARANTULA, OR
A SCORPION NOW AND THEN AS
THE SEASON GREW WARMER. . . .
THAT DESERT CAMP BELONGED TO
THE DESERT AS THOUGH IT HAD
STOOD THERE FOR CENTURIES.
AND ALSO BUILT INTO TALIESIN
WEST IS THE BEST IN THE STRONG
YOUNG LIVES OF ABOUT THIRTY
YOUNG MEN AND WOMEN FOR
THEIR WINTER SEASONS OF ABOUT
SEVEN YEARS. SOME LOCAL LABOR
WENT IN TOO, BUT NOT MUCH.
AND THE CONSTANT SUPERVISION
OF AN ARCHITECT—MYSELF,
OLGIVANNA INSPIRING AND
WORKING WITH US ALL, WORKING
AS HARD AS I—LIVING A FULL LIFE,
TOO FULL, MEANWHILE.[1]

— FRANK LLOYD WRIGHT

Living mostly indoors at Taliesin, made necessary by the harsh and seemingly relentless winters in Wisconsin, was hard on the Fellowship and even harder on Mr. Wright. In 1937, at age seventy, he was vulnerable to respiratory illnesses and cheerfully followed his doctor's orders and his wife's urgings to spend winter months in the Arizona desert. Besides, he remarked, the Fellowship was an "outdoor outfit," and given the high cost of heating the buildings at Taliesin, it was cheaper to move to the Southwest. There they could find the room they needed, so much of it that they did not have to ask anything or anybody to move over. So it was there, inspired by the character and beauty of the site he had discovered twenty-six miles from Phoenix, across Paradise Valley, that they built a winter camp, beginning in early 1938.[2]

**DESIGNED FOR THE FELLOWSHIP**—BUILT BY THE FELLOWSHIP

Apprentices in the Taliesin Fellowship played integral roles in all of the community's endeavors, but it was building the desert camp that demanded the most of them and gave them much in return. That was appropriate, for the desert camp—as it was called until 1939, when, after some debate, it was named Taliesin West—was designed for the Fellowship. In Wisconsin, Taliesin had existed for decades before the Wrights made it the Fellowship's home in 1932. There the apprentices' labors were spent in adapting and expanding the buildings for the Fellowship's purposes.

Wright's autobiographical account outlines what building Taliesin West entailed: "From first to last, hundreds of cords of stone, carloads of cement, carloads of redwood, acres of stout white canvas doubled over wood frames four feet by eight feet. For overhead balconies, terraces, and extended decks we devised a light canvas-covered redwood framework resting upon massive stone masonry that belonged to the mountain slopes all around." In the initial building stages, the Wrights and their apprentices had no well, no heating, no plumbing, and no electrical power except for that provided by a portable, diesel-powered generator, manufactured in Wisconsin by the Kohler Company. Access to electricity provided by power companies did not occur until 1951. In 1960 the camp was connected to telephone lines; the single phone (Whitney 51141) was placed in Gene Masselink's office. Life may have been difficult in Wisconsin's wintry conditions, but there was no ease to be found in the primitive circumstances the Fellowship faced in Arizona.

## HARDSHIPS

The essential feature of the new camp was its stone masonry, referred to by some as desert rubble. It consisted of large rocks dragged from the mountainside and artfully held in place by concrete containing sand collected from the desert floor. Olgivanna, Wright recalled, thought "the whole opus looked like something we had been excavating, not building." It "belonged to the desert as though it [had] stood there for centuries." The difficulty for him and the builders was that they had to live in what they were building while it was being built. Weather presented other complications: Desert winds swirled around them. Thunderstorms over the valley, with winds carrying clouds toward them, required preparations "as though they were at its mercy out on a ship at sea." Shortages of funds were a nagging concern.

Toward what he considered to be the end of this never-ending building experiment, Wright recalled, hardships "were almost more than flesh and blood could bear. Olgivanna and I, living in the midst of a rushing building operation for seven years, began to wear down." Otherwise, though, "our Fellowship life went on much the same, Taliesin or Taliesin West—except that the conspiracy of Time and Money was a little less against us."[3] Income from the other projects of these years suppressed that conspiracy, at least in part.

## MAKING NECESSITY A VIRTUE

In designing and building Taliesin West, Wright made necessity a virtue. With his practice growing again, and with his apprentices increasingly equipped to assist him, he needed a large drafting room. Additionally, of course, he and Mrs. Wright and the members of the Fellowship needed shelters of some sort, a kitchen and a dining area, and places to maintain their communal living. At Taliesin they had a playhouse for movies and artistic performances, and they needed a place for similar purposes in their new location. All this had to be built from scratch. Designing and building occurred simultaneously, and portions of what was built were put to use as soon as their purposes became recognizable.

In designing houses and commercial structures, Wright had precedents for emulation or, as he viewed them, examples to treat with contempt and avoid. For Taliesin West there were no precedents, no examples. There was nothing like it in the world, nor would replicating or imitating it in other settings have been conceivable.

Bruce Brooks Pfeiffer has provided an apt description of the beginnings of this distinctive desert camp:

. . . Taliesin West was not planned as a group of buildings or little cabins, but as one opus set on concrete terraces, surrounded by massive low masonry walls. The very first sketches for the work were those that designated how the earth was to be moved and relocated to accommodate the design of the whole building in relation

The first structure at Taliesin West, under construction here, was a lean-to designed to serve as a kitchen and dining room, storage space, and temporary studio. Courtesy of the Frank Lloyd Wright Foundation and Cornelia Brierly

to the site. Blocked-off areas, in different colors, made clear how the terraces were to conform to the topography without taking away or bringing any additional soil for fill or excavations. The total plan was set very early in the design stages. Frank Lloyd Wright, in remembering his work on these first sketches, told us that the desert was like a revelation to him.[4]

## FEE-PAYING VOLUNTEERS

One can sense the contagious nature of Wright's inspiration as he described it and as it spread among the young and eager fee-paying volunteers in his working community. He explained it again in his autobiography:

The plans were inspired by the character and beauty of that wonderful site. Just imagine what it would be like on top of the world looking over the universe at sunrise or at sunset with clear sky in between. Light and air bathing all the worlds of creation in all the color there ever was—all the shapes and outlines ever devised . . . all beyond the reach of the finite mind. Well, that was our place on the mesa and our buildings had to fit in. It was a new world to us and cleared the slate of the pastoral loveliness of our place in Southern Wisconsin. Instead came an esthetic, even ascetic, idealization of space, of breadth and height and of strange firm forms, a sweep that was a spiritual cathartic for Time if indeed Time continued to exist.

Superlatives, he continued, "are exhausting and usually a bore—but we lived, moved, and had our being in superlatives for years. And we were never bored."[5]

The apprentices had neither time nor reason to be bored, for it fell to them to do the hard work required in translating Wright's inspiration into reality. Some of them had been doing that in Wisconsin, and continuing the work in the warmth of Arizona was a welcome change.[6] In the nature of the Fellowship, there were many comings and goings, and by 1938 only ten of the fifty-six apprentices Wright listed in his 1933 brochure were still members.[7] The ten included several who were indispensable to him, three of them for years to come: Jack Howe, Gene Masselink, and Wes Peters. Edgar Tafel stayed until 1941 and Bob Mosher until 1942. Some who joined in the mid-thirties also played important roles: John Lautner and Jim Thomson until 1939; Bennie Dombar and Blaine Drake until 1941; Cary Caraway until 1942; and Cornelia Brierly until 1946 and again from 1957 into the twenty-first century. Although at times Wright engaged local construction workers to keep things moving, particularly while the Fellowship was in Wisconsin, these and more recent recruits were Taliesin West's main builders.

## BUILDING AND LIVING IN THE DESERT

Initially, Mr. and Mrs. Wright stayed at the Jokake Inn in Scottsdale. The apprentices spent their nights in sheepherder tents, nestled in sleeping bags. The tents were scattered around the desert, typically close to desert washes. That put them in jeopardy when heavy rains caused the washes to flood, as sometimes happened. Shaped like pyramids, the tents were nine feet square and nine feet high at the center, supported by a pole.[8]

Experiences with desert living conditions inspired many stories, including one recorded by Mrs. Wright: One boy, as she called him, couldn't part with comforts he had known, so he bought an air mattress and a down-filled sleeping bag. Having failed to heed admonitions to secure his tent firmly to the ground, he should not have been surprised when the wind pulled it loose on one side and threw it over a palo verde tree. As he attempted to retrieve it, the wind rolled his mattress and sleeping bag across the desert for hundreds of feet. Searching for them by lantern light, the surprised apprentice finally found his mattress impaled on a cholla cactus and his sleeping bag, farther away, torn by cactus needles. "Having learned the bitter lesson," Mrs. Wright wrote, the apprentice "gave up the idea of sleeping on an air mattress. After three winters in the desert," she continued, "he knew everything about life in it and was hopefully warning others who also did not listen, and who in turn learned by experience."

To provide places for cooking, eating, drafting, and storage, the Arizona newcomers built temporary wood and canvas structures. Among them were "sleeping boxes" for Mr. and Mrs. Wright and Iovanna. Here, as in the sheepherder tents, chilly nights made sleeping bags essential. In one of her accounts of life in the desert, Mrs. Wright recalled her own sleeping-bag experiences: In cold weather, with the temperature sometimes falling to seventeen degrees, "there are just two difficult periods—one, going into the sleeping bag at night, and the other, getting out of it in the morning. Both periods are sharp and severe but they last only a few minutes."[9]

## MR. AND MRS. WRIGHT'S LIVING QUARTERS

Herbert Fritz recalled the evolution of the Wrights' living quarters: The sleeping boxes, he said, were placed on a concrete slab about thirty-six feet square. Each of the boxes was four feet wide, eight feet long, and six feet high. Thirty-inch mattresses left space on the long sides for closets about four feet long and twenty inches wide. The lower part of the structures' sides was built of pine boards, the upper of canvas. A fence about four feet high was placed between the boxes and the edge of the slab. In one corner the apprentices built a fireplace, using stones found nearby, and in the other a small closet with a chemical toilet. In 1946 this temporary structure, known as the Sun Trap, was demolished and replaced by another one, also regarded as temporary. Known today as the Sun Cottage, it, too, has undergone several rebuildings.[10]

**BUILDING PERMANENT STRUCTURES**

Other important work that first year included building the road leading to the camp and excavating for other structures—Cornelia Brierly remarked to Ann Whiston Spirn that "all we did that first year was dig"—and digging, too, must be included with the principal accomplishments of 1938.[11]

The drafting room was the first major structure in the camp. Before it was completed in 1939, according to Bruce Pfeiffer, drawings were done outdoors on brown butcher paper to reduce glare from the sun. The drafting room included a stone vault at one end for the safekeeping of Wright's drawings.

*(right, above)* Clearing ground in preparation for a road and construction. Courtesy of the Frank Lloyd Wright Foundation

*(right, below)* The drafting room under construction at Taliesin West. Courtesy of the Frank Lloyd Wright Foundation and Cornelia Brierly

At the other end was a kitchen area, with a large fireplace. The room, ninety-six feet long and thirty feet wide, served not only for architectural work, but also for dining, concerts, and communal gatherings. Because the room was open on the north side and covered only by white canvas stretched between the large redwood beams resting on the massive walls, the chill of winter days and nights must have shattered any illusions they might have had about perpetual warmth in the desert. Rain that found its way around and through the canvas panels forming the roof destroyed any notion that the desert was perpetually dry. Still, the drafting room held appeal for those who worked in it. When completed, John Howe recalled, that room, with Wright's office alongside, "were like ships in the desert. Their white canvas roofs, sections of which were raised to admit sunlight, gave them the appearance of being under full sail. The quality of light within the enclosed spaces was indescribable, ideal for drafting."[12]

Similarly, illusions they might have had while building the camp about when it would be completed could not survive very long. The project was immense, and its innovative and experimental nature gave Wright repeated opportunities to change what had been built and to continue with one new structure after another. In 1939 the apprentices built the Sunset Terrace; Wright's office; the kitchen; the Kiva, a windowless room used primarily as a theater; the Pergola, extending along the north side of the Studio; and the Loggia/Apprentice dining room.

## ALWAYS A WORK IN PROGRESS

Through these years and in subsequent decades, Taliesin West seemed always to be a work in progress, and its unfinished look remains yet today. Looking back in the mid-1960s, Mrs. Wright explained why this is so:

[Mr. Wright] was extremely interested in supervising the details of every building he designed for others, but not for us, at Taliesin, and he would declare proudly, "You know the shoemaker's children always go without shoes." So both Taliesins were inadequately taken care of in details. I would reprimand him: "We haven't finished this wing yet and you are already working on another one."

"Anybody can do that," he would say. "Anybody can finish it—I must sketch out new ones." And we continued to add wings, terraces, pergolas, theaters, even a restaurant.

. . . He liked to do everything with speed. Nothing should take time. Consequently the execution of details was conspicuously missing. "Taliesin West is only a sketch," he would say. "Someday you are going to finish it." And we are now finishing and perfecting it. His complete design for the development of Taliesin West will take us years to finish. . . .[13]

## BUILDING PROCESSES AND MATERIALS

Considering *what* was built at Taliesin West leads to another interesting story: *how* the various structures in the camp were built. Some who were there left records of their experiences. John Howe, for example, recalled how they made the temporary shelter of two-by-fours and Sisalcraft paper. At twelve feet wide and forty-eight feet long it was large enough to accommodate eight drafting tables, a piano, the wardrobes of the entire Fellowship, and the kitchen. All else, he said, "was under the sun and stars."

In that structure the apprentices made many of the drawings for Florida Southern College, and there they continued Taliesin's Sunday evening tradition of programs and performances. Indian blankets draped over cots provided seating for themselves and guests.[14]

Edgar Tafel, in *Years with Frank Lloyd Wright: Apprentice to Genius,* wrote little about Taliesin West, recalling mainly that the rough-sawn, undried redwood, painted brown and used for trusses, was handsome against the white canvas roofs and the sky. The climate caused it to shrink in all directions, however, twisting it and even exuding nails, eventually requiring replacement by painted steel.[15]

Herbert Fritz, Jr., who had worked at Taliesin as a high school student in the early 1930s, joined the Fellowship shortly before it moved to Arizona in 1937. At Taliesin West, he recalled, the construction of the camp "made use of materials we walked over"—rocks and sand from the desert. The massive walls were built by laying rocks into forms, smooth sides exposed, and shoveling almost-dry concrete around them. Small rocks placed above the large ones as needed helped hold the materials in place and enhanced their visual appeal. Moisture that seeped from the concrete onto the rocks was scraped and scrubbed away later. The walls were as much as two to three feet thick at the bottom, sometimes tapering to narrower widths at the top. The walls supported redwood beams that held the light canvas frames constituting the roof or uprights for window openings. When the walls were in place, the wood forms were removed and the nails extracted, to be used again.[16]

To Fritz and his fellow apprentices, the work of building Taliesin West was "an adventure and a game." Preferences determined the part each one played.

Some preferred placing rock in the forms—Bennie Dombar enjoyed that. Some preferred taking the truck into the desert to get stone and sand from the washes—Fritz Benedict and Gordon Sylander enjoyed that. Wes [Peters], Cary [Caraway], and Marcus [Weston] did the form building, the difficult work, then helped with the material placing. My job was pushing a wheelbarrow. . . . I was good at it, and became very strong, being able to push the wheelbarrow filled with rock or concrete up a plank runway to the top of a chimney. Usually one person pulled a rope fastened to the wheelbarrow axle while the other handled the handles. We all took pride in our work.

Peters, Fritz wrote, "greatly accelerated the construction time of some of these walls by promising the crew a dinner out if we reached a certain distance by a certain time."

## LANDSCAPING THE CAMP

Wright assigned another task to Fritz: landscaping the camp. He and his best friend, Rowan Maiden, took the stake truck into the desert and returned with prickly pear, cholla, and staghorn. The small root systems of these plants made them easy to transplant. Those with deeper roots, such as the

ironwood, palo verde, or mesquite, they did not attempt to move. They did transplant a saguaro "that probably weighed a ton" by using a sling made by Wes Peters and Cary Caraway. All the boys, Fritz wrote, "hoisted it into a vertical position with ropes." Fritz asked Wright whether it was good to bring so many cacti into the camp area, since that seemed to be unnatural in comparison with the surrounding desert. Wright called what they were doing "an organic enrichment to the environment," and that was good.[17]

## ON THE LIGHTER SIDE

Sometimes the hard work was interrupted by humorous episodes. Fritz described one such. Charles Samson, a Harvard graduate who apprenticed from 1936 to 1942, had been away for a spell, and when he returned he was eager to be useful. Dressed in new riding jodhpurs, boots, and a Stetson hat—he later became a rancher—he offered to help Mr. Wright and other apprentices stake out an area.

Mr. Wright handed him a ball of string to take to an indicated spot, and Charles started to run with it and decided to jump over a cholla cactus. (A cholla is like a giant sandbur, with spines about one inch long, with hundreds on each burr. Each spine has an end like a fish hook—it can hardly be pulled out of the skin without pliers. . . .) Charles didn't clear the plant. His seat and thighs were covered with cholla burrs. Wes and Cary spent the rest of the afternoon pulling spines out of Charles. But Charles laughed through it the whole time and through his tears.[18]

That was not the only time Samson found himself in a predicament. It has always been the custom in the Fellowship to begin work early in the morning, and he found it difficult to wake up at the appointed hour. One morning, needing to get construction started, Wright told Peters to "go and get Charles."

So Peters found him in his bed, zipped him up in his sleeping bag, put him in a wheelbarrow, and hauled him to the swimming pool. Then Wright said, "Well, throw him into the water," which Peters did, after unzipping the sleeping bag.[19] There is no record of ensuing words and events.

## LIVING AND LEARNING IN THE DESERT

Wes Peters seems to have participated in everything in the Fellowship's early days, while also attending to his personal needs. That meant, within a day or two after arrival, building a place to sleep. Looking back on those days, he recalled that he and his wife, Svetlana, the Wrights' daughter, built two sleeping boxes about seven or eight feet long. The boxes had wood covers protected by waterproofing and attached with hinges. During the day they kept "clothes, tools, and everything else " in the boxes. In the chill of the night they had to move that out again. The comfort level? "It was fairly chilly." Before long Peters designed and built a tent, a "pyramid with a central pole." Brown in color, it had a square, white fly with red corners that went over the top of it diagonally. "It was a beautiful, charming tent," he remembered, and they spent three additional winters living in it.

The desert, too, was a marvelous place, spread out like a great lake or ocean, with cloud shadows that played patterns on the desert floor.

For years and years it was simply a wonderful combination—of going and being in Wisconsin in the summer where there was this rich, flowing green pastoral environment; and then coming out to Arizona where there was a completely different type of beauty—pristine, clear, even crystalline hard type of beauty—it was a total contrast. And it was a great thing for young students to come and see and participate in the growth of buildings which were architecturally true individually to each different environment.

Although the apprentices worked hard day after day, Wright recognized the need for diversions. One afternoon, Peters recalled years later, he said they would all have a picnic at a special place. To get to the destination he chose, he and the apprentices had to travel over rough trails, including the one used to haul the rock to build the Roosevelt dam decades earlier. As Fritz recalled the ride, so rough was the single-lane road, cut from the sides of the mountain, that he became violently carsick. Yet, he said, it was beautiful beyond description. Their destination was a lake, where they encountered a lone person, who was perhaps the caretaker. He had two small boats, one with an outboard motor on it. He piloted them through a narrow passage in the lake, one boat pulling the other. Aboard was the entire staff—"everybody who was there was on it, including Mr. and Mrs. Wright." As they sailed through the passage they observed large, horizontal serrations in the rock walls that gave Wright an idea for giving the same appearance in the walls they would pour upon returning to the camp, and he showed the apprentices how to accomplish it. Doing so, Peters observed, "showed how creatively Mr. Wright adapted to a truly different environment, a totally different design."

## DESERT ROCKS

The method of construction used, with stones placed in forms and held there with poured concrete, was a matter of necessity, for the rocks were much different from the sandstone and limestone rocks found near Taliesin in Wisconsin, where quarrying was possible and the rocks could be trimmed to the shape desired. In Arizona, Peters said, the rocks had been "formed by volcanic action, or something like that." They were so hard that they were extremely difficult to cut. Trying to do so would shatter them. The apprentices went out and gathered rocks from the foot of the mountain—big flat ones they called "face rocks."[20]

Among the rocks at the base of the McDowell Mountains behind the desert camp were some large boulders, around four feet high and quite round, into which Hohokam Indians had cut distinctive drawings known as petroglyphs. Wanting to use the boulders as sculptures, Peters had the apprentices move them, using a tractor. They managed to place one boulder near the entrance by the vault, and another near stairs leading down to a decorative pool on the prow side of the complex. There they have stood in their original orientation for more than seven decades. "When the Indians come back 2,000 years from now to claim their land," Wright remarked, "they will note we had respect for their orientation."[21] The drawing on one of the boulders, an interlocking square spiral, was adapted to become the mark, or logo, for Taliesin and Mr. Wright.

## AN APPRENTICE'S RECOLLECTIONS

In October 1939, while the Fellowship was residing at Taliesin before its third winter migration to the desert camp, Curtis Besinger began his apprenticeship. At age 25, he was already a practicing architect with a degree from the University of Kansas, where he later taught until he faced mandatory retirement in 1984. His memoir of Taliesin experiences, *Working with Mr. Wright: What It Was Like,* reveals him as a meticulous man who had carefully studied Wright's work, and particularly the architecture of both Taliesins, before beginning his tenure as an apprentice. Upon arrival at each place he analyzed what he saw, not taking anything for granted or at face value. He intended to make the most of every experience offered while working with Wright during the years 1939–1943 and 1946–1955. Traveling with the caravan in the manner established in the migrations to Arizona in 1935 and subsequent winters, Besinger arrived with the Fellowship at Taliesin West in mid-December 1939. His recollections confirm that the desert camp was really a camp. Conditions were still strikingly primitive, and he acknowledged that he never managed to live in style or comfort in a sheepherder's tent.

The building projects for the winter of 1939–1940 included those begun the previous winter, such as the Wrights' living quarters. Here, too, desert masonry formed the exterior walls and the support for ceilings, and here, again, there were races among the apprentices while building. The "form builders" competed with the "pourers," that is, "those who went with the dump truck to the washes to get the coarse sand for the concrete; those who went out with the flatbed truck to gather face rock and rubble; those who

Roadside picnics like this one were common on the Fellowship's travels between Wisconsin and Arizona. Identifiable, from left are: Herbert Fritz, Fred Benedict, Grace Scacchiatano, Wes Peters, and Hulda Drake. Courtesy of Robert C. May and the Frank Lloyd Wright Foundation

ran the wheelbarrow to haul the concrete and stone up the ramps for placing in the form; those who placed the stone and concrete in the forms; and the person running the concrete mixer." Besinger wondered how all this could be accomplished without serious accidents.

Before the masonry walls were completed, work began on the canvas and wood elements in the living quarters. He was surprised to discover that although there were roughly drawn perspectives for the rooms they were building, there were no working drawings—none for these rooms or for any other part of the camp. Details, he recalled, "were worked out as construction proceeded."

In some instances, such as the "trusses" for the canvas superstructure of the garden room, the details had already been established in the construction of the office and the drafting room. But in other instances the apprentices either received instructions from Mr. Wright, perhaps a quick drawing on a piece of board explaining how he wanted it done, or, if this was not satisfactory, were asked to make some drawing for him to work on. These drawings, also done on wrapping paper, generally consisted of a plan and section, setting down the construction already in place and any other givens. . . .

In making these drawings, an experienced apprentice might make a proposal indicating how the work could be done, based on his understanding of what had preceded it. Mr. Wright might accept this proposal, he might make a few changes, or he might reject it and use the drawing only as a basis for his own study. Some of these drawings were very much worked over, erased, and re-erased before a satisfactory solution to a particular problem was achieved.

Even when construction was in place, "there was no guarantee that Mr. Wright would not make changes."

As was his wont, Frank Lloyd Wright decided in early February 1940 that the Fellowship needed a break, so he sent them to Los Angeles for an extended "overnight picnic." Some of the apprentices rode in a station wagon that pulled a trailer loaded with food, but most rode in the back of the stake truck, along with the group's sleeping bags and overnight bags. Wright, who was driven to the city in his Cherokee-red Lincoln Continental convertible by Herb Fritz, joined them and guided them around the city to see buildings he had designed: the Storrer house, some of the cottages on Olive Hill, the Barnsdall houses, the Ennis house, and the Millard house. Even if some of these places were unoccupied and locked, the apprentices managed to get inside. The apprentices spent an evening picnicking and drinking on the beach, and the next morning they went sightseeing on their own. Late in the afternoon they began their all-night ride back to the camp. Wright was not there when they arrived, so they had a day to recover before continuing work on the living quarters.

Taliesin's stake truck, used for transporting goods and, as for the trip to Los Angeles, members of the Fellowship, who tucked themselves in sleeping bags in cold weather. Sometimes they traveled in it overnight. Courtesy of the Frank Lloyd Wright Foundation

Toward the end of that month Wright pushed the Fellowship to complete the living quarters, announcing that he intended to occupy them by Saturday, March 9. Working long hours, they almost met that deadline, and by 8:00 p.m. on March 10 the Garden Room was sufficiently completed for a dinner with distinguished guests. This experience, Besinger recalled, had a humorous aspect: Until minutes before the dinner began the apprentices were a "scruffy collection of workers," but by the time the guests arrived they had disappeared and reappeared, appropriately dressed as guests. Such experiences were always a part of the community's life.

Before leaving for Wisconsin that spring, work began on a wing to the north of the Kiva where there were to be three rooms for women and eleven for men, wrapped around the outdoor "apprentice court." The numbers reflected the gender ratio in the Fellowship at that time, a matter that played a part in an incident Besinger recounted in some detail:

One morning, when the Fellowship was shivering at breakfast, Mr. Wright came out, seated himself at the head of one of the tables, and started to talk in a general way about this problem, about the sexual instinct and its gratification. He presented his image of the Fellowship as an ideal, as a somewhat ascetic—if not monastic—community of men and women as dedicated to architecture as he was. In it, this "problem" was solved by self-discipline and sublimation through vigorous hard work out-of-doors.

He contrasted this with what he perceived to be the public image of the Fellowship—affected in part by his own marital history—as a "sex-starved community" which sought satisfaction on Saturday nights in Phoenix. It seemed that he saw Town Day [as it was called] not as an innocent opportunity to get a bath, shop, go to a movie, and get a haircut, but as an occasion for indulgence in the physical pleasures, after which some apprentices appeared at breakfast on Sunday mornings "looking like sucked oranges."

There was no response from the Fellowship. And Mr. Wright, having let his feelings be known, rose and left.

Shortly thereafter, the apprentices launched their caravan toward Wisconsin. Some had supervising responsibilities elsewhere, as noted in the previous chapter. Several with special assignments were in an advance party. The return journey was more leisurely than the one to the Southwest four months earlier, with side excursions for sightseeing.

These migrations were by this time so much a part of Fellowship life that Besinger was always surprised when people asked whether he belonged to the Wisconsin Fellowship or the one in Arizona. They could not grasp the reality that the Fellowship would move everything twice each year and that "an architect's office would load up its active files of drawing and correspondence and move twice yearly."[22] But that is what it meant to belong to Frank Lloyd Wright's working community.

## BUILDING AND LIFE CONTINUE AT TALIESIN WEST

The Fellowship returned to the desert camp in 1941 to complete the structures on three sides of the Apprentice Court and other projects, but then migrations were temporarily halted. The loss of members caused by World War II—some enlisted or were conscripted into the military, some went to prison for resisting the draft, and Curtis Besinger, a conscientious objector, was assigned to do work of "national importance under civilian direction" at camps in Colorado, Michigan, and California—delayed the further development of Taliesin West. So did a shortage of funds for cross-country transportation. After the war, construction resumed: a Water Tower, intended as protection against fires getting out of control, was built in 1946; the Cabaret Theater was a two-year project, 1949–1951; a locker room for women was built in 1952; and the Music Pavilion was the big project of 1954–1956.[23]

Through the years the apprentices transformed simple sheepherder tents into desert shelters, some of them quite elaborate. Designing and building such shelters remains a part of the apprentices' learning experiences. The shelters provide evidence that Taliesin West began as a desert camp and that it still continues to be such a place, with understandable variations.

Cornelia Brierly, who has spent winters at Taliesin West for more than half a century, takes pride in pointing out that it features the "only public buildings built by the love of so many young people. Even today they come back and point to stones they laid."[24]

# 17 THE FELLOWSHIP AT WORK

LONG AGO I PASSED THE BIBLICAL THREESCORE AND TEN, BUT I HAVE JUST BEGUN. WHEN SOMEBODY ASKED ME RECENTLY WHICH OF MY BUILDINGS I WAS MOST PROUD OF, I TOLD HIM, NATURALLY, THAT IT WAS THE NEXT ONE I WAS GOING TO DO.

I HAVE LIVED TO SEE THINGS HAPPEN THAT FEW MEN SEE. . . . I KNOW THE PRICE OF SUCCESS– UNREMITTING DEVOTION, HARD WORK, AND AN INEXTINGUISHABLE LOVE FOR THINGS YOU WANT TO HAPPEN. YOU CAN'T ACHIEVE MUCH WITHOUT THIS DEEP-SEATED FEELING FOR LIFE THAT WE CALL LOVE.[1]

—FRANK LLOYD WRIGHT

By 1940 the Taliesin Fellowship was well established in both Spring Green and Scottsdale, and its members were proving their worth to Frank Lloyd Wright. Given the flow of work in Wright's studios that year, it was reasonable to expect that the work done there would increase. And so it did. Assisted by apprentices, Wright produced designs that were executed for clients in Michigan, California, New Jersey, South Carolina, and Massachusetts, and some of the apprentices were engaged in supervising the construction of earlier designs elsewhere.

## APPRENTICES AS CONSTRUCTION SUPERVISORS

Assigning apprentices to supervise construction of his designs was prompted by Wright's refusal to put his drawings out for competitive bids. Local contractors, he had learned from experience, did not grasp what they were seeing in his drawings and therefore could not supervise construction effectively. Early on, according to Jack Howe, "he adopted the system of sending out an apprentice to get the house built. That really worked. To this day, that is how the Apprenticeship works." Howe's first assignment as a supervisor was for a small house in Kansas City. Working with the clients, he found people who could build it. If a detail did not work, he said, he used his wits to make it work.[2]

## THE BAIRD RESIDENCE

Among others using their wits for such purposes were Wes Peters and Cary Caraway. They did that in supervising the construction of a residence for Theodore Baird, a professor at Amherst College, and his wife, Frances, known as "Bertie," who taught French literature at Smith College. Baird's records of dealing with Wright and his apprentices and with design and construction problems provide another case study in the role of apprentices in Wright's work. Both Professor and Mrs. Baird read Wright's *An Autobiography,* and while they found much of it unattractive, something stayed with them when he talked about his designs: "His houses, he seemed to say, did something for people who lived in them," Baird recalled, "and what that seemed to be was what I wanted." The Bairds wondered whether one of Wright's apprentices in the Northeast might be able to design a place to satisfy their desires. They knew that Wright himself had no houses in New England and that "his attitude toward the East Coast in general was not unlike ours about California, let it drop off into the ocean and good riddance." Nonetheless, on May 24, 1939, Bertie wrote to Wright, "We want to build in the summer of 1940 in Amherst, Mass., the kind of house we should like to live in. This would require a miracle or Frank Lloyd Wright." After outlining the features they would want in a house, she concluded, "The miracle would be if you would build our house for us. But if miracles don't happen, will you tell us who else we can turn to."[3]

On June 14, 1939, Wright replied, "My dear Mrs. Baird: Of course it is possible—miracles being our specialty. Let us know more of the circumstances in detail." The Bairds responded by telling Wright who they were, how much money they had, and the furniture they would bring from their previous abode. Later they sent him photographs of the lot and a topographical map. As Wright worked on sketches, friends and kinfolk warned them that Wright was "a fool," that they "would have to live with this house," that he "was no business man," and that they were fools for engaging him.

When the blueprints arrived in late April the Bairds began looking for contractors. The bids they received, Wright agreed, were too high. In June 1940, Baird recalled, "FLLW telegraphed that the boys would be here in the middle of the week." Baird's response: "no boys." Wright invited him to meet with him in New York, and there he met not only Wright, but also Wes Peters, who rode back to Amherst with him. Before long Peters, with Wright's consent, had the contract for building the house. "If I use the archaic word gentleman in speaking of Wesley Peters," Baird wrote, "I must also add that, as I saw it, the spirit encouraged by FLLW was one of utter lawlessness, as if Taliesin had withdrawn from the Union. It was as far removed as can be imagined from that of a college, like Amherst, with its eye on the main chance and its approval of success in the world we live in. . . . Taliesin existed as a different culture, like, say, the Hopi or Navaho. . . ."

It is possible that FLLW saw very little of the apprentices individually, after all he was a practicing architect, but he could and did dominate their lives. Some never got over it. . . . Nevertheless, from the distance where I stand, is not this experience offered by the Taliesin Fellowship what we dream education ought to be? Education should be personal, in a community, making use of both body and mind, plain living and high thinking. They could watch the master sit down to his drawing board. . . . The apprentices were conscious of their privilege, and this awareness colored their attitude toward clients and the outside world. For FLLW this antagonism toward barbarians was forged in pain and humiliation and in the consciousness of his own genius. It was his by right. The claim of the apprentice was by association with genius.

Baird wrote fondly of his experiences with Peters, who supervised the construction of his house, and of Cary Caraway, who was on the scene much of the time that Peters was away, overseeing construction at Yemassee, South Carolina (Auldbrass), where apprentice Peter Berndtson was in charge; Florida Southern College; and houses Gordon Chadwick, another apprentice, was supervising in Maryland and Virginia.[4] Professor and Mrs. Baird particularly liked Caraway. Finding him an amusing companion, they would take him to dinner or feed him themselves. He was full of stories about Wright and his eccentricities, Baird recalled, "and there was much laughter. Carey's whole world had become Taliesin, presided over by FLLW."[5]

When Caraway was called back to Madison to assist Herb Fritz in finishing the Pew House, Edgar Tafel succeeded him. It was hard to speak of Edgar, Baird wrote, "without a good deal of annoyance," for he had been a real trial, as he implicitly criticized work done by Peters and Caraway. In his book, Baird claimed, Tafel had described him as being like most clients, "distraught, fit to be tied," one who "deserved not ridicule but pity."[6] That prompted Baird to remonstrate that during the longest of his occasional visits to the site Tafel had been sick in bed with the flu.

Wes Peters had good memories of working on the Baird Residence, and he considered Baird a wonderful client, even though he had to deal sharply with him on at least one occasion. Some of the pipes carrying water under the floor for heating the house were laid on the gravel. The men who installed the slab over the pipes neglected to drain them, and a very early November freeze caused the pipes to crack. When Peters or Caraway turned on the heating system they heard the pipes chattering and the water kept flowing. Checking the portion of the house that was above grade, Peters found running water. Baird panicked, causing Peters to say, "Look, Dr. Baird. You go home. You go home and don't come back here 'til I tell you. You go home, sit down, pour yourself about 4 or 5 fingers of Scotch whiskey—this is our problem, not yours. You're making it worse here. Don't come back until I call you." Putting their wits to work, and laboring all night, they developed ingenious solutions and had completed the repairs by the next afternoon.

After living in the house for about six months, Baird summarized his feelings about it in a letter to Wright, dated August 11, 1941: "I praise the house so shamelessly because it is not the creation of my imagination nor the work of my hands nor a setting for my ego. We owe it to you and Wes and Carey and Edgar. Our contribution was in wanting it with a whole heart and clear mind." So many things pleased the Bairds: the color and texture of the cypress walls, the craftsmanship of the millwright and carpenter, and the way it enlarged "the range and quality of conscious experience." The house, he said "is really an action, it works, and what it does would be felt by anybody living in it. . . ."

## WRIGHT'S "RIGHT BOWER"

In this instance and many others it was Wes Peters who got things done. Competence, dedication, leadership ability, and willingness to work hard made his accomplishments possible. If money was needed, Peters found ways to provide it, even if he had to "scrape" it from his generous sister. He recalled that she responded to his scrapings seven or eight times. As for his relationship with the master architect:

Mr. Wright was a person that was building—again, he was building a great dream. And he was making it come alive! And it was more than a pleasure to be involved with

[him]. I mean, . . . I would have paid money to just be involved in something like that. I felt it was so wonderful. . . . I appreciated it, later, when Mr. Wright had a little more money he began, periodically he'd put me on a salary. Well, it wasn't a salary. He knew that I had spent . . . probably altogether, two or three hundred thousand dollars, off and on. But when he had money he began giving it to me. . . .

I felt very good about everything. I was in a position I liked to be [in], and Mr. Wright trusted me. . . . I was just excited, when Mr. Wright start[ed] going around with me on some job and he would introduce me as his "right bower." And that was enough pay for anything.[7]

### THE COMMUNITY CHURCH, KANSAS CITY

Although houses had long been the main engine driving Wright's practice, he had also gained renown for designing several commercial buildings, particularly the Larkin Building in Buffalo, New York, and churches, most notably Unity Temple in Oak Park and the Annie Pfeiffer Chapel at Florida Southern College. A commission in 1940 to design the Community Church in Kansas City, Missouri, appeared to be an opportunity to revive that dimension of his career. He had the right apprentice for supervising its construction in Curtis Besinger. Apprentices Rowan Maiden and Davy Davison, as well as Besinger, helped prepare the working drawings and perspectives.

By Besinger's account, nothing went smoothly: initial bids were too high; some prospective builders declined to submit bids, given the building's unusual design; finding a company to do the steelwork was difficult; the building commissioner refused to issue a building permit, claiming that the drawings were incomplete and the construction details insufficient. Differences with the commission over the construction of the footings for the building resulted in an impasse, and the building committee of the church, Wright believed, was not cooperating in the quest for a permit. Moreover, local objections to engaging an architect from beyond the Kansas City area apparently stirred resentment and made Wright the center of controversy, perhaps slowing construction. When the building was well along the building commissioner ordered a number of structural tests. Although the results were favorable, or maybe *because* they were, the city prohibited publicity about them. By the time the church approached completion Wright had lost interest in it and eventually rejected it as work not attributable to him.[8]

### THE SHOW TO END ALL SHOWS

If confirmation was needed that Wright's career regeneration was progressing, it was evident in the retrospective exhibition of his work staged in 1940 by the Museum of Modern Art in New York. He intended the exhibition, "Frank Lloyd Wright: American Architect," to be "the show to end all shows." Preparing for it, Wright's apprentices "emptied all the drawings out of the vault in a rather strange disarray and put them on a truck," as one of them, Victor Cusack, recalled. Curtis Besinger identified apprentices Bob Blandin, Marcus Weston, and himself as builders of the models to be displayed, and Gene Masselink, John Hill, Davy Davison, and

Marcus Weston, along with Cusack, as the ones who transported all of this to New York and helped with installing it in the designated spaces.[9]

To accompany the drawings, photographs, and models displayed, there was to be a catalog that included a collection of essays, known as a Festschrift, paying tribute to Wright and his work. The Museum commissioned some of the best-known figures of the day to write essays in Wright's honor, among them architects Alva Aalto, Richard Neutra, and Mies van der Rohe; architectural historians and critics Henry-Russell Hitchcock, Fiske Kimball (also an architect); and Wright's clients E. J., Liliane and Edgar Kaufmann, Jr.

However, Wright objected to an essay by Walter Curt Behrendt, a German writer who had emigrated to the United States in 1934. He threatened to cancel the exhibition if Behrendt's piece was included in the exhibition catalog. After flurries of negotiations, the exhibition survived, but there was no catalog. Unfavorable reaction to its absence prompted Alfred Barr, the founding director of the Museum to issue this statement: "Mr. Wright, insisting upon 'no prejudgments in advance of the show,' refused to permit the publication of the catalog as planned, although it had been intended as a tribute to him."

Wright designed the installation for the exhibition—in fact, he had control over almost everything. However, the design drew many unfavorable criticisms, prompting Wright to request removal of the sign stating that the exhibition had been "arranged by the architect himself," and he refused to allow it to travel to other museums. He also negotiated an arrangement with Henry-Russell Hitchcock to write what Hitchcock acknowledged was "a sort of *ex post facto* catalogue of the exhibition," published in 1942 as *In the Nature of Materials: The Buildings of Frank Lloyd Wright, 1887–1941.*[10]

Wright had also hoped to build a Usonian house, modeled after the one built for the Jacobses in Madison, on a lot immediately behind the Museum. Building it would have been a choice project for Wright's apprentices, but John D. Rockefeller, Jr., had given or leased to the Museum that piece of land, and the restrictions he imposed meant that he would have to approve the building of a house there. His disapproval meant that another feature of the exhibition was unrealized. These setbacks notwithstanding, the "Show to End All Shows" removed any doubt that Frank Lloyd Wright was back.

## THE FRANK LLOYD WRIGHT FOUNDATION

Another significant event occurred the same year, 1940, when Wright consolidated his practice, the Taliesin Fellowship, and the archives holding his drawings and papers in the Frank Lloyd Wright Foundation, a new corporation under his personal control. In the late 1920s, dire financial straits and the highly publicized wrangling in his pursuit of a divorce from Miriam Noel had compelled him to place himself in the hands of shareholders of "Frank Lloyd Wright, Incorporated."[11] The terms of the incorporation compelled him, among other things, to meet from time to time with them to agree upon what expenditures were necessary and the maximum amount to be expended for any of them. He was also required to submit monthly statements of cash disbursed and to forward checks or other payments he received. That the shareholders included friends, clients, including Darwin Martin and Mrs. Avery Coonley, and kinfolk hardly made his circumstances more palatable.

### WORLD WAR II

Now, at age seventy-three, Wright was poised to move forward with the Fellowship, but World War II intervened. Several of his residential designs were executed in the years 1941 to 1945, construction continued on Florida Southern College buildings, and the research tower for the S.C. Johnson & Son Company was built, but almost all of his other clients were unable to build what he designed for them. Moreover, in 1941 the Fellowship lost several disgruntled members, including Edgar Tafel, when Wright decided not to permit them to accept work independently. He believed, according to Curtis Besinger, that what they designed would not measure up to his standards and that their outside work would dilute their contribution to the Fellowship and his practice.[12]

The most serious challenge to the Fellowship's operations, and even to its existence, resulted from the departure of apprentices for military service. In his memoir, Besinger recalled that in early 1941, after passage of the Selective Training and Service Act but before the United States entered the war, "it appeared that one by one the Fellowship was going to be reduced in size and effectiveness." With this in mind, the Fellowship sent a statement to Clarence Dykstra, president of the University of Wisconsin and director of Selective Service from 1940 to April 1941, objecting to the compulsory military draft and asserting, "To compel the breaking up of the consequences of [the Fellowship's] years of training is a far more serious loss to America at this time than the loss to the American army, of men whose convictions, education, and principles render them unfit for destruction and mass murder called war." It asked for the members "to be allowed to work as a group of interior defense rather than being compelled to waste their lives in jail."

Surmising that the statement was drafted by senior apprentices and influenced and perhaps even edited by Wright, Besinger notes that Burton Goodrich presented it at teatime for signing by members of the Fellowship. Of the twenty-five members listed with the statement, only three did not sign it.[13]

In a bitterly sarcastic letter Wright accused Dr. James Jackson, apparently the head of a Selective Service board in Madison, of perpetuating falsehoods about him and the Fellowship: "Falsehood number one: you said that I banded the young men who are my student-apprentices together as conscientious objectors. Here is a list of members of the Taliesin Fellowship now in service." Wright named six in the army, two in the marines, two in the "flying corps," one in the navy, and six doing defense work. Thus, he continued, "seventeen out of a possible thirty-one are already in service and five more are given A-1 Classification. This practically wipes out the Taliesin Fellowship and our works."[14]

By this time Wright had established a reputation as an isolationist and pacifist, in part through his diatribes against the war and President Franklin Roosevelt, delivered in broadsides known as Taliesin Square Papers.[15] Accusing

Dr. Jackson and his cohorts of gratuitously charging his young men with the dishonor of having no consciences of their own except as he dictated to them, he claimed, "that then you put it squarely up to me to see that harm likely to come to them because of your personal prejudice founded on lies and bias does not deprive them of a free trial under a free judge."

The call to military duty cost Wright the services not only of those who answered it, but also of four who declined to serve. One of them, Marcus Weston, was the son of Wright's long-time carpenter William Weston. The trial over his refusal generated considerable coverage in newspapers and was accompanied by an exchange of accusations between Wright and the United States District Judge, Patrick Stone. The judge charged that the apprentices were "living under a bad influence with that man Wright," that he was poisoning their minds. He said he intended to ask the FBI to investigate Wright and that if he was obstructing the war he should be indicted.[16]

As for Marcus Weston, following the denial of his appeal to be granted conscientious objector status, he was imprisoned in the federal penitentiary at Sandstone, Minnesota, as were Jack Howe and Davy Davison, who also refused induction into the military. Wright stayed in touch with these men and was even invited to give a lecture to Sandstone inmates. He said he "wanted to see how the democratic principle works with the individual in wartime. Or more accurately to see what happens to the individual when it does not work." While imprisoned, Howe got the job of teaching machine and architectural drafting in the library's small classrooms. The library, he said, was a good one, although the librarian didn't want to be bothered by assisting others, so he and others participated in the selection of books, and they got some good ones. Still, he added, "I didn't say it was fun."[17] The fourth apprentice who declined to serve, Besinger, was granted conscientious objector status and between July 1943 and June 1946 was assigned to "work of national importance" in Civilian Public Service camps in Colorado, Michigan, and California.[18] With the membership in the Fellowship reduced in number and with wartime shortage making travel impossible, the Fellowship did not go to Arizona in 1942–43.

## BROADACRE CITY AGAIN

An incident in Wright's practice during World War II reveals his ways of working and his continuing commitment to the principles of Broadacre City. In February 1943, more than sixty of his illustrious friends and clients, at his self-promoting instigation, signed a petition asking the government "to authorize Frank Lloyd Wright to continue the search for Democratic FORM as the basis for a true capitalistic society now known as Broadacre City." The petition expressed the belief that the work should "immediately be declared a worthy national objective and the necessary ways and means freely granted him to make such plans, models, and drawings as will enable our citizens and other peoples to comprehend the basic ideas the plans, models and drawings represent." Without political bias or influences, the signers asserted, advancing the Broadacre plans would be invaluable to the American people in postwar years.[19]

The petition yielded no results, but Wright was not completely denied opportunities to do work for the federal government. In fact, in the prior year he had designed a defense plant for Pittsfield, Massachusetts. Clark Foreman, a housing administrator, asked him to design a housing project for the same city. By Wright's account, he accepted, visited the site, went to work, and drew plans for 100 housing units, called Cloverleaf houses, no doubt keeping his few remaining apprentice draftsmen busy preparing working and detail drawings. Then, as he recalled in 1948, Foreman sent a telegram ordering him to stop. He had been replaced, but because the project was nearly completed, he was authorized to finish it. In Washington, officials were generally delighted with the plan, but some doubts concerning details had to be resolved. However, local architects claimed that by law they should be the ones to handle the project. The government offered to buy what Wright had done, but he declined to sell it, for he would have no control over the project's execution.[20]

## THE GUGGENHEIM MUSEUM

A bigger, much more significant opportunity came Wright's way in 1943. It began with a letter arriving unexpectedly at Taliesin from Hilla Rebay, curator of the S.R. Guggenheim Foundation, asking him to come to New York to discuss with her a building for their collection of nonobjective paintings. These great masterpieces "should be organized into space," she wrote, "and only you, so it seems to me, would test the possibilities to do so. It takes so much thought and loving attention, and the experience of an originator, and his wisdom, to be able to handle such a difficult task."[21]

So began an odyssey that continued with many twists and turns until after Wright's death in 1959. Essential aspects of the odyssey are documented in the vast collection of "Guggenheim correspondence" in the Frank Lloyd Wright Archives. Most of the letters in the collection are lengthy and many are repetitive, noted Bruce Brooks Pfeiffer, "because the battles won had then to be fought over and over." All of the letters, he continued, "touched to some degree with the struggle waged for seventeen years. Collectively they would stack as high as the model Frank Lloyd Wright made for Guggenheim in 1946."[22] Many of the letters confirm Pfeiffer's observation that Hilla Rebay, an immigrant from Germany, "could be dreadful in her stubbornness, obdurate over misgivings, susceptible to suspicions and doubts, fearful that her architect's building would not do her artists' work justice." Yet, they show that "a core of affection would always exist between her and Frank Lloyd Wright."[23]

Acquiring land for the new museum was an initial concern, but countless additional issues—too many to cite here—had to be negotiated. The edging aside of Hilla Rebay as curator jeopardized the negotiations, and the appointment of a successor, James Johnson Sweeney, who was not cordial to Wright or his plans, jeopardized them further. So did a protest against Wright and his design by leading New York artists. Before the negotiations had run their course, Solomon Guggenheim died. The constants in the designing and building processes were Wright, his chief engineer Wes Peters, and his principal draftsman, Jack Howe. By this time Peters and Howe and a few others were known as senior apprentices.[24] Many other apprentices

had a hand in preparing renderings, perspectives, working drawings, and presentation drawings, as well as in building the model cited above.

A chronological listing of materials prepared for the construction of the museum shows that it *had* to be a collaborative effort. In each of the years between 1944 and 1958 except 1949, 1950, and 1957, according to Pfeiffer, the studios produced drawings for one purpose or another. The Guggenheim model, like the drawings, was updated several times during these years. All this while other work was pouring into the studios at an accelerating pace, slowing the production of the Guggenheim drawings. The structure's complexity required considerable time to calculate engineering costs and Wright's frequent design changes were additional causes of delays. Wes Peters—who was assisted in engineering the structure of the building by Mendel Glickman and Tom Casey, who held a degree in architecture from the University of California at Berkeley—recalled that Wright "had more difficulty with [this building], shaping it, than . . . any other building that I know of that he worked on. As a matter of fact, he kept modifying it for years and years and years—even up to the time after the contract was let."[25]

Frank Lloyd Wright, age 90, with the contractor, clerk-of-the-works, and contract superintendent during the construction of the Guggenheim Museum in 1957. Courtesy of Donald Greenhauss.

In 1948, with costs climbing, the Guggenheim project was on temporary hold. When doubts arose about the prospect of the museum ever being built, however, Solomon Guggenheim offered this assurance: "The House of Guggenheim never goes back on its word—the museum will be built."[26] Nonetheless, Guggenheim's death the following year intensified Wright's anxieties. Soon, though, he found that he could work effectively with Harry Guggenheim, who had inherited his uncle's mantle, and in complex ways with the museum trustees. Plans for the new museum moved forward. Working with the new curator tested Wright's patience and endurance, but he found the will and ways to prevail.

Keeping the project going from Wisconsin and Arizona proved to be difficult and costly, so in 1954, more than a decade after embarking on the Guggenheim project, Wright rented an apartment on the second floor of the Plaza Hotel, remodeled it in grand fashion, and made it his residence and studio for five years while his Guggenheim plans struggled to fruition. He sometimes referred to it as Taliesin East. During the preceding decade an uncounted number of apprentices joined the Fellowship, possibly worked on Guggenheim drawings, and moved on, but his most valued assistants remained in his service. He designated Wes Peters as his associate to oversee construction when he could not be present.[27] Even after ground was broken for the museum in August 1956, Sweeney demanded changes, which placed fresh burdens on Wright and his assistants, as did continuing increases in construction costs. Wright and those assistants were also occupied in the more than fifty other commissions that came to him in 1956, even as his health became more precarious, no doubt due in part to the strain that building the Guggenheim Museum imposed on him.

## "SIXTY YEARS OF LIVING ARCHITECTURE"

In the early 1950s, as in 1940, Wright's apprentices were heavily engaged in assembling, organizing, and mounting materials for another exhibition. "Sixty Years of Living Architecture" was sponsored initially by Gimbel's Department Store in Philadelphia, through the store's owner, Arthur Kaufmann, a cousin of Edgar Kaufmann. After its premiere in Philadelphia, the exhibition moved to Florence, Italy, then to Switzerland, France, Germany, and Holland before returning to New York in 1953. There it was set up in a temporary pavilion on the site where the Guggenheim Museum was to be built. A number of apprentices traveled to New York to work on the pavilion and the exhibition it would house: Kenn Lockhart, Tom Casey, John Geiger, Robin Molny, Morton Delson, John Rattenbury, Kelly Oliver, Edward Thurman, Jim Pfefferkorn, George Thompson, David Wheatley, Herbert de Levie, and Curtis Besinger.[28]

All of these men could tell stories about their work on the exhibition pavilion in New York. Jim Pfefferkorn has recorded some of his in an unpublished memoir. The building, he said, was made up of bolted-together pipe frames with sheet metal roofing covering most of the area for the future museum. One morning when he was working on the pipes Wright called him down to give him a special assignment: He was to devise a way to install a glass ceiling where the sloping roof reached its peak, a task that the contractor said could not be done. Pfefferkorn recalled that he looked at the space for a while and "began to put together an idea." With a plank platform on the pipes, a rope elevator, and as many as fifty strap hangers to hold the glass in place for hooking over the pipe frame, it could be done. So he designed the hangers and gave it to a man designated by Wright to make them, a task that took two days.

Setting the heavy corrugated glass sheets, eight feet in length, designed for barn skylights, posed problems, Pfefferkorn recalled:

In the first place we had to work some forty feet in the air on about a four-foot-wide plank walkway. We had to watch our step. Below us were all kinds of people going back and forth. . . . One slip in handling and a sheet of glass could fall to the floor with disastrous results for those below. This was my biggest concern. We had to wear heavy gloves to keep from cutting our hands on the glass edges. . . . I insisted that only Kelly [Oliver] and I be up on the walkway doing the setting because of all of the dangers. So Morton [Delson] and a helper lifted the glass up one sheet at a time. Kelly and I being very careful carried the sheet to the end and set it in the hangers which we mounted as we went along. There were no accidents and only once as I remember did a hand slip.[29]

The pavilion was large enough to permit construction within it of a Usonian house, complete with a living/dining room, kitchen, and bedrooms. When the pavilion had to be removed from the New York site, the house was dismantled, never to be reconstructed elsewhere. The exhibition was moved to Mexico City, and then to Los Angeles, where a similar pavilion was attached to the Hollyhock House.[30] John Geiger, an apprentice since 1947, supervised the construction of the Los Angeles pavilion.

## ZIMMERMAN RESIDENCE

Earlier Wright had designated Geiger as the on-site supervisor for the construction of a home in Manchester, New Hampshire, for Dr. and Mrs. Isadore Zimmerman, commissioned in 1950. The Zimmermans paid Geiger $50.00 weekly (if the Rosenbaum fee situation provided a precedent, some of this had to be sent to Wright), and Geiger lived with the Zimmermans from June 1951 until May 1952. Attentive to details, as was Lucille Zimmerman, Geiger found that the local contractor had deviated from Wright's plans and specifications, and some of what he had done had to be done over. After a dispute over billing, the contractor parted ways with the Zimmermans and Geiger became the contractor. He prepared a new set of working drawings, proposed solutions to structural problems, and recommended significant design changes, no doubt in consultation with or at the request of the owners, all of them subject to Wright's approval.

Michael Komanecky, the curator in the Currier Gallery of Art (now the owner of the Zimmerman House), cited some of Geiger's accomplishments: "he selected cypress . . . so that a single board would continue around a corner, its handsome grain uninterrupted and thereby connecting the flow of space throughout the house," and "helped the Zimmermans find hand-woven fabrics for upholstery, pillows, and curtains throughout the house." After leaving Manchester, Geiger and Wright continued to refine the house.[31] The

Zimmermans expressed their appreciation in a letter to Wright: "Every day we see things about the house that would not be here for us to enjoy but for John. Knowing John, we can well understand your pride in the Fellowship."[32]

### TEATER'S KNOLL

A project in Idaho, tiny by Guggenheim standards, claimed inordinate amounts of Wright's time and attention. In 1951 he agreed to design a studio-residence for Archie Teater, an artist, and his wife, Patricia, to be built on a bluff overlooking the Snake River near Bliss, Idaho. In October 1953, Wes Peters flew to Twin Falls, about thirty miles east of Bliss, and made his way to the site to lay it out according to Wright's plans, as he had done for earlier projects. Wright sent apprentices Robert and Ann Pond to supervise the construction. From the beginning, Patricia Teater was a demanding, petulant, anxious, hovering, protesting client. Robert Pond's difficulties in procuring supplies from nearby lumber yards resulted in delays Mrs. Teater considered indefensible. By early March of 1954 the Ponds had had enough of her accusations, often made in letters to Wright, and left.

Tom Casey was the next apprentice sent by Wright to work with the Teaters. Neither they nor the stonemason they had hired were there when he arrived, so to get started he built a small wood frame structure adjacent to the studio, called it the Bunkhouse, and used it for his office and dwelling. He was ready to resume work on the Teaters' project when they returned. Before long Casey wrote to Wright, "She can certainly become wild and unreasonable. She gets so upset about the mason that she can't even talk to him, so I have to act as go between. So far there hasn't been any bloodshed and I intend to keep that status as peaceful as possible." Casey continued his supervision, and on May 25 he reported that all was proceeding well. However, while obtaining bids on materials while the Teaters were away, he had trouble getting suppliers to agree to allow deferred payments for lumber and other supplies. Still, the work progressed.

The explosion that ended his tenure as supervisor came when he sought and gained Wright's approval to substitute cement blocks for stones in a wall behind cabinets. Casey's explanations were to no avail, as Mrs. Teater insisted that she did not want a "mongrel house." She entered Casey's bunkhouse, upset his drafting table, scattered his documents, and sent him away. Wright did not replace him. Word of her treatment of the Ponds, Casey, other workers, and Wright himself spread through the Fellowship, leaving "a distinctly sour taste throughout Taliesin," according to Bruce Pfeiffer. However, when the couple visited Taliesin West in the 1970s "they appeared relaxed and gracious," bearing no resemblance to the "tenacious and over-anxious couple" the Fellowship had known twenty-five years earlier." The pressure of building their house on a shoestring had apparently made them "plunge out into various irrational directions."[33]

### LEWELLYN WRIGHT RESIDENCE

Another instance of an apprentice engaged in supervising the construction of a Wright design involved a client who was never asked to pay for any of his services. That client was Wright's youngest son, Lewellyn, who recalled that he first asked for a house in 1946 and received a design for a Usonian.

Told that postwar building costs would decline, he decided to delay building (if he could remember who told him that, he wrote, he would sue them, and as a lawyer, he might have). Six years later he and his wife, Elizabeth, bought a different lot, in Bethesda, Maryland, and the next year sent his father a survey of it. Soon they received "a spectacular design." At their request, Wright scaled down the house to fit their budget. Such an accommodation, Lewellyn Wright noted, was not an extraordinary favor for a son; rather, in talking with other clients he learned that what the clients wanted and could afford always came first with his father.

The apprentice assigned to supervise construction of the Lewellyn Wright house was Bob Beharka, a graduate of Arizona State University who joined the Fellowship in 1954. "I am sending out my best boy to you," Wright assured his daughter-in-law. Beharka served not only as the general contractor, but also as foreman, and he did much of the woodworking himself. Using his wits, as all apprentices were required to do in such circumstance, he figured out how to do what the drawings called for and "showed the subcontractors how almost everything should be done by first doing it himself." The workers, he said, loved working on it. Wright's son recalled that there "was nothing unique about day-to-day supervision of a Frank Lloyd Wright house by a live-in apprentice, but this one was uniquely talented, and his extraordinary efforts allowed us to stay within our budget."[34]

## LUIS MARDEN RESIDENCE AND BEYOND

Beharka's good work on Lewellyn's home earned him another assignment: supervision of the construction of the Luis Marden Residence in McLean, Virginia. When he arrived there, the Mardens pointed out two serious design flaws: one involved a lily pond on the terrace, the other, more serious, had

Bob Beharka supervised the construction of the Lewellyn Wright House and the Marden House; here Wright signs a copy of his autobiography for him. Courtesy of Robert Beharka

the terrace blocking the view of the river for those standing inside the house. So, according to Annie Gowen, a reporter for the *Washington Post,* "Beharka slunk back to Taliesin . . . to break the bad news." It was a cold night, he recalled, when he met Wright in the drafting room to tell him the terrace conundrum. "I told him exactly what they wanted—a shallow terrace that would step down." Wright, he said, bent over the drawings and quietly resketched a narrower terrace. Then he got up to leave, and Beharka helped him put on his coat. Wright sighed and said, "Don't ever get into this business."[35]

### HARRIET AND RANDALL FAWCETT RESIDENCE

When the construction in Virginia was completed, Aaron Green asked Beharka to supervise the building of the Harriet and Randall Fawcett residence in nearby Los Banos, California. Green was a former apprentice who had opened a practice in San Francisco and was managing Wright's work there as a partner. Beharka worked with Green for eighteen months, and upon completion of the house he stayed in the area and started his own practice. The Fawcetts helped him get some commissions, and he spent his entire career in Los Banos.[36]

### BETH SHOLOM SYNAGOGUE

In Frank Lloyd Wright's final years, his apprentices in the Taliesin Fellowship played increasingly important roles. While there were many houses on the drawing boards and under construction, two places of worship demanded much of Wright's assistants. One was the Beth Sholom synagogue in Pennsylvania. Beginning in 1953, Wright worked closely in the design stages with Rabbi Mortimer Cohen, who wanted Beth Sholom to be "a symbol for generations to come of the American and Jewish spirit." He was aware that although Wright knew the Bible, he needed to be educated in Judaism. The design reflected Cohen's success as Wright's educator. As the project moved toward construction, a model of the 110-foot-tall structure, itself six feet high, stirred enthusiasm. One of Cohen's collaborators exclaimed, "A jewel in the crown of Philadelphia. It will be Wright's greatest creation." Converting the concepts displayed in the model into the "mountain of light" the synagogue was designed to be was the responsibility of Wes Peters as Wright's engineer, and when construction began he was the on-site supervisor. He called on Mendel Glickmann and John Rattenbury, a relatively new apprentice, for assistance. Glickman, a structural engineer, had begun an affiliation with the Fellowship in 1932 while he was at Taliesin to study architecture with Wright. He had been a professor of engineering at the University of Oklahoma since 1949 and assisted Wright in this and other major projects while also mentoring Wright's apprentices.

The building was to be built of glass and shaped like a pyramid. Not surprisingly in a structure that was the first of its kind, and to date the last, problems developed, as Peters explained in an interview. One involved the glass used for the walls. The members of the Beth Sholom building committee insisted that it should come from a local supplier, rather than from a glass company in Wisconsin that Peters had worked with on the Johnson Wax buildings. So they had to re-detail everything. When the corrugated glass with wires imbedded was installed, the roof leaked, especially when the wind was blowing, and if the wind changed the leaking changed with it. So they sent Kenn Lockhart to diagnose the problem. He "spent weeks or months hanging, sitting on a Jacob's Ladder, or a bosun's swing, sling, sitting on the walls," Peters said, "going up these triangular inside walls, trying to find the trouble, either during rains, or before and after rains, to see what would happen." What they found was that the corrugated glass could not be sealed tightly, and changing air pressure inside the synagogue would assist the wind in creating leakage.[37]

When that problem and others were solved, more or less, construction was completed, but not before Wright's death. Olgivanna Lloyd Wright spoke at the dedication of Beth Sholom, and although a plaque mounted near the entrance to the synagogue cites Rabbi Cohen's role as co-designer, she failed to acknowledge his essential role in creating and realizing the dream the synagogue fulfilled. She repeated that omission in *The Shining Brow*. In this book, though, she called the presence of twenty young men and women from Taliesin who filled rows to her left a "glad sight."[38] Their contributions were evident in the inspiring structure surrounding them.

## ANNUNCIATION GREEK ORTHODOX CHURCH

The apprentices' role in bringing Wright's designs to fruition was perhaps most notable in the construction of the Annunciation Greek Orthodox Church in Wauwatosa, Wisconsin. Although Wright had a good grasp of Byzantine architectural traditions and a clear understanding of Orthodox liturgical practices, as well as a desire to honor Mrs. Wright's religious heritage, development of the design progressed slowly. One day in the summer of 1956, Mrs. Wright recalled, her husband exclaimed that he "had it." He "hastened into the drafting room, sharpened his pencil and the white sheet on the drafting board received his idea."

John Ottenheimer, an apprentice in the years 1953 to 1970, observed him as he "proceeded to draw the original plan and elevation . . . to scale, with T-Square, triangles and compasses. This took about one hour. Of course, he had the design already complete in his mind before he started to draw." Then his original design went to Jack Howe to produce the additional drawings the undertaking would require.[39] He had plenty of assistants, for as John Gurda, a journalist who wrote the principal work on the history of this structure, noted, the staff and apprentices at Taliesin numbered nearly ninety. The Building Committee of the new church, Gurda said, "who observed Wright with his associates described him variously as 'the king,' 'the guru,' and the 'abbot of a monastery.' The Fellowship combined elements of the medieval guild and the modern alternative community. It was a group of seekers centered around one master, steeped in his principles and devoted to his standards." When apprentices were assigned to on-site supervision, "the ideas were Wright's; turning those ideas into realities was the Fellowship's responsibility."[40]

When Wright died on April 9, 1959, five weeks before groundbreaking, it was natural for Wes Peters to take the lead in doing what remained to be done

John Ottenheimer at the site of
the Greek Annunciation Orthodox
Church, Wauwatosa, Wisconsin;
Wes Peters had named him
construction supervisor. Courtesy
of John Ottenheimer. Photo by
John Amarantides

with the Greek church. His presence gave the church's building committee
the confidence required to move forward. "All the elements were in place,"
wrote John Gurda. "The working drawings and specifications were complete,
a contractor had been selected, and construction was about to begin." Getting
to this point had not been easy: Among other considerations, fund-raising
worries increased as the cost kept climbing. The projected cost of $500,000,
set in 1952, "began to look like a down payment." By 1959 the budget was

raised to $975,000. "The financial difficulties," Gurda observed, "encouraged, if nothing else, a more active prayer life in the parish."[41] It would be up to the Taliesin Fellowship to see that God answered their prayers.

Peters designated John Ottenheimer to be the person in charge, but it was clear that Peters, who was again assisted in engineering matters by Mendel Glickman and others, would provide the essential guidance. The design called for a large dome to be placed on steel balls resting on concrete walls, to cope with expansion and contraction caused by changing temperatures. Moreover, carpenters experienced in building straight walls had to find ways to build the forms for the curving walls the design required. At age twenty-six in 1959, Ottenheimer proved to be not only a good architect and technician, but a good leader as well. He was cost-conscious and he enforced high standards, even as the builders encountered one problem after another.[42]

The Fellowship conducted itself as Wright would have expected. By this time his apprentices knew his principles so well, Peters said, that they could "interpret pretty accurately the direction he would take in filling in the details. That is the great advantage of this [Fellowship] system. Once you had a great general scheme established, a general idea, you had a trained staff who could of necessity fill in the individual details and reduce all the particulars from generals." Similarly, according to John Ottenheimer, "The building had a life of its own. People who worked on it simply cultivated that life." Mostly they followed Wright's design, under Peters's direction. Mrs. Wright selected the color of the roof, making sure that it reflected the color of the sky. There were a few departures, however, particularly in the design of the furnishings.[43]

Construction progressed and challenges were confronted and met. Finally, with dedication imminent, came the last push. Interviewed in 1984, Archbishop Iakovos recalled his impressions: "When I saw the people working, and they did continue to work until the small hours, well, I was terribly moved, deeply moved. I said to myself, 'Here we are, people of God, simple, humble, dedicated, working hard so the church may be dressed, so to speak, like a bride for the wedding day.'"

Wes Peters described the final hours of preparation:

We had been working sixteen, eighteen hours a day for two or three weeks, and we worked around the clock the last day. We were painting, laying carpet, arranging furniture and plants, erecting the icon screen. We had about forty or fifty from the Fellowship there, and maybe fifteen or twenty union electricians and laborers and so on. I said to one of the union men, "We've got to get this thing done. Are you fellows going to object if we work?" He said, "You go right ahead. We appreciate what's going on here."

. . . We were still working way up to seven or eight o'clock in the morning, hauling paint cans and ladders down below where they couldn't be seen. Late that night I got Susan Lockhart to give me a haircut because I had to get the paint and everything out of my hair. I got done with all my work maybe five or ten minutes before the ceremony ended. I changed my clothes and went out to watch the conclusion.[44]

That was not the end of the Fellowship's involvement with the church, and if its members had learned a great deal about building through the experiences with this church, they also learned about the effects of problems encountered by clients. The ceiling and the surface of the dome both failed badly, resulting in a lawsuit against the supplier of insulation and the contractor. When the contractor placed blame on the architects the parish added Taliesin to the suit and increased the claim, which was settled out of court. Gurda noted that the lawsuit was a legal necessity, and reflected no ill feelings toward Taliesin. Peters and Ottenheimer played roles in solving the problems as they continued into the mid-1970s, but as their solutions were rejected the amicability diminished and soon disappeared.[45] Even so, the men and women who worked on the church recall fondly their experiences there.

## MARIN COUNTY CIVIC CENTER

Some Wright-designed residences were under construction or proceeding in that direction, and work on them continued. Also remaining for Wright's Fellowship to complete was the large and complex Marin County Civic Center, which included a post office, an administration building, and a Hall of Justice. Wright had had his first meeting with Marin County officials in July 1957, a month after his ninetieth birthday. He accepted the commission, his 770th, on the condition that Aaron Green, who represented him in his San Francisco office, be associated with him on an equal basis. By this time Green had in some manner participated in nearly thirty of Wright's projects. The lack of a telephone at Taliesin West (until 1960) made communication between Wright and Green difficult, but they made the partnership work.

The drawings for the first stages of the Marin complex were completed in March 1958. Green recalled that they had been prepared, as was typical, by members of the Taliesin staff under Wright's supervision, but he believed that they showed a greater than usual amount of attention by Wright. "The beautiful renderings," he noted, "were by exceptionally competent staff members John Howe and Ling Po, but they also revealed much of Mr. Wright's own handiwork." Green and Peters compiled cost estimates, and Green continued to provide detailed layouts of the buildings' interiors. He also took charge of the landscape design. Before Wright's death the project was in jeopardy on several occasions, as residents of Marin County objected to the selection of Wright as architect and to his designs. After construction had begun, new members were elected to the Marin County governing board, and, in collaboration with Wright's critics, had it stopped while they made the case, unsuccessfully, for converting the administration building into a hospital. Wright's presentations, his charisma proving to be irresistible, won the project the support it needed, and construction resumed.

After Wright's death, the team members responsible for continuing his work, according to Green, were Wes Peters, Jack Howe, John de Koven Hill, John Rattenbury, Tom Casey, and Kenn Lockhart. They had to accomplish, he noted, what Wright would have done "in the matter we were trained to do." "Our responsibility to Frank Lloyd Wright," he recalled, "weighed heavily, and the future was at stake."

Mrs. Wright spoke at the groundbreaking on February 15, 1960, and the administration building was dedicated on October 13, 1962. The plaque marking the dedication identified Wright as architect, but also listed the Taliesin Associated Architects, William Wesley Peters as Chief Architect and Aaron G. Green as "associated."[46]

■    ■    ■

The sampling of names and dates and buildings presented here shows that the Fellowship performed as Wright might have scripted it when he and Mrs. Wright founded it in 1932. But there was always more to the Fellowship than architecture, and in the 1940s and 1950s the communal life they envisioned also matured and prospered, as will be evident as the story told here continues.

# 18 DAILY LIFE IN THE FELLOWSHIP

*The 1940s and 1950s*

. . . . BEING WITH MR. WRIGHT IN THE DRAUGHTING ROOM, WATCHING HIM IN ACTION, WAS, OF COURSE, THE "SPECIAL EXPERIENCE" AT THE FELLOWSHIP. HE WOULD PASS BY THE DRAWING BOARD, THEN SEEING A FAMILIAR DETAIL BEING REPEATED, WOULD SIT DOWN SAYING, "WE'VE DONE THIS BEFORE"—AND THERE AND THEN CREATE THE MOST FRESH AND LOVELY INNOVATIVE SOLUTION IMAGINABLE.[1]

**—ANDRE HOFFE, APPRENTICE**

"Take care of the luxuries," Frank Lloyd Wright liked to say, "and the necessities will take care of themselves."[2] He might have said, rather, "and the apprentices will take care of the necessities."

Most of the necessities of daily life in the Fellowship were those encountered by families and communities everywhere: shelter, work, food, clothing, daily and weekly routines, cultural and social experiences, recreation, entertainment, and having good times. Providing these necessities was the collective responsibility of the Fellowship, under the direction of Mr. and Mrs. Wright. While providing clothing was an individual responsibility, for various occasions special attire was sometimes prescribed.

## THE TRANSCENDENT NECESSITY

There was one necessity, however, not provided by the Fellowship, a transcendent one: Frank Lloyd Wright himself. From the Fellowship's founding, and now in the 1940s and 1950s, the young men and women in its membership all expected in some measure to live every day under Wright's guidance and to learn from him. For some apprentices it was not so much Wright the person, but Wright's architecture that attracted them. Passion for that architecture prompted Andre Hoffe, for example, to come to Taliesin in mid-1955. In his homeland, South Africa, he had collected every illustration of Wright's architecture that he could find, and he saw it "in vast contrast to the diet of Le Corbusier which [he] had been force-fed" while earning a Bachelor of Architecture degree from the University of Witwatersrand in Johannesburg. Now in his early thirties, he knew what he wanted. To him the Fellowship existed to support Wright's architectural practice and to provide a means for learning from him.[3]

Grattan Gill identified encountering the architecture of the Taliesins as his most important experience as an apprentice, but there were more:

. . . participating in the drafting and development of the construction documents of many important projects; the additional experience of participating in the construction, reconstruction, and alterations to both Taliesins; and the unique and

216 | COMMUNITIES OF FRANK LLOYD WRIGHT

priceless experience of listening to Mr. Wright discuss his philosophy of organic architecture in the formal setting of Sunday morning seminars after breakfast, informal discussions of a design or design issues in the drafting room, and his in-field comments on ongoing construction projects.[4]

Others would probably echo the sentiment of Robert Gorman, who had been studying at Tulane University but was not satisfied there. He remarked in an interview, "I wasn't really born until I got to Taliesin."[5]

Richard Keding no doubt reflected the views of many when he said that he came to Taliesin "in search of the key to creativity." He had grown up in Oak Park and its neighboring communities and was drawn to the beauty of Wright's buildings. Although he did not join precisely to learn how to design buildings, subconsciously that was his desire and vision. He realized that creativity would not come easily, so it was "vital to study at the source." He found Taliesin to be "a phenomenal adventure: a life apart in remote and splendid places" where he could become "intimate with Frank Lloyd Wright's architecture."[6]

For some, Wright's persona could not be separated from his architecture. Roger d'Astous, a French Canadian who was at Taliesin in 1952–1953 described his impressions of that persona:

He would ask for the moon and you would just go ahead and start making a ladder, literally to go and get it! There's nothing that he would ask that we wouldn't be ready to do. And this was not only my case; it was the case of all the apprentices. I've rarely seen a person with such a "radiation de personalité." He was electrifying—an electrifying person—stimulating a lot of admiration and energy. There's nothing that he would have asked us to do that we wouldn't have done.[7]

Some who came were well equipped for alternative or dual careers. John Amarantides, a native of Greece, arranged for Frank Lloyd Wright to lecture at the Lawrence Institute of Technology, where he was about to earn a degree in architectural engineering. Wright then invited him to visit Taliesin and, knowing that he was a musician, to play his violin for the Fellowship. Amarantides accepted and quickly realized that he *had* to be part of Taliesin's life experience. Gene Masselink arranged for him to meet with Wright, who asked him why he wanted to be an architect. In response, he mentioned, as he recalled, "this, that and the other thing." The meeting ended with Wright saying, "If you can be an architect the way you play the violin you are welcome here." John A, as he came to be known, joined, and he became director of music in 1955. He remained at Taliesin until 1973 before returning to his homeland to practice architecture. Since then, when he visits Taliesin he always brings his violin.[8]

For some, Mrs. Wright was also an attraction. When Bruce Pfeiffer was sixteen years old and living in Worcester, Massachusetts, he read an article about Frank Lloyd Wright. To discover more he went to the library at Harvard. "The librarian," he said, "or someone there, pointed out the sections of Mr. Wright's autobiography that Mrs. Wright wrote, and it just so happened that those were some of the parts that moved me the most." "So," he continued, "I knew I was coming to Taliesin as much for her as for him. It was no surprise to me to find her as powerful a driving force as he was."[9]

Some apprentices no doubt came to study with Wright because they could. Thanks to the GI Bill, veterans of World War II and the Korean War could pay the fees required of apprentices. Some may also have been encouraged by the recommendation of an advisory committee of Wisconsin's governor that, even though Taliesin could not be "evaluated in the manner normally used because of its unique concept and operations," it should be treated as an architectural training school for veterans. The committee's statement that there was "probably no other school or college in the United States comparable to it" evidently appealed to those seeking unconventional ways to become architects.

The committee's recommendation, however, did not affect a ruling made two years earlier by Circuit Judge Arthur W. Kopp of Platteville, Wisconsin. Claiming that because the Frank Lloyd Wright Foundation had no course of study, no textbooks, and no lectures except those given by Wright at breakfast or supper on Sundays, he denied it tax-exempt status. That led to appeals and a Supreme Court ruling that Taliesin was neither an educational nor a fine arts institution and that Wright must pay the $14,000 in taxes he owed. Wright protested that his native state did not appreciate what he had done for it, and he threatened to leave and even burn down his buildings. After he attended to projects in other states, his anger faded and his friends raised the funds needed to pay the taxes. More important to Wright was the adulation he received at a testimonial dinner in Madison, organized by former apprentice Cary Caraway and others, on February 10, 1955. Wright was also honored in Chicago on October 17, 1956, at a Frank Lloyd Wright Day proclaimed by Mayor Richard J. Daley.[10]

He made the most of that big day by displaying at the Merchandise Mart a line of furniture he had designed and setting up an exhibition of his work at the Sherman Hotel, where he unveiled a 24-foot-high drawing of his Mile High building. John Amarantides worked on the rendering for it, and with Louis Wiehle, John Rattenbury, Bruce Pfeiffer, and other apprentices set up what Amarantides called a fantastic, very successful exhibition.[11]

**SHELTER**

At Taliesin West the sheepherder tents so common in earlier years gave way to more durable dwellings in the 1940s and 1950s, although canvas remained an essential part of many of them. Some of the apprentices designed and built new shelters, others adapted ones built earlier.[12]

Bob Beharka's assignment to supervise the construction of the Lewellyn Wright residence and other Wright designs may have resulted from Wright's favorable impression of the desert shelter Beharka designed at Taliesin West. Built in 1954 with twelve-inch-square textile blocks he made with wood forms of his own design, this eight-feet-by-ten-feet structure had a prefabricated metal roof and an outdoor fireplace. According to one observer, there was a carryover from the design of this shelter into Beharka's long career: "The simplicity and utility of the project, the lack of pretense, its beauty derived from a clear, logical use of natural materials, with clean lines and no ornamental appliqué—all these elements became constants in his work."[13]

In an interview in 1992, Kenn Lockhart described the evolution of the shelter to which he was then building an addition. Blaine and Hulda Drake had built the original shelter in 1938, he said, using desert masonry for a large fireplace and two small closets. A hexagonal tent provided the main living space. When the Drakes left in 1941, Cary and Frances Caraway moved to the site, added a small room for their new baby on the northeast side of the fireplace, and lived in the tent. Jack Howe inherited the site in 1942 and built a living room of wood, canvas, and low masonry walls to replace the tent, with a closet to the north of the fireplace. When he married Lu Sparks in 1951, the two of them made this "cabaña" their winter home until they left the Fellowship in 1964.

Kenn and Susan Lockhart claimed the vacated site, and in 1968 they began to rebuild and expand it. Using a rented backhoe and a pick and shovel, Kenn brought utilities there, and then rebuilt everything except the fireplace. Over several "five year plans" of construction, working after 5:00 p.m. and on weekends, they increased the living space from 250 to 450 square feet, making room for a kitchen, bath, and bedroom. Susan mixed the concrete and hauled stones, and Kenn, with her assistance, did the masonry walls, carpentry, plumbing, and electrical work. By 1992 they had completed the masonry walls, roof, and under-floor utilities for an adjacent structure of 450 square feet for Susan's freestanding studio, which could also be used as

Bob Beharka's design of this desert shelter may have given Wright the confidence to charge him with supervision responsibilities at the Lewellyn Wright and Marden Houses. Courtesy of Robert Beharka a guest apartment. After Kenn's death in 1994, Joe Fabris helped Susan pour the floor in the studio and built the interior cabinetry.[14]

Jim Pfefferkorn, who arrived at Taliesin with his wife, Maxine, after having earned a degree in architecture from the University of Kansas, built a shelter for his family at Taliesin West. It began as a simple one, made of desert stone from around the site. It had a sheet-metal roof, a fireplace, and closets, but neither electricity nor running water. The bed was placed so that at night they could gaze at the stars in the desert sky. One day when Mr. and Mrs. Wright were walking past they stopped for a drink of water and a brief visit. Wright walked around the cottage, as Pfefferkorn called it, studying it on all sides. "Well, Jim," Wright remarked, "it's not what I would do, but I like it."

Soon Pfefferkorn expanded the cottage, adding a tiny room for his daughter Derice. When son Peter arrived Jim added a larger children's room. "These were simple and primitive spaces," he recalled. "Better than a tent but not luxurious." When Kenn Lockhart ran a sewer line to his cottage, Pfefferkorn extended it to his with Kenn's help. He then brought water to the cottage through a plastic line and was able to build a small bathroom. Altogether he and his family lived in this shelter for fourteen of their twenty winters in the Fellowship.[15]

The Pfefferkorns also needed lodging when the Fellowship was in Wisconsin. In their second summer there they moved to a house at a nearby farm owned by Wes Peters. Their task was to make it suitable for lodging incoming apprentices. For a number of years, until the place was no longer needed, he and Maxine served as "house parents" for younger apprentices. After moving twice they found themselves in the cottage behind the Midway barn, the central location for farming at Taliesin. After Jim had completed some remodeling, he received word that Mrs. Wright wanted his family to move, as she evidently had other plans for the house. When she arrived that afternoon he mentioned the message he had received. "I said something to the effect that I did not mind moving but that I would appreciate being asked to move rather than being told to move." She apologized, he recalled, and said that she should ask people to do things rather than order them. His reaction: "I was thoroughly shocked and amazed. Mrs. Wright was very accustomed to ordering us and telling us what to do. That was that, the whole subject was dropped, and we didn't move, which was what I wanted because I had just finished fixing up the place."[16]

At Taliesin West unusual circumstances sometimes led to the design of unusual shelters. One such was the creation of a three-tent compound in 1958 by Shreve Babcock, who had a degree in architecture from the University of California at Berkeley when he arrived at Taliesin. One tent was the bedroom he shared with his artist wife, Deirdre, a second was a nursery for their two-year-old son and the baby they were expecting, and the third was Shreve's studio. In darkness, after Fellowship duties were completed, Shreve and three other apprentices poured and finished the concrete slab for the compound. Deirdre's role as a "very eager, imminently expectant mother" was to hold flashlights as they worked.[17]

Most apprentices did not regard living in desert shelters to be a hardship. Vern Swaback probably reflected the sentiments of many of his peers:

Shreve Babcock designed this desert shelter to accommodate himself, his wife, Deirdre, their two-year-old daughter, and a daughter to be born soon. The nursery, left, was connected to the master bedroom; the freestanding tent was Babcock's studio. Courtesy of Shreve Babcock

I remember walking out to my tent, in the evening, with a sense of elegance and affluence and inspiration that no house anywhere on earth could equal. I don't care if one had the most exciting site and unlimited budget. I don't see how you could recreate that experience of walking out into a starry night—not camping out, this is not a camping-out experience, this is HOME. And knowing that here was this place, that you and the earth and the sky would commune . . . . And that somehow or other you had a hand in creating it, not through a contractor, not through subcontractors, but personally.[18]

For those who were in the Fellowship for only a few years, the shelters were as much projects as dwellings. Apprentices who stayed in the Fellowship and gained senior status could look back on having lived in many places, including desert shelters, before settling into a place with a sense of permanence.[19]

## WORK

Besides building their own shelters, apprentices continued to work on structures designed for shared activities at Taliesin West. Ling Po, who joined the Fellowship when he immigrated from China in 1948, described an experience that resembled a rite of initiation. It occurred when Wright expanded the gathering place known as the Kiva to make room for a piano. Wright ordered apprentices to knock down a concrete wall and remove the rubble. They carried it out in baskets and walked through intricate paths, up and down, dumping them, and coming back for more. As this continued for hours Ling Po felt as though one of his ribs might be broken, but Wright would not let him stop. "And that was a very good experience," Ling Po said, "because he was trying out to see how far is this fellow's endurance. Even as he used steel and concrete and wanted to find out how

After a fire destroyed part of Hillside in 1952, Wright redesigned and rebuilt it. Here, at age 85, he is with Kelly Oliver on scaffolding for rebuilding the theater roof.

Photograph © Pedro E. Guerrero

much this material can take, he in the same way tried to find out how much an individual can take. . . . Because if we don't do a little overboard how can we know what is just enough?"[20]

Joe Fabris, who also joined the Fellowship in 1948, was immediately involved in construction: "I seem to have a knack for it," he told an interviewer. "I used to work a lot—in the beginning just in the House doing odd jobs. And sometimes Mr. Wright, after his afternoon rest, would come along and just sit and watch me work and make occasional comments and direct the work a little. . . . He just seemed to enjoy being around when people were working. And he did just sit sometimes and watch me work and have his tea."[21]

Most former apprentices remember work they did at Taliesin, Taliesin West, and in Wright projects elsewhere. For example, Kelly Oliver, who joined the Fellowship in 1949, recalled that, among other things, he was in charge of the rebuilding of the Taliesin Theater and Foyer after the 1952 fire; did drawings for the concrete table, made the reusable form for the seats, was in charge of pouring the seats, and did a lot of the interior cabinetry for the Cabaret Theater at Taliesin West; was the chief electrician at Taliesin for many years; did the lighting layouts and drawings for fixtures for the Price Tower in Bartlesville, Oklahoma; laid out the lighting and designed stage lighting for the Dallas Theater Center; and supervised the construction of that theater and the John Gillin House in Dallas (assisted by David George, an apprentice from Texas, in both projects). When Oliver left the Fellowship he continued his relationship with Taliesin and in the 1960s represented the Taliesin Architects from his Denver office.[22]

Bob Broward, who apprenticed with Wright for six months in 1949–1950, recalled that his experiences at Taliesin were especially wonderful when he was directly involved with "the Master." He knew how to operate a bulldozer, and that led to his assignment to build a better road to Midway at Taliesin. As he was dragging earth back and forth "using this monster," he saw Wright on the hillside waving his cane baton to direct him. "Serge Koussevitzky had been a guest earlier," he remarked, "and I am sure that the Master thought he was conducting the Boston Symphony."[23]

## COOKING, FARMING, SERVING, AND DINING

Dining together was a major part of the communal living at Taliesin, and, as John Amarantides observed, "without communal living there could not have been a Taliesin apprenticeship system."

It was a total immersion in the "doing." A total dedication. Not the doing of one thing alone, of course; it was the multitude of activities and experiences working together which created the excitement. The excitement of learning by doing under *and with* the master. Anytime. All the time. Day and/or night. Sometimes all day and all night and all together. Only as a community living and working together under Taliesin circumstances did miracles and magic occur.[24]

Kitchen work was part of that working together, and it was always assigned to apprentices who worked under Mrs. Wright's watchful eye. Cooking, remarked Richard Keding, could never be regarded as creative work, for "Mrs. Wright considered the recipes used in the Taliesin Kitchen perfect and inviolable. Any deviation from a Taliesin recipe could provoke a sharp reprimand. Cooking was an all-consuming, high-tension experience."[25]

Jim Pfefferkorn has recorded some of his kitchen experiences: most of the menu, he said, was standard, but it had to be submitted to Mrs. Wright for approval. Pancakes were approved for some days, and Jim learned to make them so that they were "light, fluffy and delicious," and in sufficient quantity to feed sixty people. He made special pancakes for the children, shaped like animals of all kinds, with a raisin in each one for an eye. Sometimes, he said, "there would be four or five little kids all sitting on stools around me helping me to decide what kind of animal their pancakes would be."[26]

Others assigned to the kitchen also found ways to be creative. The renowned architect E. Fay Jones, who spent a summer at Taliesin with his wife and two small daughters, noted that "Mr. Wright's whole attitude was that every task was an opportunity for creative effort, for imaginative effort." What "really got that across" to him was the way Kelly [Oliver] approached his kitchen duty after getting up at 3:00 in the morning to cook breakfast, lunch, and dinner for fifty people. "Now with all these tasks to do, Kelly managed to go up the hill to an old fallen walnut tree and cut through by hand a slab for each of the tables. He treated the wood with some kind of oil and gathered some pine cones and cranberries. Instead of saying, 'God, I've got to get this damn bread baked,' slap it on a big plate and put it on the table, he went to the effort of presenting the bread in a better way.[27]

Those who were not cooks served as kitchen help for a week at a time. That meant washing dishes without a dishwasher, and occasionally, Andre Hoffe recalled, "washing up for some 30 guests in addition to the Fellowship." That "back-breaking job," he said, "at least taught the aspirant architect the importance of a kitchen sink at the right height." To have employed paid help to do the kitchen work, he added, "would have undermined the whole spirit of the Fellowship."[28]

So, presumably, was the thought of hiring someone to pick up the garbage. Mrs. Wright assigned that task to Earl Nisbet, among many others. He would dig a large pit, he said, far from the buildings, and bury the refuse. Because he was one of the newer apprentices in early 1951, he was amenable to whatever she asked. "There were stories that if one questioned anything Mrs. Wright asked to be done, she would have you for breakfast." So he dug pits and washed pots. He did the same at Taliesin West, where he had to dig through layers of rock, sand, and gravel, and the pits had to be deeper to prevent desert animals from digging it up. One day while he was completing his work as a kitchen helper, Mrs. Wright walked up to him and said abruptly, "You're not afraid of me, are you Earl?" Without hesitating he replied, "Why no, Mrs. Wright, should I be?" Her face took on a bewildered expression, he recalled, "and without responding she turned and walked away. During my years at fellowship, that was the only time I found Mrs. Wright to be speechless."[29]

Sometimes the kitchen served as a "port of entry" to the Fellowship. In the fall of 1947, Ken Peterson arrived at Taliesin and went to work in the kitchen several days before the Wrights returned from Arizona. Several days later, with Mrs. Wright resuming her place in the kitchen, he was busy cleaning and doing other chores. "Suddenly she realized I was a new face and asked in her Montenegren accent, 'and who are you?' I explained my desire to talk to Mr. Wright and she said, 'don't worry, I will talk to Mr. Wright.'" When he met with Wright several days later he was told that they had more applicants than space, Wright adding however "I hear you did well in the kitchen," so "we can always squeeze one more in."[30]

Members of the Fellowship who served Mr. and Mrs. Wright in their private dining rooms were privy to conversations between them and with their guests. All the apprentices, though, could interact with their leaders at the Tea Circle. At Taliesin it was located near Wright's studio under a huge oak tree, at Taliesin West in a shadeless corner of the desert property, a considerable distance from the main complex. Teatime was a daily event, at 4:00 p.m. Apprentices were expected to appear for it in their work clothes. Earl Nisbet has described the ritual: A teacart or table, he said, was placed at the center of the circle and apprentices would choose a snack to accompany the tea. They "would then sit on the stone bench and usually converse with others regarding their work. Should an apprentice be extremely hungry, he might be tempted to have seconds, however all eyes would fall on him and he had better be just 'pouring tea.'" Some in the Fellowship would be designated "tea cooks," whose responsibility it was to bake the snacks. Mrs. Wright might consider those who proved themselves as tea cooks for the position of breakfast cook.[31]

## WINTER WORK AT TALIESIN

Much of the food consumed by the Fellowship was produced on the farm at Taliesin. Although most of the Fellowship spent the winters of 1950–1951 and 1951–1952 in Arizona, Wright selected a few to remain at Taliesin to keep the farm going. In this group were Kenn and Polly Lockhart and their two young children, Johnny Hill, and eighteen-year-old Eric Lloyd Wright, son of Lloyd Wright. When Eric was drafted as a non-combatant conscientious objector in January 1952, Brooklyn-born Morton Delson took his place.

Lockhart had a little experience on farms as a young boy, and Eric Wright's was limited to several boyhood summers spent at Taliesin. They needed to know more, and they found it in pamphlets requested from the Department of Agriculture. Assisted by a Spring Green veterinarian, Harper Harrison, they went to work. Theirs was no small operation: Eric recalled that they had forty-two Guernseys, forty pigs, six horses, and 500 chickens.[32]

Each week Polly Lockhart scrubbed forty-five dozen eggs and shipped them to Taliesin West. To amuse herself, she recalled, she drew faces on many, "hoping a sleepy breakfast cook in Arizona would enjoy them but they never noticed."[33] They did notice something else though: the farmers in Wisconsin named all the cows after women in the Fellowship, Eric said, "and when the women apprentices heard this, there was a huge outcry against it. So we had to go back to numbering them." The eggs they shipped supplemented the canned fruit and vegetables produced in the large garden in the summer. Led by Davy Davison, the entire Fellowship worked in planting, weeding, cultivating, and harvesting the garden.

In addition to the farm work, Frank Lloyd Wright left the apprentices there with two architecture projects: repairing the Guggenheim model for an exhibition in New York, set to open in December, and finishing the working drawings for the Grant House to be built in Cedar Rapids, Iowa. They would have time to do these projects, he believed, because farmers always dried up most of the herd in winter. "Well," said Eric,

it turns out winter is one of the most productive times for milking. No cows are dried up. We would get up at 5:00 am to start the generator and begin milking by 5:30 a.m. We would spend all day milking, cleaning the barn, spreading the manure on the frozen fields, feeding the animals and chickens, and repairing the equipment, many times in sub-zero weather. At one point the temperature reached 57 degrees below zero, the coldest spot in the U.S. (Alaska was not a state then.) We would finish milking and clean up the barn by 7:00 p.m., have dinner and then go spend three hours working on the model. We were usually not into bed until 11:30.

They got the Guggenheim model to New York on time, and Kenn wrapped up the drawings and sent them back, explaining that he had done the best he could with the cows not having dried up.[34]

The hardy farmers devised ways to keep warm, or almost so, by means of fireplaces and an ineffective space heater. Most of the power provided by the diesel-powered generator was used for pumping water, operating the milking machines, and lighting the living and working quarters. When parts were needed to repair the generator, Polly Lockhart drove over winding, hilly, sometimes icy roads to Dodgeville to get them. In addition to this and other tasks, she did most of the cooking, assisted by her husband on holidays.

Life on the farm provided learning experiences for the Lockhart children. They were fascinated, their mother said, by watching the man who had an artificial inseminator service. Spotting his truck when it arrived they would call, "Mama, the 'seminator man's here! They followed him into the barn, watched him don long rubber gloves and go to work, their eyes big with wonder." The music they heard that winter also appealed to them. Brian admired Eric Wright's flute playing so much that he became a flutist himself—and an architect, too, of course.[35]

## WINTER WORK AT TALIESIN WEST

Just as these winter farmers had multiple duties at Taliesin, so did other apprentices at Taliesin West. Lynn Anderson joined the Fellowship in 1958 and arrived at Taliesin West before most of the established members. While looking at the buildings she passed the kitchen and saw a cook working over a hot range, with a mountain of pots and pans at the sink behind her. She helped out then and with the cooking the next day, but then she was asked to clean the Wrights' living quarters—washing the windows, vacuuming the concrete floors, and preparing them for scrubbing and applying a sealer. She rolled the rugs on the terrace, vacuumed, and scrubbed them; she also cleaned the chairs and built-in seats in the Garden Room. Having been unoccupied for six months, they needed a thorough cleaning.

The next day she was asked to pick up medicine for Uncle Vlado, Mrs. Wright's brother, and groceries for Aunt Sophie, and the mail at the Scottsdale post office. About a week later she found herself driving Brandoch Peters, son of Wes and his late wife Svetlana, to school. Because he had back problems, he lay flat on a mattress in the back of the station wagon until they were within a few blocks of the school; there he would move to the front seat. They followed the same procedure in reverse in the afternoons. From then on she had two additional assignments—cleaning the Wrights' living quarters and being a family server, which included washing the dishes, glassware, silverware, pots and pans, and counters and floors.

There was more: perhaps as a result of Uncle Vlado's recommendation, Anderson was asked to drive the pickup truck to the Phoenix area once or twice each week to fill the orders for construction supplies or kitchen needs. Gene made out checks to the suppliers and signed them, and she entered the amounts when the orders were filled. On one occasion she was given the names and locations of three thrift shops to buy all the bedding and pillows she could find. Entering a storefront she found herself face to face with a bentwood chair, cradling an . . . (Here the account ends with two words in red letters: "WILL ADD," but nothing was added).[36]

## MARRIAGES, DIVORCES, REMARRIAGES, CHILDREN, AND RELATIONSHIPS

From its earliest days to the present, the Taliesin Fellowship has had married couples in its membership. Some arrived as husbands and wives. Bearing and rearing children was also part of life at Taliesin, and while the parents had primary responsibility for caring for their own, the youngsters enjoyed interactions with many adults in the Fellowship. Among those who arrived as singles, courtship and marriage was a possibility. Divorces, remarriages, extramarital affairs, and homosexual relationships were regarded as unsurprising. In many respects, as members of the Fellowship have maintained, life in the Fellowship was much like life outside of it, or at least like life in communities of artists.

But there was also a significant difference: In many of the relationships Mrs. Wright played the role of manipulating matchmaker. As Kamal Amin has observed, she "needed to be in control of all situations and all people. . . . She endeavored to be a third party to every relationship," finding access through the party easiest to reach.

She inquired about the details of the relationship and invariably offered advice in an attempt to manage that relationship. Indeed, she often endeavored to disrupt the autonomy of a relationship that took place outside her sphere of control. She used a variety of means, including the denigration of one side of the relationship to the other in a transparent but often effective "divide and rule" style. She never said anything that was not true. But she either highlighted or dimmed the right features in order to accomplish her purpose. . . .

One of the tasks assigned to her group of faithful followers was to report to her at all times what was said or done anywhere and everywhere on the premises. Clearly that was an essential part of her control mechanism.[37]

Sometimes she matched gay men with straight women. The marriages of such couples were ordinarily short-lived, but they were not necessarily unhappy.

Another difference is that the Wrights' daughter Iovanna apparently engaged in more sexual affairs and was married more frequently than anyone around her in the Fellowship. That may have limited her parents' ability to impose on others the standards of conduct they might have preferred. Iovanna's first husband was Waring Simons Howe, a lieutenant in the U.S. Navy; when he left for active duty that marriage effectively ended. Subsequently she was married for nine years to Arthur Pieper, an apprentice whom, she said, she did not like all that much, but she trusted her mother's wisdom in arranging the marriage. Next she married apprentices Charles Gardiner; Andrew Binnie, who fathered her daughter, Eve; and Charles Schiffner. At one point she mentioned having paired off with apprentices "as never before," and she identified several of them as her partners, including Roland Rebay and Michael Sutton (for fifteen years), as well as a painter named George DeLacy.[38]

If members of the Fellowship regarded Iovanna's conduct as inappropriate or even scandalous, their judgments were immaterial, for she was the Wrights' daughter. It may, though, have established mores that made comparable conduct acceptable, at least as far as multiple marriages were concerned. The sense one gains from visiting with members of the Fellowship is that marriage, divorce, and remarriage were all taken in stride by the individuals involved and those around them.

Similarly, instances of homosexual relationships were generally not regarded by apprentices as troubling and, with those engaged in them likely closeted, they may not even have been known to most of the members of the Fellowship. That there were episodes of homosexual practice is attributable to some extent to the circumstances in which its members lived. They were artists, the vast majority of them men, in an experimental community. Sexual experimentation may have been seen as acceptable, and homosexual experiences provided an alternative to out-of-reach heterosexual ones. It may, in some instances, have been the second choice for sexual relations.

In early years of the Fellowship Mr. Wright registered disapproval of homosexual incidents when he learned about them, as apparently did Mrs. Wright. Although other reasons were given, such incidents apparently accounted for the expulsion of persons presumed to be culpable. Eventually, though, the disapproval diminished as the work done by gay men was essential in the operation of the Fellowship, and Mrs. Wright came to depend on a number of them as personal attendants.[39]

Remarks about homosexuality appear rarely in transcripts of interviews archived at Taliesin West and are equally rare in responses to my survey of former apprentices. Warren Biddle was one who did comment on it. He recalled that Mrs. Wright one time said to him, "you have a latent tinge of that. She'd detected that; she said that. And this has bothered me all my life. I have not had any sexual affairs with men."[40] Another who commented was Tom Olson, an apprentice from 1952 to 1961. He recalled having had some conversations with Mrs. Wright about his sexuality, tendered as help. Upon much later reflection, he said, these conversations amounted to double-dealing: "She was telling me not to act upon my feelings and others not to get caught."[41]

Tim Wright, Lewellyn's son and Frank Lloyd Wright's grandson, offered some insightful observations about homosexuality in the Fellowship. He spent his twelfth, thirteenth, and fourteenth summers at Taliesin (1950–1952), and he recalled them as having been heavenly: "To be a teenager, surrounded by attractive young men and women in their twenties and thirties from all over the world, possessing fascinating skills, passionate about their work, devoted to my grandfather and grandmother, mostly nurturing toward me—what more could one possibly ask?" At the same time, "it was Hell," probably because no adult had time to show him how to do such things as care for the ducks and get them from the lake into the coop each evening. Still, he learned how to run the tar pot when they retiled the studio roof, run the tractor with the big mower, and do other things he convinced himself were equally important. "What was so magical about Taliesin," he said, "was the incomparable vividness of every day, of the bad moments as well as the good ones. Everything we did was important, because the enterprise was important, and it was grandfather who gave us all that sense, obvious even down to the lowliest and youngest of 'apprentices' like me."

When Tim was twenty he found out that among the most nurturing apprentices were three who were gay, "but necessarily closeted." They had all behaved in exemplary fashion around him, who was not gay, but in retrospect he felt sure that there was sublimated eroticism involved, from which he benefited greatly. "In any case, as we all subsequently learned, a significant number of Taliesin apprentices were gay," most likely a greater percentage than in the population at large, but probably a typical number for an arts organization. "What's tricky," he continued, "is the time factor—there were few institutions in the '50's that would have tolerated openly gay members, hence it would be ahistorical to single out grandfather and grandmother as being unusually unsympathetic." Continuing:

Wright himself, I remember reading somewhere, may not even have known what homosexuality was. . . . When you think that he was born in 1867, this would not be so astounding as it at first sounds. But grandmother was very sophisticated about sexuality, and she vigorously regulated sexuality within the apprenticeship, which makes her role in the denial of homosexuality more interesting. Sexuality was, of course, a legitimate concern. I remember one of the apprentices later . . . saying that the Taliesin men were sexually like loaded pistols, just waiting to go off. Their lives were further complicated by the fact that seeking social/sexual companionship outside Taliesin, despite the 6 or 7 to 1 male to female ratio, was very much discouraged. . . .[42]

## PARTIES AND CELEBRATIONS

The parties and celebrations that occurred frequently often required intense labor, particularly the ones at Easter each year. Senior fellows and apprentices baked special breads, decorated hundreds of eggs, and made special table decorations. Many of their parties required elaborate costumes for skits performed by members of the Fellowship. There were parties on the lake, in Hillside, and in the residence and its courtyards at Taliesin. At Taliesin West the Fellowship partied in the Cabaret Theater and the Performing Arts Pavilion, as well as wherever else the setting seemed appropriate. Frances Nemtin recalled a party at which Ling Po showed up as a lovely Chinese girl, wearing makeup and a wig. "He glided into the party," she remembered, "and no one could identify him. Everyone thought he was a guest. Meantime Madame Po (Ling Po's mother) kept asking if anyone knew where Ling was, because here for the first time was a Chinese girl he could meet; she felt sick that he wasn't there! I don't know if he ever told her. He carried it off perfectly—the dance, the fan, beautiful robes."[43]

In a theatrical production, Cornelia Brierly is Mae West and Tom Casey is W.C. Fields. Courtesy of the Frank Lloyd Wright Foundation and Cornelia Brierly

Some of the performances became the stuff of legends, such as ones by Tom Casey as the Fiddler in "Fiddler on the Roof" and Cornelia Brierly and Tom as Mae West and W.C. Fields. One of the most elaborate was the "heaven and hell" party featuring a Spanish galleon on the lake at Taliesin. With the chorus singing "Let the heaven light shine on me" again and again, the galleon drifted toward the dam—to be saved by a gust of wind from the right direction.[44]

### GURDJIEFFIAN DANCE MOVEMENTS AND DRAMAS

The skits continued through the decades, and the apprentices had fun with them, even as a new emphasis began when Iovanna Wright returned from studying dance with Georgi Gurdjieff in 1949. The skits became dance dramas more elaborate in every way. More and more time went into rehearsals. Those who thrived on such performances dedicated themselves to participation. Moreover, while there had been some pressure to take part in the movements previously, now the expectations of Iovanna and her mother for wholehearted commitments intensified. For those who considered such things a distraction from their purpose in being at Taliesin, this was an unwelcome development. As those in the movements gained Mrs. Wright's favor, the rest were seen as being on the outs with her, or so they assumed. The division between insiders and outsiders deepened

One who regarded them a distraction was Allan Gelbin. He recalled that one Sunday after breakfast "Mrs. Wright had put Mr. Wright on my tail. . . . He started telling me some things about myself, very critically, and asked me why I had quit movements." "Well," Gelbin responded, "I would rather spend my time studying the piano and practicing." Wright replied, "Well, anyone can sit on their ass and play piano, but it takes work to do the movements, and you're lazy." Gelbin thought that was very amusing, for Wright liked to improvise on the piano. The scolding ended quickly, he said, and they started arranging branches and flowers in the theater.[45]

Curtis Besinger has presented the most detailed case concerning what many believed to be the damage done to the Fellowship by this increased emphasis on the movements. Following the death of Gurdjieff in October 1949, he sensed "an effort and intention to establish Taliesin as a center, of a kind, for the teaching of Gurdjieff philosophy." He noted that Mme. Jeanne de Salzman, Gurdjieff's longtime associate, visited the camp during the winter and asked all the senior apprentices to meet with her. She wanted to know if all of them were seriously interested in Gurdjieff and his work. Besinger said that he didn't think they were but that some were participating in the movements, not because of any interest in them, but because they were reluctant to appear uncooperative. Mme. Salzman, he said, "apparently relayed my comment to Mrs. Wright, who soon let me know that it was not appreciated."

The following summer Mr. Wright and the apprentices began to prepare drawings and models for "Sixty Years of Living Architecture," the exhibition of his work in Philadelphia and other locations,[46] but attention was diverted by the urging by Mrs. Wright and Iovanna for the members of the Fellowship to buy copies of Gurdjieff's recently published *All and Everything*. Besinger bought it but did not read it. On October 29, the anniversary of Gurdjieff's death, a demonstration of Gurdjieff's movements and a tribute to him by Wright seemed to Besinger to be "part of an ongoing effort to associate or to connect Mr. Wright with Gurdjieff." The purpose of a demonstration of the movements in Madison in the summer of 1951, he speculated, was "to publicize and proselytize for Gurdjieff's teaching."

## TENSIONS AND DIVISION IN THE FELLOWSHIP

Tensions in the community arose in the summer of 1952 over the demand for time for chorus rehearsals and for building sets for a big party, in this case a pirate party that would feature a decked-out Spanish galleon. They reached a climax, however, when work on the exhibition, then being set up in New York, conflicted with the plans of Mrs. Wright and Iovanna for dance-drama productions. Besinger and other apprentices—at various times

Fellowship members rehearsing one of the "movements," or dances, inspired by Gurdjieff and led at Taliesin West by Iovanna Wright. Courtesy of the Frank Lloyd Wright Foundation

Kenn Lockhart, Tom Casey, John Geiger, Robin Molny, Morton Delson, John Rattenbury, Kelly Oliver, Jim Pfefferkorn, George Thompson, David Wheatley, and Herbert de Levie—were in New York working on the exhibition, while Mrs. Wright wanted them back at Taliesin to rehearse for a production in Chicago. Besinger returned to Taliesin and went on to Chicago to accompany the production on the piano, but his relations with the Wrights, he recalled, were changed irreversibly.

The division in the Fellowship made evident by the two shows—the exhibition of Wright's work and the performance of movements in Chicago—continued. Although Besinger maintained a civil relationship with the Wrights, "beneath the surface it was unsettled and strained." Several conversations he had with Mrs. Wright troubled him. In one she mentioned that "the Fellowship, as it then existed, was only a scaffolding for what it was to become after Mr. Wright's death"; in another that "architecture is how we make our living," thereby suggesting that the architects were to make a living for the movement's groups. He also saw her beginning to make plans for the future of the Fellowship by taking on new roles and trying to exercise more control over the apprentices' lives. That he was the only senior apprentice not invited to the wedding or reception when Iovanna married Arthur Pieper, an apprentice, in the summer of 1954 sent him an unmistakable message. In July 1955 he decided, with mixed feelings, to leave the Fellowship. His departure was unquestionably hastened by what he regarded as the out-of-balance intrusion of the legacy of Gurdjieff into the life of the Fellowship.[47]

Granted, Besinger's account focuses on only his own experiences, but his judgments were shared by a number of his peers. One such was his friend John Geiger. He believed that Mrs. Wright was using the movements "to gain her own sort of power base." She established a body of people who were hers and not necessarily Mr. Wright's, thus dividing the Fellowship. "Over a period of time," he said, "I think she wrested control of the Fellowship from Mr. Wright." That's why Geiger quit the movements. He acknowledged that once when he went to pick up Mrs. Wright for some occasion, she seemed more gentle and vulnerable and human, not her stern self. She reached out and touched his cheek, he recalled, saying, "You're all my children." That was the only time he saw her in a sympathetic light, and it made him uncomfortable. But he saw nothing wrong with it.[48] As for the movements, those who stayed with them either enjoyed them or considered participation a price to be paid for the positive experiences they had in the Fellowship.

## PERSPECTIVES ON MRS. WRIGHT

There was a distinct line of authority between Mr. and Mrs. Wright in the management of the Fellowship. On his side was architecture. On hers was the day-to-day management of the Fellowship. The struggles between them were about who was going to do what. As Tom Casey recalled, "he wanted people to come out and build this wall or tear down something or other. And Mrs. Wright would say, 'Well, it's his turn to go in the kitchen.' 'Well, by God, how is he going to help me?' They would have pretty stiff arguments sometimes about people doing something or how they were

going to be assigned one place or another." The arguments would be resolved, but there was "a definite contest of wills."[49]

Such contests notwithstanding, Mrs. Wright's primary mission was to be attentive to Mr. Wright's needs. That meant, as she explained to Bruce Pfeiffer, to make sure that he ate well, slept well, relaxed well, and exercised well. Beyond that, she sought to ensure that the environment around him was conducive to his creative genius, to protect him where it was hazardous, and to "open the door" to him when that was beneficial. That is what she did with the Fellowship: she would exclude those whom she judged to want chiefly to be associated with Wright's name and include those who seemed to really love her husband and his work and wanted to be a part of his personal and work life.[50] The sooner apprentices grasped this, the better they fared in the Fellowship.

Some members perceived Mrs. Wright as a divider, not only with respect to the movements, but also in everyday life. In their view, she assumed this role willingly and steadfastly fulfilled it. As one of the apprentices, Deirdre Treacy Babcock, described the situation, there was an "in-group" and an "out-group." The latter were followers of Mr. Wright, and the former were Mrs. Wright's followers. As a member of the "out-group," Deirdre Babcock regarded her experiences in communal living among some seventy-five other

Wright with apprentices, including Vernon Swaback, seated, far right. Courtesy of Vernon Swaback artists, architects, and musicians as "a precious memory." But she clashed with Mrs. Wright. "The tomatoes hit the fan," she said, and she "left on a stretcher, so to speak," taking her young children to her husband's parents' home. After a hospital stay she joined them. At the end of a full year in the Fellowship and when Mr. Wright died, her husband also left.[51]

Paul Bogart, who had been at Taliesin five years before the Babcocks, has recorded a similar perspective on the division in the Fellowship but a different reaction to Mrs. Wright. Although he recognized that she "really was the controlling force in the Fellowship on a day to day basis," he had the feeling it was still Mr. Wright's Fellowship. The "young guys" were there for the architecture and "kind of 'Mr. Wright's boys,'" and thus protected from the politics of the place, or left alone. "And while a lot of people have a lot of very harsh things to say, and bad feelings," he continued, and while it was no picnic in some ways, he never felt badly treated.

Nonetheless, Mrs. Wright called him in several times and complained about his attitude. She said, "Well, Paul, you always agree and you always say yes, but you don't change." He guessed there was something in his behavior that she didn't approve, but it would have been impossible for him to change, he said, because he really didn't understand what it was that would have been expected from him that was different from the way he was behaving.[52]

Mrs. Wright made indelible impressions on most apprentices, different ones at different times. So their memories of her vary greatly. George James recalled that he was "absolutely impressed" by her background, her stature. While he was there in 1952–1953 she would talk to a group of apprentices on Tuesday evenings in the Sun Cottage, telling stories about how she got out of Russia and her life at Fontainebleau under Gurdjieff. Her studies with him, James believed, helped make her the strict person that she was. Although animosity toward her lingered among some former apprentices many years later, they may have come to Taliesin, he speculated, without realizing the amount of effort it took to understand and to learn. While Mr. Wright was deeply involved in designing, in traveling, and in getting new clients, she kept the place going and molded it so that his apprentices and assistants could all help Mr. Wright.[53]

One who saw the benefits of having both Mr. and Mrs. Wright as leaders of the Fellowship was Ling Po: "Just to think about [Mr. Wright]," he said, "is just like to think about somebody who saved my life." If not for Mrs. Wright, he continued, "there won't be the Fellowship, because Mr. Wright was an artistic, poetic master, having no wish nor patience to deal with personal problems. Mrs. Wright took up the very difficult job of keep the Fellowship going, holding it together. If not for her, there wouldn't be able for us to live with Mr. Wright, so I'm surely very thankful to her."[54]

Former apprentices with sharply differing perspectives are many. One is Bob Broward, who recalled that something he did bothered Mrs. Wright, but he couldn't remember what it was. Maybe, in fact, he simply did not know. She summoned him to her room and "lashed out at him." He remembers her saying, "Bob, you have mice on your brain," meaning that his mind was confused. He stomped out, an irreversible action, as a meeting with Wright soon confirmed. Wright's last words were imprinted in his memory: "Well, evidently you don't fit in here."[55]

Another is Milton Stricker, who remembers the incident that told him his days in the Fellowship were numbered. While he was repairing a shelf in the Living Room, a saucer slid off and shattered on the stone floor. Not wanting to bother the Wrights at dinner, he swept it up and put it in a garbage can, covered with a lid. The next morning he reported the accident to Mr. Wright, who told him not to worry about it. When Mrs. Wright came in with a stern look she said, "Frank, do you know what Milton did? He broke one of our saucers." Mr. Wright said, "Yes, Mother, Milton told me about it, and it's all right." When she asked whether it couldn't have been repaired, he told her that it was in a million pieces. Stricker believes she knew that, having gone through the garbage and finding it there. He knew then that it wouldn't be long before he had to leave. "She had a way," he said, of putting pressure on people, "trying to get them under her control, into her group."[56]

For some, bad memories of working with Mrs. Wright have not yet gone away. Bill Patrick recalled that "she early on cast [him] aside as unmalleable, though capable of being useful in the kitchen/food department." Moreover, "she made many assignments as obvious punishment for shortcomings in her one-way relationships," and after seven years in the army, he was not "seeking a second mother." There is no doubt in his mind "that many of us left Taliesin because of the intrigue and insufferable management of this matriarchal authority."[57]

Some members of the Fellowship practiced the art of accommodation. Tom Olson, for example, knew Mrs. Wright to be "a volatile person and at times difficult," as did many others, but that "her firm hand is likely what made the Fellowship function: dissidents were dispatched immediately, [not allowing] their unhappiness to fester." This preserved the unity of the Fellowship. Her involvement in the lives of Fellowship members "could be viewed as meddlesome, but was likely well intentioned."[58]

Everyone in the Fellowship recognized Mrs. Wright's complexity and the sense of royalty she conveyed. Vern Swaback thought of her as a great organist who played the people around her: "We were all kind of voicing, a 'stop' on the organ, if you will. And she would endeavor to play beautiful music, using these voices of personalities. . . . Everyone who knew Mrs. Wright had their own personal relationship; it was something known only to Mrs. Wright and that person. Every conversation was a confidential conversation—not in terms of secrecy, but in terms of meaning and purpose and intensity."[59]

## PERSPECTIVES ON MR. WRIGHT

At the distance of five decades and more, it is natural to wonder about the magic touch of Wright the octogenarian (and more) with the young men and women in the Fellowship. Vern Swaback provides an insight. On his very first day in the Taliesin West drafting room, yet a teenager, he laid out a collection of colored pencils. Seeing them, Wright paused beside his desk and said, "Doesn't that just want to make you draw?" That gave him a feeling he would never forget. Wright "had received every praise that could be granted an architect. Yet he was more enthusiastic than I was! At that moment I understood something I couldn't have learned from a textbook. I experienced the gift of a master." That experience, he says, gives him chills yet today. Swaback's only disappointment in his first days at Taliesin, he told an interviewer, was discovering that some of the new apprentices were not as excited about the program, and not as committed to it, as he was. He didn't understand their attitude. "Of course, they didn't last, they didn't stay, they didn't become part of the Fellowship."[60]

Most experiences with Wright proved unforgettable, even among those who were at Taliesin only briefly. For example, Hideo Murakami, who arrived early in 1954 and was drafted into the military later that year, recalled that late one evening in the drafting room Mr. Wright asked him, "Do you know the difference between orderly disorder and disorderly order?" Then he walked away. Another time he remarked, "Lieber Meister used to tell me, 'young man, just take care of the terminals, the rest will take care of itself.' Do you know what he meant?" Wright didn't expect answers and he didn't give any. "Just something for me to think about," Murakami concluded.[61]

Memories of experiences with Wright remained also with those at whom he aimed his wrath, including those who had been exiled. Among his most notable exiles were Paolo Soleri, Mark Mills, and Richard Salter. At his request, they resigned in 1948. Eighteen months later (March 15, 1950), Soleri asked for the reasons, so he could "ignore the vulgar gossip about my friends and myself." Wright responded, "I only hope the disagreeable character of my experience in allowing you to join my work is not characteristically Italian. I find you inclined to Rococo, arty, insolent and underground; more interested in forming a group of my weaker members around yourself than in harmonizing helpfully with my work." "So," he continued, "I asked you to leave. It is all that simple and the less said the better. . . . Get down to first principles of architecture," he continued, "instead of practicing the intrigues of a professional politician."[62]

Wright dealt with Mark Mills just as harshly, writing, "Dear Mark: Hypocrisy is a sin of which you will be accused many times in your lifetime I imagine. Taliesin held hope for you at one time. None now." Mills responded several months later, "Your accusation . . . is ill founded, it neither knows nor invites knowing my action and intensions. . . . To experience injustice from you has been a cruel burden of futility and despair inflicted because of my tenacious belief in and devotion to you."[63]

### FRANK LLOYD WRIGHT'S DEATH

Frank Lloyd Wright died on April 9, 1959, sixty days before what would have been his ninety-second birthday. The members of the Fellowship were stunned. Nobody expected him to die. According to Vern Swaback, "he was as useful and energetic as anyone could be. And when he went to the hospital we all thought he had the flu or a cold. . . . And so his death was an absolute shock, for which there was no preparation."[64]

Wright had suffered from severe pain and was taken to the hospital on April 4. Two days later, a Monday, surgeons removed what seemed to be an intestinal blockage, and he appeared to be recovering. But Thursday morning, surrounded by doctors and others, he began to fail. Mrs. Wright was brought into the room, and she was with him when he breathed his last.

Soon the entire community gathered at Taliesin West. Those present remember that Mrs. Wright sat with them on the Sunset Terrace at Taliesin West. A journalist who did a feature on Mrs. Wright noted that she showed the kind of strength "that was something other than physical—she was totally drained, almost didn't look like a person—and still sat there . . . talking about the fact that everything would be okay. We would survive. . . . She really kept Mr. Wright alive. In a very real sense he didn't die until she did. That was part of her ability, to kind of regenerate the lives of individuals. . . ."[65]

Mrs. Wright planned initially for the Fellowship to travel to Wisconsin for the funeral, but she soon decided that only the few who were closest to the family should go. But there would be a funeral in the desert. As his body lay in an open casket, surrounded by flowers and mourners, the Fellowship bade him farewell with music and eulogies. Frank Laraway described what happened next:

His body was carried out toward the front, lower parking lot where the Camaro truck with open bed, was waiting. The entire funeral crowd followed the casket to the graveled court of the entry, watching awkwardly as they slid the casket into the truck bed. It was then covered over with a custom vinyl cover, snapped tightly around all the edges. Wes, Gene and perhaps one more (Kenn Lockhart?) crowded into the front seat together and started driving toward the valley away from Taliesin West. . . .

. . . . I think we all said farewell as they headed down the dusty road toward Scottsdale. Some of us may have been saying goodbye to dreams of our own. What we had long dreaded had finally come. Our lives suddenly changed. A large number of newer apprentices would leave the Fellowship almost immediately, Mr. Wright now being gone.[66]

Procession for the burial of Frank Lloyd Wright in the Unity Chapel cemetery. Wisconsin Historical Society—Image ID 5019

Arthur Dyson had been in the Fellowship less than a year, but he stayed only a day or two after the ceremonies at Taliesin West. Having learned so much from Wright in such a short time, he experienced a palpable sense of loss: "It was just like somebody had hit you in the stomach. I think everybody kind of had that [feeling]. This was a place that had so much life in it. It had so much enthusiasm and joviality and camaraderie and all of a sudden, from my perspective, it was gone." Nobody, he recalled, knew what to say. He told Mrs. Wright he didn't want to go to the funeral, to see Mr. Wright in the casket. He wanted to remember him the way he had known him when he was alive. Not knowing what he was going to do at this point, he went home.[67]

Wright's death led many to believe that the Fellowship would dissolve. That didn't happen. Rather its members gathered to decide what to do. Most wanted to continue the course they were on, although it would be much different without Wright's presence. Those who remained carried on with the projects then underway. There were clients on the horizon, too. Tom Casey recalled that he was one of the senior assistants answering the new 24-hour-a-day phone line, where calls from all over the world arrived. When *Time Magazine* asked how many projects Wright was doing at the time of his death, Tom and others began counting—all the way to 85. That posed an enormous work level, so much so that the Fellowship turned the farming over to others.[68]

John Ottenheimer said that it took years for his thoughts about Taliesin without Mr. Wright to be clarified, to recognize the reality of the transition to the days and years without Mr. Wright:

The whole organization became dramatically different. The life, the work, personal relationships, the finances, everything. And yet the mantra was "everything is going to continue on the same. We are living the Taliesin life the same. We are doing the same architecture. There will still be apprentices learning in the same way." But that was an illusion. I returned to reside at Taliesin for a year in 1989–90. . . . It was during that time that I saw more clearly what had happened.[69]

While those thoughts were emerging, the Fellowship carried on under Mrs. Wright's leadership. It was now her Fellowship.

# 19 MRS. WRIGHT'S FELLOWSHIP

*1959–1985*

IT WAS QUITE EVIDENT AFTER THE DEATH OF HER HUSBAND THAT MRS. WRIGHT WAS THE BRAINS AND THE FORCE BEHIND THE FELLOWSHIP. SHE HELD IT TOGETHER, BOTH WITH HER BLOOD AND WITH PSYCHIC ENERGY. . . . SHE HAD GONE THROUGH THE HARD LIFE OF ESCAPE FROM THE SOVIET ZONE DURING WORLD WAR I, COMING TO FRANCE, LIVING AT FONTAINEBLEAU, COMING TO CHICAGO AND THEN TO SPRING GREEN. THE FLIGHT, PURSUIT, THE MARRIAGE TO FRANK LLOYD WRIGHT—SIXTY YEARS AT TALIESIN. AND OUT OF IT SHE HAD BECOME NOT HARD, BUT WISE: A WOMAN WHO KNEW WHAT HER LIFE WAS TO BE AND WAS SATISFIED WITH THAT LIFE.

SOMEWHAT TOWARD THE END OF HER LIFE WE CAME FOR THE FINAL VISIT. THERE WAS A DINNER. AND AFTERWARDS SHE SAID TO ME, "WHEN I MEET MY HUSBAND AGAIN, I WILL BE ABLE TO LOOK HIM IN THE EYE, BECAUSE I HAVE KEPT HIS NAME ALIVE."[1]

**—JAMES AUER**

According to Kamal Amin, who began his long tenure at Taliesin as an apprentice in 1951 and continued there as an architect until 1977, a sense of desperation set in after Frank Lloyd Wright died. It became evident, he said, "in constant anxiety about money." The administration, now concentrated in Mrs. Wright's hands, changed as she tightened her control over matters great and small. "She might or might not discuss her plans with a handful of her close, loyal, 'yes' individuals. Everything was conducted in secret. No one knew the status of any issue or indeed if there was an issue. . . . The party line was, 'We don't have any money.'" More troubling to Amin was Mrs. Wright's lack of passion for architecture as an art, although she appreciated it when it was done well. After her husband died she viewed architecture "in the context of being the only source of income."[2]

Amin's personal reaction to Wright's death was profound: "I tell you one thing I felt strongly was that I would no longer ever know what's right and what's wrong in architecture. Somehow that was the main thing in my mind. That we wouldn't ever know, really truly, what's right and what's wrong." Mr. Wright's death left him feeling "more empty than when his father or anyone else had died." When he came to Taliesin from Egypt he intended to stay about a year and then go to Europe and earn a Ph.D. in architecture. Now, though, he took Wright's passing as a signal to stay, "because there was something that was worth doing. . . . The system was going to go on."[3]

Some found consolation and hope in Mrs. Wright's continuing presence. Aubrey Banks, for example, remarked that "there was still Mrs. Wright, who was just as inspiring as Mr. Wright—and was probably more interested in me personally than Mr. Wright was." She worked with the members of the Fellowship "as individuals in a more personal way than Mr. Wright." Sometimes she "was really very hard on people," as she had been on him, but he found that it "was only to teach me something that I needed to learn. It wasn't that she particularly wanted to act that way; but it was just necessary in order to open my eyes to see things that I would otherwise not have seen."[4]

Wes Peters, Mrs. Wright, and others critiquing the box projects of apprentices, observing a practice initiated years earlier to honor Mr. Wright on his birthdays and at Christmas. Courtesy of the Frank Lloyd Wright Foundation

When the leaders of the Fellowship returned to Taliesin West after Mr. Wright's funeral, Mrs. Wright convened a meeting to tell its members her plans. Wes Peters would take Mr. Wright's place in the studio, to the extent that that was possible, and serve as male leader of the Fellowship. She would be the Fellowship's guiding authority.

**SIGNS OF CHANGE**

Frank Laraway, a relatively new apprentice, noted that many changes were evident when they returned to Wisconsin later that spring. His summary of what was to happen resembles what one might have found in college

catalogs in those days: Mendel Glickman would teach a formal academic class in structure, focusing initially on steel and wood; Jack Howe and Davy Davison would handle graphics; Gene Masselink would teach "integral, geometrical ornament and the unit system of design." The practice of reviewing apprentices' work through "birthday boxes," begun early in the life of the Fellowship, would continue, but it could not be the same. Formerly apprentices prepared designs and assembled them in elaborately crafted boxes to present to Frank Lloyd Wright for his birthday and Christmas. It was a "gift" of ideas, which he regarded affectionately. The apprentices took turns in removing each project from the box and presenting it to him. He in turn gave them feedback. Now Mrs. Wright, Jack Howe, Wes Peters, and Davy Davison would offer the critiques. Although instruction in such things as plumbing, lighting, electrical work, air conditioning, and acoustics was missing, it seemed to Laraway, who had studied architecture at the University of Michigan, that apprentice training was "evolving toward the more intensive training of the conventional classroom setting of academia, a system with which Mr. Wright was never pleased." Missing from the training, he believed, was sufficient time in the studio.[5]

## MORE CHANGES

Organizational changes in the Fellowship were perhaps most evident in the expanding role of Dick Carney, who had joined in 1948, following two years in the post-WW II military. He worked closely with Mr. and Mrs. Wright, rather than in the studio, and his extraordinary devotion to them made him the consummate insider. A year or two after he arrived, Wright's secretary, Gene Masselink, had to have his hip replaced, a procedure that limited his mobility for about a year and half. He could still serve as secretary, but he was unable to move about freely with Wright. So Mrs. Wright asked Carney to become her husband's aide. From then on he was with Wright from early in the morning until the end of the day, helping him get dressed, seeing to it that he took his medications exactly as prescribed, and driving him wherever he wanted to go. That attentiveness drew Carney into a close relationship with Mrs. Wright that remained after her husband's death.

By 1962, as treasurer of the Frank Lloyd Wright Foundation, Carney was "viceroy," so to speak, to Mrs. Wright. That placed on him the responsibility of finding ways to pay the huge tax bill that hit the Fellowship when Wright died. Cornelia Brierly recalled that "it was a tremendous sum. And it was necessary to sell off many of the art objects Mr. Wright had. That was very wrenching, to get rid of art objects so highly prized by everyone." Eventually the tax bill was paid and the foundation got a letter of praise. "The tax people," Cornelia said, "wrote us a letter saying that . . . very few people ever accomplished what we had accomplished."[6]

## SUMMERS IN EUROPE

In that instance and others, Carney explained, if Mrs. Wright said, "This needs to be done," he would provide leadership in getting it done. If he brought an idea to her and she said, "Fine, that is a good idea. Go out and do it," he would do it. One day she said she thought it would be a good idea for

Dick Carney with Mrs. Wright.

Courtesy of the Frank Lloyd Wright Foundation

the entire Fellowship to travel to Europe. Carney asked if she really wanted to do that, and she said she did. So, in consultation with her and his peers, he organized the trip, arranging cars for travel in Europe, lining up hotels, determining the itinerary, and dividing the Fellowship into two traveling parties. Apprentices who had been at Taliesin for only a year, they decided, would have to pay their own fare if they wanted to go. As things developed, everyone in the Fellowship went except for several left behind to look after things at Taliesin.

The advance party bought five Citroen station wagons in Paris, designated a driver for each of them, and met the rest of the Fellowship in Brussels. After twenty-one days in Europe they returned the cars to Paris, where they met the other half of the Fellowship and gave them the cars. At the end of that group's three-week tour they sold the cars back to Citroen and returned to the United States.

The next year, 1965, they decided that the two three-week tours had been so costly that for the same amount of money the Fellowship, if it stayed at one place, could spend the entire summer in Europe. So Carney looked for a feasible location. After visiting possible places in Paris, Florence, and Rome, and near Munich, he settled on an American school in Montagnola, Switzerland, where for six dollars a day per person they could have room and board. That cost less, Carney said, than spending the summer in Wisconsin. The arrangement worked so well that they did the same thing again the next year.

In the Fellowship's absence for three summers the buildings in Wisconsin fell into greater disrepair than usual, but there were positive effects, too. Besides creating greater cohesiveness in the Fellowship and giving it a cosmopolitan perspective that, according to Carney, never wore off, the Fellowship gained two new members: one was Anneliese Goertz, who attracted the attention of David Dodge, a member of the Fellowship for more than a dozen years. Soon she became his wife, and in 1976 a member of the Fellowship.[7] Effi Bantzer, who with her marriage to Tom Casey several years later was to become Effi Casey, connected with the Fellowship through an invitation from Frances Nemtin. Frances heard her practice her violin in the hotel room where she lived while she had served as an assistant to a German painter, Hans Purrman, and said to her, "We have a little musical group with whom you could play." Effi was aware that the Fellowship was to arrive there, for after Purrman died, a lady in the hotel said, "If you don't want to return to your academy in Germany, why don't you wait for these people from the United States? They're just your cup of tea." She accepted the invitation and soon found herself in the midst of the Fellowship, "making music together, learning about Frank Lloyd Wright, and meeting Mrs. Wright."[8]

After the Fellowship spent the summers of 1964, 1965, and 1966 in Europe, Mrs. Wright wanted to travel abroad every year. Carney, along with other members of the Fellowship, accompanied her to Montenegro (then part of Yugoslavia), South Africa (by way of Ethiopia and Kenya), Japan, Italy, Majorca, Iran, Switzerland, and other places that may have escaped Carney's memory.[9]

## CHANGES IN THE ARCHITECTURAL PRACTICE

For the Fellowship to prosper, or simply to survive, income from architectural commissions was essential. Designs already under construction or approaching that point when Wright died had to be completed. One more project merits mention. In 1957 Wright was one of about half a dozen architects brought in by the ruling regime in Baghdad to "modernize" that city. He proposed a number of structures, including an opera house and a university placed prominently in his plan for Greater Baghdad. However, a coup d'état brought a revolutionary government to power, an event that ended aspirations for building in Iraq. Not wanting that work to have been done in vain, Wright revised the plan for the opera house and used it as a basis for the Grady Gammage Auditorium at Arizona State University. After he died, his Baghdad designs were largely ignored.[10]

While that auditorium was under construction, Igor Glenn, an apprentice, assisted with preparing the drawings for it, and soon, in an unusual way, he participated in testing its acoustics. Having grown up as a chum with Stanley and Mildred Rosenbaum's four sons in Florence, Alabama, he was familiar with Wright's architecture. That probably accounts for his decision to join the Fellowship in January 1961. After a year in the Fellowship he was offered a music scholarship at Arizona State University. In 1963, while on a "construction tour" of Grady Gammage Auditorium, he "stood on the bare stage to sing and play for the workmen installing the seats—the initial live test of the interior's acoustic properties."[11]

### TALIESIN ASSOCIATED ARCHITECTS

As work on Wright's designs progressed, ranging from those under construction to some that had not moved beyond the drawing board, the Fellowship seemed to face a choice: Should its architects continue Wright's practice after the work in progress was completed, even though it would no longer be Wright's practice? Or should they finish his projects and then close the studio? With the Fellowship continuing under Mrs. Wright's leadership, they decided without debate or hesitation to continue as the Taliesin Associated Architects.[12] At some point they and other long-term members of the Fellowship became known as senior fellows; being architects was not a requirement. Those who disapproved of the new arrangement either accommodated themselves to it until they could plan an alternative future or simply moved on.

One who waited for five years after Wright's death before leaving was Jack Howe, who had shared leadership in the studio with Wes Peters. When most of Wright's designs had been built, Howe went to work with Aaron Green in San Francisco. After several years there he opened his own practice in Minneapolis. Almost forty years following the Howes' departure, Lu Sparks Howe recalled that life at Taliesin "was a life of beauty, exhilaration, and inspiration," so she was distressed to hear rumors, evidently based on remarks made by Johnny Hill in an oral history interview, that Mrs. Wright had asked them to leave. "That was *not* the case," she said. "The decision to leave was made by Jack and me." Her husband offered an explanation: "When Mrs. Wright said that she was an architect, and when she took charge of the drafting room, and had to approve of anything that was sent out . . . , I decided that it was past time for me to leave and be starting my own architectural practice."[13]

With Jack Howe's departure, John Rattenbury recalled, Mrs. Wright designated him to take over Howe's responsibilities in the studio. Because many members of the Fellowship had been there much longer than he and perhaps saw themselves as studio leaders, his seniors were not willing to allow themselves to be led. So, he explained, he worked behind the scenes.

No matter who was in charge of the studio, the practice of architecture was changing, not so much on the design side as in the management tools and procedures required for efficient operation. The architects acquired electric typewriters, copying machines, and telex, for example, and Rattenbury set up the firm's first accounting system, even though he had had no training in accounting. Many things that Wright had handled himself now had to be standardized, such as responding to requests for

proposals by prospective clients, establishing procedures for entering contracts, maintaining project records, managing the drawing and correspondence files, assigning people to work on projects, and initiating time records. Before long, he said, they had about twelve registered architects, "all home grown."

Wright's clients had been in many respects patrons. Now the architects at Taliesin dealt with developers, investors, managers, lawyers, and accountants. Their biggest concern, according to Rattenbury, was the potential for profit. They had to be convinced "that their architect would perform on schedule, within budget, and give them a building that maximized the return on their investment." Not until this was all in place could the architects get prospective clients' attention for talk about "such things as timeless beauty in architecture or sensitivity to the environment."[14]

Senior members of the Fellowship, principally those engaged in architecture, design, and administration, with Mrs. Wright shortly after Mr. Wright's death. Seated, from left: Wes Peters, Mrs. Wright, Gene Masselink, Iovanna Wright. Standing: Dick Carney, Tom Casey, Kay Rattenbury, Jim Pfefferkorn, Louis Wiehle, Davy Davison, Kenn Lockhart, Ling Po, Cornelia Brierly, John Howe, John Rattenbury, Bruce Pfeiffer, John Amarantides. Courtesy of the Frank Lloyd Wright Foundation

## PROJECTS FOR THE NEW FIRM

Rattenbury has cataloged some of the work done by the Taliesin Architects, describing its principal features and displaying it in colorful pictures. Some of the firm's buildings, completed before Mrs. Wright's death, were done in conjunction with Wright's built designs, including the Bartlesville Performing Arts Center, near the Price Tower; the Ruth Eckerd Hall at Florida Southern College; and the Arizona State University Music School. Other TAA work in these years included performing arts centers in Florida and Kentucky; a resort hotel and time-share village in California; commercial structures in Arizona, Kentucky, and Wisconsin; a community center in Arizona; park headquarters in Rocky Mountain National Park; a palace, college, and villa in Teheran, Iran; places of worship in Arizona, Michigan, and Wisconsin; a fourteen-mile pass through the Rockies at Vail, Colorado; residences in Arizona, California, and New Jersey; and master planning in Arizona.[15]

## EXPERIENCES IN IRAN

Some of the senior fellows' most interesting experiences in architecture occurred with the projects in Iran. Tom Casey agreed to go there in 1969 at Mrs. Wright's request. He was single, his wife Shirley having died, and he was well qualified to do what needed to be done. As he worked on the buildings designed by Wes Peters, some of the materials for the interiors had to be acquired in Europe, so he made a number of trips to Italy and Germany. When Effi Bantzer returned to Germany after the summer with the Fellowship at Montagnola, she corresponded with several of its members. Tom Casey, one of the correspondents, arranged a visit, and a mutual attraction developed.

In Iran, Princess Shams, the sister of the Shah in the ruling Pahlavi family, worried that Casey was there by himself, so she asked if he would like to bring his mother for a visit. He told her that there was a young lady he would rather bring. The Princess agreed, and he arranged for Effi to come. "Well," Tom recalled, "she and the Princess just hit it off perfectly. That worked out very nicely. . . . We were married then in the middle of 1971." They were in Iran almost full time while the Pearl Palace was being built, going back and forth as circumstances required.

Stephen and Frances Nemtin replaced the Caseys in November 1973 and remained there until early 1977. Frances described the time there as "wonderful totally, except for the hassle that Stephen had to go through with the bureaucracy of the Princess' cabinet. . . . But the actual work was very satisfying." By the time they arrived the palace had been built. Stephen's task was to develop the working drawings for a complex of villas Peters had designed for the little town of Chalus, overlooking the Caspian Sea, and to work with the contractor. He and Frances remained in Iran until the structural and roofing systems were in place and much of the landscaping was finished, but lack of money kept the projects from being completed. The Princess and those around her pinned the slow progress on him, Stephen said, and so with the buildings incomplete, they were asked not to return. With work yet to be done, the Princess asked Tom and Effi Casey to work there again. They did go and stayed until the latter part of 1978, when the revolution began. However, Casey said, they did not leave because of the revolution, but because they had finished what they had come to do.[16] The Caseys and the Nemtins were not the only ones from Taliesin involved in the projects in Iran. Wes Peters was the principal architect for the palace; Cornelia Brierly and Johnny Hill, assisted by others, designed its custom furnishings; and Cornelia supervised the landscaping.[17]

The projects in Iran came to the Taliesin Architects by way of Sheik Nezam Amery, a member of Iran's royal family. He had apprenticed at Taliesin from 1952 to 1954, where his royal status did not exempt him from onerous tasks, such as working with Wes Peters to empty a blocked septic tank. "Wes's enthusiastic bravado," he recalled, "kept me afloat!" After leaving Taliesin he was involved with Wright in the proposed Baghdad projects in 1957. Before those projects could materialize he was trapped in Baghdad during the 1958 Iraqi revolution, but after two months he was able to return to Teheran and open his own practice. There he worked with the Taliesin Architects on the palace for Princess Shams, for which he had recommended Peters as the principal architect, and in that role himself on the simultaneous construction of Damavand College.

Wherever the Taliesin Architects' work was done, such remuneration as it generated was critically important to the Fellowship. John Ottenheimer, who completed the design development drawings and construction documents for the Fine Arts Center at Centre College in Kentucky in 1969, recalls that the fees from that endeavor accounted for most of the significant income at Taliesin that year and that Dick Carney told him, "You supported the whole Fellowship for that year."[18]

## THE SCHOOL

The apprentices' experiences in learning changed further as a consequence of the decision to seek accreditation for what was to become the Frank Lloyd Wright School of Architecture. According to Tom Casey, who piloted the Fellowship through the accreditation processes and served as the founding dean of the School, Mrs. Wright recognized that if the learning opportunities offered by the Fellowship were to survive, they needed some level of recognition beyond the character of the people who provided them. The moves she initiated disturbed some former apprentices, who preferred Mr. Wright's informal way of doing things and disdained the thought of Taliesin becoming anything resembling a school. As a practical matter, though, Mrs. Wright anticipated the arrival of the day when, in most states, registration as architects would require degrees from accredited institutions.

In 1981, and perhaps earlier, she began to gather evidence that the learning experiences offered at Taliesin were worthy of accreditation. With a view toward gaining credibility for recognition by the National Architectural Accrediting Board, Mrs. Wright asked a number of former apprentices for testimonies concerning their learning experiences in the Fellowship. At least thirty-five responded. All of them credited their professional accomplishments in one way or another to their wide range of experiences in the Fellowship. Curtis Besinger, who had left discontentedly in 1953 to become a professor of architecture at the University of Kansas, wrote that he was happy to lend support to the quest for accreditation and that "the experience of living and working at Taliesin under the guidance of you and Mr. Wright contributed immeasurably to my education and career." Morton Delson considered accreditation to be "long overdue." Herb Fritz called the opportunity to apprentice at Taliesin "the most elevated educational opportunity" offered in his generation. John Howe remarked that the Taliesin program "certainly deserves full accreditation," and that the "unique 'learning by doing' training . . . far surpasses conventional theoretic training." And so on through the alphabet, from E. Fay Jones to Eric Lloyd Wright.[19]

With such affirmations in hand, Mrs. Wright set things in motion by inviting an architect who had experience with the National Architectural Accrediting Board (NAAB) to visit Taliesin West. She wanted him to observe the kinds of things going on there and to assess the possibility of gaining accreditation for those offerings. He responded positively, so Mrs. Wright invited the NAAB, which was meeting in Scottsdale at the time, to come to Taliesin for an informal visit. The visitors were cordial and supportive as they reviewed a description of the existing education program and enjoyed the tea Mrs. Wright arranged for them.

The next morning Tom Casey, Dick Carney, and Charles Montooth met with NAAB officials and learned that institutional accreditation by state and regional agencies was a prerequisite for program accreditation. They also heard expressions of concern that they could not discern how Taliesin measured the apprentices' progress toward unspecified goals. Following through on this conversation, a Taliesin delegation attended a North Central Association meeting and made an appointment to see Patsy Thrash, the program officer of the NCA's Commission on Institutions of Higher Education. She outlined the initial steps for gaining accreditation. The first was to get in touch with persons at another institution with an unconventional program, namely, Alverno College in Milwaukee. There Sister Austin Doherty described to Tom and Effi Casey how Alverno had brought itself out of dormancy by using an individualized approach to learning and creating methods for assessing student progress.

With Alverno, Casey noted, "there was a great commonality of circumstance," even though they had already gone through the regeneration process. As for Taliesin, "the founders were gone," and "we had this charge now to see that [their accomplishments] did not disappear." The Caseys learned much from leaders at Alverno, particularly how to formulate an assessment program that would give apprentices ways to demonstrate progress in learning.

At some point Taliesin had to designate a leader for shaping an accreditable program. Because he was involved in the effort from the very beginning, and because in the Fellowship "people make a position, so to speak," Casey concluded that it seemed to him that if they were going to be successful in preserving what they had, "somebody had to start going out there and pursuing that goal, making their way into this arena of higher education." So he said to himself, "You've got to do this; somebody's got to do it. You can do it; go and do it."

At the suggestion of Patsy Thrash, Casey got in touch with Barbara Mickey, a retired administrator at the University of Northern Colorado, as someone who might guide Taliesin through accreditation processes. After preliminary conversations with her, Casey recalled, "she came for a long weekend, and she got terribly interested in the whole program and helped us construct our self-study in a more articulated fashion." Later she came for a visit with her husband Jack, also retired from the University of Northern Colorado. The Mickeys assisted Taliesin in gaining "candidate for accreditation status" in the North Central Association in 1985. They became senior fellows and stayed in the Fellowship five years. Casey described the Mickeys' contribution to the process as "absolutely invaluable." She "really constructed for us a description of what happens when you come to learn something at Taliesin West." In due course, Taliesin was granted "candidacy" for accreditation. The Mickeys continued to assist the School in its NCA reaccreditation processes and in achieving NAAB accreditation as well.[20]

## APPRENTICES CONTINUE TO COME

Despite the changes following Mr. Wright's death, apprentices continued to come. One such was Charles Adams. He grew up in Tuskegee, Alabama, but spent his summers in Grambling, Louisiana, and attended high school there. He had deep roots in both places, as two ancestors were separately credited with the founding of Tuskegee University and Grambling State University. He learned about Wright while being tutored by a professor of art at Grambling. In the summer after graduation from high school he worked at a newsstand and was mesmerized by the pictures of Wright's work featured in a special edition of *The House Beautiful* published in 1959. Although he wanted to go to Taliesin then, his parents gave him no alternative to pursuing a college degree. So he enrolled at Michigan State University, where he not only discovered the Wright-designed Goetsch-Winckler house (1939), but was assigned Kathrine Winckler as his adviser; she and Alma Goetsch were associate professors of art at the university. Encouraged by her and inspired by Wright's architecture, he joined the Fellowship at Taliesin in September 1962—regretting, of course, that his detour through Michigan State had cost him the chance to be there while Wright was alive.[21]

Bill Schwarz had completed his fifth year of a six-year course of study in architecture at Stanford University and, by chance, was enrolled in a required class taught by Aaron Green, a former member of the Fellowship. Green took the class on a tour of the recently completed Marin County Center, and one day he brought Wes Peters, who was in San Francisco on business, to class with him. Peters spoke about Taliesin and the Fellowship and the architectural work they were involved in at the time. That Aaron and Wes "seemed to demonstrate a high level of personalized professional standards" registered with Schwarz as "intriguing and quite inspirational." He decided to follow the advice given to him earlier by Ted Eden, a Taliesin product and now a colleague in the firm where he worked, to supplement his Stanford education by enrolling for a year at Taliesin. He wound up staying in the Fellowship for about four years.[22]

For Val Cox, Mrs. Wright was the main attraction. He called her "a teacher with a capital T." She not only had "sufficient power within herself for her own evolution and growth, but had reserves to lead other people in theirs and boost them to get them started." To her, "everything else was secondary."

Looking back, he says that experiences and impressions gained in his decade and a half in the Fellowship "reside in me as whole cloth, fully informing my life and work." What counted for him and others was being at Taliesin "in the spark of the moment" and that "those whose lives have been vitalized at Taliesin carry that vitality with them in many forms and directions."[23]

As did earlier apprentices, the ones in the Fellowship in the 1970s and 1980s found much to do. Robert Mauldin, for example, besides working on projects with Charles Montooth, Vern Swaback, Cornelia Brierly, Johnny Hill, and six or seven with John Rattenbury, was involved in many on-site construction projects. At Taliesin West he was engaged in working on all the roofs; renovating the shop, laundry, locker rooms, and the Carousel (a complex of tiny rooms for women apprentices); participating in the renovations of Mrs. Wright's apartment, sun porch, and garden steps; rewiring the men's living quarters in what was known as the annex; and installing a new sound system, wiring, and controls for the projection room. At Taliesin he rewired a number of rooms, and restored floors, a number of apartments, and the Hillside galleries. This might sound mundane, but Mauldin set these activities in a distinctive context: "One thing I found to be true at Taliesin was that everyone was constantly seeking the new, unique, and highest quality approach to design, art, music, architecture and life. . . . I know of many very exciting innovations and designs created by this very small group of highly motivated and talented people. Most will remain uncelebrated and obscure but that does not diminish their talents and accomplishments. At least we know!"[24]

**TENSIONS IN COMMUNAL LIFE**

Some of the long-standing practices in the Fellowship had to be changed after Mr. Wright's death. For example, instead of hearing his inspirational talks at the Sunday breakfasts, the apprentices now listened to Mrs. Wright. But their duties in providing the necessities of daily life—cooking, working in the garden, building, and maintaining their desert shelters and other living quarters—remained largely the same. Mrs. Wright still posted the work lists, but now Mr. Wright was not there to pull apprentices away for work in the studio or in construction. Other practices, such as the semiannual migrations between Wisconsin and Arizona, continued, but as the Fellowship evolved and matured more members owned cars and provided their own transportation.

While most apprentices found communal life to be an essential part of their Taliesin experience, some looked back on it with mixed feelings. Peter Rött remembered it as strenuous, with seventy people living on fewer than 1,000 acres of land. Packing up and moving 3,000 miles twice each year was both fun and not fun. Some days life in the Fellowship could be as petty as in any small town; some days it seemed like a cooking school. But he and those around him lived in the incredible beauty of the two Taliesins. They heard comments by visitors that made the experience of being in the Fellowship "so special, so precious and fragile." Still, he wondered what drove Mrs. Wright and the seniors in the Fellowship to keep it all going. One night after he had served Mrs. Wright dinner she invited him to sit with her. "She asked me," he said, "how I felt about life at Taliesin. She said, 'sometimes all of this *really* gets to me!'"[25]

Bill Schwarz treasured and remained grateful for his participation in "a community of like-minded individuals who were devoted to a shared vision and common goals" and "manifesting those goals, day to day, in the life of the Fellowship." In time, though, he saw curious weaknesses among some senior members, particularly with respect to Iovanna, who could be "difficult, manipulative, and mean-spirited toward many." He was puzzled by Mrs. Wright's support for her in spite of the hurt she inflicted on many members. Moreover, sometimes Mrs. Wright astonished him with what he thought were "unreasonable, undeserved, or destructive criticisms of certain members. . . . She was every bit as irascible as Iovanna, and was prone towards cruel and ranting tirades." Certain individuals who had left the Fellowship were the objects of her unforgiving bitterness. More disturbing to him "was a pattern of unquestioning acceptance [of her ideas and methods] by many of the senior Fellowship members, . . . even including her habit of cruelly berating members."[26]

Schwarz's wife, Pat, whom he married two years after joining the Fellowship, has a more romantic memory of communal living. The Fellowship embraced her warmly and she merged into the routine life at Taliesin West as though she had always been there. Their honeymoon cottage was a sheepherder's tent. "The quiet, stark beauty of the desert captivated me," she recalled, "from the snow-capped mountains of winter to the dramatic, often terrifying lightning storms . . . in the summer months." In the daytime their lives were absorbed in the life of the community: "From showering and dressing with the other women in the women's locker room to the dining room where all 75 of us dined together, three meals a day, our lives were intertwined. Intertwined and interdependent." Working in the architects' office she felt "a level of excitement, a purpose, a shared vision, which ran through every fiber of life at Taliesin, from the drafting room to setting tables for lunch, a vision of beauty."

At the same time, she also felt a "diminishment of individuality of thought and action, the restriction of individual choice." So she felt also the pull of a life of her own choosing and a desire to set up a house and a life of their own. They left in 1969 (for reasons described below). Yet, she has since wondered whether leaving was perhaps a mistake. "We have our freedom now," she mused, "but we have lost that intimate connection to a larger, shared purpose."[27]

## MIXED PERSPECTIVE ON COMMUNAL LIFE

The products of the kitchen sustained the Fellowship, but not always to its members' satisfaction. Charles Adams disliked the food. Lunches were the worst: "dull and totally unappetizing." During his first week he was greeted by a baked onion on his lunch plate, which he found "totally disgusting." A senior apprentice overheard his negative comments and quickly responded with, "Mr. Wright loved baked onions." Adams was not impressed and wanted no part of it. Moreover, typical and frequent comments like this, and the "constant deification of 'The Master,'" were at times negatively overwhelming. Other meals were somewhat better, "but nothing to write home about," particularly when they included powdered milk at Taliesin West. Those who had cars would steal off secretly to the nearest fast-food stop for a quick hot dog and hamburger and beer.[28]

Stephen Gegner, who had studied engineering and psychology before joining the Fellowship in 1962, liked being the family server for the opportunity to be in the family living quarters during mealtime rather than the Hillside dining room and because he had more chances to meet guests. Mrs. Wright seemed to want to keep an eye on him, as he "was prone to getting into trouble." But he was not comfortable with her, and "an uncommon number of cliques for such a small group of people" disturbed him. He didn't seem to fit in, partly because he was, unknowingly, an alcoholic and spent time in town or alone, drinking. Moreover, he was troubled by what "seemed to be bizarre sexual partnering," with some of the couples supposedly put together by Mr. Wright and others, later, by Mrs. Wright. "There were several extramarital affairs going on—including a gay one by one of the previously mentioned couples. Then there were other gays, and even a few eunuchs." The main thing that bothered him, though, was the oligarchy, or "better said, the Olgivanna-archy. If you didn't bow down to Mrs. Wright and recognize her greatness (perhaps superior to Mr. Wright's) you were not a part of the family."[29]

For Ron Brisette, who arrived in April 1978, "the first couple of months were hell." He thought he had made a big mistake in joining and "came close to pulling the plug" as he "wondered how the things he was doing were teaching him anything about architecture." But slowly things changed, or perhaps he did, for he stayed until 1984. He is one of the few apprentices to ascribe beneficial effects to working in the kitchen, for he ended up designing many restaurants. Looking back, he cherishes the memory of his time spent with Wes Peters, not just at Taliesin, but on business trips as well. "There was not only a master-apprentice relationship," he recalled, "but something paternal, and a deep friendship that developed."[30]

Another apprentice in these years, J. T. Elbracht, who came to the Fellowship after graduating from a rural high school in Nebraska at age seventeen, welcomed the opportunities to work on real projects for real clients; to be exposed to a wide variety of projects—from working on a small house, to a multimillion-dollar resort hotel, to the interior design for law offices, to an 8,000-acre master-planned community. The studio, he said, "provided unparalleled personal growth opportunities in architecture, land planning, interior design, landscape design, client relations, business practices, practical experience, strong work ethic and a passion for design." The "awesome experiences" he had at Taliesin challenged him mentally, physically, and socially. Everything, from working in the kitchen to construction to Saturday night formal dinners, shaped his life.

There were, of course, some less positive experiences. In Elbracht's view, these involved people in or associated with the Fellowship who simply "didn't get it." Some came with unrealistically high expectations and were disappointed. Those who came to be "taught" were frustrated with the lack of structure. "At Taliesin," he said "you can't just sit back and watch—or read about it. You have to be engaged in it, and there were many opportunities for engagement."[31]

## FESTIVALS OF MUSIC AND DANCE

Some of those opportunities came in the Festivals of Music and Dance. With Mr. Wright no longer there to pull apprentices away, Mrs. Wright was free to give these activities a higher priority in Fellowship life than some of its members might have chosen. She provided the music used in the performances, drawing upon her experiences with Gurdjieff. Bruce Pfeiffer transcribed it into piano, choral, and orchestral settings and conducted the chorus or played the piano on some occasions. John Amarantides served as violinist and occasionally as conductor.

Mrs. Wright, supporting Iovanna's efforts to transform Gurdjieff's "movements" into "correlations," saw these activities as contributing to the development of each participant. While the initial focus was on those striving to be architects, according to David Dodge, that made sense, for in architecture "the whole community locks together." There is no menial job, for "everything is all part of this growing experience at becoming a better architect." But then, he said, the Fellowship accepted people who came there for the Gurdjieffian philosophy or music or painting rather than to become architects, and "things started to get a little bit fragmented. It weakened the spirit, and 'them' and 'us' started to happen."

A greater concern for him was that the Festivals were so demanding on the Fellowship's time that "basically three months were wiped out" of drafting room work. Everyone in a Festival was "rehearsing all night long; they were worthless in the daytime. The drafting room was empty most of the time, and even if you were working in there Iovanna would call a rehearsal for this or that. People had to disappear and go there." The performances drew crowds, and it helped build the Fellowship, but "it also broke it up, in a way. . . . It was definitely a major effort in a totally separate direction."[32] However, Dodge would most likely agree with his wife Anneliese's characterization of the performances as "powerful" and "beautiful," but whether he would say, as she did, that they had "fun, fun" is less certain.[33] Arnold Roy, another of the Taliesin architects, recalled that the Festivals were professional performances. "All who went through it," he said, "profited from it. It's something you wouldn't want to do again, but you're glad you went through the agony of it."[34]

Although production of the Festivals was eventually discontinued, choral and instrumental ensembles, with both senior fellows and apprentices participating, remained integral elements in the life of the Fellowship.

## LEAVING THE FELLOWSHIP

Through the years the Fellowship welcomed and integrated new members without much fanfare, and many managed their departures similarly. If they felt they had accomplished their goals, or if new opportunities presented themselves, or if they had tired of communal life, or if financial or family circumstances required a response, they moved on. Frank Laraway, for example, left because he was out of funds, a matter he found difficult to explain to Wes Peters and Gene Masselink. He had already spent most of his savings while earning a degree at Guilford College. But there was another element to his decision: He had left a girl behind in Ann Arbor. Female companionship at Taliesin, he noted, was scarce.[35] Peter Rött recalled that some of the leaving was done under unpleasant circumstances: "It was hard to leave on the best terms for many people. It was too intense for them or they got caught up in the details of trying to solve that great riddle, which came first—Taliesin or the Fellowship?"[36]

Not uncommonly, though, they left because Mrs. Wright sent them away, or made them feel unwelcome, or demanded greater submission to her will than they found acceptable. Sometimes the dismissals were effected in ways that took the members by surprise. Or rather, they would have been surprised if they had not seen it happen to others before them.

The departure of Don and Janice Kalec in mid-1969 provides an example of a chain reaction in dismissals. They had been members about as long as Bill and Pat Schwarz. When the Kalecs let it be known that they planned to leave that summer, Mrs. Wright did not conceal her disappointment. She began to probe Schwarz quite directly, hoping to discern his plans. He assured her that they did not intend to leave soon, but exercising the kind of honesty he believed she advocated, he told her that while he was flattered to know that she would like to have him and Pat stay, they had thought it most likely that they would one day move to the San Francisco area. In the meantime, though, he let her know that they wanted to continue in the Fellowship for some indefinite time, most likely a year or so.

Mrs. Wright said she didn't think it would be possible for them to continue with the required enthusiastic focus if they knew they would be leaving. They left it at that, but in a Sunday morning talk she spoke about the virtues of loyalty and stressed how essential she regarded full commitment to the Fellowship. Soon she offered Pat a position of responsibility in her private quarters, an offer that amounted to a thinly veiled sort of loyalty test. When Pat declined, she ordered them to leave immediately, " . . . right now, since the Kalecs are leaving you should too, even before they do, and don't send Bill in here to try to talk me out of it!" They quietly packed their belongings and were on their way by the end of the day.[37]

Many former apprentices have remarked that Mrs. Wright seemed to take the departure of apprentices she really wanted to hold at Taliesin as acts of betrayal. Jack Howe recalled that in 1982, on the fiftieth anniversary of the Fellowship's founding, Betty Kassler, assisted by others, compiled a list of men and women who had been at Taliesin. Her idea, he said, "was to have kind of a fiftieth anniversary thing." Mrs. Wright would have nothing to do with it. "Anybody who left Taliesin, through all the years, was deemed to have stepped off the edge of the world."[38] Edgar Tafel, like Howe one of the charter members, discussed the desirability of an anniversary reunion with Mrs. Wright. She said such a reunion would require too much work and be too costly. Tafel said all these things could be worked out and that apprentices from all over the world would want to come. Then, according to Tafel, she stated firmly, "Edgar, the problem with the whole idea for me is that too many would come who I dislike and don't want to see."[39]

## THE PASSING OF MRS. WRIGHT

Olgivanna Lloyd Wright died on March 1, 1985. Perceptions of her failing health vary. Dr. Joe Rorke, a member of the Fellowship and her personal physician, said that it was gradual, "a matter of months to a year. . . . You could see it coming both physically and mentally and you could just see her slip down, down, down."[40]

According to Bruce Pfeiffer, she could no longer be intimately involved in the affairs of the Fellowship because she had lost both her hearing and her eyesight. But she would occasionally have lunch with the Fellowship, and on one occasion she remarked to a person at the table, "Yes, I'm going blind, but I've lived a long life and I've seen a great deal, so I have nothing to regret." But then, Pfeiffer says, about a year later he came in to announce lunch to her. "She was sitting in the sun and just sort of dozing. . . . I tapped her and I said, 'Mrs. Wright, it's time for lunch,' and she said, 'Lunch, dinner, it doesn't matter. It's all darkness now.' I knew then that she really felt bad." It was a great tragedy, he said, to see that happen "to a person who was philosophically so very strong." So strongly did Mrs. Wright dislike hearing talk about anybody who had died that he couldn't mention Mr. Wright's name. That surprised him, for one of the first things she said to him more than thirty-five years earlier, when he was nineteen, was, "You should walk through life as though it's divided right down the center—half life and half death—so that when you come to that bridge the passage is very simple. It's no obstacle." But it was hard for her, he said, when her own death approached.[41]

Dick Carney, in contrast, recalled that, just as the members of the Fellowship were surprised by Mr. Wright's death almost sixteen years earlier, even when he was in the hospital undergoing surgery at age ninety-one, Mrs. Wright's death shocked him even more than her husband's. And when she died, "that sort of ended the regime of both Mr. and Mrs. Wright who . . . were benevolent dictators. They really ran the place. And so, I think it was almost harder to adjust to Mrs. Wright's death than to Mr. Wright's."[42]

## HONORING MRS. WRIGHT'S WISHES

When Frank Lloyd Wright died, his will provided for all of his worldly possessions to be passed to the Foundation he had established in 1940 and his personal belongings and effects to Mrs. Wright. After her death, honoring wishes she had expressed to them, a delegation traveled to Taliesin and surreptitiously exhumed Frank Lloyd Wright's remains from the grave in the family's cemetery by the chapel he had helped build almost one hundred years earlier. They transported those remains back to Taliesin West, where they were cremated. His ashes were interred with hers.

This incensed some of the former apprentices, and Wisconsin residents were outraged. A letter to Wes Peters from the state representative for the Spring Green area, Joseph Tregoning, described the outrage in Wisconsin and elsewhere. Petitions of protest were being circulated widely, he said, and newspaper accounts from across the country expressed displeasure. "Much more than ashes have been lost from Wisconsin," he continued, for the citizens of the state "have lost one evidence of their history, spirit, and genius." Accordingly, he was introducing and supporting "the resolution to seek return of Frank Lloyd Wright's remains and restoration of the grave site by Unity Chapel." The resolution passed in both houses of the legislature.[43]

But, not for the first time, Mrs. Wright had the last word.

# EPILOGUE

The stories told in this book affirm the thesis advanced in the introduction, that is, that Frank Lloyd Wright's communities, particularly the Taliesin Fellowship, had profound effects on his life and career. They made possible his extraordinary productivity, helped sustain his genius, provided him with crucial social outlets, and made it possible for him to remain a creative force outside the mainstream of American architecture. An ardent individualist, he flourished in communities. A fervent advocate of democracy, he presided over his communities autocratically. In the Taliesin Fellowship he shared authority with his wife Olgivanna, and after his death, her grip on its operations tightened.

Through their genius and leadership, this powerful partnership created enduring legacies. Before they met in 1924, Mr. Wright had already established many in his buildings, designs, speeches, and writings. He continued to build on these legacies during his thirty-five years with Mrs. Wright, and together they presided over the distinctive entities encompassed in the term "Taliesin." Each of these entities merits special attention.

## THE FRANK LLOYD WRIGHT SCHOOL OF ARCHITECTURE

Wright always denied being a teacher, and he rarely passed up a chance to debunk what he believed went on in American schools and universities—except when they awarded him honorary doctorates.[1] He and Mrs. Wright conceived of the Taliesin Fellowship as a sort of anti-school. Throughout their years as leaders, they established no formal admission requirements, designed no curriculum, hired no faculty, stipulated no graduation requirements, and had no graduation ceremonies.

That changed with the times, however, and in the 1980s many states required architects seeking to be registered to hold degrees from accredited institutions. This compelled the leaders in the Frank Lloyd Wright School of Architecture to concede that, whatever Taliesin had been in the past, now it had to be a school. If it had to be that, it had to be a good one, on its own terms to the extent that this was possible. In 1985, the School was granted "candidate for accreditation" status by the North Central Association, a regional agency that encompassed Arizona (Wisconsin is also in the region, but accreditation in one location covers the programs in both). Soon its Master of Architecture and Bachelor of Architectural Studies programs were accredited. Then, in intervals of three to five years, the School conducted self-studies, consultant-evaluator teams visited the School and made their recommendations, and the NCA continued its accreditation.

In 2002, after more mountains of paper and the investment of countless hours of work, the National Architectural Accrediting Board granted the School accreditation of its professional programs. However, declining enrollment, financial difficulties, administrative uncertainties, and a number of other concerns caused the NCA to place the School "on notice" in 2005. That, in turn, jeopardized NAAB accreditation. Subsequently, a number of aggressive actions and the appointment of a new dean, a registered architect and holder of both bachelor's and master's degrees from the School, resulted in a reversal of the School's fortunes and the restoration of untarnished accreditation. The Wrights' legacy was once again secure—at least until the next round of self-studies and team reviews. Mr. Wright, though, might have been chagrined by the effort required to accomplish this, and perhaps by its meaning.

## THE TALIESIN FELLOWSHIP

Mrs. Wright's death in 1985 left the Taliesin Fellowship an uncertain future. In 1994, Dick Carney, the managing trustee of the Frank Lloyd Wright Foundation, remarked that although he never thought the Fellowship would "fly apart," he was worried that if it did not take some drastic action to reverse its diminishing size, its future was not promising. He noted that in the previous thirty years the senior group had taken in only four new members—two by marriage, and two through family relationships—"so you don't quite count them as being the same as somebody who's from the outside." The failure of the Fellowship to have retained apprentices as permanent members was troubling, and "if we don't find a way . . . to start gaining younger permanent members . . ."—he paused briefly—then said, "we've been talking about this now ever since Mrs. Wright died." Carney recalled that at the time of her death the members of the Fellowship had said that they had ten years to do what needed to be done. "It's now ten years later," he continued, "and we haven't done it, and we're an aging group. And if the aging group cannot find a way to replenish itself, it's not going to exist more than another ten years."[2]

It has existed longer than that, but its membership as presently constituted, despite its dedication and willingness to work, may face challenges requiring more than they can offer. A review of the Fellowship's membership shows that in 2008 there were twenty-three senior members. Of these, fourteen had belonged to it for more than fifty years, three of them more than sixty, and one more than seventy. Only seven were admitted to membership in the 1980s and since. Its strength has been dissipated, too, by the death of nine members since Wes Peters died in 1991.[3]

Even so, Carney found reasons in 1994 to be optimistic: If you walk around through Taliesin at any point, he said, "there is a very vital life going on here, and . . . there are a lot of people who are very busy here. Those people are not all members of the Fellowship, so we have more people who are employed here . . . than are in the Fellowship"—a situation far different from earlier times. He mentioned the vital school program and the dynamic architectural firm and archives, as well as "a sort of a museum, one of the most popular tourist destinations in the country." In all of these entities of the Foundation, the Fellowship has played a vital but diminishing role.

Professionals, Carney observed, can run all of those things, "without the Fellowship being in existence." The School, though, would be in jeopardy if the Fellowship didn't exist "because one of the vital parts of the School is the interaction in the community." So, he continued, "I have no fear of suddenly Taliesin not being in operation. I have the fear that the Fellowship won't be the thing that's causing it to be in operation."[4]

Dick Carney's judgments concerning the past and future of the Fellowship may not represent a consensus—its tradition allows each of its members to "think otherwise"—but first-hand experiences with its founders will soon be gone. To have a future, the Fellowship will have to re-create itself, as it has been attempting to do, while carrying the weight of Mr. and Mrs. Wright's legacy and continuing to honor it.

## THE FRANK LLOYD WRIGHT FOUNDATION

Both the School and the Fellowship have a foundation to build on: The Frank Lloyd Wright Foundation. As a legal entity, incorporated initially in Wisconsin in 1940, and then in Arizona, it continues the work that had evolved during the Wrights' years. Dick Carney, whose leadership responsibilities increased during Mrs. Wright's declining years, remained after her death as managing trustee and CEO of the Foundation. Wes Peters was elected chairman of the board, a position he held until his death in 1991. When Nick Muller, the former executive director of the State Historical Society of Wisconsin, became the Foundation's CEO in 1996, Carney assumed the duties of chairman of the Board.

The Foundation encountered troubled times in the 1990s that continued into the new century. These involved, among other things, financial distress, and the challenge of maintaining the two Taliesins, both of them suffering from long-standing deferred maintenance.

In the decade after Carney's death in 1997, five men served as president and CEO of the Foundation. One of them retired, a second was terminated, a third was a short-term interim holder of the position, a fourth served in that role without the title while he was chairman of the board, and the fifth is in the position currently. Stability remains a goal. Financial distress has been relieved to a limited extent by revenue from tours at both Taliesin and Taliesin West and licensing agreements with companies who merchandise Wright designs, but the income from this is always unpredictable. For a time, revenue generated by the Taliesin Architects helped support the Foundation, but the firm's decline and eventual demise dried up that source. Raising funds to maintain the Taliesins, the Archives, the School, and the Fellowship is a continuing priority of the Foundation.

Significant changes in the composition of the Board have not assured success in fund-raising, but they probably increase its prospects. Until the 1990s the Foundation Board consisted entirely of members of the Fellowship. When the Foundation was chartered in 1940, the Taliesin Fellowship was its principal component. Indeed, for many years the

Foundation and the Fellowship were seen as a single entity. Gradually representatives of the public were added to the Board—a requirement for nonprofit organizations—until they held a majority of the seats. After years-long negotiations, the Fellowship agreed in 2007 to yield all the Board seats to representatives of the public.

## THE FRANK LLOYD WRIGHT ARCHIVES

Frank Lloyd Wright was always mindful of the importance of preserving his architectural drawings, correspondence, and other documents relating to his life and work. His experiences with fires that twice destroyed the living quarters at Taliesin no doubt convinced him that fireproof vaults were necessary, and they were among the first places built at Taliesin and Taliesin West. When he expanded the purposes of Taliesin West, conceived initially as a winter camp, he explained to apprentices that the only repository of his work would be there, in a single place. "If anyone wishes to learn about it or see it first-hand, authentically," he said, "this is where they are going to see it."

One might wonder, with Bruce Pfeiffer, what would have happened if Wright had not had the foresight to establish the Foundation to protect his treasures from being decimated or dispersed after his death: "The firm wants some, the family wants some, you know. What if the six of Mr. Wright's children who survived him all wanted a piece of the pie—some of the prints, some of the drawings, and some of the real estate?"[5]

When Mr. Wright died, Mrs. Wright directed that his 21,000 original drawings located at Taliesin and Taliesin West be placed in a climate-controlled vault in a commercial storage building in Arizona. In 1961, Bruce Pfeiffer went to retrieve a drawing and, upon returning to Taliesin West, mentioned to Mrs. Wright that the drawings were not filed properly. She told him to do something about it. So began his work as director-administrator-curator of the Frank Lloyd Wright Archives. Since then he and his staff have created a vast database, with records of everything in the collection, including photographs of Wright's drawings and microfiche versions of correspondence (more than 300,000 separate documents). This has required expertise in the art of preservation that Pfeiffer and others have acquired in the Taliesin manner: learning by doing. All this has enabled the Archives to provide services to researchers, including the author of this book.

A building for housing the collection and providing accessibility to researchers was built in 1985. Thanks to a gift from Aaron Green, it was enlarged in 1991. As the holdings of the Archives continue to grow, as is happening—for example, with the oral history collection—and as new technologies and the demand for services increase, space and funds to help the Archives keep pace with the demands for access to its resources are in short supply.

There is no exaggeration in the Archives' assertions that "it is now the major international resource for sustaining the Frank Lloyd Wright legacy" and that it is "the world's most complete collection of work by an individual artist housed in a single facility."[6]

## TALIESIN ARCHITECTS

Architecture, of course, had always been the raison d'être for the Fellowship and the Foundation. For more than three decades after Frank Lloyd Wright's death, the Taliesin Architects' performance was consistent with its role as a wholly owned, for-profit subsidiary of a nonprofit corporation, that is, the Foundation. In the early 1990s, several large projects provided income, but completing those projects required the hiring of persons from outside of TA, and that cut into the profits. New commissions dwindled, making it necessary for the firm to borrow from the Foundation, thus putting the nonprofit status of the Foundation at risk.

Rather than shutting down completely and doing away with the name, the Foundation's Board authorized a new arrangement: The name would be retained and Taliesin Architects would become a service entity, handling billings and clerical tasks. The architects in the firm would then practice on their own or form partnerships, retain fees earned, and, if they used the infrastructure provided by Taliesin, such as studio space and phone and copying services, pay a percentage to the Foundation. The Senior Fellowship architects continued their on-site residencies, their Fellowship status, and employee benefits. They would continue to work with apprentices in the School. Initially, eight of the architects chose to practice in pairs and four chose to be independent practitioners.[7] The results have been mixed. By 2008 the studios, once thriving centers of activity, have a ghostly feel about them. The practice of architecture at Taliesin is clearly in jeopardy, although it lives on in the successful careers of men and women who apprenticed there and in those apprenticing there now.

## THE TALIESIN FELLOWS

Unlike most schools, the Frank Lloyd Wright School of Architecture had no alumni organization until the 1980s. To former apprentices, the Fellowship had not been a school, so how could they be alumni? To them, an alumni organization would be anomalous.

That did not mean that their years in the Fellowship were of no consequence to them. Evidence of their interest in recalling the past was demonstrated in many ways through the years, but it was recorded in an unofficial way in the early 1980s. They expressed their feelings and judgments about the Fellowship in responses to a survey by Robert Siegel, a student in architecture at the City College of New York (and a resident in Usonia, the community in Pleasantville, New York, designed initially by Frank Lloyd Wright). His survey sought to ascertain the nature of their experiences as Wright's apprentices and their perception of the value of those experiences. His findings were to be used in research for a paper he was writing on the history of the Fellowship. He sent survey forms to 168 former apprentices and received 80 responses.

Among the respondents, more than half rated their experiences at Taliesin as much better than expected. Nine out of ten called being at Taliesin a life-changing experience. No one dismissed being in the Fellowship as of little importance. Four out of five claimed to be satisfied with their architectural education. Ranked as the most important aspects of their experiences were learning by doing, the master-apprentice relationship, living in a creative environment, and working with Mr. Wright. Communal living and "work lists" received lower ratings. Ninety-one percent of the respondents said that, given a chance, they would do it again.[8] Although there was no connection between Siegel's survey and the formation of an alumni organization, the nature of the responses he received helps explain why, by the late 1980s, former apprentices decided to organize the Taliesin Fellows.

The Taliesin Fellows traces its origins to a reunion at Taliesin West in 1987. One purpose of that Fellowship-hosted reunion was to dispel the notion instilled by Mrs. Wright that if you left you were not welcome to return. Some who attended were distressed by changes they saw in the buildings, but according to Paul Bogart, one of the founders of the Taliesin Fellows, "there was a really wonderful feeling of camaraderie in meeting old friends."

After the reunion several of the former apprentices in Southern California gathered to lay the groundwork for a new organization. One of them, Louis Wiehle, had always maintained a close relationship with Dick Carney, the managing trustee and CEO of the Frank Lloyd Wright Foundation, and the group soon reached an agreement with the Foundation to be known as the "Taliesin Fellows." Then, said Bogart, they were off and running. They organized a board of directors, with Dick Carney as one of the directors, and began to publish the *Journal of the Taliesin Fellows,* with Louis Wiehle as editor. The *Journal* continued through twenty-six issues, from Spring 1990 to Spring 2000. The *Taliesin Fellows Newsletter,* edited by Bill Patrick, succeeded it almost immediately. After twenty-three issues of the *Newsletter,* the organization revived its *Journal* in the Autumn 2006 with issue 27. It took a while, but the Taliesin Fellows eventually decided to accept the designation as Taliesin's alumni organization.

One of the Fellows' first goals was to accomplish the restoration of Taliesin West to the way it had been when they were in the Fellowship. That was complicated, however, by the fact that the members had been there at different times, and it would have been impractical to restore it to its most creative period. Besides, an attempt to do so would have inspired debates over when that was. In any event, they accomplished some of their goals.

Support from Dick Carney and the conscious efforts by the Fellowship to be friendly and accommodating, along with the considerable efforts of its members, made it possible for the Taliesin Fellows to achieve a measure of prosperity. In addition to its publications, the organization has supported reunions of the Fellowship at five-year intervals, beginning in 1992, and it has sustained its commitments to perpetuating the legacies of Frank Lloyd Wright and renewing the memories of its members' experiences in the Fellowship.[9]

■    ■    ■

In November 2007, the Taliesin Fellowship celebrated the 75th anniversary of its founding. Looking back, the Fellowship and the other Taliesin entities—the School, the Foundation, the Archives, the Architects, and the Taliesin Fellows—had much to celebrate. All of them have had ups and downs through the years, good times and bad, but all of them have legacies on which they now strive to build.

# NOTES

## INTRODUCTION

1. Taliesin, near Spring Green, Wisconsin, is the summer home of the Taliesin Fellowship. In the winter it resides at Taliesin West in Scottsdale, Arizona, where the business operations of the Frank Lloyd Wright Foundation are based. As you will see later in this book, however, the Taliesins are more than buildings or geographical places.

2. "What's Happening in Modern Architecture? A Symposium at the Museum of Modern Art," *Museum of Modern Art Bulletin* 15 (Spring 1948): 10, quoted in Neil Levine, *The Architecture of Frank Lloyd Wright* (Princeton: Princeton University Press, 1996), 423; in footnotes 14 and 15, page 502, Levine cites articles documenting Hitchcock's changing interpretation of the significance of Wright and traces comparisons of Wright with Michelangelo. Perhaps Wright had this in mind when he resisted calling his apprentices "students."

3. Quoted in Frederick Gutheim, ed., *Frank Lloyd Wright on Architecture: Selected Writings* (New York: Grosset and Dunlap, 1941), 136. The red square was Wright's seal—in today's terminology his logo.

4. "Frank Lloyd Wright—The Madison Years: Records versus Recollections," *Wisconsin Magazine of History* 50, no. 2 (Winter 1967): 119.

5. Thomas S. Hines, in "The Search for Frank Lloyd Wright," *Journal of the Society of Architectural Historians* 54, no. 4 (December 1995): 467–76, analyzes Wright's autobiography and provides incisive descriptions of the Wright found in works by Vincent Scully, Henry-Russell Hitchcock, Grant Manson, Norris Kelly Smith, Robert Twombly, Brendan Gill, Meryle Secrest, Anthony Alofsin, and Kevin Nute. An account of the creation of Wright's persona appears in *Frank Lloyd Wright,* by Ada Louise Huxtable (New York: Viking, 2004).

## 1—FRANK LLOYD WRIGHT, ARCHITECT

1. *A Testament* (New York: Horizon Press, 1957), 64.

2. In "The Language of an Organic Architecture," Wright elaborated on his understandings of the term and suggested parenthetically that "intrinsic" might be substituted for the term "organic." See *The Future of Architecture* (New York: Horizon Press, 1953), 320–25; also

*Frank Lloyd Wright: Collected Writings,* vol. 5 (New York: Rizzoli International Publications, 1995), 60–63. The key lines: "Organic (or intrinsic) architecture is the free architecture of ideal democracy. . . .The organic refers to *entity,* perhaps integral or intrinsic would therefore be a better word to use. As originally used in architecture, organic means *part-to-whole-as-whole-to-part. So entity as integral* is what is really meant by the word organic. INTRINSIC."

3. "An Organic Architecture: The Architecture of Democracy" (London: Lund, Humphries, 1939). Reprinted in *The Future of Architecture* (New York: Horizon Press, 1953), 238; and in Bruce Brooks Pfeiffer, ed., *Frank Lloyd Wright Collected Writings,* vol. 3 (New York: Rizzoli International Publications, 1993), 308.

4. *Frank Lloyd Wright: The Masterworks* (New York: Rizzoli International Publications, 1993), 8–9. Pfeiffer is the founder and director of the Frank Lloyd Wright Archives, editor of many volumes of Wright's writings, and author of a number of books on Wright.

5. *An Autobiography* (New York: Duell, Sloan and Pearce, 1943), 392.

6. See Bruce Brooks Pfeiffer, ed., *Frank Lloyd Wright: Collected Writings,* vols. 1 and 2 (New York: Rizzoli International, 1992). Also Frederick Gutheim, ed., *In the Cause of Architecture: Frank Lloyd Wright* (New York: Architectural Record, 1975), which includes Wright's essays published in the *Architectural Record, 1908–1952,* and brief essays presented in a symposium by eight participants who knew Wright, including three former apprentices.

7. Margaret Helen Scott, a longtime resident of Richland Center, contends that although there was no legal registry of births in that city before the 1890s, the oral traditions support claims that Wright was born there. William Weston, a longtime employee of Wright, said that Wright showed him the block on which the house stood where he was born but could not be certain of the precise location. *Frank Lloyd Wright's Warehouse in Richland Center, Wisconsin* (Richland Center: Richland County Publishers, 1984), 12–15.

8. Thomas S. Hines, Jr., cites three documents showing conclusively that Wright was born in 1867: the 1880 United

States Census for Madison, where his age is given as thirteen; a ledger-type book from Madison High School, 1884–1885, listing his birth date as June 8, 1867; and a document in his parents' divorce proceedings that gives his age as 17 on June 9, 1884. "Frank Lloyd Wright—The Madison Years: Records versus Recollections," *Journal of the Society of Architectural Historians* 26, no. 4 (December 1967): 227–28. Secrest, *Frank Lloyd Wright: A Biography* (New York: HarperCollins, 1992), 334.

9. *An Autobiography,* 57. At the urging of his wife, Frank Lloyd Wright began writing this book in 1927, and she recorded that he continued writing it in 1930. *Frank Lloyd Wright: His Life, His Work, His Words* (New York: Horizon Press, 1966), 213. The autobiography was published initially in 1932. Some portions of that edition were omitted and others were revised in the expanded and reorganized 1943 edition. An example of a revision in the 1943 edition concerns his departure from the University; the earlier edition says: ". . . the spring term of his senior year was just ended." In the later edition "spring term" is changed to "fall term." A third edition was published posthumously in 1977. Citations in this book will be to the 1943 edition, with reference to the earlier or later ones when significant differences are evident. The 1932 edition appears in Bruce Brooks Pfeiffer, ed., *Frank Lloyd Wright: Collected Writings,* vol. 2 (New York: Rizzoli International Publications, 1992), 102–382, including notes. Pfeiffer comments: "In 1943, when he added to and expanded the 1932 edition of *An Autobiography,* he glossed over, or excused, whatever importance readers might place upon the inconsistencies, the casualness of dates in the stories and narratives, be they accounts or legends, with the sweeping statement: 'I said at the beginning that the real book was between the lines. It is true of any serious book concerned with culture.'" Wright's statement appears on p. 561 of the 1943 edition.

10. Thomas S. Hines, Jr., "Frank Lloyd Wright— The Madison Years: Records versus Recollections," *Journal of the Society of Architectural Historians* 26, no. 4 (December 1967): 230–32. According to Hines, citing Wright's official transcript in the University of Wisconsin Archives, Wright received grades in only two courses, Descriptive Geometry and Drawing. The transcript shows no incompletes or audits.

11. Letters to the Editor, *Journal of the Society of Architectural Historians* 31, no. 2 (May 1972): 159.

12. "Comment on 'The Early Drawings of Frank Lloyd Wright Reconsidered,'" *Journal of the Society of Architectural Historians* 31, no. 3 (October 1972): 220.

13. "Frank Lloyd Wright—The Madison Years: Records versus Recollections," *Wisconsin Magazine of History* 50, no. 2 (Winter 1967): 119; reprinted in the *Journal of the Society of*

*Architectural Historians* 26, no. 4 (December 1967): 233.

14. Wright dated his arrival in 1887, but on the same page he mentioned shivering in front of the Chicago Opera House and seeing enormous posters announcing "Sieba," a ballet then being presented. He went in to see it and had "the roof taken off [his] unsophisticated mind." *An Autobiography,* 63–64. Joseph M. Siry, in The *Chicago Auditorium Building: Adler and Sullivan's Architecture and the City* (Chicago: University of Chicago Press, 2003), 97–98, says that this production opened in the week of August 29, 1886. Wilbert R. Hasbrouck, in "Earliest Work of Frank Lloyd Wright," *Prairie School Review* 7 (Fourth Quarter, 1970): 15, notes that the *All Souls Church Annual,* dated January 6, 1887, listed him as a member.

15. William Allin Storrer, in *The Architecture of Frank Lloyd Wright: A Complete Catalog,* 3rd ed. (Chicago: University of Chicago Press, 2002), 3, writes: "Correspondence indicates that, indeed, Wright may have done not only the perspective sketch, but the building it describes, under Silsbee's tutelage. *Unity* magazine of August 1886 states that 'a boy architect belonging to the family looked after the interior.' So this is the minimum that must be attributed to Wright." The Lloyd Joneses were Unitarian, and these structures were loosely associated with that denomination.

16. *An Autobiography,* 65–74.

17. *An Autobiography,* 71.

18. *An Autobiography,* 75.

19. Owen Jones, *The Grammar of Ornament: Illustrated by Examples from Various Styles of Ornament* (London: Bernard Quaritch, 1868), 5.

20. John Lloyd Wright, *My Father Who Is on Earth,* revised edition, Narciso Menocal, ed. (Carbondale: Southern Illinois University Press, 1994), 136–49.

21. Donald Hoffmann, "Frank Lloyd Wright and Viollet-le-Duc," *Journal of the Society of Architectural Historians* 43, no. 3 (October 1969): 173–83. Hoffmann refers to Viollet-le-Duc's influence in *Understanding Frank Lloyd Wright's Architecture* (New York: Dover, 1995), 22, 96.

22. This is identified in Wright literature as Hillside 1. The Taliesin Fellowship began to use it in the 1930s and continued to do so until it was demolished in the 1950s.

23. *An Autobiography,* 89–94.

24. *An Autobiography,* 95–96.

25. *An Autobiography,* 97.

26. *An Autobiography,* 98–102. One of Wright's fellow architects, George Elmslie, commented on this story: "Your reference to your fight with a filthy Jew, who was two-thirds your size, is a ridiculous episode to put into a serious tale of your life. I was there, as you say, but I was not scared as you imply, only fearful for you and the possibility of your

spine being injured, causing permanent injury or worse. Who would not have been, carrying as I did a great affection for you?" Letter to Wright, October 30, 1932. Ottenheimer became a principal in Ottenheimer, Stern & Reichert. Wilbert R. Hasbrouck, *The Chicago Architectural Club: Prelude to the Modern* (New York: Monacelli Press, 2005), 450.

27. Included among the clients: E. J. Kaufmann (Fallingwater), Rabbi Mordecai Cohen (Beth Sholom Synagogue), Solomon Guggenheim, and a number for whom he designed Usonian homes, such as Ben Rehbuhn (publisher of his books), Stanley and Mildred Rosenbaum, Isadore and Lucille Zimmerman, Sara and Melvyn Maxwell Smith, and Roland and Ronny Reisley. See George Goodwin, "Frank Lloyd Wright's Usonian Houses for Jewish Clients," *American Jewish Archives Journal* LI, nos. 1–2 (1999): 67–92.

28. *No Place Like Utopia: Modern Architecture and the Company We Keep* (New York: Alfred A. Knopf, 1993), 45–49.

29. Peter Blake, *The Master Builders: Le Corbusier, Mies van der Rohe, Frank Lloyd Wright* (New York: W.W. Norton, 1976), 297.

30. *No Place Like Utopia*, 45–49.

31. *Architectural Forum* 9, no. 3 (September 1943): 120, 124, 128, 132. By the time this issue appeared Blake was no longer listed as a member of the *Forum* staff. However, in a Postscript to *Form Follows Fiasco: Why Modern Architecture Hasn't Worked* (Boston: Little, Brown and Company, 1977), 165, Blake states that he served as editor-in-chief of the *Architectural Forum* and later of *Architecture Plus* "between, roughly, 1963 and 1975."

32. *An Autobiography,* 106.

33. *An Autobiography,* 107.

34. *An Autobiography,* 108. The floor plan of the Adler & Sullivan office, published in *Engineering & Building Record,* 1890, is reproduced in Robert Twombly, *Louis Sullivan: His Life and Work* (New York: Viking, 1986), 183; Wright's room (approximately 10' x 17') had doorways to both the drawing room and Mr. Sullivan's room (approximately 15' x 15').

35. *An Autobiography,* 110.

36. *An Autobiography,* 124–25. Earlier he had designed a house for another client, but it was not built. While with Adler and Sullivan he had designed about a dozen residences.

37. *An Autobiography,* 126–28. Wright's is the only account of this conversation.

38. *An Autobiography,* 130–31.

39. "In the Cause of Architecture," *Architectural Record* 33 (March 1908): 156. A number of the "younger men," including Spencer, were older than Wright.

40. *An Autobiography,* 131.

41. H. Allen Brooks, "Steinway Hall, Architects and Dreams," *Journal of the Society of Architectural Historians* 22, no. 3 (October 1963): 171–75. Brooks elaborates on the Steinway Hall group in *The Prairie School: Frank Lloyd Wright and His Midwest Contemporaries* (New York: W.W. Norton, 1972), 28–32, 37, 41–44, 45, 88–89, 146, 195. He also named others in the group from offices outside Steinway Hall: Arthur and George Dean, Hugh Garden, Alfred Granger, Richard Schmidt, and Howard Shaw; some of these had been in Steinway Hall at some point.

42. *A Testament* (New York: Horizon, 1957), 34. Beginning in 1895, Wright and Spencer had adjacent offices in the Schiller building.

43. Brooks, *The Prairie School*, 45.

44. For a detailed history of the Chicago Architectural Club, see Wilbert R. Hasbrouck, *The Chicago Architectural Club: Prelude to the Modern* (New York: Monacelli Press, 2005), particularly "Steinway Hall and the Traveling Scholarship," 277–301.

45. Brooks, "Steinway Hall, Architects and Dreams," 171–75. Dates of the exhibition are in Donald Langmead, *Frank Lloyd Wright: A Bio-Bibliography* (Westport, Conn.: Praeger, 2003), 3–7. For a brief history of the Chicago Architectural Club, the dominance of its modernist members, and the rebellion against that dominance, see Wilbert R. Hasbrouck, "The Early Years of the Chicago Architectural Club," *Chicago Architectural Club Journal* 1 (1981): 7–14. This article, Hasbrouck says, inspired him to undertake research for the book on the Club published in 2005 (see footnote 44). On pages 277–325 there are descriptions of the exhibitions and reviews treating them.

46. *The Inland Architect and News Record* 35 (June 1900): 35–40. The lecture was republished in Robert Twombly, ed., *Louis Sullivan: The Public Papers* (University of Chicago Press, 1988), 131–44.

47. *The Inland Architect and News Record* 35 (June 1900): 43.

48. *American Architect and Building News* 68 (1900): 87. Wright's address was published in *The Brickbuilder* in June 1900 and is reprinted in *Frank Lloyd Wright: Collected Writings,* vol. 1, 1894–1930, edited by Bruce Brooks Pfeiffer, pp. 45–53. Introducing it there, Pfeiffer says that Wright decried the fate of American architecture, blaming "its lack of integrity on the pressures commerce was exerting over the architect." The solution to the problem, Wright said in poetic terms, lay in the proper education of the architect.

49. *An Autobiography,* 131–32. Introducing this essay in Wright's *Collected Writings,* vol.1 (New York: Rizzoli, 1992), 58, Bruce Brooks Pfeiffer states that scholars often regard this as Wright's first great manifesto. Earlier unpublished

manuscripts suggest, however, that it was "a carefully crafted summation of ideas and concepts he had been presenting to the public for a number of years." In it Wright emphasizes the capabilities and potential of the machine in the hands of artists. For Brooks's comment on Wright's negative remarks, see *The Prairie School*, 43.

50. Listings of Wright's designs and built projects do not always agree on dates. For the most authoritative and comprehensive list, see the one compiled by Bruce Brooks Pfeiffer, director of the Frank Lloyd Wright Archives, in Robert McCarter, *The Architecture of Frank Lloyd Wright* (London: Phaidon Press Limited, 1997), 344–59. Extensive research by Paul Sprague led him to conclude that four unbuilt designs in this list were dated incorrectly. See Paul Kruty, *Prelude to the Prairie Style: Eight Models of Unbuilt Houses by Frank Lloyd Wright, 1893–1901* (Urbana-Champaign: University of Illinois School of Architecture). For pictures, some of them of building interiors and drawings, and brief descriptions of Wright's built projects, see William Allin Storrer, *The Frank Lloyd Wright Companion* (Chicago: University of Chicago Press, 1993); Storrer's *The Architecture of Frank Lloyd Wright: A Complete Catalog* (Chicago: University of Chicago Press, 3rd ed., 2002; updated 2006) has color images of most of the structures. See also Thomas A. Heinz, *Frank Lloyd Wright Field Guide* (Evanston, Ill.: Northwestern University Press, 2005).

51. *An Autobiography,* 137–38. In 1938 Romeo and Juliet was rebuilt, with horizontal board-and-batten replacing the original wood shingles. In 1992 it was rebuilt again, with board-and-batten siding.

## 2—THE OAK PARK STUDIO YEARS

1. "In the Cause of Architecture," *Architectural Record* 33 (March 1908): 163–64. As this chapter will show, this paragraph describes the Studio community as it existed after 1906.

2. Drawing information from the Lakeside City Directory of Chicago, Grant Carpenter Manson, in *Frank Lloyd Wright to 1910: The First Golden Age* (New York: Van Nostrand Reinhold Company, 1958), 215, lists downtown offices Wright occupied after beginning his career as an independent architect in 1893: 1501 Schiller Building, 1893–1896; 1107 Steinway Hall, 1897; 1123 The Rookery, 1898; 1104 The Rookery, 1899; none listed, 1900; 1106 Steinway Hall, 1901–1902; none listed, 1903; 1106 Steinway Hall, 1904–1907; 1020 Fine Arts Building, 1908; none listed, 1909; 1020 Fine Arts Building, 1910–1911; and 605 Orchestra Hall, 1912.

3. At least six of these residences have been restored and opened to the public. The Larkin Building was demolished.

Other notable projects included several apartment buildings; the Municipal Boathouse on Lake Mendota, Madison, Wisconsin; the Lake Delavan Boat Club (Wisconsin); and the River Forest Tennis Club. Avery Coonley and Queene Ferry Coonley, for whom Wright designed the expansive Coonley residence, called upon him again in 1911 to design their Gardener's Cottage and Coach House, and in 1912 the Coonley Playhouse. In her first meeting with Wright, Mrs. Coonley commented that his architecture expressed "the countenance of principle." As Christian Scientists, the Coonleys regarded "principle" as a synonym for God; accordingly, they saw Wright's houses as representing the divine order of things. See Theodore Turak, "Mr. Wright and Mrs. Coonley," in Richard Guy Wilson and Sidney K. Robinson, eds., *Modern Architecture in America: Visions and Revisions* (Ames: Iowa State University Press, 1991), 154.

4. Membership records of some sort may have existed but possibly were destroyed in a fire at Taliesin in 1914.

5. *The Chicago Architectural Club: Prelude to the Modern* (New York: Monacelli Press, 2005), 384–85. Mark L. Peisch, in *The Chicago School of Architecture: Early Followers of Sullivan and Wright* (New York: Random House, 1964), 41, writes about "Wright's Oak Park Fellowship, as he called it," but I could find no such term used by Wright or by anyone else.

6. "At Work in the Oak Park Studio," *Arris: Journal of the Southeast Chapter of the Society of Architectural Historians* 14 (2003): 18.

7. Paul Kruty, with Mati Maldre, photographer, *Walter Burley Griffin in America* (Urbana and Chicago: University of Illinois Press, 1996), 19–20. Kruty notes that among its innovative features was a brass wall sconce that pleased Wright so much that he used it in at least five houses he designed in this period.

8. *Architectural Record* 33 (March 1908): 164–65. For the opening lines of this section, see the headnote to this chapter.

9. *Frank Lloyd Wright and George Mann Niedeken: Prairie School Collaborators* (Milwaukee: Milwaukee Art Museum, and Lexington, Mass.: Museum of Our National Heritage, 1999), 20.

10. *An Autobiography,* 138–39. Byrne's recollection is in a transcript of an interview with Studs Terkel in *Division Street U.S.A.* (New York: Pantheon, 1967), 260.

11. *An Autobiography,* 236.

12. *An Autobiography,* 136.

13. *An Autobiography,* 237–38. Byrne was nineteen years old when he entered Wright's studio.

14. Scholars refer to Marion Mahony by both of her names, or as Mahony, until her marriage in 1911 to Walter Burley Griffin. Thereafter, to distinguish her from her

husband and partner, they call her Marion Mahony Griffin, or simply Mahony Griffin, or Mrs. Griffin, if they call her husband Mr. Griffin. Referring to her as "Marion," except when her name is paired with others who are denoted by first names (as in "Marion and Walter") is as inappropriate as it would be to refer to Mr. Wright as "Frank" and the others in the studio by their given names: e.g., Barry, George, Andrew, William, Charles, and so on. Recollections of Harry Robinson appear in the next chapter.

15. Paul Kruty's "At Work in the Oak Park Studio," *Arris: Journal of the Southeast Chapter of the Society of Architectural Historians* 14 (2003): 17–31, provides valuable facts and insights concerning the operation of the studio. Marking the Centennial of Frank Lloyd Wright's studio in Oak Park in 1995, the Frank Lloyd Wright Home and Studio Foundation published a 25-page booklet by Fran Martone, "In Wright's Shadow: Artists and Architects in the Oak Park Studio." The concise narrative provides a good summary of the factual information treated in a different way in this chapter. This booklet is cited only when quoted directly.

16. "In the Cause of Architecture," *Architectural Record* 39 (May 1914): 126. See also Mark L. Peisch, *The Chicago School of Architecture* (New York: Random House, 1964), 51.

17. "In the Cause of Architecture," *Architectural Record* 33 (March 1908): 164. Throughout his career there were typically women among Wright's assistants, but he counted them among his "boys."

18. "On Frank Lloyd Wright and His Atelier," *AIA Journal* 39, no. 6 (June 1963): 109–11.

19. Mark L. Peisch, *The Chicago School of Architecture* (New York: Random House, 1964), 99. Peisch cites a letter he received from Byrne, October 15, 1956.

20. "Walter Burley Griffin: An American Architect of America's Middle West," *Walter Burley Griffin in America* (Urbana: University of Illinois Press, 1996), 31.

21. Howard Dearstyne, *Inland Architect* 5 (January 1968), 10. For a summary of the early years of Byrne's career, see Sally Anderson Chappell, *Prairie School Review* 3, no. 4 (1966): 5–18.

22. Letters by White cited and quoted in the preceding paragraphs are from Nancy K. Morris Smith, "Letters, 1903–1906, by Charles E. White, Jr., from the Studio of Frank Lloyd Wright," *Journal of Architectural Education* 25 (Fall 1971): 104–12. The letters are from the Walter Ross Baumes Willcox Collection, housed in the archives of the library at the University of Oregon, where Willcox was the head of the Department of Architecture, beginning in 1922. In 1931, he organized an exhibition of Wright's work, displayed in Eugene, Oregon, and Seattle, Washington.

23. Between 1900 and 1908 Wright published an article in the catalogue of the Chicago Architectural Club, two in *The Brickbuilder* (the first being the paper he presented at the convention of the Architectural League of America cited in the previous chapter), two in *The Ladies Home Journal,* and two in *The Architectural Record.*

24. Grant Carpenter Manson, *Frank Lloyd Wright to 1910: The First Golden Years* (New York: Van Nostrand Reinhold Company, 1958), 213; Van Bergen, who was twenty-four years old at the time, had apprenticed for two years with Griffin. Fran Martone says that Isabel Roberts and van Bergen were the ones to shut the office down. See "In Wright's Shadow," published by the Frank Lloyd Wright Home and Studio Foundation, 1988, p. 19.

25. *The Prairie School: Frank Lloyd Wright and His Midwest Contemporaries* (New York: W.W. Norton, 1972), 85–86, 130, 335. For more on Drummond, see Suzanne Ganschinietz, "William Drummond: I. Talent and Sensitivity," *Prairie School Review* 6, no. 1 (1969): 4–11.

26. *1894 Class Book,* Massachusetts Institute of Technology, 1898; cited in Susan Fondiler Berkon, "Marion Mahony Griffin," in Susanna Torre, ed., *Women in American Architecture: A Historic and Contemporary Perspective* (New York: Whitney Library of Design/Watson-Guptill Publications, 1977), 75. This book accompanied an exhibition organized by the Architectural League of New York through its Archive of Women in Architecture.

27. Paul Kruty has noted that a number of architecture journals, including the *Architect* of London, reported this accomplishment. See "Chicago: The Griffins Come of Age," in Anne Watson, ed., *Beyond Architecture: Marion Mahony and Walter Burley Griffin* (Sydney: Powerhouse Publishing, 1998), 17.

28. *The Prairie School*, 79–80. Byrne's paper, November 28, 1939, cited by Brooks, exists as a typed manuscript in the Ricker Library, University of Illinois, Champaign-Urbana.

29. "The Life and Work of Marion Mahony Griffin," *The Prairie School: Design Vision for the Midwest* (Chicago: The Art Institute of Chicago; *Museum Studies* 21, no. 2 (1995): 167–69. The article provides a good overview of Mahony's career, pp. 165–92. Barry Byrne, review of Arthur Drexler, *The Drawings of Frank Lloyd Wright, Journal of the Society of Architectural Historians*, XXII, no. 2 (May 1961): 109.

30. Marion Mahony Griffin, *The Magic of America,* unpublished memoir, section IV, "The Individual Battle," 20. Two typescripts of *The Magic of America* are held in the archives of the Art Institute of Chicago and one in the New York Historical Society. They differ slightly in composition and minor details; both are available on microfilm. In 2007 the Art Institute produced an electronic edition, collating in digital form all the texts and illustrations from the three

known copies; the Institute holds the copyright. Page numbers shown in the electronic edition are the ones used here. See www.artic.edu/magicofamerica. Accessed January 29, 2008. This memoir has been aptly characterized by Judy Wells in her brief article on the "Beyond Architecture" exhibition of Walter Burley Griffin and Marion Mahony Griffin's architectural work, as "a mix of diary, letters, documents, drawings and all manner of information, assembled and reassembled by Marion late in her life" and as "an assembly of information with no real closure." Nonetheless, "because of its fragmented, eclectic structure and its contradictions, someone real does lift off the page." See "Representations of Marion Mahony Griffin," in *Architectural Theory Review* 3, no. 2 (1998): 124. According to Paul Kruty, Mahony Griffin retyped letters and other documents used in *Magic* and discarded the originals, thus denying full accessibility to the record of her life and work. (Personal conversation.)

31. Paul Kruty, with Mati Maldre, photographer, "Walter Burley Griffin: An American Architect of America's Middle West," *Walter Burley Griffin in America* (Urbana: University of Illinois Press, 1996), 26. *Western Architect* 19 (October 1913): 88, xvii, 101, includes ten pages of photos and drawings. The Irving House in Decatur is treated in the April issue, pp. 38–39, with 12 pages of photos and drawings. Von Holst, as the architect of record, also claimed credit for the Irving house. For a full treatment of this house and the two adjacent ones Mahony designed for the Muellers, see Paul Kruty and Paul E. Sprague, *Marion Mahony and Millikin Place: Creating a Prairie School Masterpiece* (St. Louis: Walter Burley Griffin Society of America, 2007).

32. *Magic of America,* Section IV, 157. For more on Mahony Griffin, see also Janice Pregliasco, "The Life and Work of Marion Mahony Griffin," *The Prairie School: Design Vision for the Midwest* (Chicago: The Art Institute of Chicago, *Museum Studies* 21, no. 2, 1995): 173.

33. Kruty summarizes Griffin's work with Wright, including while Wright was away, and Wright's reaction to it in "Walter Burley Griffin: An American Architect of America's Middle West," *Walter Burley Griffin in America* (Urbana: University of Illinois Press, 1996), 20. What may be the original copy of Wright's letter to Griffin, dated June 10, 1910, in Fiesole, Italy, is in an unpostmarked envelope in the Taylor Woolley Manuscript Collection, Rogers Library, University of Utah.

34. The address was published in *The Inland Architect and News Record* 35 (June 1900): 35–40.

35. Sullivan's address was published in *The Inland Architect and News Record* 35 (June 1900): 35–40. See Kruty's "Chicago: The Griffins Come of Age," in Anne Watson, ed., *Beyond Architecture: Marion Mahony and Walter Burley Griffin*

(Sydney: Powerhouse Publishing, 1998), 19–20; he cites as an example Wright's use of modules, that is, repeated units in a plan regulating room sizes and wall, door, and window placements, that began within a year of Griffin's entry into his employment. The same is true of the L-shaped open designs in which living rooms and dining rooms wrapped around fireplaces.

36. Mark Peisch PBS interview transcript, http://www. pbs.org/wbgriffin/piesch.html, updated June 4, 1999, p. 1. Accessed August 20, 2007. Note the misspelling of Peisch's name in this address.

37. *Magic of America,* Section IV, 329.

38. *Magic of America,* Section IV, 305, 42, 378, 215, 75b.

39. *Magic of America,* III, 174.

40. Letter from Byrne to Mark Peisch, May 3, 1951. Peisch, *The Chicago School of Architecture,* 45. Sally Anderson Chappell, who wrote her doctoral dissertation on Byrne's life and work, notes that he also had his frustrations with Wright. When he returned from a three-month absence due to illness early in 1908, she says, he found the studio in a demoralized condition. In a letter to her dated October 25, 1956, Byrne recalled: "Wright's affair with Mrs. Cheney was well underway when I entered the hospital and had progressed to a critical degree by the time I returned. Wright was rarely around and not at hand to consult on the Coonley House and Unity Temple work, which I had again taken up. As my salary was no more than an allowance to cover car fare and lunches I concluded the financial sacrifice I was making served no purpose." *Barry Byrne: Architecture and Writings,* Northwestern University Ph.D. dissertation, 1968; Ann Arbor: University Microfilms, 1969, 9.

41. Brooks, 190. In the second half of *The Prairie School,* Brooks summarizes the subsequent careers of some of those who had been assistants in the studio, particularly Barry Byrne, William Drummond, and John van Bergen. He also gives an apt accounting of the flourishing years of the Prairie School and its rather swift decline.

42. "At Work in the Oak Park Studio," *Arris: Journal of the Southeast Chapter of the Society of Architectural Historians* 14 (2003): 27. The article provides an excellent account of the Studio years, pp. 17–31.

### 3—UNSETTLED YEARS

1. *An Autobiography,* 170–71. The account in such terms continues for several pages.

2. *Executed Works and Designs of Lloyd Wright.* This publication appeared in two folio volumes in 1911. It was accompanied by a small book of photographs published in the United States as *Ausgefürte Bauten,* referred to by Wright as *Sonderheft* (special edition). Anthony Alofsin has called

these "vanity printings" and says that they were "fraught with problems." Only 100 of the folio volumes were reserved for European sale, out of a projected total of 1,250. The *Sonderheft,* he says, "was more available, with 3,900 copies in an inferior edition, titled *Frank Lloyd Wright: Chicago,* designated for European distribution." Critical response to the two folio volumes in Europe was limited to one brief review in 1913. *Frank Lloyd Wright: The Lost Years, 1910–1922: A Study of Influence* (Chicago: University of Chicago Press, 1993), 76–77. Variant versions of the Wasmuth original were published in Japan in 1916; in Germany around 1924; in the United States in 1963 and 1975. See Robert L. Sweeney, *Frank Lloyd Wright: An Annotated Bibliography* (Los Angeles: Hennessey & Ingalls, Inc., 1978), 15–18. The introductory text of *Ausgefürte Bauten und Entwürfe von Frank Lloyd Wright,* with a context-setting introduction, appears in Bruce Brooks Pfeiffer, ed., *Frank Lloyd Wright: Collected Writings,* vol. 1, 1894–1930 (New York: Rizzoli, 1992), 101–15.

3. *An Autobiography,* 162. Here again Wright misstates his age. Rather than having "almost reached [his] fortieth year," he began his forty-third year in June 1909.

4. *An Autobiography,* 163.

5. *An Autobiography,* 163–64. Here he attempted to justify his conduct, drawing on ideas of the Swedish feminist Ellen Key, whose works Mamah Borthwick Cheney translated into English. Mrs. Cheney was facile in several languages. Although Wright knew no Swedish, he claimed to have helped her. Italics are in the original.

6. *An Autobiography,* 164.

7. "Crisis and Creativity: Frank Lloyd Wright, 1904–1914," *JSAH* 25, no. 4 (December 1966): 293–94. The article was published in revised form, with much of the speculation about Anna Lloyd Jones omitted, in *9 Commentaries on Frank Lloyd Wright* (Cambridge: The MIT Press, 1989), 87–102; this version included fourteen illustrations. When Wright left, his children—Frank Lloyd Jr. (known as Lloyd), John Lloyd, Catherine Dorothy, David Samuel, Frances Barbara, and Robert Lewellyn—ranged in age from six to nineteen.

According to John Lloyd Wright, his grandmother told him often how Grandfather Wright left home: "'You can take your hat and go,' she said to him. 'And do you know what he did?' she asked, tapping me sharply on the knee with her walking stick. 'He walked right over to the hatrack, took his hat, walked politely out the door, and that was the last I ever saw or heard of him.'" Narciso G. Menocal, ed., *My Father Who Is on Earth* (Carbondale: Southern Illinois University Press, 1994), 54. This edition of John Lloyd Wright's 1946 memoir includes marginal notes by both the father and the son and additional comments and documents.

8. *Frank Lloyd Wright: A Study in Architectural Context* (Englewood Cliffs, N.J.: Prentice-Hall, Inc., 1966), 83, 98, 100. A revised, redesigned version of this book, with elaborations on its thirty-one illustrations, was published in 1979 by the American Life Foundation & Study Institute.

9. Neil Levine, *The Architecture of Frank Lloyd Wright* (Princeton, N.J.: Princeton University Press, 1996), 65.

10. Anthony Alofsin, *Frank Lloyd Wright: The Lost Years, 1910–1922* (Chicago: University of Chicago Press, 1993), 31, 306. The original contract no longer exists.

11. 32–62. Also "Appendix A: Chronology," 307–10.

12. *An Autobiography,* 366. Wright's son, John Lloyd Wright, implicitly attributes his father's apparent depression to separation from his family and his inability to live up to his ideals as a father and husband. Although the senior Wright portrayed himself as a bad father, John describes him as a lover of home, family, and fatherhood: "He just didn't like to take everything that goes with it in our complicated and restless state of society, and children become a double nuisance when a father leaves home. He tried to make himself 'Big Bad Bill' to relieve the sentimental pull on his heartstrings. . . ." "Actually," the son continued, "I can say without fear of contradiction: 'Big Bad Bill' is just Sweet William.'" Narciso G. Menocal, ed., *My Father Who Is on Earth* (Carbondale: Southern Illinois University Press, 1994), 56–57.

13. An essay by Alofsin provides a detailed analysis of the influence of Ellen Key on the philosophy of Frank Lloyd Wright and Wright's relationship with Mamah Borthwick Cheney: "Taliesin: 'To Fashion Worlds in Little,'" in Narciso G. Menocal, ed., *Taliesin 1911–1914,* Wright Studies, vol. 1 (Carbondale: Southern Illinois University Press, 1992), 44–65. A fictional account of the relationship between Wright and Mamah Borthwick Cheney by Nancy Horan treats what is known about it deftly and develops a plausible story line in which the writer's imagination necessarily comes into play. See *Loving Frank* (New York: Ballantine Books, 2007).

14. Lloyd Wright described the situation in a letter to Linn Cowles; quoted in Edgar Kauffman, Jr., *9 Commentaries on Frank Lloyd Wright* (Cambridge: The MIT Press, 1989), 96–98. He referred to Woolley as "a sensitive draughtsman, a Mormon from Salt Lake City, who, though lame, was active, helpful, and a hard worker."

15. *An Autobiography,* 165.

16. The design appears in the books by Alofsin (*Frank Lloyd Wright,* p. 52) and Levine (p. 69), and, in a beautiful rendering (in a mirror image, from a slightly different perspective, in delicately shaded colors, and with more detailed landscaping), in Bruce Brooks Pfeiffer's *Frank Lloyd Wright: Treasures of Taliesin: Seventy-Six Unbuilt*

Designs (Fresno: The Press at California State University, and Carbondale: Southern Illinois University Press, 1985), Plate 4. Pfeiffer notes that in 1957 Wright proposed the same design for a client living in Cuernavaca, Mexico, but, as in Fiesole, that one was never built.

17. Alan Crawford, "Ten Letters from Frank Lloyd Wright to Charles Robert Ashbee," *Architectural History: Journal of the Society of Architectural Historians of Great Britain* 13 (1970): 66.

18. Alofsin, *Frank Lloyd Wright,* 67.

19. Alofsin, *Frank Lloyd Wright,* 62.

20. Finis Farr, in *Frank Lloyd Wright: A Biography* (New York: Charles Scribner's Sons, 1961), 130, identifies the location but provides no documentation; Paul Kruty, in *Frank Lloyd Wright and Midway Gardens* (Urbana: University of Illinois Press, 1998) refers to it as a *pied-à-terre,* 21.

21. Levine, *The Architecture of Frank Lloyd Wright* (Princeton: Princeton University Press, 1996), 89, 90. See also Bruce Brooks Pfeiffer, *Treasures of Taliesin: Seventy-Six Unbuilt Designs* (Fresno: The Press at California State University, and Carbondale: Southern Illinois University Press, 1985), Plate 6.

22. Levine says that she shared his apartment on Cedar Street. *The Architecture of Frank Lloyd Wright,* 89.

23. *The Valley of the God-Almighty Joneses: Reminiscences of Frank Lloyd Wright's Sister, Maginel Wright Barney* (New York: Appleton-Century, 1965; republished by Unity Chapel Publications, Spring Green, Wisc., 1986), 64.

24. Levine, *The Architecture of Frank Lloyd Wright,* 76. Levine provides a detailed account of the story Taliesin was to tell; of its site, design, and construction; and of its place in Wright's life, 75–111.

25. "Crisis and Creativity: Frank Lloyd Wright, 1904–1914," *JSAH* 25, no. 4 (December 1966): 296.

26. *An Autobiography,* 172–73.

27. Antonin Raymond, *An Autobiography* (Rutland, Vt.: Charles E. Tuttle Co., 1973), 46–47, 49, 53. This work bears marks of literary license similar to those found in Wright's autobiography.

28. *Web of Life.* Privately published, 2001, pp. 27, 59. Accounts for later years are more complete.

29. James Alexander Robinson, *The Life and Work of Harry Franklin Robinson, 1883–1959* (Hong Kong: Hilross Development Ltd., 1989), 18–23.

30. Alofsin, *Frank Lloyd Wright: The Lost Years, 1910–1922: A Study of Influence* (Chicago: University of Chicago Press, 1993), 71–72, 343. Wilhelm Bernhard's entry in the planning competition appears, along with Wright's, in Alfred Yeomans, ed., *City Residential Land Development:*

*Studies in Planning* (Chicago: University of Chicago Press, 1916). The text for Wright's entry can be found also in Charles E. Aguar and Berdeana Aguar, *Wrightscapes: Frank Lloyd Wright's Landscape Designs* (New York: McGraw-Hill, 2002), 353–55.

31. *Inter alia:* Paul Kruty, *Frank Lloyd Wright and Midway Gardens* (Urbana and Chicago: University of Illinois Press, 1998), 20–21; Meryle Secrest, *Frank Lloyd Wright: A Biography* (New York: HarperPerennial, 1992), 216.

32. Shirley du Fresne McArthur, *Frank Lloyd Wright, American System-built Homes in Milwaukee* (Milwaukee, Wisc.: North Point Historical Society, 1985), 8–11. Kristin Visser, *Frank Lloyd Wright & the Prairie School of Wisconsin: An Architectural Touring Guide* (Madison, Wisc.: Prairie Oaks Press, 1992), 17–18. When Wright left for Japan, Williamson finished several projects and then left Wright's office. He continued to design Prairie Style houses until the mid-1920s before moving on to other styles. William Allin Storrer, *The Frank Lloyd Wright Companion* (Chicago: University of Chicago Press, 1993), 197, 203.

33. Thomas S. Hines, "Architecture: Reconsidering Lloyd Wright: A Brilliant Legacy of Residential Design Endures in Los Angeles," *Architectural Digest* 50, no. 5 (May 1993): 44, 48.

34. "The Blessing and the Curse: The Achievement of Lloyd Wright," in Thomas S. Hines, ed., *Lloyd Wright: The Architecture of Frank Lloyd Wright, Jr.* (New York: Harry N. Abrams, Inc., 1998), 16.

35. Antonin Raymond, *An Autobiography* (Rutland, Vt.: Charles E. Tuttle Co., 1973), 53.

36. Andrew Saint, "Frank Lloyd Wright and Paul Mueller: The Architect and His Builder of Choice," *Arq: Architectural Research Quarterly* 7, no. 2 (2003): 163. Kruty, *Frank Lloyd Wright and Midway Gardens,* 32–33. Saint's article, pp. 157–67, provides a good summary of Mueller's career. Testimony by Mueller in a court case involving the Auditorium designed by Louis Sullivan provides insights into his competence as a builder. See Edgar Kaufmann, *9 Commentaries on Frank Lloyd Wright* (Cambridge, Mass.: MIT Press, 1989), 42–62.

37. Ann Van Zanten offers a good account of John Lloyd Wright's life and career in "Barry Byrne, John Lloyd Wright: Architecture and Design" (Chicago: Chicago Historical Society and the University of Chicago Press, 1962), 42–69.

38. *An Autobiography,* 182.

39. *An Autobiography,* 185–86. The 1932 edition does not include these details. John Lloyd Wright presents a touching account of the same events in *My Father Who Is on Earth,* 80–85. Readers wanting a detailed account of these

events will find it in William R. Drennan, *Death in a Prairie House: Frank Lloyd Wright and the Taliesin Murders* (Madison, Wisc.: Terrace Books, 2007).

40. *Frank Lloyd Wright and Midway Gardens* (Urbana: University of Illinois Press, 1998), 57–59. Although Wright blamed Prohibition, problems leading to the first sale of the enterprise, Kruty says, were not related to alcohol, and the next version survived as a "dry" establishment for more than a year. He notes, though, that "there *was* a certain relationship between temperance, Prohibition, and the Gardens that merits further consideration."

## 4—UNSETTLED YEARS CONTINUE

1. *An Autobiography,* 193–94.

2. *An Autobiography,* 194. Here again Wright repeats a chronological inaccuracy. Having been born in 1867, he would have been in his twenty-fifth year at the time of the Columbian Exposition where he saw the Japanese building.

3. *An Autobiography,* 196.

4. For the 1906 text, see *Collected Writings,* vol. 1 (New York: Rizzoli, 1992), 78–80. Ralph Fletcher Seymour published *The Japanese Print* in 1912, and in 1967 Horizon Press republished it, with additional essays and plates of prints; it is reprinted also in *Collected Writings,* vol. 1, 116–25. The text for the 1917 exhibition appears in *Collected Writings,* vol. 1, 144–47.

5. "Wright's First Trip to Japan," *Frank Lloyd Wright Quarterly* 6, no. 2 (Spring 1995): 21–23; Stipe suggests that what Wright observed on this journey influenced his siting and landscaping of Taliesin. See also Melanie Birk, ed., *Frank Lloyd Wright's Fifty Views of Japan: The 1905 Photo Album* (San Francisco: Pomegranate Artbooks, 1996).

6. *Frank Lloyd Wright and the Art of Japan: The Architect's Other Passion* (New York: Japan Society and Harry N. Abrams, Inc., 2001), 38–40. This richly illustrated book provides a detailed account of Wright's lifelong connection with Japanese prints.

7. Information concerning Wright's interactions with authorities in Japan and his travels to and from there can be found in a number of publications. A well-documented chronology appears in Kathryn Smith's "Frank Lloyd Wright and the Imperial Hotel: A Postscript," *The Art Bulletin* 67, no. 2 (June 1985): 296–310. Unless otherwise noted, Wright's comings, goings, and doings are dated according to this article. In important instances sources she identified are cited. Significant dates are also listed in Bruce Brooks Pfeiffer's "A Selected Chronology of Frank Lloyd Wright's Life and Work," published in David De Long, ed., *Frank Lloyd Wright and the Living City* (Weil am Rhein: Vitra Design Museum, 1998), 313–25, and in Anthony Alofsin, *Frank*

*Lloyd Wright: The Lost Years, 1910–1922: A Study of Influence* (Chicago: University of Chicago Press, 1993), 307–10. These chronologies are generally consistent with one another, but there are slight variations.

8. Kathryn Smith, "Frank Lloyd Wright and the Imperial Hotel," 298. In the letter Wright stated his intention to leave the next day. In fact, Wright's projection of the cost was tenfold larger than that of the Japanese hotel planners. The cost eventually reached $3 million, but the fault lay largely beyond Wright's control. In David De Long, ed., *Frank Lloyd Wright and the Living City,* p. 317, Bruce Brooks Pfeiffer marks the travelers' return on June 12.

9. For this exhibition Wright brought Taylor Woolley back to assist in preparing for it. His works were shown in a separate room, creating controversy, including the charge that he had bought his way into the exhibition; the Illinois Chapter of the AIA reviewed the matter and concluded that the charges against Wright were false. Wilbert R. Hasbrouck, *Chicago Architectural Club* (New York: Monacelli Press, 2005), 424.

10. Kathryn Smith, "Frank Lloyd Wright," 299–300.

11. Julia Meech, *Frank Lloyd Wright and the Art of Japan: The Architect's Other Passion,* 100, contains a chart showing the timeline for all seven of Wright's visits to Japan, 1905 to 1922. In Katherine Smith's calculation, Wright's total time in Japan amounted to several months longer. Kathryn Smith, "Frank Lloyd Wright," 308–9.

12. *An Autobiography,* 201–2.

13. For an account of the part buying, collecting, and selling Japanese prints played in Wright's life and career, see Meech. An account of Wright's predicaments with forgeries, called revamped prints, appears on pp. 159–72.

14. See the next chapter for an account of Wright's dealings with Barnsdall.

15. *An Autobiography,* 203–5. There are no existing pictures of the Annex, although there are some of his apartment. See Meech, 154–55.

16. Quoted by Kathryn Smith, "Frank Lloyd Wright," 306; from a photocopy of the February 7, 1921, letter in the Avery Architectural and Fine Arts Library, Columbia University. Note that here he had not yet changed his year of birth from 1867 to 1869.

17. Here and in more than a dozen other instances, Smith draws her information from the *Japan Advertiser.*

18. *An Autobiography,* 220.

19. Fifteen months later (September 26, 1923), shortly after receiving good reports on the condition of the hotel after the earthquake, Wright wrote favorably of Mueller in a letter to Louis Sullivan: "Mueller's untiring attention to the execution of the details of this program counted too

in the final result. Nothing of any importance was put into place without his superintendence. I wonder how the old boy is? He will be delighted, for he was not all together sure I was right about my foundation or about a number of other things." Bruce Brooks Pfeiffer, ed., *Letters to Architects* (The Press at California State University, Fresno, 1984), 40.

20. *An Autobiography,* 220–21. Although few of his coworkers in Japan are known by name, a 1922 photograph shows about thirty men posing with Wright; they are identified as the office force in the building of the Imperial Hotel. *Collected Writings,* vol. 2, 260.

21. Others can be identified by name, but most made unrecorded contributions to Wright's work and had no subsequent relationship with him. Such information about them as had existed was lost in the fires from the earthquakes and World War II bombings, as well as, possibly, through the practice of burning belongings with the body when someone dies. Karen Severns, letter to author, February 13, 2007. For information on Endo, Tsuchiura, and two others associated with Wright, as well as images of the fourteen buildings designed by Wright in Japan (six were built, but only three remain extant), see the Web site of the Wrightian Architectural Archives in Japan (WAAJ), www.wrightinJapan.org. Accessed February 2007.

22. "Imperial Hotel, Tokyo, Japan," *Architectural Record* 55, no. 2 (February 1921): 118–23.

23. *An Autobiography* includes a photo of a telegram purportedly signed by Baron Okura, but sent from Spring Green: ". . . WIRELESS RECEIVED FROM TOKIO TODAY HOTEL STANDS UNDAMAGED AS MONUMENT OF YOUR GENIUS HUNDREDS OF HOMELESS PROVIDE BY PERFECTLY MAINTAINED SERVICE CONGRATULATONS SIGNED OKURA IMPEHO," 222. Tanigawa, "Wright's Achievement in Japan," in *Frank Lloyd Wright Retrospective,* in conjunction with an exhibition in Tokyo, Kyoto, Yokohama, and Kitahyushu, January–July 1991, 58–59. For a summary of the fate of the hotel in the earthquake, see Robert King Reitherman, "The Seismic Legend of the Imperial Hotel," *AIA Journal* 69 (June 1980): 42–46.

24. The version cited here, edited by Narciso G. Menocal (Carbondale and Edwardsville: Southern Illinois University Press, 1994), is used throughout this book. It includes also John Lloyd Wright's foreword to a revised edition, projected for 1962 but never published; three insertions intended for that edition; a new addendum; an essay by John Lloyd Wright titled "Special Problems that Befall a Son of a Great Man"; and a postscript by John's daughter, Elizabeth Wright Ingraham, also an architect. In 1992, John Lloyd Wright's memoir was reissued by Dover Publications as *My Father Frank Lloyd Wright.* The text is identical to the one edited

by Menocal, but half a dozen blank pages inserted in the later edition change the pagination, beginning at p. 75. The paragraphs cited here begin on page 94.

25. *My Father Who Is on Earth,* 94–103. The acknowledgement by Elizabeth Wright Ingram appears on pp. 230–31. For a summary of John Lloyd Wright's life and career, see Ann Van Zanten, *Barry Byrne, John Lloyd Wright: Architecture and Design* (Chicago Historical Society/University of Chicago Press, 1982), 42–69. For an account of Wright's other projects in Japan, see Masami Tanigawa, "Wright's Achievements in Japan," in *Frank Lloyd Wright Retrospective,* in conjunction with an exhibition in Tokyo, Kyoto, Yokohama, and Kitahyushu, January–July 1991, 58–62.

26. *An Autobiography,* 281.

27. Antonin Raymond, *An Autobiography* (Rutland, Vt.: Charles E. Tuttle Co., 1973), 66–67, 69–77. As with Wright's autobiography, one must look here for what is written between the lines, as autobiographers rarely avoid opportunities to cast themselves in a favorable light. Sometimes that leads to depicting others unfavorably. This autobiography includes information about work done by Wright and his assistants on projects in Japan in addition to the Imperial Hotel. Executed projects were houses for Aisaku Hayashi (1917), Arinobu Fukuhara (1918), and Tazaemon Yamamura (1918), and the Jiyu Gakuen Girls' School (1921). The Fukuhara residence was destroyed in the 1923 earthquake. Unbuilt projects included several residences, a motion picture theater, another hotel, and a commercial-residential complex (with Arata Endo).

28. Frank Riley, "Deathwatch in Tokyo," *Saturday Review,* December 16, 1967, 40.

29. Edgar Tafel, ed., *Frank Lloyd Wright: Recollections by Those Who Knew Him* (Mineola, N.Y.: Dover Publications, Inc., 2001; published originally in 1993 by John Wiley and Sons as *About Wright: An Album of Reflections by Those Who Knew Him*), 93–95. Atsuko Tanaka, "Kameki and Nobu Tsuchiura: Apprenticeship with Wright in the 1920s," presented at the annual meeting of the Frank Lloyd Wright Building Conservancy in Los Angeles, October 21, 2005; also an e-mail message to the author, May 17, 2007.

30. Dione Neutra, compiler and translator, *Richard Neutra: Promise and Fulfillment, 1919–1932: Selections from the Letters and Diaries of Richard and Dione Neutra* (Carbondale and Edwardsville: Southern Illinois University Press, 1986), 125–28; the letter was dated July 1924. The German she referred to was most likely Anton Martin Feller, who reestablished ties with Wright while living in Chicago in the 1920s. His wife, Herta, depressed following childbirth, had committed suicide in November 1923; see the *Los Angeles Times,* November 9, 1923. In *An Autobiography,*

255–56, Wright recalls that when he had no commissions in 1924, A. M. Johnson provided some hope by offering to "grubstake [him] with $20,000 to prospect in his behalf with a structural idea for a skyscraper" Wright had proposed a year earlier. He describes Johnson as "a strange mixture of the fanatic and the mystic, Shylock and the humanist. Withal he was extraordinarily intelligent." 255–56.

31. "Frank Lloyd Wright from 1921 to 1925," in Edgar Tafel, *Frank Lloyd Wright: Recollections by Those Who Knew Him* (Mineola, N.Y.: Dover Publications, Inc., 1993), 94.

32. *Erich Mendelsohn: Letters of an Architect* (London and New York: Abelard Schuman, 1967), 71.

33. These paragraphs draw on letters from the Tsuchiuras to Martin Feller, in the collection of William B. Scott, Jr., and Hannah K. Allen; used with permission.

34. *An Autobiography,* 504–5. This section is headed, "The Merry Wives of Taliesin." By 1932 Wright's attitude toward Neutra had changed markedly. In a letter to Lewis Mumford, after Neutra had established himself as a leading architect in Los Angeles, Wright protested the inclusion of work by Neutra alongside his in an exhibition at the Museum of Modern Art being planned by Philip Johnson and Henry-Russell Hitchcock. Neutra, he said, was of "a type I have learned to dislike, by cumulative experience, and to suffer from." At Taliesin in 1924, he was "worthless . . . @ $30.00 per week and a living for his family, wife, child, mother in law." By 1932 Neutra had become "the eclectic 'up to date,' copying the living." Bruce Brooks Pfeiffer and Robert Wojtowicz, eds., *Frank Lloyd Wright and Lewis Mumford: Thirty Years of Correspondence* (New York: Princeton Architectural Press, 2001), 124, 126.

## 5—TRANSITION IN CALIFORNIA

1. *An Autobiography,* 225.

2. Donald Hoffman provides a succinct summary of the careers and personalities of Aline Barnsdall's father and grandfather in *Frank Lloyd Wright's Hollyhock House* (New York: Dover Publications, 1992), 1, 4–6.

3. *Romanza: The California Architecture of Frank Lloyd Wright* (San Francisco: Chronicle Books, 1988), 3.

4. *Frank Lloyd Wright, Hollyhock House and Olive Hill: Buildings and Projects for Aline Barnsdall* (New York: Rizzoli, 1992), 43–44. Smith provides an extraordinarily detailed and richly illustrated account of the Barnsdall projects and the relationship between Aline Barnsdall and Frank Lloyd Wright. She concludes that "[a]lthough Hollyhock House is not one of Wright's best buildings, either in design or execution, it is certainly his most interesting." Correspondence between Wright and Barnsdall reveals the nature of their interactions; see Appendix 2, pp. 211–13; also Bruce Brooks Pfeiffer, ed., *Letters to Clients* (The Press at California State University, Fresno, 1984), 25–38.

5. Kathryn Smith, "Frank Lloyd Wright and the Imperial Hotel: A Postscript," *The Art Bulletin* 67, no. 2 (June 1985): 306.

6. Judith Sheine, *R. M. Schindler* (New York: Phaidon Press, 2001), 36.

7. December 31, 1931. Lloyd Wright Papers, Department of Special Collections, Research Library, University of California, Los Angeles.

8. Sheine, 36.

9. June 3, 1930. Cited by Sheine, 43.

10. June 10, 1931. Cited by Sheine, 43. Misspellings are Schindler's.

11. Sheine, 36–37, 43. The entire chapter, pp. 36–61, presents a summary of Schindler's work with Wright and that done on his own later. Schindler's response was dated June 10, 1931.

12. Bruce Brooks Pfeiffer, ed., *Letters to Architects* (Fresno: The Press at California State University, 1984), 74–75, 77–78, 113–14.

13. Smith, *Frank Lloyd Wright, Hollyhock House, and Olive Hill*, 106, 110–12, 119, 121–22, 124–26, 158, 160, 166. In 1925, when Wright's work with the Hollyhock House had ended, Schindler continued to work for Aline Barnsdall, and in 1925 he called upon Richard Neutra to design a wading pool and pergola; see Gebhard, *California Romanza,* 16.

14. Smith, *Frank Lloyd Wright,* 80, 82–84, 112, 122, 124–25. According to Eric Lloyd Wright, Lloyd Wright's son, Lloyd was removed from his role as construction supervisor and replaced by Schindler because he could not get along with contractors. A skirmish with one of them apparently precipitated the change. See Donald Hoffmann, *Frank Lloyd Wright's Hollyhock House*, 30.

15. Letter to her parents, October 25, 1919, quoted by Smith, *Frank Lloyd Wright,* 112; the letter is in the possession of Mark Schindler, Pauline Schindler's son.

16. Hoffmann, 37.

17. June 26, 1921, Lloyd Wright Papers, Department of Special Collections, Research Library, University of California, Los Angeles.

18. *An Autobiography,* 225, 227, 228, 230.

19. *Wright in Hollywood: Visions of a New Architecture* (Cambridge: The MIT Press), 5–6.

20. David Gebhard and Harriette Von Breton, *Lloyd Wright, Architect: Twentieth Century Architecture in an Organic exhibition* (Santa Barbara: University of California Press, 1971), 27–28; from an interview with Harriette Von Breton, September 1970.

21. Edgar Tafel, ed., *Frank Lloyd Wright: Recollections by Those Who Knew Him* (Mineola, N.Y.: Dover Publications, Inc., 1993), 93–94.

22. Sweeney, *Wright in Hollywood,* 3.

23. In an interview with Harriette Von Breton, Lloyd said he worked with his father on these major projects, 1921–24: Doheny Ranch Development, studies, suggested site plan, perspective renderings; Lowes house, Eagle Rock 1922, working drawings and perspective renderings; Tahoe Summer Colony, Lake Tahoe, 1922, perspective renderings; Millard House, Pasadena, 1923, on-site supervision and complete landscaping; Storer House, Hollywood, 1923, complete on-site supervision, complete landscaping; Ennis House, Los Angeles, 1924, working drawings, on-site supervision, complete landscaping; Freeman House, Hollywood, 1924, working drawings, on-site supervision, and complete landscaping. Cited in Gebhard and Von Breton, *Lloyd Wright, Architect: Twentieth Century Architecture in an Organic Exhibition,* 71.

24. Sweeney, *Wright in Hollywood,* 175.

25. "The Barnsdall Designs—An Expression of an Idea," *Frank Lloyd Wright Quarterly* 13, no. 3 (Summer 2002): 13.

26. *Madison Capital Times,* October 18, 1923.

**6—THE FELLOWSHIP**

1. *An Autobiography,* 400.

2. Mary Ann Smith, *Gustav Stickley: The Craftsman* (Syracuse, N.Y.: Syracuse University Press, 1983), xiv.

3. Published in the 1901 Chicago Architectural Club exhibition catalog. See *Collected Writings,* vol. 1, 58–69. Introducing it, Bruce Brooks Pfeiffer calls it "a most elusive and enigmatic essay," for it "recurs in different forms throughout Wright's manuscript collection file." Noting that many Wright scholars regard this as Wright's "first great manifesto," earlier manuscripts suggest that the 1901 essay was "a carefully crafted summation of ideas and concepts he had been presenting to the public for a number of years."

4. Norris Kelly Smith suggests that "Wright's conception of the Taliesin Fellowship was quasi-monastic in character, and that the idea had come to him partly, it would seem, by way of Elbert Hubbard's cooperating community . . . at East Aurora." *Frank Lloyd Wright: A Study in Architectural Content* (Watkins Glen, N.Y.: The American Life Foundation & Study Institute, 1979), 160.

5. Andrea Oppenheimer Dean, "The Roycroft Reawakening," *Preservation* (September / October 1996): 69.

6. Barry Sanders, *A Complex Fate: Gustav Stickley and the Craftsman Movement* (Washington, D.C.: Preservation Press, and New York: John Wiley, 1956), 21–23. On the use of Stickley furniture in Wright-designed homes, see David A. Hanks, *The Decorative Designs of Frank Lloyd Wright* (New York: Dutton, 1979), 42. Hanks notes that "[t]here is no difficulty in distinguishing the furniture designed by Wright and made by Ayers [his furniture builder, John W. Ayers] and the L. and J. G. Stickley furniture; Wright's furniture is far more sophisticated and relates closely to the architecture and interior woodwork of the house."

7. Mary Ann Smith, *Gustav Stickley: The Craftsman* (Syracuse, N.Y.: Syracuse University Press, 1983), 109.

8. Mary Ann Smith, 152–54.

9. *Gustav Stickley's Craftsman Farms: The Quest for an Arts and Crafts Utopia* (Syracuse, N.Y.: Syracuse University Press, 2001), 97. Hewitt notes here that "Frank Lloyd Wright constructed a comparable residence-farm-studio at Taliesin in Spring Green, Wisconsin, during the same period (1911) and eventually built a Gurdjieff-inspired commune for his apprentices there during the 1930s." How big a part inspiration from Gurdjieff played in the founding of the Fellowship is considered later in this book.

10. Wright listed Eliel Saarinen as a "Friend of the Fellowship" in 1933.

11. Accounts of portions of Cranbrook's history can be found by searching this Web site: www.cranbrook.edu/Pages/History/html (accessed August 2008). See also Kathryn Bishop Eckert, *Cranbrook: The Campus Guide* (New York: Princeton Architectural Press, 2001), 96–103.

12. Albert Christ-Janer, *Eliel Saarinen: Finnish-American Architect and Educator* (Chicago: University of Chicago Press, 1979), 79–81.

13. April 1935 and January 1936. In *Le Corbusier in America* (Cambridge: The MIT Press, 2001), Mardges Bacon notes that "Saarinen's comradeship with Wright seems evident in a photograph taken during an April 1935 visit. Informal, relaxed, and open, they confront the camera side-by-side. They are kindred spirits." Le Corbusier visited Cranbrook before Wright's second visit, and he too posed for a picture with Saarinen, but "the two appear formal, guarded, and distant. Bareheaded and pipe smoking, the dapper Parisian seems uncharacteristically tenuous and off balance" (p. 106).

14. Christ-Janer, 78.

15. *An Autobiography,* 515.

16. *Years with Frank Lloyd Wright: Apprentice to Genius* (New York: Dover Publications, 1985; published in 1979 as *Apprentice to Genius: Years with Frank Lloyd Wright),* 141.

17. John Peter, *The Oral History of Modern Architecture* (New York: Harry N. Abrams, 1994), 162, 179–80. Recorded in 1955.

18. "The Bauhaus Contribution," *AIA Journal* 39, no. 6 (June 1963): 120–21. He repeated this story five years later, almost word for word, in *Apollo in the Democracy: The Cultural Obligations of the Architect* (New York: McGraw-Hill Book Company, 1968), 169–70.

19. *Apprentice to Genius,* 66, 68.

20. *An Autobiography,* 429.

21. *Taliesin Fellowship Publication* 1, no. 1 (October 1940): 10–18. Published also in *Collected Works,* vol. 4, 50–56. Mies's reply: October 24, 1940. FLLW Foundation, fiche id M188C09. For more on Broadacre City in the life of the Fellowship, see chapter 14.

22. *Apprentice to Genius,* 69–70. Martin Pawley, in *Mies van der Rohe* (London: Thames & Hudson, 1970), 11, summarizes the difference between Mies and Wright thus: "[A] great deal of Mies' later success with comparatively conservative clients may be explained by the *conclusive* nature of his renderings. After such a clear illustration of the aesthetic feasibility of what he proposed, little beyond structural detail could be in dispute—and in the latter field Mies rapidly became uncontested master. Just as Frank Lloyd Wright was able to turn his structural triumph with the earthquake-resistant Imperial Hotel in Tokyo into a license for structural experimentation for the remainder of his career, so was Mies able to turn the clarity and intelligibility of his structural vision into a means of avoiding dispute over aesthetic or formal issues."

23. *An Autobiography,* 429.

24. Werner Blaser, *Mies van der Rohe: Continuing the Chicago School of Architecture* (Basel, Boston, Stuttgart: Birhäuser Verlag, 1981), 30. (Published originally in 1977 under the title: *Mies van der Rohe: Principles and School/Lehre und Schule*). See also Peter Blake, *The Master Builders: Le Corbusier, Mies van der Rohe, Frank Lloyd Wright* (New York: W.W. Norton, 1976), 229–32.

25. Franz Schulze, *Mies van der Rohe: A Critical Biography* (Chicago: University of Chicago Press, 1985), 259.

26. Martin Pawley, *Mies van der Rohe* (London: Thames & Hudson, 1970), 19.

27. Schulze, *Mies van der Rohe,* 219.

## 7—A HOME AT TALIESIN AND HOPE IN THE DESERT

1. *An Autobiography,* 512.

2. *In the Nature of Materials: The Buildings of Frank Lloyd Wright, 1887–1941* (New York: Da Capo Press, 1971; published initially in 1942), 86.

3. "In the Cause of Architecture," *Architectural Record* 33 (March 1908): 164–65.

4. I: 1–3, 9–10, 13, 15. The unpublished manuscript of this autobiography exists in several versions. These notes are from one dated June 18, 1983. Different dates and page-numberings will be noted as they occur. Throughout this chapter, as in Mr. Wright's autobiography, one encounters unverifiable assertions. Some may be colored by experiences in the decades between the events Mrs. Wright describes and the writing of this autobiography. Quotations from this autobiography and references to it are with the permission of the Frank Lloyd Wright Foundation.

5. I: 6–7.

6. II: 11–13 (September 30, 1981).

7. III: 2–8 (February 8, 1982).

8. IV: 1–8 (February 2, 1982).

9. IV: 9–11 (February 2, 1982).

10. IV: 10–23 (February 2, 1982).

11. VII: 9–10 (February 21, 1982). Chapters V and VI describe her experiences with Gurdjieff as they moved from city to city. In Chapters VIII–X she describes more experiences in her leadership role in the Institute.

12. X: 4–5 (May 1980).

13. X: 6–12.

14. 11: 1–3 (February 26, 1982). Chapter numbering changes from Roman to Arabic. Wright describes this first encounter in his autobiography, p. 509.

15. 11: 3–8. The references are to Catherine, Wright's first wife; Mamah Borthwick Cheney, his companion from 1909 to 1914; and Miriam Noel, his companion from 1914 to 1923, whom he married in 1923; they separated months later and were divorced in 1927.

16. 11: 13–15.

17. Michel de Salzmann, in Mircea Eliade, editor-in-chief, *The Encyclopedia of Religion* (New York: Macmillan, 1987), 6: 139–40.

18. For a detailed treatise on the Gurdjieffian influence on the Wrights and the Taliesin Fellowship, see Robert C. Twombly, "Organic Living: Frank Lloyd Wright's Taliesin Fellowship and Georgi Gurdjieff's Institute for the Harmonious Development of Man," *Wisconsin Magazine of History* (Winter 1974–1975): 126–39. See also Donald Leslie Johnson, *Frank Lloyd Wright versus America: The 1930s* (Cambridge: MIT Press, 1990), 5–9, 304–13.

19. 11: 9–15. Vladimir Hinzenburg was also known as Volodia. Wright's recollection is equally romantic but somewhat different, as he credits a "diamond-in-the-rough painter" named Jerry Blum with playing a role in bringing him together with Olgivanna. *An Autobiography,* 508–11.

20. 11: 16–19. *An Autobiography,* 511. See another recollection of the "merry wives of Taliesin" in chapter 4,

which makes no mention of Olgivanna. The women were Sylva Moser, Dione Neutra, and Nobu Tsuchiura.

21. *An Autobiography,* 510.

22. Wright chafed in his subordination to the corporate board through the months that it continued, and letters in his exchanges with his attorney, Phillip LaFollette, were frequently testy. On May 18, 1929, for example, he wrote to LaFollette: "I am, of course, legally dead already so far as any *rights,* even to myself, are concerned."

23. Maginel Wright Barney, *The Valley of the God-Almighty Joneses: Reminiscences of Frank Lloyd Wright's Sister* (Spring Green, Wisc.: Unity Chapel Publications, 1986; published initially by Appleton-Century in 1965), 113–23. See also Bruce Brooks Pfeiffer's introduction to "The Hillside Home School of the Allied Arts," *Frank Lloyd Wright Collected Writings,* vol. 3, 1931–1939, 39. Also Ellen Lloyd Jones and Jane Lloyd Jones, *The Hillside Home School* (catalog for 1913–1914, published in Hillside, Wisc.).

24. *Frank Lloyd Wright: His Life and His Architecture* (New York: John Wiley and Sons, 1979), 178–79.

25. Maginel Wright Barney, *The Valley of the God-Almighty Joneses,* 123.

26. *An Autobiography,* 303. Among those who left were Werner and Sylva Moser; Richard and Dione Neutra; Kameki and Nobu Tsuchiura; and William Smith.

27. *An Autobiography,* 306.

28. *An Autobiography,* 308–9. In the 1932 edition Wright spelled the name of the camp "Ocatilla"; in the 1943 edition it is "Ocatillo." It appears both ways in Wright literature, as well as "Ocotilla," but the preferred way among scholars is "Ocatilla."

29. Olgivanna Lloyd Wright, *Frank Lloyd Wright: His Life, His Work, His Words* (New York: Horizon Press, 1966), 103–4.

30. *An Autobiography,* 309–10.

31. *An Autobiography,* 310–11. The two for whom Wright provides only a given name were Vladimir Karfik and Cyril Jahnke. Donald Walker spelled Cy's name as Jannke; see Edgar Tafel, ed., *Frank Lloyd Wright: Recollections by Those Who Knew Him* (Mineola, N.Y.: Dover Publications, Inc., 1993), 96. Karfik, a Czech architect, was with Wright from September 1928 to December 1929. Portions of an interview with him conducted by Bruce Pfeiffer and edited by Bradley Storrer and Louis Wiehle appeared in the *Journal of the Taliesin Fellows* 11 (Summer 1993): 8–20; there Karfik recounted Ocatilla experiences.

32. Recollection by Marcus Weston, in Edgar Tafel, ed., *Frank Lloyd Wright: Recollections by Those Who Knew Him* (Mineola, N.Y.: Dover Publications, 2001; published initially by John Wiley & Sons, 1993, under the title *About Wright:*

*An Album of Recollections by Those Who Knew Frank Lloyd Wright*), 182–86. Marcus Weston joined the Fellowship in 1938.

33. For a description of the camp, a drawing of the plan for it, and photographs of the landscape and the buildings' exterior and interior, see Neil Levine, *The Architecture of Frank Lloyd Wright* (Princeton: Princeton University Press, 1996), 201–5. In subsequent pages, Levine provides a description of the plans for the resort Wright designed at Chandler, as well as drawings and a model of a portion of it.

34. *An Autobiography,* 314–15.

35. *An Autobiography,* 315.

## 8—DREAMS AND REALITIES

1. "The Taliesin Fellowship," a brochure published in December 1933; facsimile reprint 2003. © Frank Lloyd Wright Foundation. Pages are unnumbered.

2. "The Hillside Home School of the Allied Arts" (1931), 1–4. The brochure is reprinted in *Collected Writings* (New York: Rizzoli, 1993), vol. 3, 39–49. The details in the brochure are an elaboration on ideas Wright presented in "Style in Industry," the second of his Kahn Lectures to undergraduates at Princeton University in 1930, published as *Modern Architecture: Being the Kahn Lectures* (Princeton, N.J.: Princeton University Press, 1931); reprinted in *Collected Writings* (New York: Rizzoli, 1992), vol. 2, 31–42.

3. "The Hillside Home School of the Allied Arts" (1931), 4–6.

4. "The Hillside Home School of the Allied Arts" (1931), 6–7. He noted that at 6% interest this $250,000 would yield $5,000 per year, a calculation that is short by $10,000.

5. "The Hillside Home School of the Allied Arts" (1931), 8.

6. "The Hillside Home School of the Allied Arts" (1931), 9.

7. "The Hillside Home School of the Allied Arts" (1931), 10.

8. "The Hillside Home School of the Allied Arts" (1931), 11–12.

9. Jensen, one of America's most distinguished landscape architects was a sometime collaborator with Wright, as in the landscaping of the Coonley Residence in Riverside, Illinois (1907). In the 1930s, Jensen also established a school, "The Clearing," in Door County, Wisconsin. Although the methods of instruction bore similarities to those in the Taliesin Fellowship, the practices of the two masters were sharply at odds. Robert E. Grese describes the differences thus: "Unlike the students at Frank

Lloyd Wright's school, Taliesin, . . . who were taught to follow their master's directives, Jensen wanted his students at The Clearing to initiate their own studies and projects and to learn as much from each other as from their instructors." *Jens Jensen: Maker of Natural Parks and Gardens* (Baltimore: Johns Hopkins University Press, 1992), 47.

10. "The Hillside Home School of the Allied Arts" (1931), 10–13.

11. 13–14. One wonders if the pre-teens, and even the teenagers in the group, would be expected to work the standard twelve hours each week.

12. "The Hillside Home School of the Allied Arts" (1931), 13–16.

13. Mary Jane Hamilton, with Anne E. Biebel and John O. Holzhueter, "Frank Lloyd Wright's Madison Networks," in *Frank Lloyd Wright and Madison: Eight Decades of Artistic and Social Interaction* (Madison: Elvehjem Museum of Art, University of Wisconsin-Madison, 1990), 77. In his letter to President Glenn Frank, dated December 17, 1929 (Frank Lloyd Wright Archives), Wright wrote: "For more than a year . . . [n]o word of encouragement or recognition of any kind from you has reached me. I believe that in this neglect is involved involuntarily all that mocks the University—the chief characteristics that account for it as the kind of institution that can serve only a business-man's civilization."

14. Bruce Brooks Pfeiffer and Robert Wojtowicz, eds., *Frank Lloyd Wright and Lewis Mumford: Thirty Years of Correspondence* (New York: Princeton Architectural Press, 2001), 70–71. Meiklejohn, a graduate of Brown University, earned a Ph.D. at Cornell. Before coming to the University of Wisconsin, he had served as dean of the university at Brown from 1901 to 1912 and as president of Amherst College from 1913 to 1923. When he came to the University of Wisconsin, he was featured on the cover of *Time* magazine, October 1, 1928. Although the Experimental College closed in 1932, Meiklejohn continued to teach at the university until 1938. His distinguished but unconventional career continued in California; in 1964 he was awarded the Presidential Medal of Freedom. http://www.brown.edu/Administration/News_ Bureau/Encyclopedia/Meiklejohn.html (accessed September 2, 2007).

15. *Frank Lloyd Wright and Lewis Mumford,* 106–7. In a paean to his native state, "Why I Love Wisconsin," Wright had written, "I love Wisconsin because of her Meiklejohn Experiment at the university, whether it succeeded or not." Published originally in *Industrial Wisconsin* (April 1930) and reprinted in *Wisconsin Magazine* (1932), *Collected Writings,* vol. 3, 138.

16. The Dutch architect and editor of the *Wendingen* had collected a series of articles on Wright's work into a book.

17. April 6, 1931. Correspondence between Wright and Wijdeveld, along with related documents, is in the Frank Lloyd Wright Archives.

18. August 13, 1931.

19. *Frank Lloyd Wright and Lewis Mumford,* 135–40.

20. In *Frank Lloyd Wright: His Life, His Work, His Words* (New York: Horizon Press, 1966), 76–79, Olgivanna Lloyd Wright describes the Wrights' interactions with Wijdeveld differently. After commenting on Wright's appreciation and admiration for *Wendingen,* the book Wijdeveld had published, she recalled that Ben Rebhuhn, the owner of Horizon Press and a friend of the Wrights, offered to publish the book in the United States. He did so, she says, in the same exquisite form, but she does not say that Rebhuhn gave Wijdeveld no credit—an action that offended Wijdeveld. When Wijdeveld visited Taliesin, Mr. Wright suggested that he might be the director of the school he and Mrs. Wright intended to organize. Starting the school would require rebuilding Hillside, which was "in a pitiful state, ceilings and floors caving in, ruined by vandalism." As Wijdeveld looked at the ruins, his spirit "visibly collapsed within him." Mr. Wright urged him to bring his family to Taliesin and they would all work on restoring it together. But he could not consider bringing his family and burdening them with an enormous, insurmountable task. "Sad and regretful," she says, "he finally sailed back to his native Holland. We both were disappointed not to have Mr. Wijdeveld at Taliesin and we missed his cheerful spirit for quite some time." She does not provide the dates for Wijdeveld's Taliesin visit.

That his treatment of Wijdeveld weighed on Wright's conscience is evident in the multiple drafts of an apologetic letter he wrote to him in 1947. Wijdeveld and his wife, Wright wrote, would be welcome as visitors at Taliesin and he would do what he might to help him secure satisfaction somewhere. But he could not work with Wright, nor could any older men, for he was "too far gone in place and time" with his own technique to employ the technique of another. Donald Langmead and Donald Leslie Johnson, *Architectural Excursions: Frank Lloyd Wright, Holland, and Europe* (Westport Conn.: Greenwood Press, 2000), 197.

21. The ideas offered in this and subsequent brochures had been developing in Wright's mind for a while. In one of the six lectures he presented to undergraduate architecture students at Princeton University in May 1930 (published by Princeton University in 1931 as "Modern Architecture: Being the Kahn Lectures"), he outlined the principles around which he eventually established the Taliesin Fellowship. See particularly the second one, "Style in Industry," Bruce

Brooks Pfeiffer, ed., *Frank Lloyd Wright: Collected Writings*, vol. 2, 40–41.

22. This brochure, titled "The Taliesin Fellowship—An Extension of the Work at Taliesin to Include Seventy Apprentices," is archived in the papers of John Howe, one of the initial members of the Fellowship, at the State Historical Society of Wisconsin. Also there is what may be a draft of this brochure at an earlier stage. A similar copy exists in the William Wesley Peters collection in the Frank Lloyd Wright Archives; it has a receipt dated August 3, 1932. According to Bruce Brooks Pfeiffer, "This is undoubtedly the copy that must have attracted Wes Peters, Jack Howe, and others of that same first group who came in October 1932." (Letter to author from Pfeiffer dated May 1, 2006.)

23. See the next chapter for details on the initial membership.

24. This brochure is also archived in the John Howe papers. It is included in Bruce Brooks Pfeiffer, ed., *Frank Lloyd Wright: Letters to Apprentices* (Fresno: The Press at California State University, 1982), 3–7.

25. The institutions attended included the Universities of Cincinnati, Illinois, Michigan, Minnesota, Pennsylvania, and Wisconsin; Columbia, Cornell, Harvard, Marquette, Northwestern, Ohio State, Princeton, Washington, and Yale Universities; the Armour Institute of Technology (Chicago) and Massachusetts Institute of Technology; the Chicago Art Institute; Kalamazoo, Smith, Swarthmore, and Wellesley Colleges; and institutions in Switzerland, France, Germany, and Japan.

Listed among the *friends* were notable figures of the 1920s and 1930s: Jane Addams, Sherwood Anderson, Aline Barnsdall, Alexander Chandler, John Dewey, Albert Einstein, Alfonso Iannelli, Jens Jensen, Fiske Kimball, Alexander Meiklejohn, Edna St. Vincent Millay, Paul Mueller, Lewis Mumford, Georgia O'Keeffe, José Clemente Orosco, Dorothy Parker, Carl Sandburg, Edward Steichen, Alfred Stieglitz, Leopold Stokowski, Norman Thomas, William Allen White, Alexander Woollcott. *Architects* included C. R. Ashbee, Cecil Corwin, Arata Endo, Buckminster Fuller, Bruce Goff, Walter Gropius, Albert Kahn, Eric Mendelsohn, Karl and Werner Moser, J. P. Oud, Antonin Raymond, Eliel Saarinen, Kameki Tsuchiura, Mies van der Rohe, H. T. H. Wijdeveld, Lloyd Wright, and John Lloyd Wright. Among Wright's *clients*: Mr. and Mrs. Henry Allen, Mrs. Avery Coonley, Aisaku Hayashi, Richard Lloyd Jones, Susan Lawrence, Lloyd Lewis, Darwin Martin, and Alice Millard. *Countries represented* in the list included: Argentina, Austria, Brazil, China, France, Germany, Great Britain, Greece, Holland, Japan, Jugoslavia, Paraguay, Poland, Russia, Spain, and Switzerland.

26. "The Taliesin Fellowship," facsimile reprint 2003.

Frank Lloyd Wright Foundation. Pages are unnumbered. The brochure listed 56 "Fellows," some of whom were apprentices at the time, hailing from locations across the United States, and from France, Denmark, Germany, Poland, Switzerland, and Nicaragua. It also identified institutions the Fellows had attended and in some instances graduated from, including the Universities of Michigan, Pennsylvania, Cincinnati, Minnesota, and Wisconsin; Washington, Columbia, Princeton, Northwestern, Harvard, Yale, Cornell, Marquette, New York, and the Ohio State Universities; Vassar, Swarthmore, Kalamazoo, Wellesley, and Smith Colleges; the Massachusetts and Armour Institutes of Technology, and the Chicago Art Institute; and universities in Switzerland, France, Japan, and Germany. The brochure also listed 147 individuals and couples as "Friends of the Fellowship." Included among them were Wright's kinfolk and offspring; former clients and architectural associates; notable architects and designers, such as C. R. Ashbee, Buckminster Fuller, Bruce Goff, Walter Gropius, Jens Jensen, Albert Kahn, Eric Mendelsohn, J. P. Oud, Eliel Saarinen, Mies van der Rohe, and W. T. H. Wijdeveld; and other well-known persons, including Albert Einstein, John Dewey, Stanley Marcus, Edna St. Vincent Millay, Lewis Mumford, Georgia O'Keeffe, Dorothy Parker, Diego Rivera, Carl Sandburg, Edward Steichen, Alfred Stieglitz, Leopold Stokowski, Norman Thomas, William Allen White, and Alexander Woollcott.

27. *An Autobiography*, 389.

28. *An Autobiography*, 394–95. The fee, stated at $675 in the initial brochure, was increased to $1,100 the following year. The full text of the 1932 Taliesin Fellowship brochure appears in Pfeiffer, ed., *Letters to Apprentices*, 3–7. This volume also includes the brochure composed after Taliesin West was established and used until Mr. Wright's death in 1959 (pp. 38–39).

29. *An Autobiography*, 399.

## 9—FELLOWSHIP DISCOVERIES

1. *An Autobiography*, 401.

2. Liang's first-person account appears in Edgar Tafel, ed., *Frank Lloyd Wright: Recollections by Those Who Knew Him* (Mineola, N.Y.: Dover Publications, Inc., 1993), 127–32.

3. William Wesley Peters, responding to questions in a 1967 seminar for apprentices, led by Vernon Swaback, on "The Art and Philosophy of Frank Lloyd Wright" (privately printed, 1968; used by permission), 100.

4. Among the marriages: Margaret Asire and Vernon Allen; Elizabeth Bauer and Rudolph Mock; Elizabeth (Betty) Barnsdall and Irvin Shaw; and Mary Roberts and John Lautner.

5. *Letters to Apprentices: Frank Lloyd Wright* (Fresno: The Press at California State University, 1982), 18, 21. Information about the Deknatels, Dows, and Fickes is from the directory compiled by Elizabeth Kassler and others, cited later in this chapter.

6. Robert Goodall, Karl Jensen (Wright's secretary), Heinrich Klumb, Michael Kostanecki, Rudolph Mock, Takehiko Okami, and Samuel Ratensky.

7. Elyse Klumb and Svetlana Wright.

8. Robert Ebert (to whose inquiry about joining Wright responded encouragingly, through Karl Jensen) and Christel Tessa Brey.

9. Charles Morgan.

10. Mendel Glickman, Isamu Noguchi (who evidently did not participate), and Manuel Sandoval.

11. Stephen Arneson, Visscher Boyd, Willets Burnham, William Deknatel, Geraldine Deknatel, Yuan Shi Kuo, Chandler Montgomery, Louise Porch, Lewis Stevens, and Elizabeth Weber.

12. December 29, 1933. See Pfeiffer, *Letters to Apprentices,* 66–67.

13. Elizabeth Bauer (the compiler of the Fellowship Directory, who married Rudolph Mock while in the Fellowship), William Bernoudy, Robert Bishop, Abe Dombar, James Drought, Charles Edman, William Beye Fyfe, Philip Holiday, Frederick Langhurst, Yen Liang, and Irving Shaw.

14. No longer listed: Robert Ebert, Robert Goodall, Yuan Hsi Kuo, Charles Morgan, and Isamu Noguchi. Additions: Margaret Asire, Yvonne Bannelier Wood, Betty Barnsdall, Paul Beidler, Ernest Brooks, Alfred Bush, Alden Dow, Vada Dow, George Dutton, Ruth Dutton, A. C. Van Elston, Stanhope Ficke, Sally Ficke, John Lautner, Charles Martin, Eugene Masselink, Nicholas Ray, Mary (Marybud) Roberts, Henry Schubart, Thomas Wigle, and Harry Yardley.

15. The 29-page directory compiled by Kassler was privately published in September 1981. It elicited sufficient additional information to warrant publication of a 12-page supplement in July 1982. The supplement included corrections, amplifications, and new entries, along with a five-page list of about 150 apprentices enrolled in classes in design and planning taught by John Rattenbury, a senior fellow, between 1963 and 1981, and a list of almost 40 other apprentices enrolled in the Frank Lloyd Wright School of Architecture in 1959–1962. Drawing upon publications of former apprentices Curtis Besinger, Andrew Devane, Herb Fritz, Pedro Guerrero, John Howe, Henry Klumb, and Edgar Tafel, and with the cooperation of others, some of whom had compiled rosters for specific periods, Kassler identified about 691 persons as Fellowship members. Sixty-two were reported as having died, and 272 returned information

sufficiently useful to be included. She acknowledged that the length of entries reflected only the availability of information or the lack of it and indicated nothing about an individual's importance in the Fellowship; that if an entry included data that had not come from the person listed or from Taliesin it might be wholly erroneous; and that by not including information about ex-fellows' responsibilities in the Fellowship—as in the case of John Howe, for example—the entries would be inappropriately skimpy.

Included among those listed are not only Wright's experienced draftsmen and architectural apprentices, but also "women accompanying their husbands, musicians of a summer, Mr. Wright's adolescent grandchildren, [and] others who for one reason or another were privileged to share a holistic way of life that was even more rewarding than it was demanding." Through participation in the working community, everyone was "an apprentice in the art of living, which for Mr. Wright was inseparable from the art of architecture."

Kassler called her directory "a first faulty effort toward the proper directory which someone some day will prepare, perhaps in connection with a definitive history of our extraordinary alma mater, Mr. and Mrs. Frank Lloyd Wright's Taliesin Fellowship."

16. In the six years preceding the founding of the Fellowship, in addition to *An Autobiography* (London, New York, and Toronto: Longmans, Green and Company, 1932), Wright published *The Disappearing City* (New York: William Farquhar Payson, 1932) and *Modern Architecture: Being the Kahn Lectures for 1930* (Princeton: Princeton University Press, 1931). Articles published in 1927–1932 included, among others, fourteen in the *Architectural Record* titled "In the Cause of Architecture," all with subtitles; two others in the *Architectural Record* with different titles; three in Wasmuth's *Monatshefte für Baukunst* (in German); two each in *Architectural Forum, Liberty* magazine, *World Unity,* and *Architectural Progress*; and one in *Country Life, American Architect, Die Form, Annual of American Design, Architects' Journal, American Architect(ure), Creative Art,* and *London Studio.* For lists of articles by and about Frank Lloyd Wright in these years, see Robert L. Sweeney, *Frank Lloyd Wright: An Annotated Bibliography* (Los Angeles: Hennessey & Ingalls, Inc., 1978), 35–54; and Donald Langmead, *Frank Lloyd Wright: A Bio-Bibliography* (Westport, Conn.: Praeger, 2003), 64–81. *An Autobiography* and *The Disappearing City* and a number of these articles have been reprinted in other publications, including: Bruce Brooks Pfeiffer, ed., *Frank Lloyd Wright: Collected Writings,* vols. 1–3 (New York: Rizzoli, 1992–1993); Frederick Gutheim, ed., *In the Cause of Architecture: Essays by Frank Lloyd Wright for the Architectural*

*Record, 1908–1952, with a Symposium on Architecture with and without Wright by Eight who Knew Him* (New York: Architectural Record Books, 1975). Excerpts from Wright's writings appear in Frederick Gutheim, ed., *Frank Lloyd Wright on Architecture: Selected Writings (1894–1940)* (New York: Grosset and Dunlap, 1941).

17. Author interview, November 28, 1994.

18. This account draws upon Wright's autobiography, pp. 431–33, and papers in the John Howe Collection, State Historical Society of Wisconsin, cited by Osmund Overby, *William Adair Bernoudy, Architect: Bringing the Legacy of Frank Lloyd Wright to St. Louis* (Columbia: University of Missouri Press, 1999), 11–12.

19. August 15, 1932. See Pfeiffer, *Letters to Apprentices,* 57.

20. October 27, 1932. Edman's arrival was delayed by eye problems, with which Wright also sympathized.

21. (New York: Dover Publications), 16. Published initially in 1979, with the title and subtitle inverted, by the McGraw-Hill Book Company. Tafel included a copy of this telegram and his letter to Wright that prompted it in a book he edited: *Frank Lloyd Wright: Recollections by Those who Knew Him* (Mineola, N.Y.: Dover Publications, Inc., 1993); also included, spanning 1933–1948, are thirteen additional letters from Wright to Tafel, a telegram, and an exchange of letters between Wright and Samuel Tafel, Edgar's father.

22. Undated interview, *Frank Lloyd Wright: Recollections,* 124.

23. Bruce Brooks Pfeiffer described the origins of *An Autobiography* in *Frank Lloyd Wright: Collected Writings,* vol. 2, 1930–1932 (New York: Rizzoli, 1992), 102–4. In an interview with the author on November 28, 1994, he recalled that, when he was in high school, someone at Harvard's architecture library pointed out the sections of the autobiography that Mrs. Wright wrote, and that "it just so happened that those were some of the parts that moved me the most." On file in the FLLW Archives.

24. The most recent reprints of the 1943 edition were by Barnes & Noble Books in 1998 and Pomegranate Communications in 2005.

25. *An Autobiography,* 365–66.

26. *Frank Lloyd Wright versus America: The 1930s* (Cambridge: The MIT Press, 1990), 29.

27. "Builder and Poet—Frank Lloyd Wright," LXXI (June 1932): 379–80.

28. "The Autobiography of a Fighting Architect," April 3, 1932, p. 4.

29. Tafel, ed., *Frank Lloyd Wright: Recollections,* 15.

30. Patrick Meehan, ed., *Frank Lloyd Wright Remembered* (Washington, D.C.: Preservation Press, 1991), 125. Based on an extemporaneous talk given by Howe at a professional

conference in 1977 and updated for this book in 1989.

31. "Reflections of Taliesin," *Northwest Architect,* July–August 1969, p. 26.

32. Patrick Meehan, ed., *Frank Lloyd Wright Remembered,* 125. Based on an extemporaneous talk given by Howe at a professional conference in 1977 and updated for this book in 1989.

33. *An Autobiography,* 443–44.

## 10—GETTING STARTED

1. *An Autobiography,* 392–93.

2. *An Autobiography,* 384–85. The term "Taliesin" applies to: a) the house Wright began building in 1911; b) the land around that house, including where the Hillside buildings are located; c) the spirit and other intangibles engendered by and associated with the house and the land; and d) the community that lived there.

3. *An Autobiography,* 388.

4. *An Autobiography,* 389.

5. Olgivanna Lloyd Wright, *Frank Lloyd Wright: His Life, His Work, His Words* (New York: Horizon Press, 1966), 79–81. Apprentices unfailingly referred to their leaders as Mr. Wright and Mrs. Wright. In her writing and speaking, Mrs. Wright always called her husband "Mr. Wright."

6. Edgar Tafel, *Years with Frank Lloyd Wright: Apprentice to Genius* (New York: Dover Publications, Inc., 1979), 37–39.

7. Transcript of remarks at Peters' funeral, July 20, 1991, p. 4. Frank Lloyd Wright Archives.

8. William Wesley Peters, responding to questions in a 1967 seminar for apprentices, led by Vernon Swaback, on "The Art and Philosophy of Frank Lloyd Wright" (privately printed, 1968; used by permission), 100–5. A copy is filed in the FLLW Archives. Swaback joined the Fellowship as an apprentice in 1957 and remained in it until 1979.

9. October 11, 1932, cited in Osmund Overby, *William Adair Bernoudy, Architect: Bringing the Legacy of Frank Lloyd Wright to St. Louis* (Columbia: University of Missouri Press, 1999), 7.

10. *An Autobiography,* 402–4.

11. Fritz, "At Taliesin," in Edna Meudt and Betsy Strand, eds., *An Uplands Reader* (Dodgeville, Wisc., June 1979), 129, 131. Bannelier is Rannelier in Fritz's piece.

12. Rosa D. Otero, *Permeable Walls and Place Recognition in Henry Klumb's Architecture of Social Concern.* Ph.D. dissertation, University of Pennsylvania (2005), 24, 29, 43, 44, 45; cited with the writer's permission.

13. Fritz, "At Taliesin," in Edna Meudt and Betsy Strand, eds., *An Uplands Reader,* 131–38. This essay contains an excellent description of apprentices' and workers' lives at Taliesin.

14. William Wesley Peters and Vernon Swaback, 106–7.

15. Author interview, November 23, 1994, p. 2. Frank Lloyd Wright Archives.

## 11—BEYOND SCHOOLING

1. Newspapers helped spread the good word about the Fellowship by carrying the "At Taliesin" columns without charge. Their editors' good relationships with Wright prompted them to do so. The columns also served as advertisements for Sunday afternoon film showings in the Taliesin Playhouse. According to Cornelia Brierly, Mr. or Mrs. Wright sometimes suggested the topics, and after apprentices wrote them, Gene Masselink usually typed them. Mr. Wright may have occasionally edited them. Author interview, September 2, 2006. Langhorst's column was dated April 14, 1934, Henning, 36–37. See note 4 for details on this source.

2. "At Taliesin," February 27, 1936. Howe was a charter apprentice, that is, a member of the group that joined in 1932; he remained in the Fellowship until 1962.

3. April 12, 1934. Fred Langhorst was a charter apprentice who left the Fellowship in 1935.

4. Wright wrote thirty-one of the "At Taliesin" columns that appeared in print, and Taliesin visitors about half a dozen; the remaining ones were signed by those who wrote them or published anonymously. After the Fellowship began its annual treks to and from Arizona, the *Chandler Arizonan* printed a few of the columns. In a painstaking effort, with the cooperation of archivists, newspaper editors, and librarians, Randolph C. Henning "rediscovered" a total of 285 columns. An architect with a long-standing interest in Wright and his architecture, Henning transcribed, assembled, and provided commentary on 112 of them in *"At Taliesin": Newspaper Columns by Frank Lloyd Wright and the Taliesin Fellowship* (Carbondale and Edwardsville: Southern Illinois University Press, 1992). In his Afterword (279–81), Henning asserts that the columns are more than a historic diary or even a "graphically written 'home movie'" of Taliesin life during the four short but eventful years of the Fellowship's infancy." On a more important level, he continues, they provide a valuable and unique insight into years in Wright's life that "began in crisis but ended in an explosion of renewed activity." Their use here obviously employs the second of these alternative ways of viewing them.

Henning generously gave me a complete set of the transcribed columns, including those not proofread for publication; he has also deposited a set in the Frank Lloyd Wright Archives. When citing columns included in Henning's book, I identify them by date, writer, title (if there is one), and page number. For the rest, I simply give the names of the writers, if they do not appear in the text, and the publication dates. In some instances I have corrected errors in punctuation and typographical errors in the transcriptions of the original columns. Occasionally I have inserted bracketed words or phrases in attempts to clarify the writers' meaning. For information about the writers, I draw upon Henning's Appendix E, pp. 309–14, *The Taliesin Fellowship: A Directory of Members,* compiled by Elizabeth Kassler, and miscellaneous other sources.

5. February 16, 1934. Bishop was a charter apprentice. He left the Fellowship in 1935. When he wrote this column, at least a dozen of the charter apprentices had already left.

6. February 16, 1934. Henning, "The New Education," 26. Nicholas Ray was the stage name for Raymond Nicholas Kienzle, who left Taliesin in 1934 for a career in theater and film.

7. March 8, 1934. Schubart was eighteen years old when he wrote this column after seven months in the Fellowship. He left six months later. His mother came to stay with him at Taliesin while he was ill, and she wrote two "At Taliesin" columns.

8. October 4, 1934. Goodrich was in the Fellowship from 1934 to 1942 and again from 1944 to 1946. The writer of thirteen columns, he was the third most prolific contributor to "At Taliesin."

9. June 7, 1934. Beidler was in the Fellowship 1933–1934.

10. *Tales of Taliesin: A Memoir of Fellowship* (Tempe, Ariz.: Herberger Center for Design Excellence, Arizona State University, 1999), 4.

11. May 22, 1935. Henning, 126–28. Cornelia Brierly was in the Fellowship 1934 to 1946 and again since 1957. She wrote twelve "At Taliesin" columns.

12. September 20, 1934. Henning, 78–80. This song was the wedding march for the marriage ceremony of apprentices Blaine Drake and Hulda Brierly in May 1936. Benny Dombar, May 22, 1936. Henning, 194, 202.

In the 1943 edition of his autobiography (p. 379), Wright remarked on the need for a work-song "that is a thing of the militant work-spirit." He did not include it in the earlier edition because, he said, the song seemed, and still does, to be shouting "damn." But it takes an ego shouting "damn," he continued, "to withstand emasculation by such imitative erudition as ours and the 'cultivation' any true ego, upright, is sure to receive at our very best hands." And so he included it in this version, and even used it as the frontispiece for Book Five, "not as literature whatsoever, but for better or for worse." Although he says the song had long been in hiding, its words, set to music by Mrs. Wright, conveyed the spirit displayed by the apprentices. A "poster" with the song's text hangs yet today in the entry to the Hillside studio.

13. July 12, 1935. Earl Friar was at Taliesin 1935–1937. Cary Caraway was a member of the Fellowship 1935–1942.

14. December 6, 1935. Everett Burgess Baker was at Taliesin 1935–1936. A theater man, his stage name was Edward Burgess.

15. June 29, 1934.

16. May 28, 1937. Marybud Roberts Lautner, the daughter of a Wright client, Abby Beecher Roberts, was in the Fellowship 1933–1935. On January 1, 1934, she married fellow apprentice John Lautner.

17. In *Tales of Taliesin,* 16, Brierly recalled that Carmody had told her she would surely make some farmer a good wife. What Carmody did not know, she added, was that she would occasionally get so tired that she would hide behind a bush and have a good cry to release her total exhaustion. When Hulda Brierly arrived at Taliesin she was identified by an anonymous writer as "the sister of our million dollar Cornelia." January 10, 1935. Henning, 103.

18. February 2, 1934. Henning, 19. Masselink was in the Fellowship from 1932 until his untimely death in 1962.

19. February 2, 1934. Holliday was a charter apprentice who left in August 1934.

20. *Tales of Taliesin,* 10.

21. March 15, 1934.

22. August 7, 1936. Musson had attended Ohio State University with Gene Masselink and had a degree in architecture from Oklahoma State University; he joined the Fellowship in 1935 and left in 1937.

23. "The Scullerite," November 15, 1935. Henning, 162–63.

24. September 12, 1936. Henning, 216–17. Mabel Morgan, the daughter of a mason who helped build Taliesin, was employed from 1934 to 1936 and possibly beyond.

25. March 22, 1934. Henning, 29. Alfred Bush, age seventeen when he wrote this, was in the Fellowship 1933–1935.

26. October 27, 1935.

27. February 9, 1933.

28. "Frank Lloyd Wright Realizes Another Dream at Unique Theater: Opening at Taliesin Tonight—Building Constructed by Apprentices from Native Materials." Henning, 285, 288.

29. February 9, 1934. Henning, 20–21. Abe Dombar was a charter apprentice who remained in the Fellowship until 1935.

30. September 5, 1937. Unsigned.

31. William Wesley Peters, responding to questions in a 1967 seminar for apprentices, led by Vernon Swaback, on "The Art and Philosophy of Frank Lloyd Wright" (privately printed, 1968; used by permission), 107.

32. "Reflections of Taliesin," *Northwest Architect,* July–August 1969, 29.

33. *Working with Mr. Wright: What It Was Like* (Cambridge: Cambridge University Press, 1995), 27.

34. "Reflections of Taliesin," *Northwest Architect,* July–August 1969, 26.

## 12—REACHING IN ALL DIRECTIONS

1. April 14, 1934. Henning, 36–37. This chapter continues to rely on the "At Taliesin" articles as a principal source of information regarding the daily lives of the Fellowship's apprentices. See footnote number 4 in the previous chapter for a description of this source and the citation method practiced here.

2. November 13, 1936.

3. Unsigned, January 25, 1934, and February 1, 1934; Gene Masselink, February 2, 1934; Henning, 19–20. James Drought had studied with Alexander Meiklejohn at the University of Wisconsin; Everett Baker later joined the Fellowship; Baker Brownell collaborated on a book with Wright (*Architecture and American Life,* 1937); Ferdinand Scheville was in the group that incorporated Frank Lloyd Wright and rescued him from financial ruin in the 1920s; Franz Aust was one of the faculty members who participated in the negotiations in 1929 concerning possible ties between Wright and the University of Wisconsin and was a frequent guest.

4. Bob Bishop, March 1, 1934. Bishop wrote two columns on this date, one with more elaboration and editorializing than the other. One dated March 2 contained even more elaboration.

5. Gene Masselink, October 4, 1934. Masselink was probably referring to the Rural Division of the Emergency Relief Administration, a New Deal program established in March 1934; it evolved into the Farm Security Administration.

6. June 28, 1934. Henning, 61, 52. Peter Frankl accompanied the Fellowship on its journey to Arizona the following winter (see the next chapter).

7. February 16, 1934. Henning, 25.

8. February 16, 1934. Henning, 28. Meyer's column, "Making Light of the Times," reporting on that evening appears in an appendix in Henning's book. Also included in this appendix are a poem dedicated to Wright and a three-part column recounting Meyer's experiences while living with the Fellowship for a week in midsummer 1934. *"At Taliesin,"* 298–306.

9. July 25, 1935. Henning, 143–44.

10. November 22, 1934. Henning, 87. For the account of the Janesville visit, see Edgar Tafel's column, July 25, 1935. Henning, 143–44.

11. July 30, 1937.

12. November 22, 1934. Henning, 87. On September 27, 1934, Marybud Lautner wrote that Edgar Kaufmann, Jr., came as an apprentice "to see if we lived up to all that he had read about the Fellowship and wound up signing up for himself and one of his friends." She noted that Cornelia Brierly, also from Pittsburgh, had arrived. Henning, 82.

13. For details on the Broadacre City model and Wright's plans for ideal communities, see chapter 14.

14. December 20, 1934. Henning, 94–95. Jensen had been the landscape architect for Wright's Coonley House (1907) in Riverside, Illinois, and the Sherman Booth project (1911–1912) in Glencoe, Illinois. Wright may also have consulted him concerning plantings at Taliesin in 1912. See Charles E. Aguar and Berdena Aguar, *Wrightscapes: Frank Lloyd Wright's Landscape Designs* (New York: McGraw-Hill, 2002), 117–19, 144–49, 155–57, 159.

15. March 11, 1935. Henning, 216.

16. December 9, 1934. Henning, 92.

17. "Frank Lloyd Wright: And the Significance of the Taliesin Fellowship," *Architectural Review* (January 1935): 1–2.

18. December 10, 1934. Henning, 93.

19. Bruce Richards, June 8, 1934. Henning, 50–51. Richards was new to the Fellowship when he wrote this column; he remained a member for a year or two.

20. The letter appears in David Larkin and Bruce Brooks Pfeiffer, eds., *Frank Lloyd Wright Masterworks* (New York: Rizzoli International Publications, 1993), 292.

21. October 25, 1934. For a history of Tan-y-deri and the Porters' years there, see Mary Jane Hamilton, "Tan-y-deri: Another view of Taliesin's Unfolding Narrative," *Frank Lloyd Wright Quarterly* 17, no. 3 (Summer 2006): 4–21. The Porters lived with Mrs. Porter's mother until 1920, when they purchased the Arthur Heurtley residence, a 1902 design by Wright.

22. Bruce Brooks Pfeiffer identifies the arrival of fifteen-year-old Cornelia (Kay) Schneider in 1935 as a turning point in Mrs. Wright's role in the Fellowship. Kay was young enough to be attracted to Mrs. Wright as a source of guidance, and during the next several years "other young apprentices arrived who along with Kay formed a nucleus of people impressed by Mrs. Wright's knowledge of philosophy and human nature. They found they could learn from her as well as from Mr. Wright, and she in turn made it possible for them to gain closer contact with her architect husband."

*Frank Lloyd Wright in the Realm of Ideas* (Carbondale and Edwardsville: Southern Illinois University Press, 1988), 171.

23. August 8, 1934. Henning, 68. A. R. Orage was a London literary critic who abandoned his career in 1922 to join Gurdjieff at Fontainebleau and was sent by Gurdjieff in 1924 to organize groups of followers in the United States. See Jacob Needleman and George Baker, eds., *Gurdjieff: Essays and Reflections on the Man and His Teaching* (New York: Continuum, 1996).

24. August 17, 1934.

25. February 8, 1934.

26. William "Beye" Fyfe, a charter apprentice, left the Fellowship in late 1934.

27. March 1, 1934.

28. John Howe, March 8, 1934. The reference to Spengler was appropriate, for he had recently been a subject of discussion in the Fellowship. Fred Langhorst, March 2, 1934.

29. Alfred Bush, March 22, 1934. Henning, 29–30.

30. May 6, 1934.

31. June 28, 1934.

32. Edgar Tafel, April 26, 1934.

33. May 17, 1934.

34. Bob Mosher, March 29, 1934.

35. Edgar Tafel, May 10, 1934.

36. May 13, 1934. Henning, 44.

37. June 21, 1934. Bisser (Elizabeth) Lloyd Jones was the sister of Jenkin Lloyd Jones, cited earlier in this chapter.

38. Bob Mosher, December 9, 1934. Henning, 91–92.

39. December 10, 1934.

40. December 23, 1934. Henning, 96–97.

41. January 10, 1935. Brierly's characterization of Goodrich was in an author interview, September 2, 2006.

42. January 25, 1935.

43. June 1, 1935.

44. Edgar Tafel, July 4, 1935. Henning, 140. Thompson provided a summary in a July 14, 1935, column.

45. July 21, 1935.

46. September 6, 1935.

47. Contributions to "At Taliesin" were also less frequent. In 1934 there had been 106; in 1935, 61; and in 1936 and 1937, 51 each year. Henning has discovered several published in 1938.

48. January 3, 1936. Henning, 171–72.

## 13—EACH DAY AN EXCITEMENT

1. Eugene Masselink, February 2, 1934, in Randolph C. Henning, ed., *"At Taliesin": Newspaper Columns by Frank Lloyd Wright and the Taliesin Fellowship, 1934–1937* (Carbondale and Edwardsville: Southern Illinois University

Press, 1991), 18–19. For citation practices regarding material drawn from *At Taliesin* articles, see footnote 3, Chapter 11.

2. February 2, 1934. Henning, 19. "Pathe News" refers to *Pathe-Journal* newsreels developed initially by Charles Pathe, a French industrialist. By the 1930s, these newsreels were shown in theaters across America.

3. Henning, 321–22.

4. Unsigned, November 1, 1934.

5. October 30, 1936. Henning, 218–20. The Fellowship had been in Arizona, where it worked on the model for Broadacre City.

6. Unsigned, February 1, 1934.

7. February 22, 1934.

8. March 1, 1934.

9. January 25, 1934.

10. April 26, 1934.

11. May 24, 1934.

12. Edgar Tafel, July 4, 1935. Henning, 139. Others in the trio were Edgar Neukrug, violinist, and Youry Bilstin, cellist.

13. August 23, 1935. Henning, 155–58.

14. August 20, 1937. Members of the string quartet were violinists Mark Kondratieff and William Faldner, violist Anton Bek, and cellist Sam Sciacchastano. Other musicians present around that time were Margaret Cree, a cellist, and composer Adolph Hoffman.

15. January 25, 1934.

16. February 2, 1934. Henning, 20.

17. February 16, 1934. Edman, a charter apprentice, left the Fellowship in 1934 or 1935.

18. October 4, 1934.

19. November 1, 1935. *The Japanese Print* was published in 1912 and republished in expanded form, with illustrations, in 1967. The text appears in Bruce Brooks Pfeiffer, ed., *Frank Lloyd Wright: Collected Writings,* vol. 1, 1894–1930 (New York: Rizzoli International Publications, 1992), 116–25.

20. December 4, 1936. Marya Lilien returned to Poland in mid-1937. In 1941 she became a professor and head of the department of interior architecture in the School of the Chicago Art Institute. When she retired her former students established the Mary Lilien Foundation for the advancement of interior design.

21. Gene Masselink, October 4, 1934. The Dana gallery was named for Mrs. Susan Lawrence Dana, who provided funds for it. Wright had designed her large Prairie-style home in Springfield, Illinois, in 1902. Across a hallway is the room dedicated to the patronage of Charles E. Roberts, whose Oak Park home was remodeled according to a Wright design in 1896. Renovation of these rooms occurred in the

summer of 1934. Bob Mosher reported on this on July 12, 1934. Henning, 62.

22. August 11, 1934.

23. September 27, 1934. Henning, 81–82.

24. Cornelia Brierly, October 19, 1934. Henning, 87–88.

25. October 25, 1934.

26. June 20, 1935.

27. July 19, 1935.

28. March 1, 1934.

29. This issue of *Taliesin* is undated and the pages are not numbered.

30. November 20, 1936.

31. January 15, 1937.

32. March 26, 1937. Henning, 257–59. For an illustrated account of the building of the Jacobs house, see Herbert Jacobs, with Katherine Jacobs, *Building with Frank Lloyd Wright: An Illustrated Memoir* (San Francisco: Chronicle Books, 1978).

33. Henning, 232–34. Edgar Tafel briefly recorded his experiences at Fallingwater in *Years with Frank Lloyd Wright: Apprentice to Genius* (New York: Dover Publications, Inc., 1979), 174–75.

34. January 29, 1937. Henning, 235–36.

35. January 31, 1937.

36. February 6, 1937. Henning, 237–38.

37. March 5, 1937. Henning, 243–45. The Johnson Wax buildings are treated in more detail in Chapter 17. The Larkin building was designed in 1903 and demolished in 1950.

38. Henning, 276–77.

39. December 10, 1937. Henning, 277–78. William Cheaney was in the Fellowship from August to December 1937 and served as assistant secretary, specifically working on this project.

## 14—BROADACRE ADVENTURES

1. Frank Lloyd Wright, *The Disappearing City* (New York: William Farquar Payson, 1932), 3.

2. March, Lionel, "An Architect in Search of Democracy: Broadacre City," in H. Allen Brooks, ed., *Writings on Wright: Selected Comments on Frank Lloyd Wright* (Cambridge: MIT Press, 1981), 196, 205. Transcribed from a broadcast on the BBC, January 7 and 15, 1970.

3. *An Autobiography,* 320, 329.

4. *An Autobiography,* 430.

5. The $1,100 charged apprentices in 1934 would amount to more than $17,600 in 2008 dollars.

6. Somewhat uncharacteristically for Wright, in the course of lecturing and writing about Broadacre City,

according to George R. Collins, he "openly and generously acknowledged his debt to more than thirty individuals." Collins called Wright's proposal "an orgy of eclecticism, in fact a creaky eclecticism which Wright would never have countenanced in his architectural designs." His misleadingly titled essay, "Broadacre City: Wright's Utopia Reconsidered," appears in *Four Great Makers of Modern Architecture: Gropius, Le Corbusier, Mies van der Rohe, Wright* (New York: Da Capo Press, 1970; published initially by Columbia University Press, 1961), 68.

7. *Disappearing City*, 3.

8. These paragraphs draw on Anthony Alofsin, "Broadacre City: The Reception of a Modernist Vision, 1932–1988," *Center: A Journal of Architecture in America* 5 (1989): 8–9.

9. Cited in George R. Collins, "Broadacre City: Wright's Utopia Reconsidered," 58–59. A similar list appears in the essay by Alofsin, "Broadacre City," 10.

10. Henning, 91.

11. Henning, 93.

12. Henning, 104–5. Neil Levine has remarked that the Broadacre model "was a kind of private WPA program to provide work for the Taliesin Fellows during the Depression." *The Architecture of Frank Lloyd Wright* (Princeton: Princeton University Press, 1996), 220. The apprentices, however, did not seem to regard it as a "make-work" enterprise.

13. Gene Masselink, February 10, 1935. Henning, 106–7.

14. January 10, 1935. Henning, 102.

15. Henning, 102–3.

16. Eugene Masselink, "The Arizona Trek," February 10, 1935. Henning 106–10.

17. "The Arizona Trek," February 10, 1935, Henning, 106–10.

18. Henning, 110–11. Twenty of the twenty-five had written "At Taliesin" columns.

19. Henning, 111.

20. Interview with Cornelia Brierly, Wes Peters, and Kay Rattenbury, by Jay Pace, May 10, 1989, pp. 25–26. Oral history archive, Taliesin West.

21. Cited in Anthony Alofsin, "Broadacre City: The Reception of a Modernist Vision, 1932–1988," *Center: A Journal of Architecture in America* 5 (1989): 18.

22. *Tales of Taliesin*, 98.

23. Charles E. Aguar and Berdeana Aguar, *Wrightscapes: Frank Lloyd Wright's Landscape Designs* (McGraw-Hill, 2002), 226–27.

24. *In the Nature of Materials: The Buildings of Frank Lloyd Wright, 1887–1941* (New York: Da Capo Press, 1973; published initially in 1942 by Meredith Press), 86.

25. Weil am Rhein, Germany: Vitra Design Museum, 1998), 204–7; 23–24. The book accompanies the exhibition curated by David De Long and features essays on many of Wright's built and unbuilt projects. Similarly, George R. Collins, in "Broadacre City: Wright's Utopia Reconsidered," in *Four Great Makers of Modern Architecture: Gropius, Le Corbusier, Mies van der Rohe, Wright* (New York: Da Capo Press, 1970), observed: "It may also be noteworthy that the Broadacre plan included at least a dozen of Wright's unsold building projects of the nineteen-twenties" (p. 66).

26. *The Creative Community: Designing for Life* (Mulgrave, Victoria: The Images Publishing Group, 2003). 197, 193.

27. Interview at Taliesin West, November 23, 1992, pp. 15–16, Frank Lloyd Wright Archives. For a brief account of Soleri's expulsion see chapter 18.

28. Eugene Masselink, January 24, 1936; Henning, 175–76; Bennie Dombar, February 7, 1936; Henning, 177–78.

## 15—LANDMARK BUILDINGS

1. *An Autobiography*, 448. "Little Sunshine" was Wright's term of endearment for Bob Mosher.

2. See particularly: Donald Hoffmann, *Frank Lloyd Wright's Fallingwater: The House and Its History* (New York: Dover Publications, Inc., second, revised edition, 1993); Edgar Kaufmann, Jr., *Fallingwater: A Frank Lloyd Wright Country House* (New York: Abbeville Press, 1986); Robert McCarter, *Fallingwater: Frank Lloyd Wright* (London: Phaidon Press, 1994, 2002); Narciso G. Menocal, ed., *Fallingwater and Pittsburgh*, Wright Studies, vol. 2 (Carbondale and Edwardsville: Southern Illinois University Press, 2000); Bruce Brooks Pfeiffer (with Yukio Futagawa), *Frank Lloyd Wright: Selected Houses: Fallingwater*, vol. 4 (Tokyo: A.D.A EDITA, 1990, 2004); Edgar Tafel, *Years with Frank Lloyd Wright: Apprentice to Genius* (New York: Dover Publications, Inc., 1979); and Franklin Toker, *Fallingwater Rising: Frank Lloyd Wright, E. J. Kaufmann, and America's Most Extraordinary House* (New York: Alfred A. Knopf, 2003). This portion of the chapter follows the chronology constructed by Hoffman. Quotations in the text are cited by author's names.

3. Toker, 102. Wright's alleged "humiliation" at the Museum of Modern Art concerned his antagonism toward the International Style, to be represented in the exhibition by the work of Richard Neutra, whom he had come to detest. It took much cajoling to keep Wright from withdrawing. At issue in controversies over Toker's book are such matters as whether Edgar or E. J. initiated the contacts with Wright that led to the agreement to build, and whether Wright had completed drawings in private before impressing his apprentices by sketching them quickly in their presence.

4. See a sampling of the Fallingwater correspondence in Bruce Brooks Pfeiffer, ed., *Letters to Clients: Frank Lloyd Wright* (Fresno: The Press at California State University, 1986), 82–108.

5. Hoffmann, 13.

6. Peter Reed and William Kaizen, eds., "To Meet—To Know—To Battle—To Love—Frank Lloyd Wright," *The Show to End All Shows: Frank Lloyd Wright and the Museum of Modern Art, 1940* (New York: Museum of Modern Art, 2004), 172; written for a catalog that was not published at the time.

7. Hoffmann, 17.

8. Tafel provides a dramatic account of this version, 1–3, 7.

9. Hoffmann, 17.

10. September 27, 1935. Quoted by Hoffmann, 25.

11. For an account of this journey, see Tafel, 84–93.

12. Wright to Kaufmann. February 1, 1937.

13. Wright to Mosher, August 27, 1936. Bruce Brooks Pfeiffer, ed., *Letters to Clients: Frank Lloyd Wright* (Fresno: the Press at California State University, 1986), 96.

14. Kaufmann to Wright, August 28, 1935. "To Meet—To Know—To Battle—To Love—Frank Lloyd Wright," Peter Reed and William Kaizen, eds., *The Show to End All Shows: Frank Lloyd Wright and the Museum of Modern Art, 1940* (New York: Museum of Modern Art, 2004), 176.

15. Hoffmann, 53.

16. Hoffmann, 81. Adjusted for inflation, the cost for Fallingwater in 2007 dollars would be about $5,500,000.

17. Hoffman, 30.

18. Tafel, 175.

19. *An Autobiography,* 468–69. The unbuilt project Wright referred to was for the *Capital Journal* in Salem, Oregon, designed in 1931.

20. Tafel, 175–76.

21. The chronology of this portion draws principally on Jonathon Lipman, *Frank Lloyd Wright and the Johnson Wax Buildings* (Mineola, N.Y.: Dover Publications, 2003; published originally in 1982 by Rizzoli International Publications) and the chapter on these buildings in Pfeiffer, ed., *Letters to Clients: Frank Lloyd Wright*, 130–57. Quotations from these and other sources are cited individually.

22. *An Autobiography,* 469–71.

23. Lipman, 56–63.

24. Lipman, 37.

25. In 2007 dollars, this would be about $7,000,000.

26. "Mr. Wright and the Johnsons of Racine, Wisc.," *AIA Journal* 79, no. 1 (January 1979): 65.

27. http://www/fllwctr//history.htm. Accessed January 2007.

28. For details, see Steven B. Rogers, "The Frank Lloyd Wright Campus at Florida Southern College: A Child of the Sun," *Frank Lloyd Wright Quarterly* 12, no. 3 (Summer 2001): 4–23.

29. Author interview with Frances Nemtin (formerly Polly Lockhart), March 1, 2007. She said that Wright was "holding them hostage" at Taliesin. In the summer of 1948, Robert Broward, inspired by the articles and photographs of Wright's work in the January 1948 issue of the *Architectural Forum*, went to Lakeland to work in the construction of the Administration Building, first as a laborer, then as a welder and block mason. Lockhart suggested that he should contact Wright about joining the Fellowship. He did so, and after completing his architectural studies at Georgia Tech he was in the Fellowship in 1949–1950. "Robert C. Broward: Some Notations Concerning My Life," *Friends of Kebyar* 10.2, no. 53 (May–September 1992): 4; response to author survey, June 20, 2002.

30. Letters cited are in Pfeiffer, ed., *Letters to Clients: Frank Lloyd Wright*, 158–84.

31. Herbert Jacobs and Katherine Jacobs, *Building with Frank Lloyd Wright: An Illustrated Memoir* (San Francisco: Chronicle Books, 1978), 18. The contract between "Mr. and Mrs. Herbert Jacobs and the Taliesin Fellowship Architect," dictated by Wright and written by Mrs. Jacobs, is reproduced on pp. 19–20; it dealt mainly with how Wright was to be paid.

32. Jacobs, 53. After World War II the Jacobses built a second Wright-designed house. By this time their relations with him had cooled, and they built it themselves.

33. John Lautner supervised the construction of the George D. Sturges Residence in Brentwood Heights, California, and the Abby Beecher Roberts Residence (Deertrack) in Marquette, Michigan; Edgar Tafel the Lloyd Lewis Residence in Libertyville, Illinois, the Bernard Schwartz Residence in Two Rivers, Wisconsin, and the Charles Manson Residence in Wausau, Wisconsin; Blaine Drake the Sidney Bazett Residence, Hillsborough, California; Bob Mosher the Rose Pauson Residence (Shiprock) in Phoenix, Arizona; and Wes Peters and Cary Caraway the John Clarence Pew Residence, Shorewood Hills, Wisconsin. Other residences designed in these years were for Ben Rebhuhn, Great Neck Estates, New York; Otto Tod Mallery (Suntop Homes), Ardmore, Pennsylvania; Andrew F. Armstrong, Ogden Dunes, Indiana; Loren B. Pope, Falls Church, Virginia; Alma Goetsch and Kathrine Winkler, Okemos, Michigan; Joseph Euchtman, Baltimore, Maryland; and Clarence Sondern, Kansas City, Missouri. Wright also designed a complex of buildings for Leigh Stevens's Auldbrass Plantation at Yemassee, South Carolina. A number of them were constructed in 1940 and 1941, and design and construction of more continued

in 1946–1962. More than a dozen other designs in these years were not built.

34. This account follows the reconstruction of events provided in *Frank Lloyd Wright's Rosenbaum House: The Birth and Rebirth of an American Treasure,* by Barbara Kimberlin Broach, Donald E. Lambert, and Milton Bagby (San Francisco: Pomegranate, 2006), 19–36.

35. Electric heating was installed but proved to be so expensive that it had to be replaced with an oil-fueled system. Rosenbaum to Wright, March 21, 1941.

36. Wright to Goodrich, January 8, 1940.

37. Broach et al., 24.

## 16—THE DESERT CAMP

1. *An Autobiography,* 454.

2. *An Autobiography,* 453. The high cost of heating Taliesin was perhaps most evident in the deep holes in the woods surrounding Taliesin as the apprentices cut trees and split logs for firewood; the time and labor required in the process must also have been a concern. Gene Masselink, "At Taliesin," February 10, 1935, 106–7.

3. *An Autobiography,* 454–55.

4. *Frank Lloyd Wright: Selected Houses: Taliesin West,* text by Bruce Brooks Pfeiffer, edited and photographed by Yukio Futagawa (Tokyo: A.D.A. EDITA, Ltd., 1989), 11–12.

5. *An Autobiography,* 453.

6. In a discussion with apprentices at Taliesin West in 1994 I asked what Jefferson's Monticello and Wright's Taliesin West had in common. The instant response: "Both were built by slave labor."

7. This should not be construed as a negative, nor is it surprising, for most who left had accomplished their purpose in joining. Some remained as senior draftsmen or, as in the case of Gene Masselink, in other roles.

8. Described by Herbert Fritz, "At Taliesin," in Edna Meudt and Betsy Strand, eds., *An Uplands Reader* (Dodgeville, Wisc., n.d.), 140–41. A copy in the State Historical Society of Wisconsin is signed by Fritz for Jack and Lu Howe, June 1979.

9. *The Shining Brow: Frank Lloyd Wright* (New York: Horizon Press, 1960), 49–50.

10. "At Taliesin," in *An Uplands Reader,* 141.

11. "Frank Lloyd Wright: Architect of the Landscape," in David De Long, *Designs for the American Landscape, 1922–1932* (New York: Harry N. Abrams, 1996), 152. The lack of accurate building records, understandable in the circumstances in which the builders worked, makes precise dating of the construction projects impossible.

12. "Reflections of Taliesin," *Northwest Architect,* July–August 1969, 63.

13. *Frank Lloyd Wright: His Life, His Work, His Words* (New York: Horizon Press, 1966), 106–7.

14. "Reflections of Taliesin," *Northwest Architect,* July–August 1969, 62–63. Sisalcraft in its simplest form is made of hemp.

15. Tafel, 194–95.

16. When Tony Puttnam arrived as an apprentice in the 1950s the reuse of nails continued: "[W]e were building a building and there was absolutely no money. We were pouring concrete, so the second morning we had to straighten the nails that we pulled out of the forms and put in the new form. By the third morning we took up a collection and sent someone into town to buy some new nails, but Gene said, 'Don't even think about it. There's no money. We will not buy nails.'" Author interview, June 21, 1995. On file in the FLLW Archives.

17. P. 142.

18. Pp. 140–41.

19. Interview with Cornelia Brierly, Wes Peters, and Kay Rattenbury, by Jay Pace, May 10, 1989, p. 24. Oral history archive, Taliesin West.

20. William Wesley Peters interview. Frank Lloyd Wright Archives. Interviewed by Indira Berndtson and Greg Williams, December 9, 1988, pp. 5–6, 8–10. Fritz, 143.

21. *Years with Frank Lloyd Wright: Apprentice to Genius* (New York: Dover Publications, 1985), 196.

22. *Working with Mr. Wright: What It Was Like* (Cambridge, U.K.: Cambridge University Press, 1995), 7–78; specific quotations from pp. 62–63, 65, 68, 72, and 76.

23. This paragraph, and earlier ones, draw on Neil Levine's detailed account of the designing and building of Taliesin West, pp. 263–72, in *The Architecture of Frank Lloyd Wright* (Princeton: Princeton University Press, 1996); Levine also provides a fascinating description of the camp (pp. 272–90), some of it in what might be called a virtual walking tour. The "Building Condition Assessment" by Eifler & Associates—Architects, for the restoration of the Wrights' living quarters, is an additional source. For a vivid account of the essence of Taliesin West, join Philip Johnson's virtual procession through it in John Peter, *The Oral History of Modern Architecture: Interviews with the Greatest Architects of the Twentieth Century* (New York: Harry N. Adams, Inc., 1994), 84–85; at the conclusion, Johnson writes, "you realize that you've been handled, and petted, and twisted much as a symphony will caress you, or an opera, until you get to the crisis."

24. Author interview, February 28, 2007.

## 17—THE FELLOWSHIP AT WORK

1. "Is It Good-by to Gothic?" *Frank Lloyd Wright: Collected Writings,* vol. 5 (New York: Rizzoli International

Publications, 1995), 231–32. Published originally in *Together,* May 1958.

2. Tobias S. Guggenheimer, *A Taliesin Legacy: The Architecture of Frank Lloyd Wright's Apprentices* (New York: Van Nostrand Reinhold, 1995), 152; based on a conversation with Howe, July 1991. The house referred to by Howe was the one for Clarence Sondern, designed in 1939. There are no formal or systematic records as to who among the apprentices worked on which buildings, but it is possible to make connections by drawing upon recollections and compilations by former apprentices, correspondence, interviews, responses to surveys, oral histories, and published works. John W. Geiger, an apprentice from 1947 to 1954, has assiduously sought to establish and maintain records concerning former apprentices. His admittedly incomplete list shows 67 structures on which 31 apprentices worked part-time or full-time between 1936 and 1959. I am grateful to him for providing me with useful information.

3. Unless otherwise noted, information and quotations in these paragraphs are drawn from Theodore Baird's 50-page booklet, "On Building in Amherst a House Designed by Frank Lloyd Wright," November 20, 1989 (pp. 16, 17, 21, 22, 30, 31, 32), and from letters preserved in the Baird House archive. I am grateful to Jean Hoffman and Jim Phaneuf, to whom Baird willed the house upon his death at age 95 in late 1996, for giving me a tour of the house, a copy of Baird's booklet, correspondence between Wright and the Bairds (1939–1941), and clippings from the October 22, 1997, *Daily Hampshire Gazette* describing how they came to be owners of the house. Included in the newspaper account is an excerpt from a letter from Baird to his beneficiaries: "This is not in my mind a personal matter. Our interest is not in doing something for you but in doing something that will, I hope and trust, be good for the house. It is our belief that you would care for it, maintain it, and value it as it should be." These documents are cited with the owners' permission.

4. William Wesley Peters interview by Indira Berndtson and Greg Williams, November 20, 1989, pp. 15–16. Oral history collection, Frank Lloyd Wright Archives. The houses Chadwick was supervising were for Joseph Euchtman in Baltimore and Loren Pope in Falls Church, Virginia.

5. Caraway's given name was "Jesse Claude." At Taliesin he was known as "Cary"; Baird and others occasionally spelled it "Carey."

6. I looked in vain for this insult in Tafel's *Years with Frank Lloyd Wright.*

7. Peters interview by Indira Berndtson and Greg Williams, May 15, 1991, 5–6. Oral history collection, Frank Lloyd Wright Archives.

8. Curtis Besinger, *Working with Mr. Wright: What It Was Like.* (Cambridge, U.K.: Cambridge University Press, 1995), 88–94, 119–23.

9. These paragraphs draw upon an essay by Kathryn Smith, "The Show to End All Shows: Frank Lloyd Wright and the Museum of Modern Art, 1940," in a book by that title, edited by Peter Reed and William Kaizen (New York: Museum of Modern Art, 2004), especially pp. 46–47, 50–51, 53, 56–59; pages 52 and 54–55 contain pictures of the exhibition. Besinger describes the model-building process in *Working with Mr. Wright* (Cambridge: Cambridge University Press, 1995), 97–100.

10. (New York: Da Capo Press, 1942). In the preface, Hitchcock acknowledges the cooperation of the Taliesin Fellowship.

11. In his autobiography Wright described the circumstances of those years and the resentment they caused, calling them "disgraceful to my country as to myself," resulting from "persecution aroused by my own indiscretion," 291–99.

12. Besinger, 118. Some of those he mentioned as leaving disgruntled in fact went into military service, and at least one of them returned after being discharged.

13. Besinger, 111–13. If there was a response from Dykstra, Besinger did not hear of it.

14. *Letters to Apprentices* (Fresno: The Press at California State University, Fresno, 1982), 146–47. Wright's list misplaces some of the persons named as to their branch of service, and it is misleading in other respects. Some who were listed as being in defense work actually served in the military.

15. Six *Square Papers* were published in 1941, one in 1944, and nine after the war. They can be found in *Collected Writings,* vols. 4 and 5.

16. "Stone to Ask FBI Probe Frank Lloyd Wright," *Capital Times,* December 22, 1942. Photocopy in Frank Lloyd Wright Archives, #8005.001/1701 906.

17. "Address at Sandstone Prison," n.d., *Frank Lloyd Wright: Collected Writings,* vol. 4 (New York: Rizzoli International Publications, 1994), 106. John Howe, interviewed by Indira Berndtson and Greg Williams, March 12, 1991, p. 40.

18. Besinger, 151–52.

19. Cited in Alvin Rosenbaum, *Usonia: Frank Lloyd Wright's Design for America* (Washington, D.C.: Preservation Press, 1993), 171, 177. A list of the signers appears in John Sergeant, *Frank Lloyd Wright's Usonian Houses: Designs for Moderate Cost One-Family Homes* (New York: Watson-Guptil Publications, 1976, 1984), 201. It included notable figures of mid-twentieth-century

America: Thurman Arnold, Charles Beard, Thomas Hart Benton, John Dewey, Marshall Field, Buckminster Fuller, Walter Gropius, Henry-Russell Hitchcock, Robert Hutchins, Albert Kahn, Edgar Kaufmann, Sr., Fiske Kimball, Alexander Meiklejohn, Carl Miles, Robert Moses, Georgia O'Keeffe, Nelson Rockefeller, Mies van der Rohe, Alexander Woollcott, William Allen White, and many others.

20. *Architectural Forum* 88, no. 1 (January 1948): 80. For a first-hand account by an observer of Wright's encounter with the Chief of the Planning Section of the Federal Works Agency in which the project was canceled, see Talbot Wegg, "FLLW versus the USA," *AIA Journal* 53, no. 2 (February 1970): 48–52. Rosenbaum, *Usonia: Frank Lloyd Wright's Design for America* (Washington, D.C.: Preservation Press, 1993), 176. Drawings of the Cloverleaf design appear in Bruce Brooks Pfeiffer, *Frank Lloyd Wright: Treasures of Taliesin: Seventy-Six Unbuilt Designs* (Carbondale and Edwardsville: Southern Illinois University Press, 1985), plates 28a and 28b. This design was a further development of his 1938 plan for the Suntop Quadruple Homes in Ardmore, Pennsylvania (suburban Philadelphia).

21. June 1, 1943. *Frank Lloyd Wright: The Guggenheim Correspondence,* selected and with commentary by Bruce Brooks Pfeiffer (Fresno, California: The Press at California State University; and Carbondale and Edwardsville: Southern Illinois University Press, 1986), 4. Further citations of letters and commentary are to this book.

22. *Guggenheim Correspondence,* ix–x.

23. *Guggenheim Correspondence,* 29.

24. Others included Curtis Besinger, Davy and Kay Davison, Johnny Hill, Kenn and Polly Lockhart, and Gene Masselink.

25. Peters interview, by Greg Williams and Indira Berndtson, December 29, 1989. Oral history collection, Frank Lloyd Wright Archives.

26. *Guggenheim Correspondence,* 112.

27. *Guggenheim Correspondence,* 195. For a richly illustrated account of Wright's years in New York, see Jane King Hession and Debra Pickrel (Salt Lake City: Gibbs Smith, Publisher, 2007). A chronology of Wright's executed works, projects, exhibitions, and awards in New York City appears on pp. 124–25.

28. Identified by Besinger, 253–54.

29. G. Jim Pfefferkorn, *Taliesin Stories: Autobiographical* (Spring Green, Wisc.: privately printed, n.d.), chapter 1, 16–17. Used with permission.

30. Bruce Brooks Pfeiffer, *Frank Lloyd Wright Drawings* (New York: Harry N. Abrams, 1990), 152; a perspective drawing appears on this page.

31. "Realizing Wright's Usonian Design for the Zimmermans: Architect, Apprentice, Client," *Journal of the Taliesin Fellows* 2 (Fall 1990): 22–23.

32. Portions of the June 16, 1953, letter appear in David Larkin and Bruce Brooks Pfeiffer, eds., *Frank Lloyd Wright: The Masterworks* (New York: Rizzoli International Publications, 1993), 245.

33. Henry Whiting, II, *Teater's Knoll: Frank Lloyd Wright's Idaho Legacy* (Midland, Mich.: Northwood Institute Press, 1987), 29, 34, 37, 45, 50–52, 55, 57–58; also unnumbered pages in the Foreword.

34. Robert Lewellyn Wright, "A Son as Client," *Frank Lloyd Wright Newsletter* 3, no. 2 (1980): 7–8. Robert Beharka, "Retrospection: A Personal Recollection," *Journal of the Taliesin Fellows* 22 (Summer 1997): 16–17. Beharka interview by Indira Berndtson, November 9, 1997, Oral history collection, Frank Lloyd Wright Archives. Response to author survey, October 29, 2002. Although Lewellyn Wright gave the design a 1955 date, others date it 1953.

35. "The Wright Way," *The Washington Post Magazine,* August 21, 2005, 44.

36. Robert Beharka, "Retrospection: A Personal Recollection," *Journal of the Taliesin Fellows* 22 (Summer 1997): 17.

37. William Wesley Peters interview, by Indira Berndtson and Greg Williams, January 31, 1990, pp. 2–3. Oral history collection. Frank Lloyd Wright Archives.

38. Patricia Talbot David, *Together They Built a Mountain* (Lititz, Pa., 1974), 43, 88, 101, 144. *The Shining Brow* (New York: Horizon Press, 1960), 189.

39. John Gurda, *New World Odyssey: The Annunciation Greek Orthodox Church and Frank Lloyd Wright* (Milwaukee: Milwaukee Hellenic Community, 1986), 58.

40. Gurda, 86.

41. Gurda, 87.

42. Gurda, 90.

43. Gurda, 101.

44. Gurda, 102–3.

45. Gurda, 114–17. About the leaking roof Wes Peters remarked: "If a conventional roof leaks, it's assumed to be the contractor's fault. If an unusual roof leaks, it's automatically assumed to be the architect's fault." Gurda says that the Annunciation parish fared better than the Beth Sholom Synagogue congregation, where projected costs tripled, construction took five years to complete, and the people were "deluged during heavy rains until a technical problem was corrected."

46. Aaron G. Green, *An Architecture for Democracy: The Marin County Civic Center* (San Francisco: Grendon Publishing, 1990), 66–68, 70–71, 73, 94.

## 18—DAILY LIFE IN THE FELLOWSHIP

1. Response to author's survey, May 31, 2002, 1.

2. This aphorism may have originated with Dorothy Parker. Bruce Pfeiffer gives an example of its application: "When Wright collected a check from Kaufmann he was over in Philadelphia and he telephoned Mrs. Wright and said, 'We've got some money, Mother, what do we need?' She needed a new carpet sweeper, so she said, 'It would be nice if we had an electric vacuum cleaner.' He said, 'Well, I've found a harpsichord.' And she said, 'Well, for heaven's sake get the harpsichord.' They both had that same feeling. You can always push an old carpet sweeper a little bit longer but you can't always get a fine harpsichord on sale." Author interview, November 28, 1994, p. 11.

3. Response to author's survey, May 31, 2002, 1. Hoffe was in the Fellowship 1955–1956.

4. Response to author's survey, September 19, 2002, 3. Gill was in the Fellowship in 1952 and 1955–1957.

5. Interviewed by Indira Berndtson, August 10, 1995, 2. FLLW Archives. Gorman was in the Fellowship 1952–1955.

6. Response to author's survey, September 13, 2002, 1. Keding was in the Fellowship 1958–1960 and 1963–1970.

7. Interviewed by Indira Berndtson, November 14, 1995, 4, FLLW Archives.

8. Response to author's survey, August 15, 2002, 1. John A's 11-page eloquent statement is one of several that are sufficiently packed with information and insights that publishing them in their entirety would be desirable. He was in the Fellowship 1951–1973.

9. Author interview, November 28, 1994, 6, Frank Lloyd Wright Archives. Pfeiffer joined the Fellowship in 1949 and continues in it yet today.

10. *Capital Times,* October 16, 1953, 9; May 18, 1955, 1–2; Robert Twombly, *Frank Lloyd Wright: His Life and His Architecture* (New York: John Wiley and Sons, 1979), 377–80; testimonial invitation, John Howe Collection, State Historical Society of Wisconsin, box 26, folder 28.

11. Response to author's survey, August 15, 2002, 7.

12. The building of desert shelters, their transformation through the years, and their genealogies are important parts of the Fellowship's history, and it is impossible to do justice to them here. For an illustrated account of the continuing tradition of building desert shelters, see Dixie Legler, "Desert Shelters: Learning by Doing," *Frank Lloyd Wright Quarterly* 18, no. 2 (Spring 2007): 4–15.

13. Roderick Grant, "Robert Beharka and the Countenance of Principle," *Journal of the Taliesin Fellows* 22 (Summer 1997): 4.

14. Kenn Lockhart, interviewed by Indira Berndtson and Greg Williams, January 22, 1992; Frank Lloyd Wright Archives; Susan Jacobs Lockhart, e-mail message to the author, July 19, 2007; Lu Howe, letter accompanied by pictures, to the author, August 7, 2007. The story of the Lockhart Cottage, with illustrations, appears in Diane Maddex, *Wright-Sized Houses* (New York: Harry N. Abrams, Inc., 2003), 148–53.

15. G. Jim Pfefferkorn, *Taliesin Stories: Autobiographical,* privately printed, 1997. "Building at Taliesin West," 7–8. "Our Arizona Cottage," 2–6. Letter to the author, August 27, 2007. Jim had come to Taliesin to interview for a position as a draftsman and was surprised to find himself and his wife as apprentices to Wright.

16. G. Jim Pfefferkorn, *Taliesin Stories: Autobiographical,* privately printed, 1997. "Work at Taliesin East–Wisconsin," 14–17. Letter to the author, August 27, 2007.

17. Deirdre Treacy Babcock, response to author's survey, May 24, 2002. "Desert Shelters: Learning by Doing," *Frank Lloyd Wright Quarterly* 18, no. 2 (Spring 2007): 18.

18. Interviewed by Indira Berndtson and Greg Williams, January 15, 1991, 13. Swaback was in the Fellowship 1957 to 1979.

19. In mid-2008, 14 of the 23 senior fellows had been members of the Fellowship for at least 50 years, and 3 more than 40; they attest to their difficulty in identifying all their various abodes. Six have entered in the past 25 years. Admission of new members has apparently been halted.

20. Interview by Indira Berndtson and Greg Williams, April 20, 1989, Frank Lloyd Wright Archives; included in "Save America's Treasures: To Document the Historic Buildings at Taliesin West," 125.

21. Interview by Indira Berndtson and Greg Williams, May 4, 1989, Frank Lloyd Wright Archives; included in "Save America's Treasures: To Document the Historic Buildings at Taliesin West," 21.

22. Summary of interviews by Indira Berndtson, by phone, August 5, 1994. Frank Lloyd Wright Archives, pp. 1–2; response to author's survey, July 7, 2002.

23. *Friends of Kebyar* 10.2, no. 53 (May–September 1992): 3.

24. Response to author's survey, August 15, 2002, 4.

25. Response to author's survey, September 13, 2002, 2.

26. "Work at Taliesin East," *Taliesin Stories: Autobiographical,* 6.

27. Tobias S. Guggenheimer, *A Taliesin Legacy: The Architecture of Frank Lloyd Wright's Apprentices* (New York: Van Nostrand and Reinhold, 1995, from a conversation with E. Fay Jones, 1991), 167.

28. Response to author's survey, May 31, 2002, 2.

29. *Taliesin Reflections: My Years Before, During, and After*

*Living with Frank Lloyd Wright* (Petaluma, Calif.: Meridian Press, 2006), 49, 67, 68.

30. Response to author's survey, September 22, 2002, 3–4.

31. *Taliesin Reflections: My Years Before, During, and after Living with Frank Lloyd Wright* (Petaluma, Cal.: Meridian Press, 2006), 46–47.

32. E-mail to the author, July 25, 2007. See also Michael Komanecky, "Morton Delson and the Kalil House: The Making of a 'Usonian Automatic,'" *Journal of the Taliesin Fellows* 6 (Spring 1992): 8, for an account of Delson's recollections.

33. Frances Nemtin (who was known as Polly Lockhart in the years of which she wrote), "Life on Midway Farm" (privately printed, 1999), 4–5.

34. Email to the author, July 25, 2007.

35. Frances Nemtin, "Life on Midway Farm" (privately printed, 1999), 4–5. Wright had left apprentices at Taliesin in some of the winters in the 1940s; among them were Ted Bower, John Rattenbury, and Kay Davison, whose husband Davy was imprisoned in Minnesota for refusing to be drafted. Ted Bower, telephone interview by Indira Berndtson, August 17, 1994, 37–38, Frank Lloyd Wright Archives.

36. Response to author's survey, undated (ca. August 15, 2002). Uncle Vlado was Mrs. Wright's brother. Accompanying the handwritten account drawn upon here, Anderson included several hundred pages of portfolio materials that, unfortunately, were not labeled. Attempts to reach her by phone were unsuccessful, and regrettably, she passed away in 2007, before I could get in touch with her at this point in my writing.

37. *Reflections from the Shining Brow: My Years with Frank Lloyd Wright and Olgivanna Lazovich* (Santa Barbara: Fithian Press, 2004), 72–73. Amin was a member of the Fellowship from 1951 to 1977.

38. "'My Life': An Autobiography by Iovanna Lloyd Wright," unpublished, pp. 130, 167, 172, 224, 238–42, 246, 248. Cited with the permission of the Frank Lloyd Wright Foundation.

39. Mentioned in personal conversations by several who so served.

40. Interviewed by Indira Berndtson and Greg Williams, October 16, 1992, 5, Frank Lloyd Wright Archives. Biddle was in the Fellowship 1952–1955.

41. Response to author's survey, July 23, 2002, 1.

42. Response to author's survey, March 24, 2003, unnumbered pages. There are no official statistics on the ratio of men to women, but perusal of such membership rosters as exist suggests that in the early days it was about 4:1. In later years the preponderance of men was far greater.

43. Interviewed by Indira Berndtson, January 30, 1990, 8.

44. For summaries and photos of some of the skits, see Cornelia Brierly, *Tales of Taliesin* (Tempe, Ariz.: Herberger Center for Design Excellence, Arizona State University), 58–63.

45. Interviewed by Indira Berndtson and Greg Williams, December 17, 1990, 13, Frank Lloyd Wright Archives.

46. This exhibition previewed in Philadelphia in 1951 traveled to Florence that year; to Zurich, Paris, Munich, and Rotterdam in 1952; to Mexico City and New York in 1953; and to Los Angeles in 1954.

47. Besinger, 212, 214, 219, 220, 232, 243, 253–54, 260, 267, 271, 288–91.

48. Interviewed by Indira Berndtson and Greg Williams, April 29, 1992, 62, Frank Lloyd Wright Archives.

49. Interviewed by the author, November 28, 1994, p. 17.

50. Interviewed by James Auer, for the video "Partner to Genius," Milwaukee: WMVS/WMVT, 1991; in Frank Lloyd Wright Archives; used in part in the video.

51. Deirdre Treacy Babcock, interviewed by Greg Williams, August 11, 1993, Frank Lloyd Wright Archives, 9, 16.

52. Paul and Phyllis Bogart, telephone interview by Greg Williams, May 3, 1992, 18–19, Frank Lloyd Wright Archives.

53. Interviewed by Indira Berndtson, at the 1997 Fellowship Reunion, Taliesin West, November 7, 1994, 8–9, Frank Lloyd Wright Archives.

54. Interviewed by the author, November 21, 1994, 5;

55. Interview by Indira Berndtson, September 11, 1992, 3, Frank Lloyd Wright Archives.

56. Interview by the author, June 21, 1995.

57. E-mail message, August 17, 2007.

58. Response to author's survey, July 23, 2002, 2.

59. From a transcript for the video "Partner to Genius: Olgivanna Lloyd Wright." Milwaukee: WMVS/WMVT. Frank Lloyd Wright Archives. (The "organ" metaphor was not used in the production.)

60. Patrick J. Meehan, ed., *Frank Lloyd Wright Remembered* (Washington, D.C.: Preservation Press, 1991), 167; the interview by Hoyt Johnson appeared initially in *Scottsdale Scene Magazine,* 1986. Telephone conversation with the author, July 17, 2007.

61. Response to author's survey, January 7, 2003. "Lieber Meister" was Wright's term of endearment for Louis Sullivan.

62. Letter to Soleri, March 22, 1950. Soleri recounted this experience in an interview excerpted by Edgar Tafel in *Frank Lloyd Wright: Recollections by Those Who Knew Him*

(Mineola, N.Y.: Dover Publications, Inc., 2001), 180–81. He relates his departure to Wright's belief that he was trying to lure other apprentices to go to Italy with him to establish something similar to Taliesin. Wright was also upset that they had built a house at Canyon de Chelley without his authorization while they were supposed to be caring for Uncle Vlado and Aunt Sophie at Taliesin West.

63. September 8, 1948, and November 29, 1948.

64. From a transcript for the video "Partner to Genius: Olgivanna Lloyd Wright." Milwaukee: WMVS/WMVT. Frank Lloyd Wright Archives.

65. "Partner to Genius."

66. "New Beginnings: Death and Aftermath," response to author's survey; undated, 1–2.

67. Interviewed by Indira Berndtson, February 4, 1993, 20–21, Frank Lloyd Wright Archives. Through the years Dyson maintained cordial relations with the Taliesin, and from September 1999 to April 2002 he served as dean of the Frank Lloyd Wright School of Architecture.

68. From a conversation with E. Thomas Casey, 1991, published in Tobias Guggenheimer, *A Taliesin Legacy: The Architecture of Frank Lloyd Wright's Apprentices* (New York: Van Nostrand Reinhold, 1995), 102.

69. Response to author's survey, May 13, 2002, 2.

## 19—MRS. WRIGHT'S FELLOWSHIP

1. Conclusion to "Partner to Genius," a video narrated by James Auer. Milwaukee: WMVS/WMVT, 1991. The escape was from Russia, for there was no Soviet Zone then.

2. *Reflections from the Shining Brow: My Years with Frank Lloyd Wright and Olgivanna Lazovich* (Santa Barbara: Fithian Press, 2002), 146–48. Amin was in the Fellowship 1951 to 1977.

3. Interview by Indira Berndtson and Greg Williams, July 29, 1992, 13, Frank Lloyd Wright Archives.

4. Interview by Indira and Greg Williams, February 6, 1992, 15, Frank Lloyd Wright Archives. Banks was in the Fellowship from 1952 to 1990; later, as a resident of Spring Green he remained in close touch.

5. "New Beginnings: Death and Aftermath," 3, submitted in response to the author's survey, May 13, 2002. Interview by Indira Berndtson, by phone, February 27, 1996, 39–40, Frank Lloyd Wright Archives.

6. Interview by the author, November 16, 1994, 3; Frank Lloyd Wright Archives; Marty and Marty, 106–7.

7. Interview by the author, November 15, 1994, 7–8, 2–4, Frank Lloyd Wright Archives. Carney incorrectly identified Lugano, instead of Montagnola, as the location of the American School.

8. Effi Casey interview by the author, November 22, 1994, 1; Frank Lloyd Wright Archives. Also remarks by Effi Casey at a Senior Fellowship presentation at Taliesin West, undated.

9. Interview by the author, June 21, 1995 (transcript revised March 2, 1996, and March 20, 1997), 1–3, Frank Lloyd Wright Archives.

10. See Bruce Brooks Pfeiffer, "Frank Lloyd Wright and Baghdad," *Frank Lloyd Wright Quarterly* 15, no. 1 (Winter 2004): 4–17; for the larger context of Wright and Baghdad, see Neil Levine, *The Architecture of Frank Lloyd Wright* (Princeton: Princeton University Press, 1996), 383–93.

11. Response to author's survey, May 3, 2003, 1–4.

12. The term "Associated" gradually slipped out of usage, and in 1993 the firm officially became "Taliesin Architects."

13. Letters to the author from Mrs. Howe, November 9, 2002 and June 18, 2003. Interview of Jack Howe by Indira Berndtson and Greg Williams, March 21, 1991, 50, Frank Lloyd Wright Archives. Cited with Mrs. Howe's permission.

14. Interview by the author, November 16, 1994, 8–9, Frank Lloyd Wright Archives; Marty and Marty, 183–84.

15. *A Living Architecture: Frank Lloyd Wright and Taliesin Architects* (San Francisco: Pomegranate, 2000). Wes Peters was listed as the principal architect for sixteen of these structures, Rattenbury for five, and Tom Casey and Charles Montooth for one each.

16. Casey interview by the author, November 28, 1994, 13–14, Frank Lloyd Wright Archives. Frances Nemtin interview with the author, November 30, 1994, 16; Stephen Nemtin, interview with the author, June 20, 1995, 3–4. Details confirmed by Effi Casey, phone conversation, July 31, 2007. The revolution referred to is the one in which Muhammed Reza Shah Pahlavi was overthrown on January 16, 1979. He fled the country, and in October 1979 Iranian students stormed the U.S. embassy in Teheran, demanding his return in exchange for the American hostages being held in the embassy. The Shah died in Egypt in July 1980 and the hostages were released in January 1981 after 444 days in captivity.

17. Brierly, *Tales of Taliesin*, 153–55.

18. Response to author's survey, May 13, 2002, 1.

19. The letters are on file in the William Wesley Peters Library at Taliesin West. Twenty-six of the thirty-five writers are cited in this book. In addition to those mentioned here, the contributors included John Amarantides, Nezam Amery, Kamal Amin, Ernst Anderegg, William Bernoudy, William Calvert, Richard Ciceri, Benjamin Dombar, Alden Dow, Grattan Gill, Aaron Green, Mark Heyman, Elizabeth Wright Ingraham, Donald Kalec, Elizabeth Kassler, Edgar Kaufmann, John Lautner, Robert Mosher, David Lamar

Oliver, John Ottenheimer, Jim Pfefferkorn, Bill Schwartz, Milton Stricker, Vernon Swaback, Edgar Tafel, Alvin Louis Wiehle, and Jeffrey Scott Will.

20. Interview by the author, November 28, 1994; Frank Lloyd Wright Archives, 1–7.

21. "Recollections and Reflections of My Membership in the Taliesin Fellowship," response to author's survey, May 5, 2002, 1–2, 6. Adams was in the Fellowship for two years, and upon leaving began a nine-year stint as an instructor in architecture at Tuskegee University.

22. Response to author's survey, July 14, 2002, 1.

23. Interview by Indira Berndtson and Greg Williams, February 28, 1992, 7, Frank Lloyd Wright Archives; e-mail correspondence with the author, June 28, 2003.

24. Response to author's survey, May 10, 2002, 2.

25. Response to author's survey, May 24, 2003, 2.

26. Response to author's survey, July 14, 2002, 2–3.

27. Response to author's survey, July 5, 2002, 2, 3.

28. Response to author's survey, May 5, 2002, 3.

29. Response to author's survey, May 8, 2003, 1–2. For more on the sexual practices and ethos in the Fellowship, see the previous chapter.

30. Response to author's survey, July 14, 2002.

31. Response to author's survey, July 4, 2002, 1–4.

32. Interview by the author, November 17, 1994, 3–4, Frank Lloyd Wright Archives.

33. Interview by the author, December 1, 1994, 7–8, Frank Lloyd Wright Archives.

34. Interview by the author, November 22, 1994, 4; Frank Lloyd Wright Archives.

35. "New Beginnings: Death and Aftermath," 4, submitted in response to the author's survey, May 13, 2002.

36. Response to author's survey, May 24, 2003, 1.

37. Response to author's survey, July 14, 2002, 7. In her response, Pat Schwarz made no reference to the couple's expulsion.

38. Richard L. Knonick interview of John Howe, June 4, 1987, *Journal of the Taliesin Fellows* 23 (Summer 1998): 17–18.

39. Tafel, *Frank Lloyd Wright: Recollections by Those Who Knew Him* (Mineola, N.Y.: Dover Publications, 1993), 302.

40. Interview by the author, November 16, 1994, 7, Frank Lloyd Wright Archives.

41. Interview by the author, November 28, 1994, 7, Frank Lloyd Wright Archives.

42. Interview by the author, November 15, 1994, 9, Frank Lloyd Wright Archives.

43. Letter from Tregoning to Peters, April 17, 1985. Joint Resolution #32, passed by the Wisconsin State Assembly, April 25, 1985, and concurred in by the Senate, May 7, 1985.

## EPILOGUE

1. Princeton University, 1947; Florida Southern College, 1950; Yale University, 1954; and the University of Wisconsin, 1955.

2. Interview by the author, November 15, 1994, 6.

3. The numbers cited here are compiled by observation, not drawn from official records (such records may not exist). The nine who have died are: Dick Carney, Tom Casey, Anneliese Dodge, Johnny Hill, Marion Kanouse, Bill Logue, Kenn Lockhart, Kay Rattenbury, and Dori Roy.

4. Interview by the author, November 15, 1994, 6.

5. Interview by the author, November 28, 1994, 10.

6. Information here was gained from interaction with Pfeiffer and his staff and from an article in the *Frank Lloyd Wright Quarterly* 5, no. 1 (Spring 2000): 16–19.

7. Jim Goulka, "Taliesin Architects Reorganized," *Taliesin Fellows Newsletter* 12 (July 15, 2003): 1, 3.

8. I am grateful to Robert Siegel for allowing me to read and cite his paper, "The Taliesin Experience," and to review the survey responses. Because he had not sought permission to quote from them he could not grant that permission to me. Siegel's paper is in the Frank Lloyd Wright Archives.

9. These paragraphs draw upon the author's wide-ranging interview with Paul Bogart, April 25, 2001.

# SELECTED BIBLIOGRAPHY

The books, journal and magazine articles, interviews, and other sources cited in this book are identified in the chapter endnotes. The most significant are also listed here.

## BOOKS BY FRANK LLOYD WRIGHT

*An Autobiography*. New York: Duell, Sloan and Pearce, 1943 (a revision and expansion of *An Autobiography,* published in 1932).

*The Disappearing City*. New York: William Farquhar Payson, 1932.

*The Future of Architecture*. New York: Horizon Press, 1953.

*The Living City*. New York: Horizon Press, 1958.

*A Testament*. New York: Horizon Press, 1957.

*When Democracy Builds*. Chicago: University of Chicago Press, 1945.

## COLLECTIONS OF WRITINGS BY FRANK LLOYD WRIGHT

*Frank Lloyd Wright: Collected Writings,* Vols. 1–5, Bruce Brooks Pfeiffer, ed. New York: Rizzoli International Publications, 1992–1995. Included here are some of the books listed above and his most significant articles published in the years 1900 to 1959.

*Frank Lloyd Wright: The Guggenheim Correspondence,* Bruce Brooks Pfeiffer, ed. Fresno: The Press at California State University; and Carbondale and Edwardsville, Illinois: Southern Illinois University Press, 1986.

*Frank Lloyd Wright: Letters to Apprentices,* Bruce Brooks Pfeiffer, ed. Fresno: The Press at California State University, 1982.

*Frank Lloyd Wright: Letters to Architects,* Bruce Brooks Pfeiffer, ed. Fresno: The Press at California State University, 1984.

*Frank Lloyd Wright: Letters to Clients,* Bruce Brooks Pfeiffer, ed. Fresno: The Press at California State University, 1984.

## INTERVIEWS BY THE AUTHOR

Paul Bogart, Cornelia Brierly, Richard Carney, Effi Casey, Tom Casey, Anneliese Dodge, David Dodge, Ling Po, Frances Nemtin, Stephen Nemtin, Bruce Brooks Pfeiffer, Tony Puttnam, John Rattenbury, Joseph Rorke, Arnold Roy, and Milton Stricker.

## INTERVIEWS BY FRANK LLOYD WRIGHT ARCHIVES STAFF MEMBERS

Kamal Amin, Deirdre Babcock, Aubrey Banks, Robert Beharka, Warren Biddle, Paul and Phyllis Bogart, Ted Bower, Robert Broward, Cornelia Brierly, Val Cox, Roger d'Astous, Arthur Dyson, Joe Fabris, John Geiger, Allan Gelbin, Robert Gorman, John Howe, George James, Frank Laraway, Ling Po, Kenn Lockhart, Frances Nemtin, Kelly Oliver, William Wesley Peters, Bruce Brooks Pfeiffer, Kay Rattenbury, and Vernon Swaback.

## LETTERS AND E-MAILS TO THE AUTHOR

Lu Howe (Mrs. John Howe), Susan Jacobs Lockhart, William Patrick, G. Jim Pfefferkorn, Karen Severns, Atsuko Tanaka, and Eric Lloyd Wright.

Severns, Karen, February 13, 2007.

Tanaka, Atsuko, May 17, 2007.

Wright, Eric Lloyd, July 25, 2007.

Wright, Tim, March 24, 2003.

## OTHER CORRESPONDENCE—ON MICROFICHE IN THE FRANK LLOYD WRIGHT ARCHIVES

George Elmslie to Wright, Mark Mills to Wright, Joseph Tregoning to William Wesley Peters, Kameki Tsuchiura to Martin Feller, H. Th. Wijdeveld to Wright. Also Frank Lloyd Wright to H. Th. Wijdeveld, Lloyd Wright, Mark Mills, Paolo Soleri, Philip LaFollette, R. M. Schindler (archived with the Lloyd Wright Papers, Department of Special Collections, Research Library, University of California, Los Angeles).

## UNPUBLISHED MANUSCRIPTS AND PRIVATELY PRINTED WORKS

Copies of most of the following are in the Frank Lloyd Wright Archives:

Baird, Theodore, "On Building in Amherst a House Designed by Frank Lloyd Wright," privately printed, November 20, 1989, and accompanying correspondence.

Siegel, Robert, "The Taliesin Experience," May 1985.

Wright, Iovanna Lloyd, "'My Life': An Autobiography" (undated).

Wright, Olgivanna Lloyd, an autobiography (parts dated 1980, 1981, and 1982).

## WEB SITES

Florida Southern College, http://www.flsouthern.edu/fllwctr/index.htm. Accessed December 4, 2008.

Griffin, Marion Mahony, *The Magic of America*. Art Institute of Chicago, www.artic.edu/magicofamerica, 2007). Accessed December 4, 2008.

Peisch, Mark, PBS interview transcript for "Walter Burley Griffin in His Own Right," http://www.pbs.org/wbgriffin/piesch.html. Accessed December 4, 2008.

## SELECTED WORKS BY PRESENT OR FORMER MEMBERS OF THE TALIESIN FELLOWSHIP

Amin, Kamal. *Reflections from the Shining Brow: My Years with Frank Lloyd Wright and Olgivanna Lazovich*. Santa Barbara, Calif.: Fithian Press, 2002.

Besinger, Curtis. *Working with Mr. Wright: What It Was Like*. Cambridge: Cambridge University Press, 1995.

Brierly, Cornelia. *Tales of Taliesin: A Memoir of Fellowship*. Tempe, Ariz.: Herberger Center for Design Excellence, Arizona State University, 1999.

Fritz, Herbert, Jr. "At Taliesin," in Edna Meudt and Betsy Strand, eds., *An Uplands Reader*. Dodgeville, Wisc. (June 1979): 129, 131.

Gottlieb, Lois Davidson. *A Way of Life: An Apprenticeship with Frank Lloyd Wright*. Mulgrave, Victoria, Australia: Images Publishing Group, 2001.

Green, Aaron G. *An Architecture for Democracy: The Marin County Civic Center*. San Francisco: Grendon Publishing, 1990.

Howe, John. "Reflections of Taliesin," *Northwest Architect*, July–August 1969.

Kassler, Elizabeth Bauer, compiler. "The Taliesin Fellowship: 1932–1982: A Directory of Members." Privately printed and distributed by the compiler, 1981; supplement, 1982.

Nemtin, Frances. "Life on Midway Farm." Privately printed, 1999.

———. "Web of Life." Privately printed, 2001.

Nesbit, Earl. *Taliesin Reflections: My Years Before, During, and After Living with Frank Lloyd Wright*. Petaluma, Calif.: Meridian Press, 2006.

Pfefferkorn, G. Jim. *Taliesin Stories: Autobiographical*. Privately printed, Spring Green, Wisc., n.d.

Tafel, Edgar. *Frank Lloyd Wright: Apprentice to Genius*. New York: Dover Publications 1985; published in 1979 as *Apprentice to Genius: Years with Frank Lloyd Wright*.

Tafel, Edgar, ed. *Frank Lloyd Wright: Recollections by Those Who Knew Him*. Mineola, N.Y.: Dover Publications, 2001; published initially by John Wiley & Sons, 1993, under the title *About Wright: An Album of Recollections by Those Who Knew Frank Lloyd Wright*.

## SELECTED WORKS BY OTHERS

Alofsin, Anthony. *Frank Lloyd Wright: The Lost Years, 1910–1922: A Study of Influence*. Chicago: University of Chicago Press, 1993.

———. "Taliesin: 'To Fashion Worlds in Little.'" In *Taliesin 1911–1914*, Narciso G. Menocal, ed., *Wright Studies Volume One*. Carbondale: Southern Illinois University Press, 1992, pp. 44–65.

Barney, Maginel Wright. *The Valley of the God-Almighty Joneses: Reminiscences of Frank Lloyd Wright's Sister, Maginel Wright Barney*. New York: Appleton-Century, 1965; republished by Unity Chapel Publications, Spring Green, Wisc., 1986.

Brooks, H. Allen. *The Prairie School: Frank Lloyd Wright and His Contemporaries*. New York: W.W. Norton, 1972.

Byrne, Barry. "On Frank Lloyd Wright and His Atelier." *AIA Journal* 39, no. 6 (June 1963): 109–12.

———. "The Life and Work of Marion Mahony Griffin." *The Prairie School: Design Vision for the Midwest*. Museum Studies 21, no. 2 (1995): Chicago: The Art Institute of Chicago, 167–69.

De Long, David G., ed. *Designs for the American Landscape, 1922–1932*. New York: Harry N. Abrams, 1996.

———, ed. *Frank Lloyd Wright and the Living City*. Weil am Rhein, Germany: Vitra Design Museum, 1998.

Gebhard, David. *Romanza: The California Architecture of Frank Lloyd Wright*. San Francisco: Chronicle Books, 1988.

Gloag, John. "Frank Lloyd Wright: And the Significance of the Taliesin Fellowship." *The Architectural Review* (January 1935): 1–2.

Goodwin, George. "Frank Lloyd Wright's Usonian Houses for Jewish Clients." *American Jewish Archives Journal*, LI, nos. 1-2 (1999): 67-92.

Guggenheimer, Tobias S. *A Taliesin Legacy: The Architecture of Frank Lloyd Wright's Apprentices*. New York: Van Nostrand Reinhold, 1995.

Gurda, John. *New World Odyssey: The Annunciation Greek Orthodox Church and Frank Lloyd Wright*. Milwaukee: Milwaukee Hellenic Community, 1986.

Henning, Randolph. *"At Taliesin": Newspaper Columns by Frank Lloyd Wright and the Taliesin Fellowship*. Carbondale and Edwardsville: Southern Illinois University Press, 1992.

Hoffmann, Donald. *Frank Lloyd Wright's Fallingwater: The House and Its History*. New York: Dover Publications, Inc., second, revised edition, 1993.

———. *Frank Lloyd Wright's Hollyhock House*. New York: Dover Publications, 1992.

Jacobs, Herbert, with Katherine Jacobs. *Building with Frank Lloyd Wright: An Illustrated Memoir*. San Francisco: Chronicle Books, 1978.

Kaufmann, Edgar. "Crisis and Creativity: Frank Lloyd Wright, 1904–1914." *JSAH* 25, no. 4 (December 1966): 293–94; published in revised form, with illustrations, in Kaufmann's *9 Commentaries on Frank Lloyd Wright* (Cambridge: The MIT Press, 1989), 87–102.

Kruty, Paul. "At Work in the Oak Park Studio." *Arris: Journal of the Southeast Chapter of the Society of Architectural Historians* 14 (2003): 18.

———. *Frank Lloyd Wright and Midway Gardens.* Urbana: University of Illinois Press, 1998.

Kruty, Paul, with Mati Maldre, photographer. *Walter Burley Griffin in America.* Urbana and Chicago: University of Illinois Press, 1996.

Levine, Neil. *The Architecture of Frank Lloyd Wright.* Princeton, N.J.: Princeton University Press, 1996.

Lipman, Jonathon. *Frank Lloyd Wright and the Johnson Wax Buildings.* Mineola, N.Y., Dover Publications, 2003; New York: Rizzoli International Publications, 1982.

Manson, Grant Carpenter. *Frank Lloyd Wright to 1910: The First Golden Age.* New York: Van Nostrand Reinhold Company, 1958.

Marty, Myron A., and Shirley L. Marty. *Frank Lloyd Wright's Taliesin Fellowship.* Kirksville, Mo.: Truman State University Press, 1999.

Meech, Julia. *Frank Lloyd Wright and the Art of Japan: The Architect's Other Passion.* New York: Japan Society and Harry N. Abrams, Inc., 2001.

Neutra, Dione, compiler and translator. *Promise and Fulfillment, 1919–1932: Selections from the Letters and Diaries of Richard and Dione Neutra.* Carbondale and Edwardsville: Southern Illinois University Press, 1986.

Overby, Osmund. *William Adair Bernoudy, Architect: Bringing the Legacy of Frank Lloyd Wright to St. Louis.* Columbia: University of Missouri Press, 1999.

Pfeiffer, Bruce Brooks. *Frank Lloyd Wright: Treasures of Taliesin: Seventy-Six Unbuilt Designs.* Carbondale and Edwardsville: Southern Illinois University Press, 1985.

Pfeiffer, Bruce Brooks, and Gerald Nordland. *Frank Lloyd Wright in the Realm of Ideas.* Carbondale and Edwardsville: Southern Illinois University Press, 1988.

Rosenbaum, Alvin. *Usonia: Frank Lloyd Wright's Design for America.* Washington, D.C.: Preservation Press, 1993.

Saint, Andrew. "Frank Lloyd Wright and Paul Mueller: The Architect and His Builder of Choice." *Arq: Architectural Research Quarterly* 7, no. 2 (2003): 163.

Secrest, Meryl. *Frank Lloyd Wright: A Biography.* New York: HarperCollins, 1992.

Sergeant, John. *Frank Lloyd Wright's Usonian Houses: Designs for Moderate Cost One-Family Homes.* New York: Watson-Guptil Publications, 1976, 1984.

Smith, Kathryn. *Frank Lloyd Wright, Hollyhock House and Olive Hill: Buildings and Projects for Aline Barnsdall.* New York: Rizzoli, 1992.

———. "Frank Lloyd Wright and the Imperial Hotel: A Postscript." *The Art Bulletin* 67, no. 2 (June 1985): 296–310.

Smith, Nancy K. Morris. "Letters, 1903–1906, by Charles E. White, Jr., from the Studio of Frank Lloyd Wright." *Journal of Architectural Education* 25 (Fall 1971): 104–12.

Smith, Norris Kelly. *Frank Lloyd Wright: A Study in Architectural Context.* Englewood Cliffs, N.J.: Prentice-Hall, Inc., 1966; revised version published by the American Life Foundation & Study Institute, 1979.

Stipe, Margo. "Wright's First Trip to Japan." *Frank Lloyd Wright Quarterly* 6, no. 2 (Spring 1995): 21–23.

Storrer, William Allin. *The Architecture of Frank Lloyd Wright: A Complete Catalog,* 3rd ed. Chicago: University of Chicago Press, 2002; updated 2006.

———. *The Frank Lloyd Wright Companion.* Chicago: University of Chicago Press, 1993.

Sweeney, Robert L. *Frank Lloyd Wright: An Annotated Bibliography.* Los Angeles: Hennessey & Ingalls, Inc., 1978.

Tanaka, Atsuko. "Kameki and Nobu Tsuchiura: Apprenticeship with Wright in the 1920s." Presented at the annual meeting of the Frank Lloyd Wright Building Conservancy in Los Angeles, October 21, 2005.

Twombly, Robert. *Frank Lloyd Wright: His Life and His Architecture.* New York: John Wiley and Sons, 1979.

———. "Organic Living: Frank Lloyd Wright's Taliesin Fellowship and Georgi Gurdjieff's Institute for the Harmonious Development of Man." *Wisconsin Magazine of History* (Winter 1974/75): 126–39.

Wright, John Lloyd. *My Father Who Is on Earth.* Narciso G. Menocal, ed. 1946; reprinted Carbondale: Southern Illinois University Press, 1994.

# ACKNOWLEDGMENTS

Research for this book began in the concluding year of my tenure as the Ann G. and Sigurd E. Anderson University Professor at Drake University. I am grateful to the Andersons for the financial support that made undertaking a second book on Frank Lloyd Wright's communities feasible, as well as for the benefits of the professorship that supported my earlier work on *Frank Lloyd Wright's Taliesin Fellowship* (1999), coauthored with Shirley Marty.

The resources of the Frank Lloyd Wright Archives at Taliesin West and the help provided by the Archives staff members have been indispensable in my research. My appreciation for the generous spirit displayed in their offers of assistance and in granting me permission to draw upon the Archives' extensive holdings runs deep. I am particularly grateful to Bruce Brooks Pfeiffer, director and prolific Wright scholar; Oskar Muñoz, assistant director and curator of the photograph collection, who was especially helpful in procuring many of the images in this book, identifying the subject in them, and providing guidance on their use; Indira Berndtson, who has created and maintained an extremely valuable and still-growing oral history collection; and Margo Stipe, curator and registrar of collections, who cheerfully provided good counsel. Also to Sara Hammond, assistant in the oral history collection, who assisted me many times as I engaged in researching the transcripts of interviews; and other assistants throughout the Archives who were always ready to help. Elizabeth Dawsari, librarian at Taliesin West, and Dennis Madden, the library's archivist, were also generous in offering valuable support.

Staff members of Drake's Cowles Library, led by Dean Rod Henshaw, provided assistance in many ways. Diane Collett merits special mention for her considerable help in acquiring copies of articles from other libraries and archives. At the University of Illinois in Champaign-Urbana, where I did much of my research, I benefited from assistance by staff members in the Architecture and Art Library, which is in a building named for the founder of the School of Architecture, Nathan Ricker, mentor more than a century ago to three of Frank Lloyd Wright's early assistants. (Wright would have liked the inscription above the entrance to Ricker Hall: "ARCHITECTURE AND KINDRED SUBJECTS.") Jane Block, the head librarian, provided assistance on a number of occasions, as did Chris Quinn, Jing Liao, Dorfredia Williams-Robinson, and several graduate assistants. Also helpful in my research were the resources and staff members in the archives of the State Historical Society of Wisconsin; the Frank Lloyd Wright Preservation Trust in Oak Park; the Ryerson and Burnham Archives in the Art Institute of Chicago; the Department of Special Collections in the UCLA Research Library; and the library of the Frank Lloyd Wright Building Conservancy. Gary Ingersoll of Monticello, Illinois, expertly scanned twenty-two images from various sources and burned them to a CD for use in this book.

A number of persons read and commented on portions of the manuscript, including Randolph Henning, who merits special mention, as he provided me with the research materials he compiled in writing *"At Taliesin": Newspaper Columns by Frank Lloyd Wright and the Taliesin Fellowship, 1934–1937*; more than 100 of these columns provided stories for Chapters 11 to 14. Other readers of a chapter or more were John Geiger, Paul Kruty, Karen Severns, Margo Stipe, Atsuko Tanaka, and Carl and Roberta Volkmann. Most helpful were two scholars who critiqued the complete manuscript and offered many insightful suggestions: David Kyvig, a distinguished professor of American history at Northern Illinois University and my friend and scholarly collaborator for more than three decades, and my brother, Martin Marty, a prolific historian while on the faculty of the University of Chicago, 1963–1998, and in his retirement years.

I am grateful to members of the Taliesin Fellowship for their assistance, particularly Effi Casey, the late Tom Casey, Cornelia Brierly, Bruce Brooks Pfeiffer, and Indira Berndtson. Others who were helpful in many ways, but most tangibly in allowing me to record interviews with them, include Richard Carney (CEO of the Frank Lloyd Wright Foundation), Heloise Crista, Anneliese and David Dodge, Joe Fabris, Ari Georges, John DeKoven Hill, Marion Kanouse, Julie and Paul Kardatske, Jay Jensen, Ling Po, Susan Jacobs Lockhart, Sarah and Bill Logue, Charles and Minerva Montooth, Frances and Stephen Nemtin, Anthony Puttnam, John and Kay Rattenbury, Dr. Joe Rorke, Shawn Rorke-Davis, and Arnold and Doris Roy. Tom Casey, Anneliese Dodge, Carney, Hill, Kay Rattenbury, and Doris Roy are now deceased and Jay Jensen, Julie and Paul Kardatzke, and Ling Po have left the Fellowship but maintain strong ties with it. Penny Fowler, H. Nicholas Muller, Ryc Loope, June Hill, and John Wyatt, who were associated with the Fellowship in the 1990s, were also helpful, as were Suzette Lucas and Margo Stipe, who continue in key positions.

Members of the Taliesin Fellows, the Taliesin Fellowship's alumni organization, have become friends through the years, and some have provided special assistance in interviews, personal conversations (some occurring at Fellowship reunions in 1997, 2002, and 2007), and survey responses, particularly John Amarantides, Paul and Phyllis Bogart, Larry Brink, Val Cox, Arthur Dyson, Don Fairweather, John Geiger, Grattan Gill, Frank Laraway, Jack Lee, Jerry Morosco, Kelly Oliver, Tom Olson, Bill Patrick, Peter Rött, Charles Schiffner, Vernon Swaback, and Eric Lloyd Wright. Additionally, I appreciated the responses to the survey I conducted in the early stages of my research, and I regret that I could not incorporate specific information from all of them in the text of this book. Respondents included, in addition to those mentioned above, Charles Adams, Nazam Amery, the late Lynn Anderson, Deirdre Babcock, Bruce Barrett, Bob Beharka, Nicola Bingel-Hecht, Ted Bower, Douglas Boyd, Ron Brissette, Robert C. Broward, Victor Cusack, Russell Dixon, A. Jane Duncombe, J. T. Elbracht, Stephen Gegner, David George, Igor Glen, Lois Gottlieb, Floyd Hamblen, Monika Herman, Norman

Hill, Andre Hoffe, Julie Kardatzke, Richard Keding, Daniel Lieberman, José Marcial, Robert Mauldin, Mark Mills, Hideo Murakami, John Ottenheimer, Charles Paterson, Kenneth Peterson, Ling Ming Poliandro, Robert Rasmussen, Sara Robinson, Patricia and William Schwarz, Victor Sidy, Milton Stricker, and Edgar Tafel.

I have appreciated the good work done by the Northern Illinois University Press in making this book a reality: J. Alex Schwartz, director, and, in their various roles, Susan Bean, Barbara Berg, Julia Fauci, Sara Hoerdeman, Linda Manning, and Gary Von Euer.

This book is dedicated to Shirley Marty, who has been my partner and collaborator in everything for more than five decades. She accompanied me on research missions while we worked on this book and joined me in many participant-observer experiences. She edited draft after draft of the manuscript with inexplicably good cheer. Her patience, understanding, and unfailing love were essential in bringing the book to completion. Although her name does not appear on the title page, she deserves to be considered the book's coauthor.

Myron Marty
Monticello, Illinois

# INDEX